KEEPERS OF LIFE

TRAIL

footfalls through crystal autumn air
over brown earth loam
broken rock
and duff leaf litter

dancing with sunlit tree shadow veins
the lifeblood of sun journeys

path leading back to
hillfarm hayfield
logging road
moccasin feet of a life
connected to Earth and Sky

crossing rock walls and fire pits
built by those who have long since
closed the circle of life

path over soil of
flesh and bone
fur and feather
leaf and twig

I try to walk a good trail
treading lightly
rooting deeply

until I once again become
leaf and limb
reaching to the sky
                              — Michael J. Caduto

KEEPERS OF LIFE

Discovering Plants Through Native American Stories
and Earth Activities for Children

Michael J. Caduto and Joseph Bruchac

Foreword by Marilou Awiakta
Story illustrations by John Kahionhes Fadden and David Kanietakeron Fadden
Chapter illustrations by Marjorie C. Leggitt and Carol Wood

Fulcrum Publishing
Golden, Colorado

Library of Congress Cataloging-in-Publication Data
    Caduto, Michael J.
        Keepers of life : discovering plants through Native American stories and earth activities for children /
    by Michael J. Caduto and Joseph Bruchac ; story illustrations by John Kahionhes Fadden and David
    Kanietakeron Fadden ; chapter illustrations by Marjorie C. Leggitt and Carol Wood.
            p.   cm.
        Includes bibliographical references and index.
        ISBN 1-55591-186-2
        1. Indians of North America—Folklore. 2. Tales—North America. 3. Plant ecology—Study and
    teaching (Elementary). 4. Human ecology—Study and teaching (Elementary) 5. Nature study—Activity
    programs. I. Bruchac, Joseph, 1942– . II. Title.
    E98.F6C117 1994
    372.3'57044—dc20   94–12584
                                                                                           CIP

Printed in the United States of America
0 9 8 7 6 5 4 3 2

Fulcrum Publishing
350 Indiana Street, Suite 350
Golden, Colorado 80401-5093
800-992-2908

To all our grandparents.
In the Native tradition of the circle,
the elders are closest to the children
and to all our relations.

Permissions

Permission to reprint the following is gratefully acknowledged:

The map, "Native North America" on pages xiv–xv, showing the culture regions of the Native North American groups discussed in this book, is printed with permission of Michael J. Caduto (©1994). Cartography by Stacy Miller, Upper Marlboro, Maryland.

The poem "Trail" by Michael J. Caduto on page ii is reprinted with permission of the author.

The photograph on page 5 by Dale S. Turner is reprinted with his permission.

The photographs on pages 7, 18, 21, 80, 107, 188, 207 and 224 by Alan C. Graham are reprinted with his permission.

The Haudenosaunee prophesy on page 7 and the list of Haudenosaunee seasonal ceremonies on page 47 are from Barbara Barnes (Kawenehe), Mike (Kanentakeron) Mitchell, Joyce (Konwahwihon) Thompson et al.'s *Traditional Teachings* (1984), and are reprinted with permission of the North American Indian Traveling College, Cornwall Island, Ontario.

The quote from Vernon Cooper on page 8, the quote from Audrey Shenandoah on page 47, the quote from Charlie Knight on page 48, the quote from Chief Oren Lyons on page 48, the quote by Harriet Starleaf Gumbs on page 64 and the quote from Chief Oren Lyons on page 240 are from Steve Wall and Harvey Arden's *Wisdomkeepers: Meetings With Native American Spiritual Elders* (©1990) and are reprinted with permission of Beyond Words Pub., Inc., Hillsboro, Oregon.

The photograph on page 12 by Jack Wandell is reprinted with his permission.

The photograph on page 15 by Cecil B. Hoisington is reprinted with her permission.

The list of problem-solving skills on page 16 was adapted from William B. Stapp and Dorothy A. Cox's *Environmental Education Activities Manual* (©1970), published by Thomson-Shore, Inc., Dexter, Michigan, and is reprinted with permission of the authors.

The map of North American biomes on page 35 is adapted from the *Biogeographical Provinces Map* by Dr. M.D.F. Udvardy and is used with permission of the International Union for the Conservation of Nature and Natural Resources, Gland, Switzerland.

The illustration of the Circles and Cycles of Life on page 46, concept and design ©1994 by Michael J. Caduto, is used with his permission.

The photographs on pages 49, 83, 106, 107, 165, 202, 207, 212 and 230 ©1994 by Michael J. Caduto are reprinted with his permission.

The quote by Ten Bears on page 48, the quote by Ohiyesa on page 112 and the quote by Chief Luther Standing Bear on page 129 are from Kent Nerburn and Louise Mengelkoch's (eds.) *Native American Wisdom* (1991) and are reprinted with permission of New World Library, San Rafael, California.

The excerpt of the speech by Chief Jake Swamp on page 49 is reprinted with his permission.

The Round Dance of Unity and Thanksgiving on page 50 is used with permission of Dr. Ella Sekatau, DHL, Ethno-historian and Cultural Education Consultant of the Narragansett Indian Tribe, Charlestown, Rhode Island.

The illustration of kelp on page 62 is adapted from R. F. Scagel et. al.'s *Plant Diversity: An Evolutionary Survey* (1965) and is used with permission of Wadsworth Publishing Co., Inc., Belmont, California.

The illustration on page 68 is adapted from K. Esser's *Cryptograms* (1982) and is used here with permission of Cambridge University Press, New York.

The illustrations on pages 96 (top) and 113 (left) are adapted from William A. Jensen and Frank B. Salisbury's *Botany: An Ecological Approach* (1972) and are used here with permission of Wadsworth Publishing Co., Inc., Belmont, California.

The illustrations on pages 96 (bottom) and 132 are adapted from Friedrich G. Barth's *Insects and Flowers* and are used here with permission, ©1991 Princeton University Press, New Jersey.

The photograph on page 100 is reprinted from P. V. Glob's *The Bog People: Iron Age Man Preserved* (©1965) by P. V. Glob, English translation ©1969 by Faber and Faber Limited, London, and is used here with permission of Faber and Faber Limited, Publishers, and P. V. Glob, Director of the Danish National Museum, Denmark.

The illustration on page 113 (left) is adapted with permission from Floyd S. Shuttleworth and Herbert S. Zim's *MUSHROOMS AND OTHER NON-FLOWERING PLANTS* (A Golden Guide), ©1987 and ©1967 by Western Publishing Co., Inc., Racine, Wisconsin. Original illustration by Dorothea Barlowe, Sy Barlowe, Jack Kunz, Barbara Wolff and Jean Zallinger.

The illustration on page 113 (right) is adapted with permission from Trudi Hammel Garland's *Fascinating Fibonaccis* (1987), published by Dale Seymour Publications, Palo Alto, California.

The photograph on page 120 by Alexander Lowry is reprinted here with his permission.

The photograph on page 137 by William S. Lea is reprinted here with his permission.

The grasslands map on page 151 is adapted from P. G. Risser et al.'s *The True Prairie Ecosystem* (1981), published by Hutchinson Ross Publishing Co., Stroudsburg, Pennsylvania, and is used with permission from Van Nostrand Reinhold Publishers, New York.

The illustration on page 152 is adapted from Lauren Brown's *Grasses: An Identification Guide* (1979) and is used here with permission of Houghton Mifflin Co., Boston, Massachusetts.

The photograph on page 154 by Kenneth W. Wood is reprinted here with his permission.

Brief portions of the "Discussion" in Chapter 11 describing urban plants are adapted from Michael J. Caduto and Lori D. Mann's *Ann Arbor Alive: The Ecology of a City* (1981), published by the Ecology Center of Ann Arbor, Michigan, and are used with permission of the authors.

The photograph on page 183 by Peter Hope is reprinted here with his permission.

The photograph on page 210 by Will and Jane Curtis is reprinted here with their permission.

The photograph on page 216 is reprinted here with permission of the Missouri Botanical Garden, St. Louis.

The photograph on page 221 by Richard York is reprinted here with permission of the California Native Plant Society, Sacramento.

The photograph of the child on page 243 by Nancy Fellows is reprinted here with her permission.

The activities and information throughout this book by Michael J. Caduto are reprinted with his permission.

The stories by Joseph Bruchac throughout this book are reprinted with his permission.

The story illustrations by John Kahionhes Fadden and David Kanietakeron Fadden throughout this book are reprinted with their permission.

The illustrations by Carol Wood that accompany the activities and discussion throughout this book are reprinted with her permission.

The illustrations by Marjorie C. Leggitt throughout this book are reprinted with her permission.

The illustration of the hand used in the Introduction, in the symbols that precede each activity and at the end of the "Discussion" in Chapter 15, is a registered trademark of Michael J. Caduto and P.E.A.C.E.®, Programs for Environmental Awareness and Cultural Exchange. ®1993 by Michael J. Caduto.

Contents

SURVIVAL

HEALING OUR RELATIONS

✤ Foreword ✤

A bridge is a gift to the people. A life line.

Living near the mighty Mississippi River, I'm constantly thankful for our two bridges. An old maxim says, "We see what we are taught to perceive." My father taught me to appreciate the skill of bridge builders, emphasizing that they must work in harmony with the laws of nature. So when I look at the two bridges I see that their long spans are well grounded in both banks and their lengths are held in balance by supports below and above. Because they are strong yet flexible, the bridges hold fast in the elements. They were built with respect. They are beautiful. They are reliable.

It is the same with the books of the Keepers series. Using the ancient wisdom of Native North American stories as the connecting span, Michael J. Caduto and Joseph Bruchac have respectfully built bridges of understanding between people and the natural world—first in *Keepers of the Earth,* then in *Keepers of the Animals* and *Keepers of the Night.* Now comes *Keepers of Life,* which unifies humans, plants and all that lives in the great cycle of coming and going, giving and receiving that is life itself. As the authors say, "Plants stand between all life on Earth and eternity." Because of this scope, the balances in the book are necessarily complex and intricate.

Chief among them is the authors' very careful choice of stories. As I began the book I thought, "How are they going to choose? The distance to be spanned is so great, not only between plants and people, but also between cultural perceptions." When I finished reading, I realized that Caduto and Bruchac had chosen the stories by working in harmony with the laws that Nature taught Native North Americans to perceive millennia ago: *Everything in the universe is related in one family. All life is equal. Generative power is gender-balanced—male and female. And to keep life going, all these relationships must be kept in balance.* These are Original Instructions, laws instilled in Nature by the Creator. In presenting the stories, Caduto and Bruchac faithfully adhered to the laws and to the language Native peoples use to express them, a language which is gendered and familial—Mother Earth, Father Sky and so on. For fun, and also to have a visual pattern, I marked the stories with male and female symbols. Clearly, the authors have preserved the healthful traditional balance, where both genders are equally vigorous Keepers of Life. I saw what I have been taught to perceive—an inclusiveness that begins in the very heart of the universe and extends to "all our relations."

Corn—*Zea mays*—exemplifies this concept and has upheld it to Native peoples for seven thousand years. In his beautiful and extraordinary cover illustration, John Kahionhes Fadden has rendered what they perceived in the plant. From the union of male tassel and female silks comes the nutritious ear, whose seeds continue the generations. And so it is with humans. In their creation story, the Mayans say that the Creator and the Maker made human beings from cornmeal, from maize. In the stories of all Native peoples, the spirit of the plant teaches the wisdom of respect; sometimes the spirit is female, sometimes male. Appropriately, Fadden has portrayed the spirit in a form that could be either gender and holds in the outstretched hand an unmistakable message: balance.

The span of stories is well grounded in knowledge of science and human cultures. All along its length, it is supported by supplemental text and activities. Readers—adults and children alike—will understand how all life is interconnected in one continuous cycle and requires respectful care. However, teaching students to perceive the balance and mutual respect of genders may need special emphasis because, comparatively speaking, contemporary society is just beginning to teach perception of female presence and roles. From a Native North American perspective, what are women doing in the stories?

Women continue the generative power of Mother Earth, renewing, nourishing and sustaining the life of the people. Traditionally with food, men have been the hunters and women have been the principal caretakers of plants, which comprise 80 percent of human food. Women, as well as men, act decisively to preserve life.

In the Huron creation story, "The Sky Tree," the people lived in the sky land where a great tree furnished all their food. The old chief was sick. In a dream he saw that fruit from the top of the great tree would cure him. He told his wife Aataentsic, "Ancient Woman," to cut down the tree and bring him the fruit. At the first stroke of her axe, the tree split and fell through a hole in the sky. Aataentsic told her husband what had happened, then said these very important words: *"Without the tree, there can be no life. I must follow it."*

Looking up from the waters below, Turtle saw Aataentsic falling. Like a clan mother, she organized help, telling the other animals to bring up soil from beneath the waters and pile it on her back. "Aataentsic settled down gently on the new earth and the pieces of the tree fell beside her and took root."

Immediately following this story is "How Kishelemukong (the Great Mystery) Made the People and the Seasons." He caused the first men and the first women to sprout from the branches of an elder tree. Then he "created the four directions and the seasons that would come from these directions. The West, North and East were Grandfathers, governing the times of Fall, Winter and Summer. The South was a Grandmother, bringing the warmth and new life of Spring." To make sure the divisions among the seasons were fair and acceptable, Kishelemukong decided to have Grandfather North and Grandmother South play a handgame that would hold the seasons in balance. "And so it is to this day."

And so the balance continues in the stories.

Like men, women teach the law of respect to the people—and sometimes have to relearn the law themselves. In an Inuit story, Nunan-shua, "the Woman Who Dwells in the Earth," punished a disrespectful hunter. To a hunter whom she had observed to be respectful, Nunan-shua gave the gift of success. In "The First Basket," the mother cedar gave some of her slender roots to a woman and showed her how to make a basket. The basket was cedar's daughter. When the woman sang her thanks, the basket walked beside her and carried her load. Another woman was not so wise. She didn't sing thanks to her basket, and was greedy besides. The basket refused to walk. "From that time on, no basket ever again carried a burden for the people on its own."

Women teach children their first lessons in survival and well-being. They also gage the cycles of life and ceremony. The story of how Waynabozho brought wild rice to the people begins with his grandmother calling him to her lodge. "Grandson," Nokomis said, "it is time for you to go to some distant place in the forest and fast. Then a dream may come to you to help the people yet to come." She helped him plant the first rice seeds he found, then sent him out again to learn the further good he needed to know. Thus the generations cooperate in bringing a new food for the people.

As *Keepers of Life* circles toward completion, the Osage story of "Buffalo Bull and the Cedar Tree" brings a vision of healing for the people and "all our relations." At the beginning of the story a man from the Peace Clan "uses an arrow flecked with feathers stained red from pokeberry juice to bring peace to Buffalo Bull. Healing plants grow where Buffalo rolls on the ground. He gives the people different kinds of corn and squash to eat and, finally, Buffalo offers himself as food, shelter, clothing and tools." The people then find the cedar. She stands in the midst of the four winds, sending forth her fragrance. "'I stand here on this cliff,' Cedar said, 'so that the Little Ones may make of me their medicine.'" And she shows the people her gnarled roots and bending branches with their feathery white tips as symbols of long life. "Cedar becomes medicine, a symbol of longevity to the people and is their Tree of Life." Because Buffalo Bull and Cedar give openly of themselves, the Osage people ultimately discover ways to live well. And they continually express their thanks to the Creator for these gifts.

The stories teach us to perceive our relatives in the universe as bridges from the Creator, life lines that sustain us in body and spirit. Our relatives are beautiful. They are reliable. And if we keep them with respect, maintaining the balance of giving and receiving, they will hold us in balance so that we, in turn, can help heal Mother Earth and our people. This is the message and the hope of *Keepers of Life*. It is a gift to the people. And to the "seeds of the people"—our children.

—MARILOU AWIAKTA

✦ Acknowledgments ✦

From the Authors: Our thanks to Bob Baron, publisher, Carmel Huestis, editor, as well as all staff involved with the design, production and sales of this book at Fulcrum Publishing. The illustrators—John Kahionhes Fadden, David Kanietakeron Fadden, Marjorie C. Leggitt and Carol Wood—have enhanced the text with beautiful imagery. Their respective work can be distinguished as follows: Kahionhes and Kanietakeron have illustrated all of the stories and signed their artwork; Marjorie C. Leggitt's plant illustrations are credited as such in the captions; and Carol Wood's artwork comprises the balance of the illustrations that accompany the chapters, especially those in the "Activities" and "Discussion" sections. Thanks to the many people whose striking photographs appear on these pages. We are grateful to Marilou Awiakta for her thoughtfulness in agreeing to write the Foreword.

There is a long list of people whose help was crucial during the thorough and extensive process by which the manuscript was reviewed, and to whom we are greatly indebted. The following people reviewed the overall manuscript for accuracy: Dr. James F. Hornig, Professor of Chemistry and Environmental Studies, Dartmouth College; John Moody, Ethnohistorian and Independent Scholar; and Charles E. Roth, Naturalist/Educator. Thank you also to these experts in their respective fields for reviewing the various chapters of the manuscript for accuracy: Jim A. Bartel, Chief of the Division of Listing, U.S. Fish and Wildlife Service, Portland, Oregon; Dr. Robert Betz, Biology Department, Northeastern Illinois University; Carol Cochran, Director of Education, Arizona–Sonora Desert Museum; Dr. Laura E. Conkey, Associate Professor of Geography and Biological Sciences, Dartmouth College; Dr. Philip W. Cook; Alan D. Copsey, J.D., Ph.D.; Kevin Dahl, Associate Director, Native Seeds/SEARCH; David Daugharty, Assistant Dean, Faculty of Forestry, University of New Brunswick, Canada; Elliot Gimble, Director of Rivers Program, Atlantic Center for the Environment; Frank Golet, Professor of Wetland Ecology, University of Rhode Island; Erich Haber, Canadian Museum of Nature; Dr. Dennis Hall, Biology Department, Northeastern Illinois University; Peter Hope, Botanist; Professor Hugh H. Iltis, Department of Botany, University of Wisconsin–Madison; J. James Kielbaso, Professor of Forestry, Michigan State University; Dr. Ralph H. Lutts, Virginia Museum of Natural History; Peter J. Marchand, Research and Teaching Fellow, Plant Sciences Department, University of Arizona; Dr. Cyrus B. McQueen, Associate Professor of Biology, Johnson State College, Vermont; Carlene A. Raper, Ph.D., Research Associate Professor, Department of Microbiology and Molecular Genetics, University of Vermont; Alan D. Rossman, Ph.D., Manager of Education, Chicago Botanic Garden; Helen Ross Russell, Environmental Education Consultant; Dr. Karen B. Searcy, Herbarium Curator, Biology Department, University of Massachusetts; Dr. Floyd A. Swink, Morton Arboretum, Lyle, Illinois; Erik van Lennep, Director, Arctic to Amazonia Alliance; Dr. H. W. Vogelmann; Fred Wiseman, Johnson State College, Vermont; and Brock Woods, Earthkeeping Program Manager, University of Wisconsin–Madison Arboretum.

A number of people offered important logistical help in organizing the field-testing for this book, including Heather Dundas, Program Coordinator, Nature Saskatchewan; Chuck and Marli Hagen of the Native Art Center, Wiscasset, Maine; Lori D. Mann, Education Director, Coyote Point Museum, California; Trica Oshant; Pamela Pirio, Coordinator, Stupp Teacher Resource Center, Missouri Botanical Garden; and Jeffrey Schwartz, Director of Education, Audubon Society of New Hampshire. Thank you to the following parents, teachers, naturalists, environmental educators and youth leaders who donated large amounts of their time and consideration as they field-tested and evaluated the activities newly designed for this book: Linda K. Arms, Camp Fire Leader, Wakan Dan-de Camp Fire Club, Santa Clara, California; Carli Carrara, Instructor, Third-Grade, Henry Barnard Lab School, Rhode Island College; Susan Caswell, Teacher; Steven Cleaver, Program Director, Horizons for Youth; Cheryl Boynton Cleeves, Science Specialist, Clifford School, Redwood City, California; Ann Collacchi; Deborah E. Crawford; Nancy Dowey, Director, White Wing School; Nancy Fellows, Hopkinton Independent School; Mary K. Fitzgerald; Christine Fowler; Claudia Jane Hall, Philomath, Oregon; Lucy Hanouille; Alan Harris, Education Coordinator, Lloyd Center for Environmental Studies; Laura K. Hathorn, Educator; Diane Hoppe; Leonora Isaak, Naturalist/Educator, Beaver Brook Association; Lucille Keegan; Enid Kelly; Joyce Kutaka Kennedy, Teacher; Pamela A. Korejwa, Science Director, St. Joseph's School and Ocean Quest, Woods Hole, Massachusetts; Paul E. Lavasseur; Karen Leavitt, Fourth-Grade Teacher, Deerfield Community School, New Hampshire; Cynthia LeBlanc; Judi Lee, Montessori Teacher; Diane Lonergan; Diane MacDonald; Diane Miner; Jean Minnich; Linda Nichols, Teacher; Cheryl C. Norton, Director of Education, Audubon Society of Rhode Island; Lynn Peters; Cindy Pierce, Teacher; Ann Podlipny; Vicky Price, Teacher; JoAnn Riecke; Sharon MacLean Robinson, Second-Grade Teacher, K.R.E.S., Bradford, New Hampshire; Kathryn Schmeiser, Elementary Science Teacher; Claire Schwarzbach, South Road School; Bora Simmons, Associate Professor, Northern Illinois University; Theresa Symancyk; Gwendolyn G. Thompson and her Fourth-Grade Class; Bill Tyler, Refuge Manager, Audubon Society of Rhode Island; Joanna Waldman; Deborah Watson-Kimball; and Brock Woods, Earthkeeping Program Manager, University of Wisconsin–Madison Arboretum.

From Michael Caduto: For the enthusiasm of all the children who helped to make this book come to life, I am greatly appreciative. I am also indebted to the scientists, naturalists, Native North Americans and all observers of Earth whose eyes and writings have helped me to see farther and understand more than my own direct observations and research into the wonders of the natural world make possible. I appreciate the openness of Dr. Ella Sekatau, DHL, Ethno-Historian and Cultural Education Consultant of the Narragansett Indian Tribe, and her willingness to share the Round Dance of Unity and Thanksgiving. Thank you to my wife, Marie, for her support and patient tolerance of my long creative absences. My gratitude to LightHawk, the Wilderness Society of Seattle and Alan Copsey, J.D., Ph.D., for helping me to fly over and venture into the Olympic Mountains and Cascade Mountains during my research on the temperate rainforest. Invaluable assistance was provided by my mom, Esther Caduto, Gail Vernazza, as well as by the staff of the Hathorn/Olson Photographic Laboratories. I also thank Joseph Kennedy, Esquire, for providing me with a quiet place in which to write the first part of the manuscript. And thanks to Squirrel, my companion during many long days of writing.

From Joseph Bruchac: Ktsi wliwini, "great thanks" to all the Native storytellers, too numerous to mention, who continue to help me find my way along this road I've chosen. Ktsi wliwini to the men and women of the Abenaki Nation for their courage and to Cecile Wawanolet for her ageless devotion to preserving our language. Ktsi wliwini to my sons, Jim and Jesse, for their faith and their commitment to the old ways in this hardest of times. Wlipamkaani, nitobak! Travel well, my friends.

LEGEND

—— BOUNDARIES OF CULTURAL AREAS

INNU NATIVE NORTH AMERICAN GROUPS DISCUSSED IN BOOK (CAPITAL LETTERS)

Arapaho OTHER NATIVE NORTH AMERICAN GROUPS (INCLINED AND LOWER CASE LETTERS)

– – – NATIONAL BOUNDARIES

········ STATE AND PROVINCIAL BOUNDARIES

CARTOGRAPHY BY STACY MILLER, UPPER MARLBORO, MD.
COPYRIGHT © 1994 MICHAEL J. CADUTO.

SCALE

0   100   200   400 STATUTE
                          MILES

⟶ ◈ NATIVE ◈ ⟵
NORTH AMERICA
◈

ATLANTIC

OCEAN

Cultural areas and tribal locations of Native North Americans. This map shows tribal locations as they appeared around 1600, except for the Seminole culture in the Southeast and the Tuscaroras in the Northeast. The Seminoles formed from a group which withdrew from the Muskogee (Creek) and joined with several other groups on the Georgia/Florida border to form the Seminoles, a name which has been used since about 1775. In the eastern woodlands the Haudenosaunee (Iroquois) consist of six nations, the Cayuga, Mohawk, Oneida, Onondaga, Seneca and Tuscarora. The Tuscaroras were admitted to the Iroquois League in 1722 after many refugees from the Tuscarora Wars (1711–1713) in the Southeast fled northward. There are hundreds of other Cultures/Nations that are not included due to limited space. The generally recognized name of at least one distinct Culture is given in each area, emphasizing those with large populations, past and/or present. Traditional names are used where possible because many names in general use are not preferred by Native North Americans.

Introduction

Keepers of Life is a seed waiting to be planted. You—the parent, educator, naturalist, camp counselor or storyteller—provide the soil, water, sunlight and caring that enable the seed to sprout and bloom, the moments of discovery, excitement and sharing that bring the stories and lessons to life. Stories, facts and activities are a pathway into the mysterious world of plants—giving voice to their need to be understood and nurtured by human beings. In the magic of the stories, Earth is created on Turtle's back; the first People are made from maize; Kehtean, the Creator, changes the giant Maushop into a great white whale; Koluskap creates the flowering and fruiting plants and beds of soft moss for People to sleep on; a redbird gives the gift of the bitterroot to an old woman for survival; Corn Spirit shows People how to respect the corn and give thanks for its many gifts; and "Indian Summer" is given to People as a time to be thankful for the gifts from Earth and the Creator.

Keepers of Life continues the tradition begun by its highly popular and critically acclaimed predecessors, *Keepers of the Earth* and *Keepers of the Animals*. This is a book about learning to understand, live with and care for plants: a gathering of carefully selected Native North American stories and hands-on activities promote an understanding of, appreciation for, empathy with and responsible stewardship toward all plants on Earth. *Keepers of Life* is a valuable aid for those who want children to be excited by and connected with plants and "all our relations," the term used by many Native North Americans to refer to life on Earth, including people. When the stories and activities in this book, and resources in its companion teacher's guide, are followed carefully as children progress from kindergarten through the primary grades (roughly ages 5 through 12), a complete program of study will be provided. This program covers the important concepts and topics of botany; plant ecology; the environmental and stewardship issues that are particularly important to plants; and the natural history of every kind of North American plant and plant-like organism from algae to flowering plants, and from all North American habitats from desert to seashore and from rainforest to alpine tundra. Children are also introduced to such crucial environmental issues as the "greenhouse effect" and global warming, ozone depletion, acid rain, endangered species and extinction.

Tell children a story and they listen with their whole beings. Lead children to touch, smell and understand a flower, to listen to the wind sighing in a pine grove, to see the waving blades of seaweed along the shore or to taste a sweet wild edible berry and you begin to establish connections between children and the plants in their surroundings. Have children listen to and look at a seed—feel the seed, study the way it grows and how it develops flowers that attract bees, butterflies and other insects that pollinate the flower and help new seeds to develop. Help children to understand how the flower is part of a field or vacant-lot community of plants, animals, rocks, soil and water—all fueled by the plant-growing energy of the sun. Visit places where people have affected the flower's home to help children appreciate their stewardship role in the world and how all things are intertwined. Keep the children at the center of their learning encounters. Build on these experiences with activities that help children to care for and take care of plants so they may develop a conservation ethic.

As the stories unfold and you help the children bring the activities to life, a holistic, interdisciplinary approach to teaching about the plants and Native North American cultures begins. With their close ties to the plants, and all parts of Earth, Native North American cultures are a crucial link between human society and plants. The story characters are voices through which the wisdom of Native North Americans speaks in today's language, fostering listening and reading skills and enhancing understanding of how the Native people traditionally live close to plants. Each story is a natural teaching tool that becomes a springboard as you dive into the activities, which are designed to provoke curiosity among children and facilitate discovery of plants and their environments and the influence that people have on those surroundings. Pedagogically sound, these activities have been extensively field-tested. They involve the children in creative arts, theater, reading, writing, science, social studies, mathematics and sensory awareness, among other subjects. The activities engage a child's whole self: emotions, senses, thoughts and actions. They emphasize creative thinking and synthesis of knowledge and experiences. Because of the active and involving nature of the experiences found in this book, children who have special needs physically, mentally and emotionally will respond well with proper care and skilled instruction.

These stories and activities have been used and enjoyed by families and children at home and in camp settings, nature centers, environmental education programs, public and private schools and library story hours, in both rural and urban settings. Churches and other spiritual groups have found Native North American traditions to be an inspiration for developing environmental stewardship and deeper ties with plants and Earth as part of Creation. While the

---

*As used here, *Earth* refers to all of our surroundings: plants, animals and the physical environment, which includes air, water, soil, rocks and sky. Although, by convention, people are often referred to separately in the text, here they are considered to be a *part* of Earth, as Native North Americans believe them to be.

stories and activities arise from North America, with some adaptations for local conditions, they are relevant and useful to people and places in other lands as well.

Native North Americans see themselves as *part* of nature, not apart from it. Their stories use natural images to teach about relationships among people and among people, plants and the rest of Earth. To the Native peoples of North America, what is done to a tree, a flower, a bird, a rock or a river is done to a brother or sister. This perspective has important implications throughout this book where it deals with endangered species, plant stewardship and related environmental problems and solutions.

Native North Americans emphasize a close relationship with nature versus control over the natural world. In many stories the lessons are taught both directly and through metaphors. A good example of this is the Mayan story "The People of Maize" in Chapter 13. The first people, who are made of wood, cut down the trees without showing thanks and hunt the animals without mercy. They do not give thanks to the Creator and the Maker. These first people are destroyed, except for a few who become the howler monkeys of the rainforest. People are then made out of maize, cornmeal dough. These people are thankful, they take care of the rainforest and all goes well for them as long as they remember to live in this way. Like the People of Maize, we each need to take a journey into the realm of our plant relations to better understand them and their needs for survival. *Keepers of Life* provides a path for this journey, and the means for sharing these insights and this knowledge with children so they may learn to live in a healing relationship with the world of plants.

STEPS FOR USING
THIS BOOK EFFECTIVELY

The book is divided into two parts, and there is a separate teacher's guide. Part I offers thoughts and suggestions for facilitating the use of stories, guided fantasies, puppet shows and activities, as well as for planting trees and shrubs. If you would like to further round out your background in certain areas before beginning Part II, the teacher's guide discusses the nature of Native North American stories and the cultures from which these particular stories come. It also considers the important educational philosophies and approaches upon which this book is based.

Part II is the heart of the book. In this section, we use stories as an introduction to the subjects explored in the activities. In some cases the activities follow directly from the story, while in others the story is a stepping stone that leads into the activities in a more general way. Stories and activities are arranged under broad topical headings in the Contents. The "Index of Activities Arranged by Subject" describes the specific lessons taught by each activity and the locations of activities throughout the book.

Each story is followed by a "Discussion" section that provides background information on the topics the story introduces. These discussion sections in themselves constitute a unique collection of essays that enhance understanding of the Native North American context of the stories. They also cover the natural history and environmental issues related to every major group of North American plants. Relevant questions then offer further help in bridging the stories and activities. Chapters end with the section "Extending the Experience."

Following the title of each activity are several symbols that provide a quick reference to both the setting(s) and the topic(s) of that activity.

These two symbols identify activities that occur

 outdoors

 indoors (Many indoor activities can be done outdoors, but it is not necessary to do so.)

When an activity is marked with both the indoor *and* outdoor symbols, it means parts of the activity are better conducted outdoors while other parts are better conducted indoors.

In addition, the activities focus on one or more of the following four subject areas, each of which is represented by a corresponding symbol:

 sensory awareness of plants

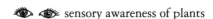 understanding of plants

 caring for plants and Earth

 caring for people

Begin by sharing a story and illustrations with the children or by having them present the story. Lead a discussion using the background information from the "Discussion" section and the "Questions" section at the end of the story. Some leaders prefer to conduct some or all of the activities before sharing the story, to give the children background in that subject. Use the approach that works best with your group.

The "Discussion" sections contain much information for the leader's reference. Use what you need for your children's level, and keep it simple. The ideas in the "Discussion," "Questions" and "Activities" sections are provided to encourage appreciation, celebration and stewardship as well as understanding. Do not try to "have all the right answers," or to get the children to memorize lots of facts and terms.

Concentrate on having children master the goals of each activity.

Each "Activity" begins with a title and a brief description of what the children will do during the activity. Broad educational "Goals" are also included. Conduct the activities that are at the appropriate "Age" level, as indicated in the text. Activities are marked as being appropriate for younger children (roughly ages 5 to 8) or older children (roughly ages 9 to 12). Some activities are appropriate for both age groups and are so marked. Many activities can be adapted to work well with different ages, and this book also has been widely adapted for use with children from 13 to 15 years of age and up. All of the "Materials" you will need to conduct the activity are also listed. Virtually all of the materials can be found outdoors, in the learning center and at home: they are simple, common and inexpensive.

Each activity has a detailed "Procedure." These sections use a simple, cookbook-like approach that has been found to work very well with leaders from all backgrounds working in every kind of learning situation. Use the activities described under "Extending the Experience" at the end of each chapter to reinforce and supplement the lessons of the stories and activities. Another valuable tool is the "Glossary and Pronunciation Key to Native North American Worlds and Names."

Explore, with the children, the Native North American group from which the story comes. The map on pages xiv to xv shows the cultural areas and tribal locations of the Native North American groups discussed in this book. These specific cultures, and their larger cultural groupings, are described in detail in the teacher's guide.

Be creative and use this book as a complement to your family experiences or your educational program for elementary-age children. The section "Further Resources on Native North Americans and Environmental Studies," in the teacher's guide, provides lists of books for learning and teaching about Native North Americans, plants and Earth. It also includes guides to environmental and outdoor education; to values education; and to facilitating storytelling, guided fantasies, puppet shows and interdisciplinary studies. An extensive section in the teacher's guide lists "Further Reading by Chapter for *Keepers of Life.*" This chapter-by-chapter list includes books for both children (categorized as being appropriate for either younger or older children, or both) and adults, covering the Native North American group(s) from which the story(ies) in each chapter come and the plants and other environmental topics addressed in each chapter.

AUTHORS' NOTES
Use of Gender and Terms for Native Peoples

The use of gender varies among individuals and cultures. To maintain the accuracy and spirit of word usage and meaning among the writings contributed to this book by other authors, we include these writings in their unedited forms. The balance of the text avoids gender bias.

In this book, we use the term *Native North American* to refer to Native peoples of the United States, Canada and Central America. These peoples are often, by convention, called "Native American" and "American Indian." Not all Native North Americans are American Indians. The Inuit (Eskimo) peoples of the far north (Chapter 12) comprise a culture that is distinct from the North American Indians who inhabit this continent.

In the United States, *American Indian* and *Native American* are terms used interchangeably to refer to the Native, aboriginal inhabitants of North, Central and South America. In Canada, the terms *Native Indian, First Nation* or *Aboriginal* are commonly used rather than *Native American.* In all cases, it is best to refer first to peoples with regard to their individual tribal nation, such as "Inuit," "O'odham," "Anishinabe" or "Wampanoag."

Hunting as a Subject of Ecological Education

A number of the stories in *Keepers of Life*, as well as the "Discussion" and "Questions" sections in several chapters (particularly Chapters 9, 12, 13 and 15) address, among other subjects, the topic of hunting. Hunting is and has been integral to the lives and cultures of Native North Americans. For these peoples hunting was, and in some cases still is, a matter of survival. For animals, hunting is always a matter of survival. Traditionally, Native North Americans do not hunt for sport, they hunt only for survival.

Hunting is one part of the relationship between people and animals. We neither advocate nor condemn hunting. Hunting needs to be taught about because it is a reality in our world, and education should be inclusive and not gloss over controversial subjects. Those who want their children to be exposed to and understand the differences between traditional Native North American hunting practices, the realities of modern hunting and the important issues related to each are encouraged to explore Chapters 20 and 21 in *Keepers of the Earth* as well as Chapters 9, 13, 15, 16 and 17 in *Keepers of the Animals.* We want to show in these chapters that, since hunting is commonplace, there are ways it can be managed to assure that animal populations are maintained in a healthy state. We encourage users of this book to study the methods offered in Chapter 2 under "Conducting the Activities," and in the various values education resources listed in the teacher's guide, for approaching values and controversial issues in education.

The same kinds of skills that enable hunters to stalk and capture their prey can help children to become more aware and sensitive in their relationships with animals, such as trying to get close to an animal in the wild to observe it and learn about it.

PART I

A GUIDE FOR USING AND ENJOYING THIS BOOK

In front of the elm bark lodge, an old man dressed in torn clothing sat weeping.

CHAPTER 1

✤ Seeds of Wisdom: Keepers of Life on Earth ✤

The Corn Spirit

(Tuscarora—Eastern Woodland)

Long ago, they say, there was a village of people whose cornfields were blessed with good harvests, year after year. They had so much corn each year that they began to take it for granted. They stopped weeding the fields and the children trampled the cornstalks as they played. When harvest time came, the people picked, but they did not do it well. Much of the corn was left unpicked and only the birds ate it. The people wasted more than they ate. They threw ears of corn to their dogs. As they had always done, they dried some of the corn to eat in the winter and use for seed corn the next spring. They placed this corn in storage baskets to bury for the winter, but they did everything carelessly. The corn baskets were not well made. The storage holes were not dug deeply or well covered.

"There is much game in the forest," the people said. "We can always hunt to survive, even if the stored corn spoils."

So the people went on without showing respect for the corn that gave them life. They even forgot to say thanks to the Creator for their good fortune.

Only one man remembered to show respect. His name was Dayohagwenda. Dayohagwenda cared for his fields and weeded them. He harvested his corn carefully and gave thanks for his good harvest. He stored his corn with great care. He was sad about the way the others acted.

That autumn, after the harvest moon, the people went hunting. But the hunters had bad luck. Animals were hard to find. It seemed that the deer and moose and even the rabbits had all disappeared from the forest. The people tried to fish, but the streams and lakes were empty. Finally, the people dug up their stored corn. But the poorly made baskets had fallen apart. Much of the corn had been eaten by mice. The rest had rotted away.

"What shall we do?" the people said. "We will starve."

Meanwhile, Dayohagwenda was walking in the forest. He was thinking about the way his people no longer showed respect for the corn or gave thanks. As he walked, he found an old trail. It led to a clearing in the forest. In that clearing was a lodge made of elm bark and built on top of a mound of earth. Weeds grew all around the lodge. In front of the lodge, an old man dressed in torn clothing sat weeping.

"Grandfather," Dayohagwenda said, "why are you weeping?"

"I am weeping because your people have forgotten me."

"Why are your clothes torn?"

"They are torn because your people threw me to their dogs."

"Why are you so dirty?"

"I am dirty because your people let their children trample me."

"Why are there weeds around your lodge?"

"Your people no longer take care of me. Now I must go away and I can never return again to help them."

Now Dayohagwenda knew who the old man was. He was Corn Spirit.

"Grandfather," Dayohagwenda said, "do not leave us. I still respect you. I will go back and remind my people how to treat you."

The old man stopped weeping. "Grandson," he said, "I will stay with *you*. If your people show me respect, I will not leave them."

Dayohagwenda went back to the village.

"We are going to starve," the people said. "Our corn is gone and we have no other food."

"Listen," said Dayohagwenda, "I have been in the forest. There I found a lodge surrounded by weeds and an old man wearing torn clothing the color of cornhusks. He said his people deserted him and he was going to leave forever."

The people understood. "It is Corn Spirit," they said. "He has left us and now we will surely die."

"No," said Dayohagwenda, "I spoke with Corn Spirit. I told him we would treat him with respect. He said that if we respect him, he will help us through the winter."

Then Dayohagwenda dug up his own stored corn. His baskets had been well made. He had dug his granary deep and covered it properly. All of his harvest was there. There was more than he had remembered storing, much more. There was enough to feed the whole village through the winter. There was even enough left to use as seed corn for planting in the spring when the leaves of the maple tree were the size of a squirrel's ear.

From then on, Dayohagwenda's people always showed respect for the corn. They planted with care and hoed and weeded. They sang songs of thanksgiving as they harvested. They made strong baskets and deep storage pits for their granaries. Most of all, they remembered to give thanks for the blessing of corn and all of the other good things they had been given. They taught their children and their children's children to do the same. So it is to this day.

Stories are the living legacy of a people by which the wisdom of the ages is passed to each new generation. The germ of the seed corn in "The Corn Spirit" contains the genetic memory of countless generations, which ensures that the nascent plants possess the traits needed to survive; in the same way, a story is part of the cumulative, collected wisdom of the ancestors that teaches each new generation how to live in balance. In these tenuous times, when the survival of Earth and humankind is being pushed to the brink, we need to visit the storehouse of oral tradition, to retrieve and cultivate the ancient seeds of wisdom contained in the stories of Native North Americans and to combine these lessons with the knowledge of ecological science.

The traditional Native North American relationship with nature is one of dynamic balance, of sacred respect and worship, of practical give-and-take in response to changes in population levels and habitat conditions. Survival exists along a continuum between the spiritual and the pragmatic. The Native way of conservation "has worked longer than any modern conservation programs."[1]

Mother Earth hears the call; she awakes; she arises; she feels the breath of the new born Dawn. The leaves and the grass stir ... all things move with the breath of the new day; everywhere life is renewed. This is very mysterious; we are speaking of something very sacred, although it happens every day.[2]

—The Kurahus, *Hako, Birth of Dawn*
Pawnee

The indigenous cultures of the Americas are based on some of the most sophisticated knowledge and uses of native plants ever known. The Incas used beans as a form of code by which messages were relayed by runners. The ancients who were versed in the reading of beans deciphered the meaning contained in the colors, sizes and shapes of the beans (Figure 1-1). Astute ecologists, Native North Americans used the plants growing in a certain area as environmental indicators of the kinds of soils, clays, minerals and ores that would be present, as well as the game animals that would be found associated with those plants and that kind of habitat.[3] Traditionally, Native North Americans have encountered plants with a seemingly endless variety of uses, including

- food
- clothing (cotton)
- shelter
- beverages
- weapons
- cosmetics
- paper
- preservatives
- medicines
- birth control
- anesthetics
- art
- dyes
- smoking ingredients
- aromatics
- musical instruments (flutes, drums, etc.)
- treatment of mental disorders
- tools (ropes, handles, etc.)
- crafts and craft materials
- canoes (bark and dugout)
- glues
- paint fixatives
- vessels (wooden bowls, baskets, bark buckets)

Native knowledge of plants grew over the millennia and became the basis of intensive agriculture and systematic forms of environmental management. Forestry practices were used to encourage the growth of trees and other plants that were found useful and to discourage plants that were not wanted.[4] *Fire* was the most powerful tool wielded to manage the forest.[5] Each year, in parts of what is now called New England, Natives burned away the undergrowth to regenerate the growth of annual plants and green shrubs. Localized burning was used in many parts of Native North America to facilitate moving about in the forest, to decrease the populations of biting insects, to make it easier to spot prey while hunting as well as enemies that might approach the village, to encourage prey animals (such as deer) by creating new growth for browse and to decrease the likelihood that an enemy might burn out one's village. Fire-resistant pines and other trees flourished. Firs and other species that were smaller and less fire-resistant were often killed back.[6] Tracts of pitch pine were maintained on Cape Cod by regular burning. In California, forests were burned to kill parasitic mistletoe on oak and mesquite, and some bushes were burned so the straight branches that grew back could be used to make baskets. Fire was used by the Native peoples of the plains to maintain open prairies, to provide browse and open land for bison and to control the migratory herds of these great animals.

Fire is but one—probably the most dramatic—of the many ways Native North Americans managed their environments. Because the survival of Natives has depended directly on the land and the plants and animals that live here, Natives have developed a thorough, practical knowledge of conservation. The traditions of Native North America include an intimate connection to the physical aspects of the environments as well as a deep respect for Earth and all of Creation. The traditional practices in forestry, agriculture, hunting and gathering are accompanied by prayers, rituals and taboos to show respect for all aspects of Earth, with special thanks to those that are a source of survival. An intimate knowledge of plant and animal populations allows for changes in harvest and hunting pressures so as to conserve resources and assure the survival and diversity of species. "Peoples who mix

Figure 1-1. A palette of native seeds. Corn: (left) chin-mark flour corn and (right) Hopi blue and white corn. Loose seeds (clockwise from upper left) red dye amaranth, scarlet runner beans, domesticated devil's claw, Tarahumara asufrado bean, Hopi red lima bean and Mayo blusher squash. (Photo by Dale S. Turner, courtesy Native Seeds/SEARCH)

farming with gathering and hunting have retained a rich knowledge and appreciation of wild diversity."[7]

When Europeans first landed on the magnificent shores of eastern North America, they found old-growth forests that were "open" and "park-like."[8] Stands of white pine had an average height of more than 100 feet (30.5 meters), containing some individual trees vaulting to a height of 250 feet (76.2 meters) with a diameter of up to 5 feet (1.5 meters).[9] However, soon after Europeans arrived in North America, they began using plants for profit because they had long ago denuded much of their own countryside of trees big enough to be cut for lumber. The forests of North America, then, were seen through mercantile eyes. Sassafras became the first commodity shipped back to Europe from North America, for use as flavoring and medicine (it was thought to cure syphilis), as early as 1602 to 1603. Fish (salted cod), furs and ship timbers were among the first trade goods that sailed for Europe.[10] Trees still standing after cutting for export, for local use or to clear farmland were often burned indiscriminately. Similarly, unsuccessful attempts were made to remove and destroy those Native peoples who had survived the devastating plagues of smallpox, tuberculosis, influenza, measles, chicken pox, scarlet fever and bubonic and pneumonic plagues that swept through Native populations after initial contact with Europeans. While Native North Americans used fire as a tool to *manage* their environment, European settlers used fire and cutting to *remove* the forest.

There are still places in Native North America and throughout the world where social and economic pressures conspire to create the kind of exploitive environmental practices that characterized the early European settlement of the North American continent. The messages inherent in the rich oral tradition of Native North Americans have never been more important than in these times when the plant world is under siege from myriad human activities. Acid precipitation (including rain) has created thousands of lifeless lakes and ponds by destroying the growth of algae, which comprises the base of the aquatic food chain. The toxic aluminum dissolved into solution by acid waters is the most likely factor that kills aquatic mayflies, minnows and mollusks and then kills a variety of fish including trout, bass, pike, walleye and others. Vast regions of temperate forest are in decline due to the effects of acid rain and ozone pollution in the lower atmosphere.[11] As many as half of the trees in some alpine forests have died outright.[12,13] Other forms of toxic industrial air pollution have killed extensive plant communities downwind. Air pollution in the lower atmosphere is thought to be reacting synergistically with the effects of ozone destruction in the upper atmosphere, causing, in particular, the depression of plant immune systems and concomitant increased susceptibility to disease and insect damage. On a broader scale, plants are the green tissue that greatly affects, and is dramatically affected by, the global environmental events of our times. Global warming,

if it continues apace, will alter regional climates and affect associated plant communities, particularly in cold temperate and polar ecosystems. Many plant species will not be able to "migrate" or adapt fast enough to rapidly changing temperatures and amounts of rainfall along shifting climatic boundaries.

There may not, however, be many forests left to suffer this fate. Clear-cutting, slash-and-burn agriculture, cattle ranching and other unwise uses of forest lands are denuding millions of acres of temperate and tropical rainforests, dryland forests and old-growth forests. The natural vegetation is often replaced with a monoculture of coniferous trees, or the land is left a virtual desert. Many plant communities native to North America, such as the tallgrass prairies, having been plowed under and grazed to near extinction, are now relegated to a few small islands of protected conservation areas. More than 55 percent of the original acreage of wetland habitats that were found in the United States when Europeans first arrived have been filled, drained, grazed, farmed, built upon or otherwise altered so that they no longer possess their important ecological, recreational, aesthetic and other natural values. Worldwide, subhumid and semiarid land is being destroyed and reduced to a desert-like state at the rate of 2.4 million acres (972,000 hectares) each year.[14] The loss of tropical forests, both rainforests and arid plant communities, continues at an alarming pace, bringing with it the ensuing loss of habitat, a parade of newly extinct and endangered species, a staggering loss of genetic diversity among associated plants and animals, an increasing imbalance in atmospheric gases (particularly the so-called greenhouse gases) and the loss of traditional ways of life for many indigenous peoples who dwell in these habitats.

Rainforests shelter more than one-half of all the plant and animal species on Earth, and more than 50 percent of Earth's original rainforest has been destroyed to date, mostly in the past 40 years (Figure 1-2). A stand of tropical rainforest the size of a football field is destroyed every second.[15] Roughly one-half of the 20 million acres (8.1 million hectares) of tropical rainforests that are cleared each year for slash-and-burn agriculture are cut into virgin forest.[16] Among the species of plants being lost in tropical forests are the genetic forebears of half of the roughly one dozen leading food crops worldwide that provide 90 percent of humankind's food. Not only are rainforests home to plants used to manufacture hundreds of modern prescription drugs, but rainforests also store a vast amount of carbon. As a rainforest is cut, the stored carbon dioxide is released into the atmosphere when the wood is burned and as stems and root systems decay. This carbon dioxide, a major "greenhouse gas," contributes to global warming. The most serious threat to tropical rainforests is slash-and-burn agriculture. Other activities that destroy millions of acres of tropical rainforest each year include logging and cattle ranching. There is also an illegal, widespread black market trade in threatened and endangered species, which is depleting endangered plant and animal populations and driving them closer to extinction.

Farther to the north, running like a precious green vein thousands of miles up the Pacific Coast from California's Sierra Nevada through Oregon, Washington, British Columbia and north to the fjords of Alaska's Inside Passage, are the vast, vaulting canopies of the remaining ancient, old-growth forests and temperate rainforests. These magnificent natural communities are the domain of the great conifers, including Douglas fir, sugar pine, incense cedar, Pacific yew, Sitka spruce, western hemlock and western red cedar. One of the redwood spires in the fog belt of coastal California, the tallest tree on Earth, stands at 375 feet (114.3 meters) high. These ancient forests contain a rich diversity of plant and animal life and are some of the most productive forests anywhere outside of the tropics.

Yet, in northern California, Oregon, Washington, British Columbia and Alaska, nearly 200,000 acres (81,000 hectares) of ancient forests are cleared each year—a rate amounting to the clear-cutting of a patch of forest the size of 500 football fields every day.[17] Roughly 90 percent of the Pacific coastal forests have been cleared to date in heavily logged areas, and most of the remaining forest is on publicly owned land. At the current rate of cutting, all of these ancient, irreplaceable forests will be gone in just 20 years.

Deep in the cool, moist habitats of the mixed evergreen forests of the Klamath and Siskiyou mountains along the California-Oregon border grows the Pacific yew. The bark of this small, slow-growing tree contains a potent cancer-fighting substance known as *taxol* that has the power to stop cancer cells from dividing. Taxol has been used to successfully treat advanced ovarian cancer and studies indicate that it may help to cure other cancers, such as those of the breast and lung. Although a partially synthetic version of taxol is now being produced from the needles of yews in Europe and Asia, and the harvesting pressure on the Pacific yew has been relieved, this tree's existence remains threatened as ancient forests disappear.

Taxol is just one utilitarian example of the importance of plants and of species diversity. Each species possesses a range of values, from the intrinsic, ethical and spiritual values of life itself to the values of aesthetics, science, ecology, history, research, education, recreation and more. In addition, every species of plant possesses unique qualities including climatic and ecological adaptability, pest resistance, nutritional value, flavor and medicinal properties. It has been estimated that, if current trends continue and the tropical forests of North, Central and South America are reduced to those protected in parks, reserves and refuges, by the year 2000, 66 percent of all plant species and 14 percent of all plant families would be destroyed forever.[18]

According to the Haudenosaunee (Iroquois) peoples, these human-caused ecological disasters will continue if we do not change current ways of relating to and caring for the natural world. One notable sign of damage to deciduous forests in the northeastern states and maritime provinces is a decline in the vigor and health of sugar maple trees.[19] A widespread symptom of this decline, which has become more pronounced over the past decade, is the thinning of foliage and the death of branches at the tops of sugar maple crowns. These ecological events have been hauntingly presaged in a Haudenosaunee prophesy told for many generations:

> There will be a day coming when you will see the trees start dying from the top down: the rivers will become unfit to drink or swim in, and the fish will float on top of the water. Our wells will be unfit to drink.[20]

Figure 1-2. Tropical rainforests are stunningly beautiful and diverse environments. They are home to an array of plants and animals; more than half of all species worldwide live in rainforests. (Photo by Alan C. Graham)

Given the pressures exerted by the one-half billion people inhabiting North and Central America[21] and the accelerating demands being placed on the environment, we have little time left in which to establish a balanced relationship with Earth. At the current rate in which tropical vegetation is being destroyed, for instance, there is time for just one more generation of research regarding the traditional farming/gathering peoples of the Neotropics in Central America and the rare plants they use.[22]

Ultimately, we must have a balanced relationship with Earth that recognizes the importance and interrelatedness of all life, as well as the limits of our ability to fully understand Earth and the living things with which we share our home. Science spurs our intellectual development even as it confirms our ignorance—the impossibility of ever knowing all that is. Herein lies "The Great Mystery" of Native North American cultures, which goes by many names. A rational, compassionate mind would conclude that, since we do not really know the effects of our actions, humility and a desire for care and caution in our actions toward Earth and other peoples is the only wise course to take.

These days people seek knowledge, not wisdom. Knowledge is of the past; wisdom is of the future.[23]
—Vernon Cooper
Lumbee

Science continues to reaffirm the great truths echoed in the teachings of the elders throughout the cultures of Native North America—that "we are all related," at cultural, ecological, evolutionary and even molecular levels. Whether plant, animal, rock, air or water, we are, in essence, all composed of the same subatomic particles; even the densest of materials consists mostly of space. Native North American traditional cultures view nature as a relative, as a *subject,* whereas Western cultures tend to perceive the natural world as *object.*

We humans see the world a certain way because of the limitations of our sensory and perceptual abilities. Most people empathize with animals because they are, in appearance, more like us than trees and other plants. Hurt an animal, and it will react quickly and violently, often by writhing in pain and crying out. Yet, simply because humans can experience the language of one being and not another, does this mean, in terms of *being,* that one is necessarily of a higher value? We place artificial human distinctions of value on the world around us by assigning greater importance to those things that look and appear to *feel* more like us. Observations made of the sensory awareness of plants, however, seem to demonstrate that they, too, react when a leaf is torn or burned and when an animal or another plant is harmed nearby.[24]

Today the global environment itself—the living Earth—is crying out with a multitude of signs of our misuse. The same principles and Earth wisdom used by a traditional agriculturalist in prehistory who read the signs of poor health in crops growing near the village can be used in these times to respond to the full range of environmental problems, from taking the steps needed to protect a locally rare

plant species to changing the personal habits of consumption that contribute to the stratospheric ozone destruction that threatens plant communities around the world.

Listening to plants for guidance and using plants as symbols of healing and peace is an ancient tradition in Native North America. Long ago in prehistory, east across the continent to what is now upper New York State and southeastern Ontario along the shores of Lake Ontario, the Peacemaker and Hiawatha* brought peace to the long-warring five nations of the Haudenosaunee. A great white pine, the Tree of Peace, was planted, in whose shade, from that day on, the Sachems would sit to hold council. The four roots of the "Great White Root" (*Oktehrakenrahkowa*) grew out to each of the four directions to symbolize peace and charity and to lead other nations and individuals to the Council of the League.[25] All weapons were buried beneath the Great Tree and an eagle, perched atop its branches or soaring above, keeps watch to warn others of approaching danger (Figure 1-3). If danger comes, the Sachems and Council will meet to discuss and find the truth, and then people will find and meet at the Great Swamp Elm Tree to put their minds together to discover a way to restore peace and happiness.[26]

Black Elk, the great Oglala Lakota visionary, shared his vision of the daybreak star herb. Two men from the east gave it to him, saying, "With this on earth you shall undertake anything and do it."[27] They told him to drop this "herb of understanding" on Earth, where it rooted, grew and formed four blossoms of different color on its stems: blue, white, scarlet and yellow. "The rays from these streamed upwards to the heavens so that all creatures saw it and in no place was there darkness."[28]

Living in balance, in many Native North American cultures, means to live within and honor the circles of life. A circle of giving and receiving becomes part of our relationship with the natural world when we take only what is necessary to survive and return the remains of plants and animals to Earth with gratitude. There are natural laws to guide our actions—the cycles of night and day, of the moons and seasons. These in turn relate to ecological concepts such as the nutrient cycle, water cycle and gas cycles. Traditional circles of life include ceremonial circles, the circles of the family and community and the circle of life and death.

Each generation continues the circle of wisdom handed down by the elders. Time and again throughout Native North America, traditions speak of caring for Earth, and each other, in the tradition of Seven Generations: among the Shinnecock, Lenni Lenape, Lakota, Anishinabe, Haudenosaunee and others. Some say we need to consider how each of our actions, today, will affect the next seven generations to

*This is the true Hiawatha in Haudenosaunee tradition. Longfellow's famous "Song of Hiawatha" in fact recalls tales of the great Anishinabe being called Manabozho, whom Longfellow mistakenly called "Hiawatha."

Figure 1-3. The Haudenosaunee Tree of Peace, the League of Peace and the principles that they embody have inspired agreements for peaceful coexistence among many peoples and nations throughout the world. The United Nations Charter and the United States Constitution are but two notable legacies of the League. (Illustration by John Kahionhes Fadden)

come, and they remind us that we are all part of a Seventh Generation. Others also consider how the wisdom of their ancestors, who lived seven generations ago, would guide them about a course of action being taken today. Another perspective heard is that we are the fourth generation, and that we should use the wisdom of three generations ago to care for the children of three generations to come. Let us grow the future in the hearts and minds of children, for each child is a fertile bed anxiously awaiting the seeds and nurturing needed for growth, sustenance and the skills of survival.

In their roles as producers of food energy, green plants, along with the sun, are the Keepers of Life. Other plants are vitally important for recycling waste and making it available as nutrients for new growth. Plants stand between all life on Earth and eternity. Native North Americans are and have been the original people in North America: deeply rooted Keepers of Life through the millennia. The Keepers of Life are calling us to action. By their stewardship and wisdom traditions, in conjunction with the knowledge of ecology, we are all asked to be and live in balance, to become Keepers of Life—living each day with care for the next seven generations in our hearts.

NOTES

1. Gary Paul Nabhan, *Enduring Seeds: Native American Agriculture and Wild Plant Cultivation* (San Francisco: North Point, 1989), 42.

2. Frances G. Lombardi and Gerald Scott Lombardi, *Circle Without End: A Sourcebook of American Indian Ethics* (Happy Camp, Calif.: Naturegraph Publishers, 1982), 17–18.

3. E. Barrie Kavasch, "Herbal Traditions," in Richard G. Carlson (ed.), *Rooted Like the Ash Trees: New England Indians and the Land* (Naugatuck, Conn.: Eagle Wing Press, 1987), 22.

4. Jack Weatherford, *Native Roots: How the Indians Enriched America* (New York: Crown, 1991), 41.

5. Ibid.

6. Ibid.

7. Nabhan, *Enduring Seeds,* 42.

8. William Cronon, *Changes in the Land: Indians, Colonists and the Ecology of New England* (New York: Hill and Wang, 1983), 25.

9. Ibid., 30.

10. Ibid., 20.

11. Charles E. Little, "Report from Lucy's Woods," *American Forests* (March–April 1992): 25–27, 68–69.

12. Hubert W. Vogelmann, "Catastrophe on Camel's Hump," *Natural History,* vol. 91, no. 11 (November 1982): 8–14.

13. Hubert W. Vogelmann, G. J. Badger, M. Bliss and R. M. Klein, "Forest Decline on Camel's Hump," *Vermont Bulletin of the Torrey Botany Club,* vol. 112 (1985): 274–287.

14. Nabhan, *Enduring Seeds,* 28.

15. Edward O. Wilson, *The Diversity of Life* (Cambridge, Mass.: Belknap Press, 1992), 275.

16. World Wildlife Fund figures.

17. Seth Zuckerman, *Saving Our Ancient Forests* (Venice, Calif.: Living Planet Press, 1991), ix.

18. Nabhan, *Enduring Seeds,* 28.

19. Brent Mitchell, "Air Pollution and Maple Decline," *Nexus,* vol. 3, no. 9 (Summer 1987): 1–13.

20. Barbara (Kawenehe) Barnes, Mike (Kanentakeron) Mitchell, Joyce (Konwahwihon) Thompson et al., *Traditional Teachings* (Cornwall Island, Ont.: North American Indian Traveling College, 1984), 81.

21. Population Reference Bureau, 1994 World Population Data Sheet (Washington, D.C.: Population Reference Bureau, 1994).

22. Nabhan, *Enduring Seeds,* 28.

23. Harvey Arden and Steve Wall, *Wisdomkeepers: Meetings With Native American Spiritual Elders* (Hillsboro, Ore.: Beyond Words, 1990), 59.

24. Peter Tompkins and Christopher Bird, *The Secret Life of Plants* (New York: Harper & Row, 1973), 5–6, 13–14, 19.

25. Barnes et al., *Traditional Teachings,* 31.

26. Ibid., 32.

27. John G. Neihardt, *Black Elk Speaks: Being the Life Story of a Holy Man of the Oglala Sioux* (Lincoln, Nebr.: University of Nebraska Press, 1979), 43.

28. Ibid.

CHAPTER 2

Tips and Techniques for
❖ Bringing This Book to Life ❖

"The myth is the public dream."[1]
—Joseph Campbell
The Power of Myth

It has been said that story and myth carry the wisdom of the collective *subconscious* of the world down through the ages. This wisdom, derived from cultural experiences that are part of the universal human condition, teaches us how to live, to integrate our lives into society and to exist in balance as part of an ecological community. Myth helps us to realize the wonder and mystery of the universe, shows us the nature of the world around us and illuminates our place in the social order.[2]

Science brings to light the knowledge gathered by the collective *consciousness* of humanity up to the present time. By explaining how the universe functions, science increases our understanding of nature and human nature. Science tells us *how* it all works but does not answer the universal question, "*What* is it?"[3] Science tells us how the heart beats, but myth helps us to understand why.

Knowing to a certain degree how Earth works, but lacking the wisdom of who we are and how to live in balance with Earth, means that we do not know where we are going. We are lost: walking a trail through thick forest without a map, a destination or even a clue to tell us what lies ahead around the next bend. What are our individual stories? What are the stories of our cultures? What is the contemporary story of Earth? Madeleine L'Engle, in *Walking on Water: Reflections on Faith and Art,* quotes Laurens Van Der Post on the Kalahari Bushmen: "These people know what we do not: That without a story you have not got a nation, or a culture, or a civilization. Without a story of your own to live you haven't got a life of your own."[4]

A synthesis of story and science brings together the subconscious and conscious aspects of human beings and human cultures. It is a profound union that helps each part of us to become more fully aware of what the other parts know and are doing. This integration of our personal and collective beings is an essential step toward the healing of our selves and our relationships with Earth and other people. This is the seminal purpose of the *Keepers* books.

TELLING THE STORIES

Stories are a link between our imagination and our surroundings. They reach deep into a child's inner world, to the places where dreams and fantasies are constantly sculpting an ever-growing worldview. The emotional identification a child forms with a story character—such as Fallen Star in Chapter 6, the woman who makes the first basket in Chapter 10, Blue Dawn in Chapter 11 or Waynabozho and his grandmother in Chapter 14—lead that child to momentarily *become* that character, to experience the sounds, sights, smells, sensations and emotions through which the character lives. Stories are a bridge between a child's life and the lessons the stories teach.

Each chapter in Part II of *Keepers of Life* begins with a Native North American story that is the key to unlocking a child's imagination while evoking useful images and exciting interest in the subjects that are then explored in the activities. The natural curiosity with which children regard Native North Americans is a window to educational opportunities. Several chapters contain supplemental stories that introduce or enhance the lessons of the activities.

Although none of the Native stories appears in the original language in which it was first told, we have tried in our retellings to capture the motion and the imagery of the original tales and to make sure the central message of each story is kept intact, for stories are powerful tools used for teaching and discipline in Native North American cultures. If you decide to retell these stories, to memorize them rather than read from the book, or to develop them into puppet shows, plays or skits, we urge you to pay close attention to the way these stories work. They are, however, meant to be *told,* rather than read silently.

Among Native North American cultures, certain stories were usually told at specific times of the year. Northeastern peoples told stories during the long cold season between the first and last frosts. Although you may not be able to restrict your use of these stories to this period of time, it is good to point out to children the traditional storytelling seasons. With this in mind, we suggest some ways to approach the oral use of these stories.

Seeing the Story

To begin with, read each story aloud to yourself several times before you try to read it to children or to tell it from memory. Let the story become a part of you. This was the method of the old-time Native North American storytellers, who listened again and again to each tale, rehearsing the story alone before trying to share it with an audience. After a story has become part of you, you may find yourself "seeing" the story as you tell it. At that point you may wish to bring your telling to life with descriptions of those things you see as you tell the tales aloud. When the story is a part of you and you are sharing it effectively with the listeners—creating the "reality" of that story—the characters and events will live and move in the mind's eye of the listeners.

But be careful as you do this, and do not try to change the endings or combine these stories. The elements of a story create a whole, a living being unto itself. Stories, to many Native North Americans, are *life;* they help to maintain the cultural integrity of the people and to keep the world in balance. When you "see" a story, it is like seeing an animal after having only heard about it before. It suddenly comes alive for you. But one animal is different from another, and so, too, is each story. Some stories may be wolves. Some may be turtles. But to combine the two does not work.

Be sure to look up the meaning of any unfamiliar Native words or names that appear in the story before you share the story with children. These terms are identified and explained in the glossary at the end of this book. This way, when children ask, "What is a Clan Mother?" or "What is a longhouse?" you will be ready with an informed response.

Once you "see" a story and feel comfortable with its telling, you may find it helpful to have a way of recalling the story at the proper time (Figure 2-1). The Iroquois storyteller, or *Hage'ota,* carried a bag full of items that acted as mnemonic devices—each item represented a story. The Hageota, or perhaps a child in the audience, would pull an item out of the bag, the item would be shown to the people and the story would begin. This process also transforms the storytelling into a shared experience by bringing the children into the act of choosing the stories to be told.

Making a storyteller's bag is an easy project. You and your children can gather things from the natural world or make things to add to the bag. Feathers, stones, nuts, small carvings—anything that can be jostled around in a bag without breaking can be part of your collection. Read the stories in this book carefully and then use your imagination.

The Setting of the Story

In many Native North American cultures, everyone was allowed to have a say and people listened with patience. People would sit in a circle during the time of storytelling because in a circle no person is at the head. All are "the same height." Remembering this may help you, and it is good to remind your listeners—who are not just an audience but also are part of the story—of that.

Pay close attention to the setting in which you read or tell a story. A quiet place where people can sit comfortably in a circle, whether in chairs or on the floor, is the best choice. Be very careful about this: if other things are going on around you, or if some people are seated outside the group

Figure 2-1. Pictographic symbols woven into beaded belts, such as this one at the Six Nations Indian Museum in Onchiota, New York, are used to record and retell important stories among the Haudenosaunee. (Photo by Jack Wandell)

or where they cannot hear well, your story will lose power. Someone who is standing outside a group and acting uninterested or hostile can become amazingly quiet and involved when "brought in." Also, be sure you are comfortable as you tell the story. Pay attention to how you feel as you speak from a standing position or while seated in a chair. There is no *one* right way for everyone. Some people do best while sitting in a chair or on the floor, whereas others feel more assured while standing or even walking around. Find *your* way.

Speaking the Story

Breathing is one of the most important things for a storyteller. Too many people try to speak while breathing from high in the chest. This tightens your chest and can strain your voice. Your breath—and your voice—should come from your diaphragm, the part of your body that is just below your ribs and above your stomach. Place the tips of your fingers there and breathe in. If your diaphragm does not move out, then your breathing is wrong. Native North American peoples see that area as the center of power for the body, and it is certainly the source of power for oral presentations. Your voice will be stronger, project farther and sound better when it comes from the diaphragm.

Resonance is a vital part of a good speaking voice. Try humming as an exercise to develop your natural resonance. One common method of voice training is to hum the vowel sounds, first with the letter "M" before them and then with the letter "B." Clarity is as important as resonance, so when you read or tell stories, be careful not to let your voice trail away, especially on significant words. Remember that you are the *carrier* of the story, and you must bring it to everyone in the room. Lift your chin up as you speak and look to the very back of the room (but don't forget to make eye contact with your audience). Imagine your voice as beginning in front of your mouth and reaching to the farthest wall. You do not have to shout to be heard.

Pace is also important in telling a story. Many people tend to speak either too fast or too slowly. If the story has truly become a part of you, then you should be able to sense the appropriate pace and follow that pace in your reading or telling. You may wish to practice by tape recording yourself as you read or retell a story from memory. Then listen for places where you speak too quickly, for words that are not well enunciated and for correct emphasis on important points in the story.

You may want to use any one of a number of formulaic beginnings and endings traditionally used by Native North American people when telling stories. One way the Abenaki people begin a story is with the words, "Here my story camps." They then close the story with such phrases as "That is the end" or "Then I left." The Iroquois often begin by saying, "Would you like to hear a story?" as do many other Native North American people. They then end with the words, "*Da neho!*" which means, "That is all." Such simple beginnings and endings may help you as a storyteller because they provide clear ways into and out of the tale.

Involving the Listeners

A good story cannot exist without a good listener. As a reader or teller, you can help your listeners be more effective and more involved. We have already mentioned the setting in which the story is told; there are also other ways to bring listeners into the tale. One device is the use of "response words." Tell the listeners that whenever you say "Ho?" they are to respond with "Hey!" Response words let you know that listeners are still awake and listening. Response words also can be used as pacing elements in the story or to make listeners feel themselves entering the tale. For example:

"Moon began to climb down the rope. … Ho?"
"HEY!"
"He climbed lower and lower. … Ho?"
"HEY!"
"But his weight was so great. … Ho?"
"HEY!"
"That the rope broke and he fell down to Earth below. …
     Ho?"
"HEY!"

As you tell your story, do not look at the same person in your audience all the time. If you are telling stories to a large group of children, make eye contact with different people and see them as individuals, not just a faceless mass. Ask questions that can be answered by someone who has been listening to the story. For example:

"And so that bright red suit of feathers went to whom?"
"Cardinal!"
"Yes! Then Buzzard tried on another suit of feathers. It
     was blue with a black-streaked crest. But that suit
     was not fine enough, either, for the messenger of all
     the birds. So that blue suit went to whom?"
"Bluejay!"

If there is singing, chanting, movement or hand clapping in your story, teach it to the children before the story begins. Then, at the appropriate time in the story, have everyone join in.

As you tell a story, be aware of how you use your hands, your facial expressions and the motions of your body. Some storytellers or readers prefer to sit quite still and let their voices do all of the work. Others become very theatrical. Again, you should find the way you are most comfortable. Flailing your arms about aimlessly can be distracting or overly dramatic. You can make your hand gestures more meaningful and give your listeners something really significant to focus on by incorporating Native North American sign language in your tellings. Many of these signs are the same as those used by the deaf, and the lingua franca sign language that Native North Americans developed because of widespread trade across pre-Columbian America is both effective and beautiful to watch. Two inexpensive and easy-to-use books that teach Native North American sign language through photographs and simple drawings are *Indian Sign Language,* by William Tomkins (New York: Dover, 1969), and *Indian Talk: Hand Signals of the North American Indians*, by Iron Eyes Cody (Happy Camp, Calif.: Naturegraph Publishers, 1970).

When sharing longer stories with very young children, we find it sometimes helps to take a brief break halfway through. Use this interlude to share and discuss the story illustration(s) as they relate to events that are unfolding. This technique prolongs the children's attention spans.

LEADING THE GUIDED FANTASIES

Guided fantasies create firsthand learning experiences that would not otherwise be possible. Some examples are *"Flower Fantasy"* (Chapter 9), *"Into a Grassland"* (Chapter 10), *"An Arctic Day"* (Chapter 12) and *"Growing Your Green Heart"* (Chapter 15). All the guided fantasies build upon the subjects introduced by Native North American stories that open the chapter.

While reading the fantasies, have the children:
• assume a comfortable position (we often have them lie on their backs)
• close their eyes
• relax
• take a few slow deep breaths
• clear their minds to make them more receptive to the images conjured up

Have children visualize that they are in a safe quiet place, or one they love best, to help them relax. Ask everyone to remain quiet throughout the story so those who are into the journey will not be disturbed. Reassure children who have difficulty sitting still and imagining the fantasy—not every kind of activity works well with everyone. Incorporate sounds into the fantasy, such as music, a drumbeat or sound effects to enhance the experience. Use different voices and be dramatic!

PERFORMING THE PUPPET SHOWS

Prepare children for puppeteering by having them make stick puppets or finger puppets of plants or animals with which to practice puppet motions (Figure 2-2). For finger puppets, sculpt the head out of clay or salt dough. Each child will use his or her thumb to press into the bottom of the puppet's head, going about as far as the length of a fingertip. This leaves a hole just large enough for a finger to fit into. Paint the puppet head after it hardens. The "body" or "stem" of the puppet will be a simple, tube-shaped piece of cloth (an infant's sock works well), with the closed end pressed up and glued into the hole in the bottom of the puppet's head.

The puppets can be simple, one-sided or two-sided, crayon-colored cardboard-on-a-stick puppets (Figure 2-2), or elaborate three-dimensional puppets with flowers that talk, seeds that are thrown or arms and wings that move. Larger puppets are more visible to an audience. Have children take turns acting out different plant and animal movements in front of the group while those watching work their puppets to mimic those actions, such as floating, drifting on the wind, being rooted in place, blooming, dropping seeds, sprouting, growing, hopping, skipping, crawling, walking, climbing and jumping. Have the puppets talk to each other and express being sad, surprised, happy, shy and other emotional states.

As children practice working their puppets behind a stage, have them imagine that they *are* that puppet—doing, thinking and feeling all that it does, thinks and feels. Have them look up at their puppets as they bring the puppets to life. Encourage children to develop a puppet's character and voice and to try to be consistent. Energy and movement make a puppet expressive. Puppets also should enter the stage from an appropriate place. A flower should sprout from the ground, fruit should be found in tree branches, seeds may blow in from the side, a groundhog may pop up from a burrow, a bat may fly in from above and a squirrel could climb down from a tree.

Special effects enhance the performance. Crack a walnut shell with a nutcracker to make a sound simulating a seed breaking out of its seed coat. Shake a piece of metal flashing to create thunder. Spray mist from a bottle from behind the stage to mimic fog or a rainstorm. Rap on a hollow coconut shell to imitate a woodpecker's pecking. Make your own original sound effects!

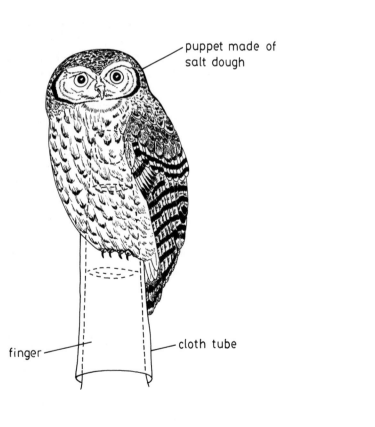

puppet made of salt dough

finger

cloth tube

Finger Puppet

paint stirring stick sandwiched between two poster board halves of puppet

Stick Puppet

Figure 2-2. Two kinds of puppets you can make: a finger puppet (left) and a double-sided stick puppet (right). These puppets depict an elf owl and a stinkhorn mushroom.

A number of useful books are available on puppeteering, including *Puppets: Methods and Materials*, by Cedric Flower and Alan Jon Fortney (Worcester, Mass.: Davis Publications, 1983); *Introducing Puppetry*, by Peter Fraser (New York: Watson-Guptill, Inc., 1968); and *Puppet Shows Made Easy!* and *Puppetry and the Art of Story Creation*, both by Nancy Renfro (Austin, Tex.: Nancy Renfro Studios, 1979).

CONDUCTING THE ACTIVITIES

The following checklist provides specific ideas for creating experiences that are meaningful, informative and fun.

Plan Wisely and in Detail

Consider the time available. List activities and the time needed for each one. Plan extra activities so there is always something to do. If some children or groups finish a project earlier than others, provide meaningful tasks or projects for them to work on while waiting for others to finish. Prioritize in case you begin to run out of time so you can be sure to include the most important activities. Allow enough time to lead the final activity without rushing through it.

Choose and Adapt Activities for the Children's Levels

Young children need shorter, active, hands-on, concrete experiences. Older children, too, need direct involvement. Older children also understand concepts more readily and are challenged by longer activities that probe a subject in greater depth.

Allow time for discussion and questions, including the ubiquitous "But why?"

Set the Stage

Prepare the children with one or two pre-activities to help them focus on the intended theme. Use a story, a puppet show, a slide show, a filmstrip, a movie or an activity.

Link the Activities in a Meaningful Way

Provide connections between activities. Discussion and leading questions help children to discover these links. Tie each activity in with the overall theme. A focused summary at the end of each activity is a good way to do this. Ask, "What happened?" and "What does it mean?"

Put Children Into the Center of the Experience

Facilitating and sharing the experience is more effective and exciting than show-and-tell. Establish goals and let children participate in the planning to reach those goals. Early involvement increases motivation. Let children take turns leading or co-leading the group.

Teach by Example: Model Positive Behaviors

Children love to imitate adults. Consistency between your actions and words is crucial. Being a role model is among the most powerful teaching tools.

Use Firsthand, Sensory Experiences Whenever Possible

Help children to experience the subject firsthand (Figure 2-3). Avoid prolonged discussion. To see it, smell it, hear it, touch it or taste it is to know it better. Active involvement also sharpens motor skills.

Use Creative Questions and Answers

Emphasize children's own discoveries. Use questions to direct children's attention to important objects or subjects of inquiry. Avoid giving the answers away. Here is an example:

Child: "Why do trees have bark?"
Leader: "Well, do you have anything that covers the outside of your body?"
Child: "Yes, I've got my skin."
Leader: "What does your skin do for your body?"

Figure 2-3. This child, surrounded by a sea of grass, is intently focused on the grasshopper cradled in her hand. Firsthand experience is the best teacher. (Photo by Cecil B. Hoisington)

Child: "I think it keeps germs and other things that are bad for me from getting inside. It protects my insides from getting hurt and helps me to heal when I do hurt myself."

Leader: "So what good is a tree's bark?"

Child: "Maybe it keeps a tree healthy, kind of like a tree's skin."

Leader: "Right! Bark is one way that a tree protects itself from diseases, insects, decay, injury, even fire and other things in its environment that might be harmful. And like your skin, only much more slowly, if bark is injured it heals in time. Good thinking!"

If you do not know the answer to a question, it is okay to say so. Children and adults alike can usually tell if you are faking it. Search together for solutions to unanswered questions.

Emphasize Positive Feelings as Well as Knowledge

A child who empathizes with someone or something is more likely to want to learn about that person or thing. You can *say* that a tree or other plant is a living thing, that it interacts with and senses its environment, that it grows better and stronger if it is talked to in a caring way or exposed to soothing music and that it needs the care of human beings to survive. But watch what happens when you have children take charge and care for specific trees or a patch of forest, giving them the responsibility for the welfare of those living things. Have children practice giving to their trees. Have children read *The Great Kapok Tree* by Lynne Cherry (New York: Harcourt Brace, 1990); *Just a Dream* by Chris Van Allsburg (Boston: Houghton Mifflin, 1990); or *The Lorax* by Dr. Seuss (New York: Random House, 1971). How do the various characters in *The Lorax* treat the trees and animals in that story? Who are the good models of stewardship with the natural world in this story? What lessons do the boy in *Just a Dream* and the woodcutter in *The Great Kapok Tree* learn in their dreams? With these activities children become excited and motivated; they laugh at times, and some even cry if their tree is hurt or damaged by someone else. They learn what it means to care.

Provide a supportive atmosphere, a trusting and respectful experience and a compassionate means to a compassionate end. This approach fosters positive self-esteem, behavior and environmental attitudes. Children who love themselves are more likely to value Earth and trust other people.

Foster Aesthetic Appreciation

Set a contemplative tone for the day by beginning with an appropriate story. Build slow, quiet moments for observation into the rhythms of each day. Late afternoons are good times for this, when energy starts to wane. Share your poetry, photographs and memories with the children, and have them share theirs as well.

Emphasize Group Work and Positive Social Interaction

Use teams and small groups to practice positive communication, cooperation, conflict resolution and other social skills. This approach promotes self-knowledge and a sense of connection with others—of feeling safe, open and confident in social interaction. Involve everyone. The recognition given each child's contribution helps to build his or her self-esteem.

Foster Problem-Solving/Research Skills

Here is a process to facilitate decision making and problem solving for environmental and social concerns as well as personal problems:

1. Recognize the problem(s).
2. Define the problem(s).
3. Listen with comprehension.
4. Collect information about the problem(s).
5. Organize the information.
6. Analyze the information.
7. Generate alternatives for possible solutions to the problem(s).
8. Develop a plan of action.
9. Implement the plan of action.[5]

Use Long-term Projects

Watch migrating birds and find out what you can do to protect the tropical rainforest where many of these birds winter. Keep a pet and learn responsible caring. Make a commitment to do all you can to save an endangered species. If you have lots of children come through your home or learning center for short periods of time, design projects that can be passed on from child to child. A garden tended by many children over time establishes a tradition of nurturing the green world.

Include a Connection With Other Communities and Countries

Environmental issues transcend cultural and political boundaries. Teach children to understand their relationships with other cultures, both here and in distant lands. How does our heavy reliance in North America on the natural resources imported from other countries affect those societies, their environments and the plants that live there? What are the ecological problems associated with acid rain, nuclear energy, global warming, ozone destruction and other issues that link North Americans to other people and environments around the world?

Include Moral Issues: Environmental and Social Ethics

Native North American stories and Earth activities involve values and moral issues as well as knowledge because they teach about relationships—our thoughts, feelings and actions toward ourselves, other people and the environment. Foster caring, nurturing and compassion in children's lives. Empathy is the tangible sense of our interconnectedness. When we feel what another person feels and when we understand that Earth is a living organism whose parts also have an awareness, even though that awareness may be different from our own, we want to help because we share that emotional experience. A child's level of moral development is another important consideration when planning values activities.[6]

> We are one in relationship with the Earth and other people. Doing good supports this relationship. Love and moral goodness are inseparable; they are the elemental components of a life ethic.[7]

Deal With Problems and Controversy Constructively and Positively

Accept problems as part of reality when studying Earth and other cultures. Emphasize positive approaches to problems. Approach controversial issues directly yet cautiously. Avoid biased teaching by identifying and discussing bias, prejudice and ideology. Children who understand controversy are better able to approach moral issues objectively. Experience with controversial issues motivates and involves children in seeking solutions to problems such as water pollution, acid rain, cross-cultural misunderstandings, world hunger and AIDS.

Respect Spiritual and Religious Beliefs

Spirituality is an important part of environmental activities in appropriate settings. Spiritual beliefs and religious practices are major factors in determining a child's orientation and conscience toward Earth and other people.[8] Each individual's spirituality needs to be acknowledged and respected. A child may say, "This story says that Earth was created on Turtle's back (Chapter 3), but that's not what I was taught to believe." We have found a good response to be: "Yes, people believe in different accounts of creation. This story tells us about the beliefs of certain Native North American cultures."

Respect the Privacy of Personal Beliefs and Feelings

Give children the right not to answer questions if the response will reveal sensitive personal beliefs or self-knowledge. One example is Study Question 2 in Chapter 3, which asks children how they believe the world was created.

Discipline Compassionately and Decisively

Involve attention-seeking children in the discussion or activity by asking them for help. Stand near an overly active child and put your arm around her or his shoulders. These techniques comfort or give attention to the attention

seekers in a positive way while avoiding a confrontation. If a rule is questioned, explain the meaning behind the rule and turn the experience into a constructive dialogue. This approach fosters the development of positive personal moral standards.

Avoid using power plays or demeaning methods of punishment. A child who is a severe problem and a continual distraction may have to leave the group so the learning can continue. Ask the child to reflect on what has happened, why and how he or she could learn from the experience.

Don't send mixed messages. Establish the rules and the consequences of excessively disruptive behavior early in the lesson and be consistent in applying both.

Keep a Sense of Humor, Joy and Appreciation

A light touch opens hearts and minds. Be watchful for "teachable moments" in nature that can captivate and enthrall—a flower bud bursting forth or a seed blowing by on the wind. You may want to build a repertoire of nature puns for older children, such as:

Question: "What did the tree say after someone cut it down and its neighbor asked, 'Why did they do that?' "
Answer: "It said, 'How should I know? I'm stumped.' "
Some children will laugh and some will groan (just like adults), but they love it!

Be Yourself

Use whatever works best for you. Some adults take a high-energy approach to leading activities, while others use a more low-key style. There are many ways of leading; if you are well prepared and promoting a positive relationship with the children, you are doing well.

Provide a Culminating Activity or Experience

Wrap up and summarize with an activity that creates a sense of closure. *"Seventh-Generation Stewardship"* in Chapter 15 is a good example.

TAKING YOUR CHILDREN OUTDOORS

Waves break on a rocky shore; wind rushes across the prairie; flowers scent the breeze at the edge of a marsh; a pungent smell wafts from the pavement near a vacant lot after a rain. Field trips are a chance to study the environment firsthand. You can visit plants and animals in their homes, learn wilderness survival skills on an extended camping trip or take a trip to a botanical garden and experience plants that come from distant lands. There is adventure in the unknown, and even familiar places look different when visited in the spirit of discovery. Whether in the backyard, the school grounds, a vacant lot, nature-center lands, a residential camp, a wilderness area or a city park, there are discoveries awaiting (Figure 2-4).

Of course, not every experience will be filled with wonder and aesthetic beauty; fear is also a natural part of discovering the new. Some fears, such as being afraid to disturb a bees' nest, are well founded. Other fears are irrational. No matter how a worm feels to the touch, it is not going to hurt anyone and is an extremely important animal that helps to maintain soil fertility.

Planning the Outdoor Excursion

Conduct the whole program in your mind's eye beforehand and plan for all contingencies such as transportation and proper attire for seasonal weather conditions, especially rain, snow, cold and extreme heat. If you are planning a program at a nature center, send a letter home beforehand to parents, or to the visiting classroom teacher, to help ensure that the children come prepared with proper clothing. Parents, teachers, seniors, older students or other community volunteers are excellent resources for helping with the excursion. Keep the ratio of adults to children in each group at around 1 to 5 or 1 to 6.

Choose activities that fulfill your goals and objectives. Think of a theme for the entire program; something broad such as "survival" allows for focus and flexibility. Once you have arranged for your site and chosen your activities, gather name tags and all necessary materials and then make a brief outline of the day's activities and other important reminders on index cards that fit easily into a pocket.

Scout the area where you intend to take the children and become familiar with the site. Note the plants, animals and physical aspects of that place and include them in your activities. Do not use trails along which children might encounter poisonous or irritating plants such as poison ivy, oak and sumac. Avoid areas where ticks that carry diseases, such as Lyme disease, are found, particularly during the seasons when ticks are most likely to transmit diseases. If a nature trail is present, use it. If not, plan a route that will do minimal damage to the plant and animal communities. When multiple trips are planned into a wild area, establish a path to reduce widespread trampling of the plants, or vary the route in and out to disperse the traffic. Consider access carefully if your group includes children in wheelchairs or with other special needs: no one wants to be left behind.

Above all, be prepared! Bring along a complete portable first-aid kit. Include anti–bee sting serum and a snake-bite kit and know how to use them. It is best if you or a co-leader is certified in first aid as well as CPR for both children and adults.

Include in your trail kit:
- small, sharp knife
- matches packed in a waterproof container
- compass
- map of the area, preferably a topographic map
- insect repellent
- water, especially during hot days and on long walks
- trash bags
- hand lenses for viewing small details in nature

Since most kinds of weather can be enjoyed if you are properly prepared, it is a good policy to go outside under all but the worst conditions. Heavy rains, winds, lightning or other severe weather can come unexpectedly depending upon the weather patterns in your region. Be ready with a full complement of "rainy day" activities just in case.

Figure 2-4. Dramatic discoveries reward the close observer of plants in the wild. This flower spider, a kind of crab spider, waits on a violet to ambush a bee or other pollinating insect. The spider's toxin affects bees, flies and other insects, which, once bitten, are held overhead while the spider sucks them dry. Size: body, .1 to .2 in. (2.5 to 5.1 mm). (Photo by Alan C. Graham)

Conducting the Field Trip (With Special Tips for Larger Groups)

It's time to go! The children are anxious to begin and energy is high.

"There are a few things I want to say before we go outside," you begin. "We're visiting the plants and animals in *their* homes, so how do you think we should act?"

"On our good behavior," someone says.

"Right. If you pull a leaf off a plant, you're tearing off part of a living thing. When you take a rock off the path or turn a log over, you're removing the roof of an animal's home. Do you think you'd like it if someone walked by and ripped a piece off of *you,* such as your arm, or visited your home and tore the roof off?"

"No!" they respond.

"Okay. So, what should you do if you see a beautiful flower or a colorful leaf that you want to pick?"

"We should look at it where it is growing and leave it there."

"Exactly—then you can always come back and visit it later on. And what should you do if you look under a rock or log?"

"Put it back the way we found it!"

You continue, "Since there are so many of us, we need to respect each other when someone is talking. Please raise your hand if you want to say something and listen whenever someone is talking. If you see me raise my hand, that is the signal to raise your hand and listen because there's something to see, do or discuss."

The tone of empathy and caring is set for the whole walk during the crucial first few minutes. This is also a good time to orient the children, in a general way, to the theme of the field trip and to what they can expect. Don't forget to keep plenty of surprises up your sleeve!

Children love to play games en route. You can use the "deer walk" to create suspense and interest. First have them cup their hands behind their ears to create "deer ears." Have children listen carefully and compare the intensity of sounds heard with and without the deer ears. Ask the children why deer can usually hear people coming before the people notice the deer.

"Because they listen quietly?"

"Right, and that's how we'll walk, with our deer ears alert and as quiet as can be," you reply. "Deer will signal danger by raising their tails and showing the white patch underneath. Whenever you see a white flag (hold up a sample flag), quietly gather around and we'll look at whatever our fellow deer thinks is interesting to see." (Pass out white flags to everyone.) In this way the walk becomes part of the experience. Puppets, such as a talking flower, stuffed animals, stories or other fun props keep the children's interest.

You are on the trail now and there is something you want to point out. Walk past that spot far enough so that roughly one-half of the group has passed it. Then backtrack to the spot, and you will be standing in the middle of the group to make it easier for the children to hear. Always try to stand facing the sun so it falls on their backs and does not glare in their eyes. Ask questions to help children discover what you want them to see. Draw the children in and include everyone. These are great times to tell stories or to listen to one of the children's stories. But be careful! You will need to limit their storytelling. Children love to share *long* stories. Handle this tricky issue by allowing special times for their stories toward the end of the field trip.

Approach the excursion with "structured flexibility," being open to the unexpected find or event. Dusk is a magical time of day to take an excursion. An exciting prelude to or part of a nocturnal excursion is the activity called "Disappearing Trees." If, without blinking, the children stand about 20 feet (6.1 meters) away and look at a small, distant tree during the twilight hours, they will see the tree "disappear"!

The camouflage game is another exciting activity that brings suspense into a field trip. Begin with a brief discussion period about what camouflage is and how animals use camouflage, such as cryptic coloration, hiding behind or

under things or being shaped like another natural object. Be sure to have pictures of some well-camouflaged animals to hold up as you talk. Tell children you want them to camouflage themselves whenever you yell "Camouflage!" Give them 10 seconds to hide and tell them not to go more than 20 feet (6.1 meters) away. Close your eyes as you count. Call out the names or locations of children whom you can see from where you are standing when you open your eyes.

After you have played the game once, tell the children that the counting time will be shortened by one second during each round of the game, which can come at any time along the trail when you yell "Camouflage!" This adds an undertone of anticipation to the entire excursion.

When children are quiet and listening, they often see special things. Suppose a child comes up to you after the camouflage game and says, "I saw a stick and it was walking! It's over there on that bush." Postpone the next planned activity and use the occasion as a time to marvel at the "walking stick" insect while letting the children generate their own questions. Or, use some creative questioning to tie the sighting in with your camouflage lesson. This is a good way to quell some fears about insects and, at the same time, increase children's understanding of the fascinating interrelationships among plants and animals.

Snack breaks are good times to share special moments. They are also opportune for reading or telling one of the stories in this book that relates to the theme of your walk.

Include quiet time during the outdoor excursion. Children enjoy keeping a journal in which they write, draw pictures, make leaf or bark rubbings or practice other creative forms of expression. Their sketches and writings range from humorous stories and comic-strip variety pictures to beautiful drawings and sensitive poetic verse.

Projects also get children involved. Plant some trees, pile brush for small mammal homes or pick up trash. For a long-term study with multiple visits, design and sow a garden of flowers and vegetables, plan and implement a recycling program or even set up an acid rain monitoring station. These kinds of activities are found throughout this book. Projects, along with team activities, provide the means for small-group cooperation and social development.

When you are ready to wrap up the visit, it is more effective to conduct a summarizing activity onsite or on the way back *before* you come within sight of the house, school bus, learning center or other final destination. While the children are in the midst of the excitement and involvement at the site, their attention is still focused there. If you try to wrap up away from the site, the element of concentration on that place and the day's events is weakened and the children's thoughts are already turning to their next experience.

KEEPING A FIELD JOURNAL

Include quiet time in your trips. Children enjoy keeping a journal in which they make entries on the spot while out on an excursion. Have them record outdoor experiences as a log of natural events, an irreplaceable and accurate learning tool that reveals patterns in nature as well as unusual sightings. Ask them to write down a simple observation, illustrate something seen, make leaf or bark rubbings, create a poem or record a tune that comes to mind while hiking or photograph special places and paste the photographs in the journal. Tailor the format to the children's level.

Have children build on their journals over time. They should include, if possible:
- date, time, place and conditions
- observations, answering the questions of who, what, when, where, how and why
- thoughts and interpretations of what is seen
- sketches, illustrations or photographs to accompany the written observations
- connections between natural life in the field: a bird eating a certain insect or the remains of a particular animal in another animal's droppings

Enhance the experience by having children research and record the natural history and ecology of the plants, animals and other aspects of nature observed.

CLASSIFYING AND IDENTIFYING PLANTS

In *Keepers of Life* we encourage a knowledge of plants through observation, experience, stewardship and story. We also realize the value of learning how plants are related to one another. This section is more technical than the balance of the book because it provides a general overview of plant classification.

Identification is simply a tool to help us understand relationships. *Be careful to not get caught up in naming for its own sake.* The goal is to further children's understanding of and appreciation for each plant's natural history and its ecological connections, as well as to inspire, excite and motivate children to develop both empathy and stewardship toward plants. Field guides are available for identifying plants in the wild and you are encouraged to make use of these.

A brief, clear summary of the six major groups of plants and plant-like organisms studied in this book is provided in the outline near the end of this section. Chapters 5 through 9 study these six groups.

Taxonomy is the branch of biology concerned with the systematic classification of living things. It is easy to see the differences between an animal such as a buffalo and a plant such as a pine tree, but not all living things are so easily categorized. Certain mostly one-celled organisms called *dinoflagellates* ("whistling whips"), for example, have characteristics of both plants and animals. Some marine-dwelling, photosynthetic species of dinoflagellate are among the most important producers found in the world's oceans. Yet many species also possess two whip-like *flagella* that they use for locomotion, a characteristic often considered to be unplant-like. Most of the luminescence seen in ocean water is caused by these remarkable creatures. Today, dinoflagellates are usually classified in the Kingdom Protoctista. Certain kinds of algae, too, such as *Euglena* and some species of green algae, are sometimes classified by zoologists in the Kingdom Protoctista because they also have flagella in addition to the ability to photosynthesize. *Viruses* are not usually listed in a classification of living things because they consist only of a strand of nucleic acid—either RNA or DNA (never both)—enclosed in a coat of protein; as a result, they cannot exist outside of the host organism that they parasitize. Viruses infect life forms ranging from bacteria to flowering plants and people.

Through time many systems have been devised for grouping living things according to such distinctions as cell structure, evolutionary relationships and details of reproductive cycles. At one time, two major groupings, or *kingdoms*, were recognized—*Plantae* and *Animalia*. Then it was noted that *bacteria* have cells that are more simplified and smaller than those of other organisms, reproduce almost exclusively by asexual cell division and almost always occur as single-celled individuals. These *prokaryotic* cells lack an organized nucleus. They are distinguished from *eukaryotic* cells, which are larger and more highly evolved, reproduce by relatively complex sexual and asexual means and are often parts of multicellular organisms. Eukaryotic cells possess a membrane-enclosed nucleus that contains chromosomes of DNA and protein. Bacteria, therefore, were reclassified, sometimes along with blue-green algae (which are also prokaryotic), into a third kingdom called the *Monera*.

Today, at least six classification systems are used, but it is widely recognized that organisms can be divided into as many as five kingdoms, based on a system first proposed by Robert H. Whittaker: *Monera* (bacteria and blue-green algae), *Protoctista* (algae, protozoans and sponges), *Fungi* (molds and mushrooms), *Plantae* (flowering plants, conifers, ferns and mosses) and *Animalia* (animals with and without backbones).[9] The names of the different divisions used to classify organisms, moving from the broadest category to the most specific, are as follows: kingdom, division (zoologists use "phylum"), class, order, family, genus and species. A *species* is a population of organisms that are closely related through similarities in their anatomy and historical evolutionary development and are capable of reproducing among themselves but cannot successfully breed with members of another species.

This book, as well as *Keepers of the Earth* and *Keepers of the Animals,* uses the terms *plant* and *animal* frequently. Where helpful, specifics are given to indicate a more detailed classification of organisms. Although algae and fungi often are not classified as members of the plant kingdom, they do possess many plant-like characteristics and for many years were classified as plants, and so are studied in this book along with plants. Algae and fungi also are included here because younger children are not yet ready for the specifics of taxonomic classification, which can be quite confusing. We encourage educators to explore a more detailed classification system of living things with children as they grow into the upper elementary and junior high grades.

There are more than 375,000 kinds of plants and plant-like organisms, and they are diverse and challenging to identify (Figure 2-5). *Embryophytes* produce an embryo at some stage of reproduction and their structures are more complex than those of thallophytes. This group includes flowering plants and conifers (*spermatophytes* or "seed plants"), ferns (*pteridophytes* or "spore producers") and mosses (*bryophytes*). Flowering plants are called the *angiosperms* ("enclosed seeds") and conifers are known as the *gymnosperms* ("naked seeds"). Those plants with which people are most familiar, including the ferns, conifers and flowering plants, are called *tracheophytes*. These plants contain plumbing systems composed of conductive (vascular) tissues: *xylem* carries water and dissolved substances, such as minerals, upward in the plant; *phloem* transports primarily carbohydrates and other organic materials both up and down the plant body. Mosses and related plants are embryophytes that do not possess conductive tissue.

The fascinating *thallophytes*, nonvascular plants and plant-like organisms, range from microscopic, single-celled algae to some species of fungi that may be the largest living things on Earth. The body of a thallophyte is called a *thallus*, which lacks true roots, stems and leaves and does not possess conductive tissue. They do not grow flowers, fruits or seeds and do not produce an embryo during reproduction. *Lichens*, each of which is a symbiotic association of a fungus and an alga, are studied along with the fungi in Chapter 6.

All six major groups of plants and plant-like organisms are listed below, arranged by easily recognizable groupings that are based on their relationships.

- *algae and related organisms,* including diatoms, stone-worts, dinoflagellates and euglenoids
- *fungi and related organisms,* including true fungi, water molds, mildews, sac fungi, pin molds, club fungi, imperfect fungi and slime molds
- lichens
- *mosses and related plants:* true mosses, bog mosses, rock mosses, liverworts and hornworts
- *ferns and related plants,* including whisk ferns, clubmosses, spikemosses, horsetails, quillworts and psilopsids
- *conifers and related plants,* including gingko ("maiden-hair tree"), cycads and gnetophytes
- *flowering plants:* monocotyledons and dicotyledons

While glancing down this list you may find a number of plant groups with which you are not familiar. Just as most people tend to focus on vertebrate animals when we think of animals, we orient mostly to flowering plants and conifers

Figure 2-5. Flowering plants, like these delicate yellow lady's slippers, are the most familiar plants to many people. Yet more than 350,000 species of plants may be found in a seemingly endless variety of sizes, shapes and colors. Size: height, 4 to 28 in. (10.2 to 71.1 cm); flowers, 2 in. (5.1 cm). (Photo by Alan C. Graham)

when considering plants. And even though most people do naturally separate animals according to taxonomic groups, such as birds, reptiles, amphibians and mammals, we do not usually do this with plants. If someone shows a snake to a fourth grader and asks her or him to identify what kind of animal the snake is, most children will say "a reptile." Yet, lead a child up to an oak tree and ask what kind of plant he or she is looking at and you may hear "an oak tree" or even just "a tree." But you are not likely to have the response be "a flowering plant." We tend to orient to the *growth form* of a plant rather than to the *kind* of plant it is. Therefore, the chapters of this book that address specific groups of plants are organized according to taxonomic plant groups aligned as closely as possible to the kinds of plants that are commonly and easily recognized.

PLANTS IN THE WILD:
TO COLLECT OR NOT TO COLLECT

Plants are living beings that breathe, get nourishment, grow, struggle to survive and reproduce just as animals and people do. They just do these things more slowly. *We strongly recommend that children be discouraged from picking any parts of plants or uprooting plants of any kind.* Children can "capture" a plant with a photograph or an illustration instead. Our philosophy is to protect, enjoy and observe plants in their own homes/habitats, which is where we learn the most about them (Figure 2-5). Treat the leaves, stems, roots, flowers, bark, logs, soil, forests, fields, wetlands, deserts and other parts of plants and their homes with respect.

The only way to collect live plants, or parts of them, is to pull pieces off the plants or to transplant them. Plant pieces are taken from a living thing. Many wild plants have a low rate of survival when transplanted and it is illegal to pick or dig up protected species, including many wildflowers. By picking or transplanting, you could inadvertently contribute to the decline of a rare or endangered species.

It *is* fine, and fun, to participate in the natural process of gathering live, attached, ripe seeds, berries and other fruits. The experience can be incorporated into a lesson about the co-evolution of plants and animals, demonstrating how plants have developed fruits and seeds that attract and entice animals into spreading seeds, thereby aiding in the survival of plant species.

Be sure of the identity of the plants you are picking to avoid poisonous plants that cause painful skin irritations. Also, do not allow the children to eat any plant parts unless you have picked them ahead of time and are absolutely certain that what you have in hand is edible.

It takes an adult's determination and patience to instill a respect for the natural world. As a simple nervous habit, for instance, some children and adults will tear up and destroy the grass and many other plants all around where they are sitting. Gathering plant parts that have *naturally* died or fallen off, such as seeds, autumn leaves or beautiful winter weed stalks, is okay as long as the children treat even these plant parts with respect and take only what they need.

> Flowers are for our souls to enjoy; not for our bodies to wear. Leave them alone and they will live out their lives and reproduce themselves as the Great Gardener intended.[10]
> —Oral Tradition
> *Lakota (Sioux)*

In those cases where you, the educational facilitator, *must* collect plant parts to be used by you and the children during activities, we offer the following suggestions.
• Obtain permission to collect on private or public land.
• Pick only what you *need.*
• Only pick from common species of plants and where there is a healthy population.
• Thin out, lightly, from several different patches of the plant you are picking to allow the plants to replenish themselves and to avoid depleting a particular population.
• *Never collect any rare, threatened or endangered species or parts of them.* Become acquainted with all laws governing the collection of wild plants, particularly rare species. Keep rare plant sightings a secret and report them to the appropriate conservation group.
• Refrain from conducting experiments involving wild plants, unless this involves something harmless and unintrusive, such as gathering seeds of a plant that is abundant and trying to understand how to grow this plant. Have children learn by observing a brief period of the wild plant's growth, development and behavior.
• Never take the largest plant, leaf, berry, flower or other plant part found amid those you are gathering. This is the "Grandmother" and should be left out of respect.
• Gather plant parts that you need ahead of time. It is better to not have children watch you do the picking, which would set the example that it is all right for them to pick, too. If you must pick plants when the children are present as part of an activity, use the occasion to teach the ideas and practices for good stewardship that follow.
• Always use sharp pruning shears to collect plant parts. Cut back to the nearest living part of the stem to allow the plant to grow over and heal the wound. Openings left in a plant's protective outer tissues allow insects and diseases to enter and damage the plant.
• Bring along a small cooler with a bit of water and ice in the bottom to keep the plants fresh and cool until you either are ready to use them or can get them to a refrigerator.
• Do not collect wild plants or plant parts that someone is selling. It is hard to be *sure* of how the items were obtained.
• Restore all areas you disturb to their natural state. Replace rolled-over rocks and logs, put back leaf litter and so on.

Whether gathering live plant parts yourself, picking live berries or accompanying children as they gather dead leaves or weeds, we offer a way of relating to the plants. Forms of these simple practices are used by a number of Native North American peoples to keep strong the circle of giving and receiving with the "plant people."
• Ask permission of the plants to show respect.
• Say "thank you" to the plants. Take the first of your gift from the plants, such as the first handful of berries or colorful leaves gathered, place it on the ground near the plants that created that gift and express your appreciation. Leave your gift there and gather what you need. You also might bring a special gift, such as seeds, to leave for the plants. Many Native North American cultures show their appreciation to plants in this way.
• Take and use only what you need: thin out but never take all from any given patch. This is sharing with other animals or humans who come along later looking for the same thing you need now. Thinning allows a healthy growth of plants to maintain the population.
• Complete the circle of giving and receiving. Thank the plants as you return unused plant parts to the soil where they were found, beneath the plants that produced them.

PLANTING TREES AND SHRUBS

Planting and nurturing a tree, shrub or other plant outdoors creates a powerful connection to the plant world and helps children to practice caring and stewardship toward plants. If possible, find a source of plants that are grown using chemical-free, organic methods to ensure a natural hardiness and to preserve the ecological balance. Use healthy, vigorous plants with lush foliage that is free of insect pests and diseases. Make sure the plant does not have any dead branches or deformities. Choose plants that are abundant and widespread in the wild: do not purchase a plant that is rare, threatened or endangered. Plants that are native to your region are best. Create a good match between the tree or shrub and the site. Consult a local nursery for advice and information. Consider also:

• *local climate and microclimate.* Know the growth needs of your plant: light, water, soil, air circulation and so on. Choose a tree that is adapted to your climate. Make sure the tree has sufficient space, fertile well-drained soil to grow in and the proper amount of sunlight. Some plants, for instance, prefer full sun while others do well in partial shade.

• *the size and shape of the plant in relation to available growing space.* Plant trees and shrubs far enough apart and sufficiently away from other objects to allow the growth of full, mature crowns. Generally, a tree or shrub will grow as wide as it does tall. Plant a tree that is expected to attain a height of 30 feet (9.1 meters), for example, about 15 feet (4.6 meters)—one-half of its mature height—from the nearest tree or object. Consider nearby buildings, fences, intersections, sidewalks, windows and so on. Make sure the tree has enough root space as well as overhead space. Never place a tree under powerlines, where its crown will have to be constantly pruned back and deformed, or along walks or roads where bicycles and other traffic are likely to cause injuries.

• *hardiness and susceptibility to diseases and insects*

• *tolerance to pollution,* such as air pollution, salt spray and runoff, etc.

• *maintenance requirements.* Pick a plant that does not require a lot of pruning and special care. Native plants are best.

• *appearance.* Finally, consider the plant's shape, color, texture and size and how that plant blends with its surroundings.

Late fall or early spring, while the plant is dormant, are the best times to plant trees and shrubs. Do not plant during the summer. Here are some basic tips for planting a tree or shrub:

1. Dig a hole that is at least twice the diameter and the same depth as the plant's root system.
2. Obtain more than enough rich, brown soil to fill the hole around the plant's roots.
3. Inspect the plant for broken roots and dead or damaged branches. Prune these carefully and cleanly back to the nearest

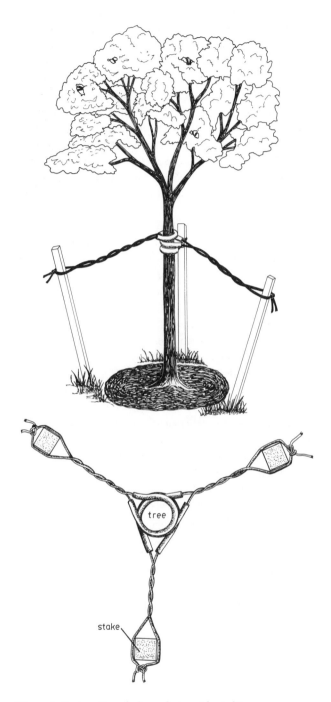

Figure 2-6. A well-staked, newly transplanted tree.

intersection with a living root or branch. *Do not prune at this time other than to remove dead and damaged roots and branches.*

4. Spread a few inches of rich native soil over the bottom of the hole. Add enough soil to make sure the plant is set in the ground at its original growing level. *Do not use fertilizer* until the tree is well established in its new home. (At that time, use composted manure, which is available at most gardening supply stores.)

5. Gently lower the plant into the hole and pack soil

around and under the roots. *Lift the plant by the ball of roots, never by the trunk.* Shovel a layer of soil into the bottom of the hole and tamp this soil down gently but firmly with your hands to eliminate air pockets. This is the time to carefully eye the plant from all angles to make sure its trunk is vertically straight and is not leaning. Add and gently tamp down several more layers of soil until the hole is full. Eliminate air pockets around the roots. Bury the tree so the old surface layer of the roots is even with the surface of the new soil. Create a ridge of soil around the edge of the now-filled hole to retain water above the roots while watering.

6.   Mulch the surface of the soil around the plant's base with a 2- to 4-inch (5- to 10-centimeter) layer of leaves, compost or wood chips to control weeds, keep moisture in and moderate soil temperature over the roots.

7.   Place a small stone or piece of wood on the surface of the mulch within the raised circle of soil and direct the flow onto this surface when watering to prevent erosion. Give the tree a slow, thorough soaking until the water stops sinking in quickly and begins to pool on the surface. Depending on the weather, give the plant a deep watering weekly or when the soil becomes dry 4 inches (10 centimeters) below the surface. Water as needed to keep the soil *moist,* not soaked. Gradually reduce watering after midautumn as the plant prepares for winter dormancy.

8.   Stake and brace trees that are about 6 feet (1.8 meters) or taller for support (Figure 2-6). Drive three sturdy stakes firmly into the ground around the tree about 2 feet (.6 meter) or more away from the trunk on the outside of the planting hole. Angle the top of the stakes slightly away from the tree. Tie a piece of rope onto each stake. Make the ropes about 2 feet (.6 meter) longer than twice the distance between the tree and the stake. String a piece of rubber tubing onto each piece of rope. Run each rope *around* the tree trunk but *do not tie it onto* the trunk. Use the tubing for padding where the rope circles the trunk to prevent injury and chafing on the tree. Tie the rope onto the stake. Repeat this procedure for the other two stakes, creating a gentle tension on the ropes so the tree trunk is held up straight but has a little room for movement.

* * *

You now have both the ideas and practical suggestions needed for effectively using and integrating the Native North American stories and Earth activities found in Part II. It is time to begin a journey into the intriguing world of plants. We hope these stories and activities bring you and your children the kind of fascination and enjoyment that we experience while sharing them.

NOTES

1. Joseph Campbell with Bill Moyers, *The Power of Myth* (New York: Doubleday, 1988), 40.

2. Ibid., 31.

3. Ibid.

4. Madeleine L'Engle, *Walking on Water: Reflections on Faith and Art* (Wheaton, Ill.: Harold Shaw, 1980), 140.

5. William B. Stapp and Dorothy A. Cox, *Environmental Education Activities Manual* (Dexter, Mich.: Thomson-Shore, 1979), 16. To obtain a copy write to Environmental Education Activities Manual, 2050 Delaware, Ann Arbor, MI 48103.

6. Michael J. Caduto, *A Guide on Environmental Values Education* (Paris: United Nations Education, Scientific and Cultural Organization [UNESCO], 1985), general reference.

7. Ibid., 34.

8. Robert Coles, *The Spiritual Life of Children* (Boston: Houghton Mifflin, 1990), 119–120.

9. L. Margulis and K. V. Schwartz, *Five Kingdoms: An Illustrated Guide to the Phyla of Life on Earth* (San Francisco: W. H. Freeman, 1981), general reference.

10. Frances G. Lombardi and Gerald Scott Lombardi, *Circle Without End* (Happy Camp, Calif.: Naturegraph Publishers, 1982), 18.

PART II

NATIVE AMERICAN STORIES AND PLANT ACTIVITIES

✢ CREATION ✢

"You must cut down the Sky Tree and bring the fruit to me," said the old chief.
Aataentsic took her husband's stone ax and went to the great tree.

Chapter 3

✢ The Sky Tree ✢

(Huron—Eastern Woodland)

In the beginning, Earth was covered with water. In Sky Land, there were people living as they do now on Earth. In the middle of that land was the great Sky Tree. All of the food which the people in that Sky Land ate came from the great tree.

The old chief of that land lived with his wife, whose name was Aataentsic, meaning "Ancient Woman," in their longhouse near the great tree. It came to be that the old chief became sick and nothing could cure him. He grew weaker and weaker until it seemed he would die. Then a dream came to him and he called Aataentsic to him.

"I have dreamed," he said, "and in my dream I saw how I can be healed. I must be given the fruit which grows at the very top of Sky Tree. You must cut it down and bring that fruit to me."

Aataentsic took her husband's stone ax and went to the great tree. As soon as she struck it, it split in half and toppled over. As it fell a hole opened in Sky Land and the tree fell through the hole. Aataentsic returned to the place where the old chief waited.

"My husband," she said, "when I cut the tree it split in half and then fell through a great hole. Without the tree, there can be no life. I must follow it."

Then, leaving her husband she went back to the hole in Sky Land and threw herself after the great tree.

As Aataentsic fell, Turtle looked up and saw her. Immediately Turtle called together all the water animals and told them what she had seen.

"What should be done?" Turtle said.

Beaver answered her. "You are the one who saw this happen. Tell us what to do."

"All of you must dive down," Turtle said. "Bring up soil from the bottom, and place it on my back."

Immediately all of the water animals began to dive down and bring up soil. Beaver, Mink, Muskrat and Otter each brought up pawfuls of wet soil and placed the soil on the Turtle's back until they had made an island of great size. When they were through, Aataentsic settled down gently on the new Earth and the pieces of the great tree fell beside her and took root.

Each year there will be a contest between Grandfather North and Grandmother South. They will play the hand game.

How Kishelemukong Made the People and the Seasons

(Lenni Lenape—Eastern Woodland)

Long ago, Kishelemukong, the Great Mystery, built the world. First Kishelemukong caused a great turtle to rise up from the depths of the water and float on the surface. Then Kishelemukong took moist earth and placed it on the back of the giant turtle as the turtle floated in the endless ocean. The ridges of Turtle's back turned into mountains, and grass and shrubs and trees of all kinds began to grow from the soil.

It went on this way for some time, but Kishelemukong felt that something was yet to be made. There were birds and animals and living things of all kinds, but there was something yet to be made. Kishelemukong considered shaping beings from the stones of Earth. But such beings would be heavy-footed and they would crush the plants beneath them.

Instead, Kishelemukong made a straight ash tree grow up tall. From its branches the first men and the first women sprouted.

Then Kishelemukong placed the sun in the day sky and the moon in the night sky. And so that all would grow and rest in its proper time, Kishelemukong created the four directions and the seasons which would come from each of those directions. West and North and East were Grandfathers, governing the times of Fall and Winter and Spring. South was a Grandmother, bringing the warmth and new life of Summer. Like the trees and the plants, human beings grew to love that time of the year and their Grandmother South the best of all.

Then Kishelemukong decided to make sure the divisions between the seasons were fair and acceptable.

"It will be this way," Kishelemukong said. "Each year there will be a contest between Grandfather North and Grandmother South. They will play the hand game. One will take a bead and hide it in one hand or the other so that the opponent must guess which hand it is held in. Each will have 12 sticks and each time a winning guess is made, one stick will be taken. Whenever Grandmother South begins to win more sticks, the weather will begin to turn warm and Spring will come. But when her luck begins to change, Autumn will be a signal that Grandfather North is winning his sticks back again."

And so it is to this day. Because the game between Grandmother South and Grandfather North is so evenly matched, the seasons are always about the same length, but as in every game, sometimes one of them has better luck than the other and so we never know for sure when each season will end or begin.

DISCUSSION
The Giving Plants

Plants are the difference between a living, breathing, green Earth and a stark sphere of dead seas surrounding barren continents of rock, sand and gravel. In the Huron story "The Sky Tree," everything the people in Sky Land eat comes from the great Sky Tree. Even the fruit that will heal the old chief is borne on the tree's highest branches. As soon as Aataentsic plunges down and steps onto the fresh soil of the new Earth on Turtle's back, pieces of the great tree take root there and the new Earth comes to life.

The thin skin of living things on Earth's surface—the *biosphere*—is largely determined by the range of plant growth. On land, the biosphere extends down to the deepest roots and up to the crowns of the California redwoods, the tallest trees at more than 375 feet (114.3 meters). In the oceans and seas, which cover 71 percent of Earth's 8,000-mile (12,875-kilometer) girth, the biosphere is concentrated in the top 600 feet (182.9 meters), including the tidal zone, where sufficient light penetrates to support photosynthesis for plant growth. Some living things, however, can be found down to 6 miles (9.7 kilometers) deep in the cold, eternal ocean night of total darkness. These living things are fed by dead plant and animal matter that sinks down from above, as well as by nutrients from hot springs welling up from within Earth.

The Lenni Lenape story "How Kishelemukong Made the People and the Seasons" begins with a new Earth on Turtle's back. *Kishelemukong,* the Great Mystery, does not make people out of stone because they would crush the plants. He makes the first people sprout from branches of an ash tree. He then creates the sun and moon, the four directions and seasons, and brings all of these into balance. This shows a clear intuitive knowledge and understanding of how the survival and sustenance of human beings is rooted in the world of green plants, and of how all life is attuned to the rhythms of the sun, moon and seasons. Plants are our breath of life through the oxygen they create in green tissues. In addition to needing oxygen, nearly all forms of animal life depend on green plants for energy to sustain, grow and reproduce. Only certain *anaerobic* bacteria can survive without oxygen, while some kinds of bacteria and the aforementioned deep-sea animals do not need energy from plants. As the green links between the sun and the survival of virtually all life on Earth, plants are the unifying life force in our world.

Human survival and livelihood are the most widely recognized gifts that we receive from plants. Photosynthesis is the direct and indirect producer of an astounding array of resources that people use for making everything from furniture to drugs, including:
• all of our food, from bread to meat and from fruits and vegetables to milk, cheese, seeds, nuts and eggs. Even the meat consumed by people is from animals that either eat plants directly or have plants at the base of their food chains.
• drink
• clothing, such as that produced from animal hides, feathers and wool
• medicine
• alcohol and other intoxicants
• oils and other fats
• starches
• waxes
• perfumes

Cellulose, a substance produced in plant cell walls, is an essential fiber from which we produce:
• shelters, made of wood, bark, branches, leaves

• clothing from cotton and other plant fibers
• paper from pulp
• fuel, including fossil fuels formed from the ancient remains of giant horsetails, ferns and clubmosses from the Carboniferous period
• cordage from fibers, such as hemp
• baskets, from bark and wood splints
• all other products made from wood

The *real* economic base of North America is not gold, it is green. Even our currency bills are printed on materials made from plant fibers.

We take the common plants for granted, seeming to give them less value, yet we regard the rarest plants as the most valuable of all. In fact, each plant species is endowed with its own unique, irreplaceable *values* (see "Discussion" in Chapter 14).

Plant Symbols

Among traditional Native peoples of the Americas, plants are integral to the human relationship with nature. Botany is not a separate "field of study." Plants are important components of art, music, ceremony and symbolism. Many Haudenosaunee (Iroquois) thanksgiving ceremonies are based on gratitude for the gifts of corn, strawberries and other useful plants. Sunflower seeds are a sacred food to Plains peoples, who place a ceremonial bowl of sunflower seeds on the grave to sustain the deceased during the difficult journey to the spirit world. Incas believe the sunflower is the sacred symbol of the sun god. The priestesses—"Maidens of the Sun"—wore sunflower disks of gold on their breasts. Certain Native North American cultures regard the cactus as an emblem of endurance and bravery and the cattail as a symbol of peace and prosperity. In southwestern North America and Central America, some Native cultures, including the Mayans, worship the water lily as the sacred Earth symbol.

Individuals and families in many Native North American cultures are closely associated with plants and plant families. Many creation stories say that people first formed from plants. In the Lacandon Mayan tradition, people are fashioned from maize by the Creator and the Maker. The first Abenaki people step alive from an ash tree, with hearts growing and green, each time Gluscabe, the Transformer, shoots an arrow of life into the tree. Among the Abenaki of the Northeast, certain families have adopted the butternut tree as their family name.

Much can be understood about other cultures through their adopted plant symbolism and lore. Plants are used as symbols in every area of our lives, from expressing love and desire with roses, offering peace with an olive branch or representing a nation with the sugar maple leaf on Canada's flag. Each of the 50 states in the United States has an official state flower or state plant of some kind; each Canadian province has a provincial flower as well. Often the chosen plant symbol reveals the values of a culture or nation—something considered important enough for people to choose to identify with. The poinsettia, a flower of Native America, was adopted as the flower of Christmas by European immigrants. Plants appear as family crests; ceremonial decorations; expressions of condolence; colors of celebration; badges for saints and heroes; and symbols of reverence, gratitude and admiration. Our expressions, beliefs, passions, affections, fears, religions and superstitions are all symbolized with plants.[1]

Human fears of plants are, perhaps, more rational than our fears of animals. With the exception of an occasional horror movie depicting gargantuan, people-eating plants or aliens emerging from giant seed pods, most fears are focused upon the real threats posed by plant defenses: injury by thorns, rashes from irritants or even poisons in deadly berries or fungi. People do not actively fear plants as much as they fear animals because plants appear sedentary to the untrained eye, and thus unalarming. This common, erroneous image of plants as passive beings has even led to stereotypical characterizations of people as being physically slow like "a vegetable," or even a bit psychologically off balance—"a fruit." Someone who sits idle for long, unimaginative hours in front of a television set is a "couch potato."

The Plants

Plants are living beings that grow, "breathe," sense and interact with their surroundings, reproduce, live out their lives and die. The six major groups of plants and plant-like organisms include the **algae, fungi, mosses, ferns, conifers** and **flowering plants**, plus a number of related, less-familiar groups. (See Chapter 2 for a detailed classification of plants.) Plants, however, are often recognized by their form or appearance, such as a tree, shrub, herb, wildflower or mushroom.

No other living things are self-feeding like green plants, which can produce nutrients, and release both oxygen and water, through a process called photosynthesis (see "Discussion" in Chapter 5). The green chlorophyll in plants—the site of photosynthesis—is the color most often seen, but it can be masked by other pigments such as oranges and reds. Land plants take up available soil water and minerals through roots. A few specialized plants, called *epiphytes,* are able to trap these life-giving essentials directly from the air. Many aquatic plants absorb water and minerals through other tissues besides roots. Fungi are *saprophytic*—they consume the remains of dead plants and animals. *Parasitic* plants, such as mistletoe and dodder, extract staples for living from sap in the stems, roots or leaves of living *host* plants.

PLANT LINEAGE. More than 3 billion years ago, some tiny plant-like organisms were the first and only forms of life on Earth. These first "primitive" living things were similar to the blue-green algae of today. It was not until 420 million years ago that the first land plants evolved from a group of aquatic green algae. Ferns and related plants, such as horsetails, clubmosses and psilophytes, eventually evolved to become the first *vascular plants* (those with internal plumbing systems). Over millions of years a fantastic landscape formed of tree-size ferns and clubmosses, plants that reproduced via millions of tiny spores.

Seed plants appeared about 300 million years ago when cone-bearing *conifers* evolved. These hardy plants spread all over the world and are so successful that they have changed little over the millennia. Today, about one-third of the forests on Earth consist of spruce, fir and pine. Many conifers survive in harsh desert border country, in Arctic and in mountainous regions.

With the development of *flowering plants* around 136 million years ago,* a great period of co-evolution between plants and animals began. Of particular importance are the relationships that formed between flowers and pollinating insects. Flowering plants have become so prevalent that they comprise about 250,000 of the total 375,000 plant species (in 300 families) alive today, and they have the greatest diversity and geographic range found in the plant world.

From Home to Biome

A plant's home or *habitat* is the particular surrounding physical environment that meets its survival needs. Although all plants need food, water, oxygen and carbon dioxide (green plants), the survival needs of different kinds of plants vary greatly. Every plant needs space in which to grow, a certain amount of direct sunlight (green plants) or shade and a specific range of temperature and moisture. Seeds of the sugar maple will sprout in the deep shade of the forest. Aspen seeds, however, require open space and direct sunlight. As an aspen grove develops it casts its own shade and alters the environment, making the understory more suitable for trees and other plants that favor filtered shade. The composition of plant communities is the result of both the preexisting conditions of those habitats as well as the changes brought about by the growing plants themselves. All living things, both plants and animals, are engaged in a delicate circle of life with the environment, using their habitat for survival and changing that habitat with their activities.

Some plants have other specific needs to complete their life cycles. Cones of the jack pine must be exposed to an intense fire before they will open. Many seeds and trees require a prolonged spell of below-freezing weather to sprout, or leaf out respectively, in the springtime. Some seeds cannot sprout unless they pass through the digestive tract of an animal, a process that *scarifies* and weakens the seed coat.

Plants need the animals with which they share their habitats. Earthworms till the soil, improving both the fertility and aeration essential to growing roots. Bees, wasps

---

*Fossil evidence that has been discovered in Virginia indicates that flowering plants may have evolved about 100 million years earlier than is generally believed.[2, 3]

and other insects pollinate the flowers from which seeds form. Insects also chew up leaves or suck on root juices. Plants provide animals with shelter in a hollow tree; food of seeds, berries and nuts; and even water in a succulent cactus stem or in a pool in a hollow where two branches diverge.

Ecology, which comes from the Greek word *oikas* meaning "a house," is the study of the relationships among plants, animals and their environments. An expanse of forest, desert, mountainside, prairie, ocean, pond or other habitat is home for an *ecological community*. This community is made up of the plants and animals that live *interdependently* in a particular environment, sharing the available food, water, air, shelter and other resources needed for survival. The plants, themselves, in this locale are known as a *plant community*. All of these essential resources, along with the organisms that live in a particular habitat, comprise an *ecosystem*.

Interrelationships abound in every ecosystem: these are dynamic interconnections among both the living and the nonliving parts of an ecosystem. If plants produce the food that is the basis for all life on Earth, then soil—whether found on land or as liquid soil in the waters of an ocean, lake, pond or stream—is the seedbed for these life-giving plants. Speckled alder and sweet gale grow in wet soils, where decomposition is poor and so nutrients are not readily available. Bacteria associated with nodules in the roots of these shrubs are able to extract nitrogen directly from the atmosphere, thus enriching the plants' diets and raising the levels of organic nitrogen in the surrounding soil.

The very rootedness and interrelatedness of plants, and their particular ranges of tolerance to temperature, rainfall, soil conditions, wind, sunlight, elevation, length of growing seasons and other factors, have resulted in the formation of large-scale plant communities called *biomes* that cover vast territories (Figure 3-1). These biomes can be clearly marked on a map of North America. The range of a plant can be affected by all of the above-mentioned factors, plus geographical barriers such as mountain ranges and oceans, competition for resources with other plants, animals (including people) and even by the absence of a beneficial insect that the plant may need to successfully pollinate its flowers.

Plant communities in North America are greatly affected by large-scale events of the past and present, such as glaciers and dominant weather patterns. There have been four major glaciations over the past billion years. The latest began 2 million years ago during the Pleistocene Epoch and retreated about 12,000 years ago—a mere blink of an eye in geologic time. At the height of the latest glaciation, ice covered North America as far south as the Ohio and Missouri river valleys. Today, 10 percent of Earth's land surface is covered with ice, with Antarctica and Greenland lying under a glacier up to 2 miles thick. Antarctica's mantle of ice—the largest in the world—is so heavy that one-third of its land mass is depressed more than 1,000 feet (304.8

meters) below sea level. The Arctic Ocean is covered with ice year-round except for a brief summer period. Glaciers and ice sheets hold 75 percent of the world's freshwater.

Only those North American plant communities that lie south of the reach of the most recent glacier are older than about 12,000 years. As the glacier grew and crept southward, it gouged, ground and scraped the hills, mountains and valleys, sculpting such breathtaking geologic features as California's Yosemite Valley. Gradually, with the movement of the glacier and advancing cold before it, species of plants and animals migrated farther south until even the southern Appalachians were carpeted with tundra and boreal forest. The glacier itself, however, never reached that region.

The climate has warmed considerably since the glacier melted. Although there was a period between then and now when the weather was milder than at the present time, we are, overall, in the midst of a warming trend. Since about the year 1700, global temperature has been climbing and polar ice cover has decreased. Average sea level has risen 4 to 6 inches (10.2 to 15.2 centimeters) during the past century.[4] Today, 75 percent of Earth is under water and ice.

Large-scale weather patterns, which are impacted heavily by polar regions and ocean currents, have a dramatic effect on the location and composition of North America's plant biomes. Tropical air, being warmer, lighter and more humid than polar air, rises and carries its moisture toward the poles, while the heavier, drier polar air circulates southward to replace the rising tropical air. The wind currents formed by this exchange of heat and moisture between north and south are deflected to the right in the Northern Hemisphere and the left in the Southern Hemisphere by the *Coriolis effect,* a force created by Earth's spinning motion. *Westerlies* are created in this way—those general wind patterns blowing from west to east in the middle latitudes. Ocean currents tend to mirror the movement of global air masses. For instance, the warm Gulf Stream flows northward over the surface while deep frigid polar water moves south beneath it. Rain falls from moisture-laden air blowing inland from the oceans. This phenomenon is especially pronounced where coastal mountains force ocean air masses up, cool the air and create heavy rainfall. The temperate rainforests of the Pacific Northwest are watered in this way. Typically, a *rain shadow* forms east of these mountains, where the relatively dry air has little rain to give as it moves downslope and warms, as in the case of the desert biome east of the Rocky Mountains. As this air continues eastward it picks up moisture and rainfall increases, supporting the grasslands of the Great Plains. Rainfall also is slight in places where cold ocean currents well up, cooling the air above and discouraging precipitation.

All of these geographical and climatic elements interact to influence the composition of plant biomes in North America. Biomes have their own distinct dominant vegetation, associ-

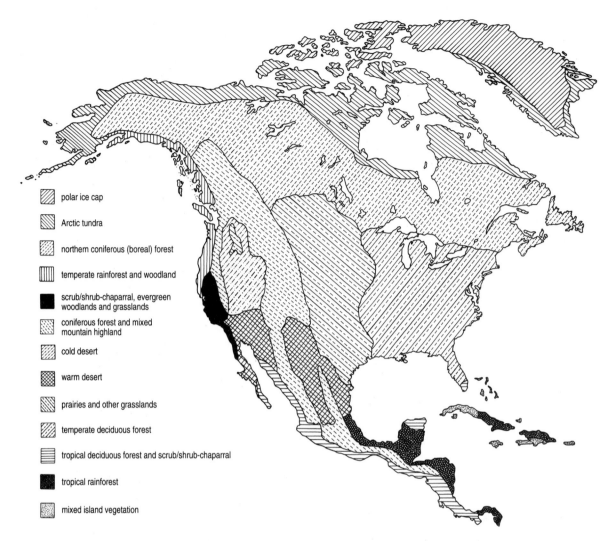

Legend:

- polar ice cap
- Arctic tundra
- northern coniferous (boreal) forest
- temperate rainforest and woodland
- scrub/shrub-chaparral, evergreen woodlands and grasslands
- coniferous forest and mixed mountain highland
- cold desert
- warm desert
- prairies and other grasslands
- temperate deciduous forest
- tropical deciduous forest and scrub/shrub-chaparral
- tropical rainforest
- mixed island vegetation

Figure 3-1. Map of the major North American Biomes: a generalized view of biomes identified by plant communities. Boundaries between biomes are not as well defined as shown here; the transition between biomes often occurs over a great distance. There is much diversity as well as an intermixing of plant communities within each biome. For example, a complex mosaic of plant habitats is found within the western biome called "coniferous forest and mixed mountain highland." The "temperate deciduous forest" biome in the east actually contains large regions of prairie to the west, pine forests in the southeast as well as mixed forests of coniferous and deciduous trees throughout.

ated animals and particular stages of ecological succession (see Chapter 8) that lead to a characteristic community. This community tends to persist in dynamic equilibrium with agents of change, such as fire, insects, disease or human activity. If any of these factors become overwhelming, they can alter the community dramatically.

The following terrestrial biomes found in North America, including Middle America, are covered in this book:

- tundra—Arctic and alpine (Chapter 12)
- northern coniferous (boreal) forest (Chapter 8)
- deciduous forest (Chapter 9)
- prairies and other grasslands (Chapter 10)
- scrub/shrub-chaparral (Chapter 12)
- desert (Chapter 12)
- temperate rainforest (Chapter 13)
- tropical rainforest (Chapter 13)

North America's aquatic environments include:

- ocean (Chapter 5)
- freshwater (Chapters 5 and 7)

North America's oceans and freshwater environments are dominated by prolific and diverse forms of algae. The continent's freshwater ecosystems, such as lakes, ponds, streams and rivers, encompass some of the largest bodies of water and river systems in the world. Wetlands, lying between dry land and deep water, include such rich and ecologically vital habitats as freshwater marshes, swamps, bogs and meadows (Chapter 7), as well as seashores, including salt marshes, estuaries, rocky shores, sandy beaches and coral reefs (Chapter 5).

Every major biome of the world is found in North America except for the tropical savannah, which is an

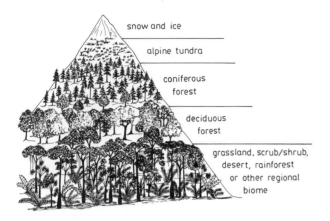

Figure 3-2. Plant zonation along a mountain slope. In reality, these zones are not as clearly defined as shown here; they grade into one another where plant growth varies in response to climatic differences that correspond with elevation.

expansive grassland habitat with scattered trees. Tundra is found farthest to the north, south of the polar ice and snow, and to its south the northern coniferous forest stretches in a band across the continent from the Pacific to the Atlantic. Roughly south of the Canadian border lies a complex ecological tapestry of biomes woven by wind currents, mountain ranges, rainfall patterns and all of the aforementioned factors. From west to east, the predominant pattern is coastal temperate rainforest, desert, grassland or prairie and deciduous forest. Patches of a smaller biome, the scrub/shrub or chaparral, are interspersed in desert and grassland communities. The northern coniferous forest, and patches of alpine tundra in highest elevations, reach southward in fingers along the spines of the Sierras, Cascades, Rockies and Appalachians.[5] Tropical rainforest is found in southern Mexico. Each North American biome is presented in greater detail in the various chapters of this book.

The plant communities of mountain slopes follow, with decreasing elevation, patterns similar to what is found on a journey from north to south (Figure 3-2). Higher elevations bring the colder equivalent of more northerly latitudes. Starting at the top of a tall mountain range in North America, the biomes encountered moving downslope are, generally, alpine tundra, northern coniferous forest, deciduous forest and then, depending on the prevailing climate at low altitudes, any one of the other biomes of grassland, scrub/shrub, desert, coastal temperate rainforest or tropical rainforest. Climatically, descending 1,000 feet (304.8 meters) in altitude is roughly equivalent to moving 300 miles (482.8 kilometers) away from the nearest pole. Other terrestrial habitats in North America include fields, agricultural lands and urban and suburban environments.

QUESTIONS

1.   In the Huron story "The Sky Tree," why would someone cut down the Sky Tree because of a message that appears in a dream? Why are dreams so powerful to the Huron?

2.   Who creates the new Earth on the back of Turtle? What are some other stories of creation that you know? How do *you* believe the world was created?

3.   Who creates the world and the living things on Turtle's back in the Lenni Lenape story "How Kishelemukong Made the People and the Seasons"? What kind of tree do people come from in this story? Who comes first, people or other living things?

4.   How does Kishelemukong create the four directions and the seasons? Which season comes from which direction?

5.   What kind of game does Kishelemukong create for Grandfather North and Grandmother South to compete in to keep the seasons evenly matched?

6.   What is a plant? How is a plant different from an animal?

7.   What *kinds* of plants can you think of? Do any of these plants live near your home?

8.   What do plants need to survive? How are these things the same as, or different from, those things that people and other animals need to live?

9.   Why are plants important? Could animals live without plants?

10.   How are plants used as symbols in art, music, stories and advertising and by states, provinces, national governments and individuals? Do you use any plants as symbols in your life?

11.   What plants do you like? Why? Which plants do you dislike? Why? Are you afraid of any plants? Is there any reason you are afraid?

12.   What is a plant's habitat? Why does a plant need a habitat? What does a plant get from its habitat? Why does a plant grow in a particular place? Does a growing plant change its habitat?

13.   Why is soil important to plants? Could plants survive without soil?

14.   What is ecology? What makes up an ecosystem?

15.   What does it mean to say living things are interdependent? What are some interrelationships among living things found in a habitat?

16.   Why do very large habitats, such as deserts, oceans, lakes, forests, mountains and marshes, have particular plants growing in them? Can you name other large habitats?

17.   Does a plant's habitat always stay the same? What can cause changes in a habitat? Will the same plants always be found there? Where do plants go to? Where do they come from?

18.   What does it mean to say we share our Earth home with all other people, plants, animals and nonliving things such as sun, air and water?

ACTIVITIES
Perplexing Plants

ACTIVITY: Solve some riddles about each of the six major groups of plants and plant-like organisms. Take the children on an excursion to a natural area, park or botanical garden to observe and identify representatives of these six groups.

GOALS: Understand certain characteristics that distinguish each of the major kinds of plants and plant-like organisms.

AGE: Younger children and older children

MATERIALS: Copy of plant riddles from the activity, photographs, illustrations and/or samples of several examples of plants and plant-like organisms from each group, Figure 3-3.

PROCEDURE: Ask the children to solve the following riddle. Ask them to listen to the whole riddle all the way through and to raise their hands with responses *after* you are done reading if they think they know the answer. What group of living things:

- often stay in one place for life but may send their children on journeys of thousands of miles (kilometers)?
- can be as small as the smallest living thing on Earth, yet are also the largest?
- give new life when they die?
- may be soft as mush or harder than some rocks?
- feed nearly every animal on Earth?
- can survive in the ocean, Arctic or desert?
- move, but appear to be still?
- are usually green, but can be any color of the rainbow?

If no one guesses "plants" right away, offer some hints until someone guesses correctly. As the riddle shows, plants are such a diverse group of living things that it is difficult to answer the question, "What is a plant?"

Now follow the same procedure with the following six riddles. Tell the children that the riddles identify plants and plant-like organisms from each of the six major groups. The answers are given in parentheses after each riddle. Hold up some photographs, illustrations and/or samples of organisms from each group right after the children guess the answer to that particular riddle. Allow children to ask questions about each *group* before moving on to the next riddle.

- We are often very tall.
- Your pencils are made from one of us.
- We never make flowers.
- We have leaves of green needles.
- We make seeds in cones.
   We are the (conifers).

- We come in all colors.
- We live in the water.
- We can be microscopic or as tal
- Some of us are attached to the bott
- Some of our kind are called seaweed.
- We feed, directly or indirectly, all ocean life.
- We make a slippery coating on rocks in the stream. Be careful you don't step on us!
- Snails like to graze on us.
   We are the (algae).

- We can be many different colors but are rarely green.
- You might find one kind of us growing on an old piece of bread, and another out of a decaying log.
- We rot.
- We would not eat you alive, but we may devour you after you've died.
- Our spores are floating in the air in front of you right now, looking for the right place to land and grow.
- Some people say that toads like to use some of our fruit as stools.
- Our puffballs give off clouds of smokey spores when you step on them.
   We are the (fungi).

- We are the most common group of plants on Earth.
- You eat our seeds, fruits and nuts all the time.
- You love to eat our vegetables!
- Our leaves are mostly green but can be other colors, too.
- You climb in our branches, pick off our heads and burn us in your fireplace.
- We make the bowl of cherries that no one ever told you your life would be.
   We are the (flowering plants).

- We are green and not so tall.
- Our leaves are often delicate and lacy.
- Some people say we grow in "beds."
- When we sprout in the springtime we look like little "fiddleheads."
- You often get one of our green sprigs when you buy a bouquet of flowers.
- Coal and oil formed from the remains of our ancestors millions of years ago.
- We make spores instead of seeds.
   We are the (ferns).

- We like to grow where it is damp and shady.
- You like to lie down on our green carpets in the woods.
- We are short and usually soft.
- Some people say we only grow on the north side of trees.
- We sprout from spores.
- A rolling stone gathers none of us.
   We are the (mosses).

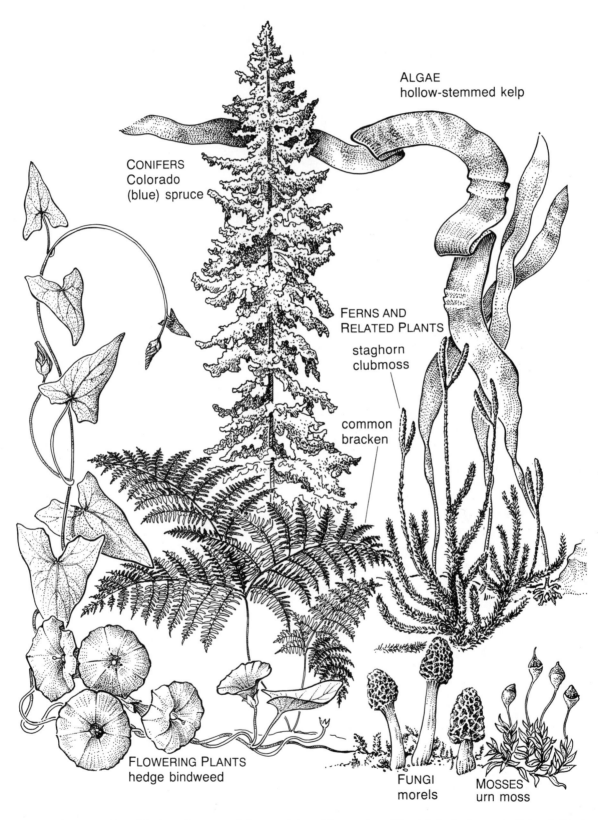

Figure 3-3. Representatives of the six major groups of plants and plant-like organisms. Sizes (clockwise from top): Colorado (blue) spruce, 70 to 100 ft. (21 to 30 m); hollow-stemmed kelp, to 15 ft. (4.6 m); staghorn clubmoss, 10 in. (25.4 cm); urn moss, .1 to .5 in. (.3 to 1.3 cm); morels, 2 to 5 in. (5.1 to 12.7 cm); common bracken, 2 to 5 ft. (.6 to 1.5 m); hedge bindweed, 1 to 3 ft. (30.5 to 91.4 cm). (Illustration by Marjorie C. Leggitt)

Share Figure 3-3 with the children; it shows representatives of these six major groups. Use the section called "Classifying and Identifying Plants" in Chapter 2 to share with older children the reasons that algae and fungi are often classified outside the plant kingdom. Now take the children on a brief field excursion to a natural area, park or botanical garden. Have them focus on the characteristics of the plants and plant-like organisms they are seeing as they decide which of the six groups each belongs in.

Tree of Plants

ACTIVITY: Create a mural of a tree with six branches, one for each major group of plants and plant-like organisms. Illustrate representatives of each of the six groups and place them on the appropriate branch of the Tree of Plants mural.
GOALS: Understand the characteristics of each of the six major groups of plants and plant-like organisms. Recognize where familiar plants fit on the Tree of Plants.
AGE: Younger children and older children
MATERIALS: Construction paper, pieces of light cardboard, roll of brown parcel-post paper, writing paper, scissors, crayons, pencils, staples, paste, tape, clay, balloons, pipe cleaners, straws, empty egg cartons, toothpicks, cardboard tubes (from paper towels and toilet paper), photographs and illustrations of plants from each of the six major groups or samples of actual plants, copy of plant classification section from Chapter 2 and Figure 3-3.
PROCEDURE: Use the roll of brown paper to create a large mural silhouette of a tree with six major branches. Stuff rolled-up newspaper behind the trunk and branches to lend a three-dimensional effect. Refer to the section on plant classification in Chapter 2 and describe the characteristics of each group of plants and plant-like organisms while holding up photographs or illustrations of each kind, or while referring to samples of actual plants. Share Figure 3-3 with the children and take them on a field trip outdoors to see and discuss plants firsthand.

Have the children create large illustrations or models of plants and plant-like organisms from all six groups using supplies listed in the "Materials." When the artwork is completed, ask the children to take turns sharing their creations with the group and to describe all they know about that plant and why it fits into its particular group. Use questions to help guide the children toward the characteristics that are especially important, and then help each child to attach her or his creation to the Tree of Plants.

Refer back to the Tree of Plants whenever necessary during the course of the stories and activities in this book. Children can add to or change the Tree over time to reflect new knowledge and discoveries, such as photographs clipped from magazines, calendars and so on.

A Harvest of Symbols

ACTIVITY: Create collages showing images of how particular plants are used as symbols by contemporary cultures and in Native North American traditions. Write a report describing the things symbolized by that plant and why the plant is used as a symbol. Examine the values and attitudes toward plants of both Native cultures and modern cultures as revealed by the way plants are used as symbols.
GOALS: Observe how and why plants are used as symbols by traditional Native North Americans and other cultures. Understand the values different cultures hold toward plants.
AGE: Older children
MATERIALS: Sources of information about plant symbols such as magazines, atlases, encyclopedias, gardening journals, newspapers, maps, billboards and other signs; light cardboard such as oak tag; pencils, crayons, markers; scissors; paste; paint, brushes and containers of water; and chalk and chalkboard or markers and newsprint.
PROCEDURE: Have all of the children read (or *read to* younger children) the two sections of the "Discussion" called "Plant Symbols" and "The Giving Plants." Lead a brainstorming session on how plants are used as symbols by Native North Americans, such as the strawberry, maize, sunflower, cattail and water lily. Ask the children to think of ways plants are used as symbols by contemporary society, such as in art, advertising or music or by governments. Discuss the kinds of values plants hold for people, including intrinsic values, cultural, ecological, practical and commercial (see the section called "The Values of Species" in the "Discussion" of Chapter 14.)

Now have the children divide into two groups: those who want to explore traditional Native North American plant symbols and those preferring to examine plant symbols used by contemporary society at large. Have each child research ways that plants are used as symbols by examining the encyclopedia, magazines, maps, atlases, newspapers, signs, journals, works of art and other media. Individuals in each group could choose to focus on one or two sources of symbols, such as signs and billboards or magazines and newspapers. As the children work, they should record their findings in both images and notes, demonstrating and explaining how the plant is used as a symbol, what this use reveals about the values those people assign to that plant, and any stereotypes or other attitudes those people demonstrate by using the plant that way. Images can take the form of magazine clippings, photographs or illustrations made in the field. A collage provides a good visual record of plant symbols. Each child will compile the field notes into a brief written report of their findings and observations based on those findings.

Once their collages and reports are complete, have the members of first one group and then the other come up to present their collages and read the accompanying reports. As they do this, record in two columns on newsprint or a chalkboard the values held toward plants that are revealed from the findings of each group: the traditional Native researchers and those researching society at large. When all reports have been given, facilitate a question-and-answer discussion comparing and contrasting the traditional Native values with the contemporary values held toward plants as revealed by the two groups' symbols.

Making Earth on Turtle's Back

ACTIVITY: Create a model of Earth on Turtle's back, including some of the major North American biomes (younger children and older children). Research and present a report describing the biomes you constructed (older children).

GOALS: Understand the living and nonliving components that make up the biomes found in North America, and that the location of those biomes is determined by climate, rainfall, geography, soil type and other factors. Understand that Earth is our common home, a habitat that provides for the survival of all plants, animals and people. Visualize how Earth is made up of many ecosystems. Understand the meaning of ecology, interdependence, interrelationships and ecological community. Understand that plants influence their environments and that habitats are constantly changing. Discover how the thin skin of soil supports life on Earth.

AGE: Younger children and older children

MATERIALS: One sheet of plywood measuring 4 feet (1.2 meters) by 4 feet by 1/2 inch (1.3 centimeters) thick; chicken wire or window screening; one 12-inch (31-centimeter) wooden support and eight 7-inch (18-centimeter) wooden supports (strong sticks will do); wire-cutting pliers; thin wire; measuring stick or tape; lots of newspaper; wheat paste; water; modeling clay; tempera paints and brushes; pipe cleaners; cloth scraps; toothpicks; construction paper; crayons; paste; scissors; hammer; nails; fence staples; pencils; writing paper; a 2-foot (.6-meter) sheet of plastic; yellow beachball; golfball; string; Figure 3-4; pictures of the different biomes that will appear on Earth; list of common plants and animals found in each biome; information about biomes from the "Discussion" sections throughout this book.

PROCEDURE: Create the turtle-shell base for Earth out of the plywood, support sticks, nails and chicken wire (Figure 3-4). Drive a nail into the center of the plywood from the bottom and into the 1-foot (31-centimeter) tall stick while holding the stick on top of the plywood. Draw a circle with a 2-foot (.6-meter) radius onto the wood using the support

stick as the center. Nail a ring of eight 7-inch (18-centimeter) tall sticks halfway between the center and the edge of the circle. Now form the chicken wire or window screening over the supports to make a dome. If you use window screening, you will need to stuff crumpled newspaper under the screening for extra support. Staple the wire or screening down along the edges and on the tops of the wooden supports. Add wire sculpture where Turtle's head, tail and four legs will be.

Divide the children into small groups and assign each group a specific biome (Figure 3-1) to design and build. Divide up Turtle's back and show the children in each group how much space they have in which to create their biomes. Provide them with descriptions of the biomes, and life found in each one, from the "Discussion" sections throughout this book. Obtain illustrations of the biomes, and life therein, from reference books. Have the children draw out a plan for Earth including all landforms and water. Use the pictures of the different biomes to help the children visualize the environments as they plan. Spend some time working on methods for how to draw pictures that will become three-dimensional objects.

Mix the wheat paste, adding just enough water to form the consistency of wallpaper paste. Have the children tear up strips of newspaper several inches wide. If they tear the paper from top to bottom the sheets will tear evenly. Thoroughly coat the paper strips with the paste and drape them over the chicken wire, pulling them tight to form a smooth surface. Then make the mountains, hills, valleys, rivers and streams out of the papier-mâché. Push in on the chicken wire near the top of Earth to make a depression for a lake. Line this hole with papier-mâché. Stick toothpicks standing upright in Earth wherever

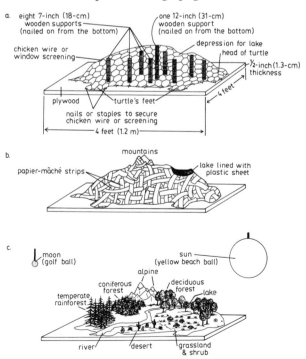

Figure 3-4. Creating "Earth on Turtle's Back"

forests will be constructed. The toothpicks will become trunks for trees. Remember to leave large flat areas surrounding the continents. These will become the oceans. Allow to dry for several days.

Paint the landscape with tempera paints and let this dry. Do not forget to paint in the rivers, streams, open green areas for fields, and the oceans and deserts. Paint the lakebed blue. Once the paint is dry, line the lakebed with the plastic sheet and secure the edges with fine strips of papier-mâché. When this is dry, fill the lake with water.

Now have the children use the other materials to make people, animals, trees, other plants and other life appropriate for their biomes. Have them add some human settlements as well. You will need to state that each of the different biomes they have created on Turtle contains many *habitats,* homes for the plants and animals that live in that specific biome. Generate a list of four or five common plants and animals for each biome to get the children started. Emphasize that Earth provides the survival needs of all life.

Hang the sun (yellow beachball) and moon (golfball) above Earth and thank the sun for bringing life to the green plants, which in turn keep people and animals alive.

Have older children research the natural history of their biomes as the basis for a written report. When the research is completed, they will orally present the findings to the group.

Describe how Earth is an ever-changing place, and that plants grow in these particular biomes because the conditions such as temperature, rainfall, wind, elevation and soil type all meet plants' need for survival. Discuss the importance of soil to continued life on Earth, and the ways that plants change their environments as they grow and develop. Have the children describe the biomes they built and the plants and animals that live there. During their discussion, point out the interrelationships among the living things found in their biomes. Introduce children to the meaning of a few terms: *ecology, ecosystem, ecological community, habitat* and *plant community.* Relate all these lessons back to the stories that begin the chapter. Help the children to understand that, as they look at Earth on Turtle's back, all life is interdependent on the Earth home we share with each other and with all living things.

EXTENDING THE EXPERIENCE

• Set up six art stations: one for each of the six different kinds of plants and plant-like organisms. Illustrate what you see at each station using crayons, pastels or paints and bind this artwork into booklets. Or, use photographs cut from magazines, seed catalogs, calendars, etc.

• Create your own symbols using plants.

• Make word meanings out of plant symbols and create a picture story using this new language.

• Invent and create a model of an entirely new group of plants and describe its adaptations.

• Share other stories in which plants are important, such as *The Secret Garden* and *Jack and the Beanstalk.* What roles do plants play in these stories? How do the stories turn out?

• Visit plants from your biome and from distant biomes during a visit to a botanical garden. Incorporate some of these new plants into your *"Earth on Turtle's Back"* model.

• List the reasons *you* think plants are important. Illustrate a small book showing these values.

• Read about biomes in other parts of the world and the plants, animals and people who live in them. How are we interrelated to all of them?

• Create a gallery of the plant world, with models and illustrations of representatives from each of the six major groups of plants and plant-like organisms.

• Continue the seasonal themes in "How Kishelemukong Made the People and the Seasons" by exploring Chapter 15 in *Keepers of the Earth.*

NOTES

1. Ernst Lehner and Johanna Lehner, *Folklore and Symbolism of Flowers, Plants and Trees* (New York: Tudor, 1960), 12.

2. Bruce Cornet, "Dicot-Like Leaf and Flowers from the Late Triassic Tropical Newark Supergroup Rift Zone, U.S.A.," *Modern Geology,* vol. 19, no. 1 (August 1993): 81–99.

3. Nicholas C. Fraser, "Cascade: A Triassic Treasure Trove," *Virginia Explorer,* vol. 9, no. 1 (Winter/Spring 1993): 15–18.

4. National Geographic Society, *Our Awesome Earth* (Washington, D.C.: National Geographic Society, 1986), 38.

5. Peter Farb and the Editors of Time-Life Books, *Ecology* (New York: Time-Life Books, 1970), 14.

CELEBRATION, THANKSGIVING AND STEWARDSHIP

*Our Creator decided, "When it becomes warm, the wind, it is then that the sap will flow, so it is that the maple trees
will be tapped, from there it will be collected that it may be boiled down by the people."*

Chapter 4

✦ The Thanks to the Trees ✦

(Seneca—Eastern Woodland)

(This comes from the traditional Seneca Thanksgiving Address, adapted and translated from a Long Opening Thanksgiving Address given in 1972 by Enos Williams/Quivering Leaves at Seneca Longhouse, Six Nations, Ontario.)

And now we will speak again.

Our Creator decided trees will be on Earth, growing here and there; also forests will be growing of trees, groves will be growing on Earth. And it is still true that trees grow here and there. Our Creator decided this will be something important, for from these trees medicines can come. And certain it is, they are still growing, all of them are different in the way they grow.

Our Creator decided all of the trees will have names, every one of them that people will know them, the people who will live here on Earth. And it is possible that from those trees, within their families, people will grow well. It is possible that people will draw on those trees when it changes, the wind, when it grows colder, the wind. It is possible that then people will be kept warm and they will work together as one, kept warm by that which he left, the live coals on Earth.

Our Creator decided the trees will work together well to bring happiness to families on Earth. And we still think it is coming to pass in this manner. And carefully now, the Creator decided, "The trees will have this one to lead them. People living on Earth will say, 'That tree standing there, the Maple, it is a special tree'."

Our Creator decided "When it becomes warm, the wind, it is then that the sap will flow, so it is that the maple trees will be tapped, from there it will be collected that it may be boiled down by the people. And so then it will be possible for the people to drink the maple syrup again."

And it is possible then that people will be gathered; it is important also that people gather together then. Medicine will be made from the maple syrup, and people moving about, people on Earth will be helped. And when it became warm, the wind, it is true that we saw again this new sap was rising. And it came to pass that we drank the maple syrup again. And it was possible that we were gathered together at what we call Maple Sugar Gathering, the Maple Festival.

And so it is we thank our Creator in the way that he left it we should always thank him at ceremonies. And we think this ceremony has come to pass. Let us put together our thoughts that we will always be grateful, for it is certain that he is sending them to us, the trees which are standing on Earth. We are the ones our Creator thought of; those trees were meant to be used well by those of us moving about on Earth.

Carefully now, it is that we thank him, the one who dwells in the sky, Sonkwaiatison.

DISCUSSION

Among the Haudenosaunee (Iroquois), the ability to speak well is very important and is regarded as a special gift from the Creator. At the start of any gathering, a "Thanksgiving Address" of greater or lesser length must be given in one of the Haudenosaunee languages by someone who is a good speaker, possessed of a strong voice and the right delivery, the memory necessary to remember everything, and the fluency in the Native language to say the right words.

Each address has a formal progression, moving from Earth to Sky. It always begins by gathering the people together and then acknowledging, in turn, Earth, the Water, the Grasses, the Hanging Fruit, the Trees, the Birds, the Three Sisters Who Sustain Us (Corn, Beans and Squash), the Wind, the Thunderers, the Sun, the Moon, the Stars, the Four Beings, Handsome Lake (a Haudenosaunee prophet of the early 1800s who brought a Good Message from the Creator) and the Creator. There is a deep awareness of the relationship among all things and the responsibility of human beings to be thankful and careful in the way we live within this natural balance.

In the address thanking and acknowledging the trees, the Maple has a special place. It is the leader tree, the first to give something to the people each year in the form of its syrup, which is both sweet to the taste and used as a medicine. Added to boiling water, the Haudenosaunee say, maple sugar soothes stomach problems. They also use maple syrup to counteract diarrhea, as a cough medicine and as a diuretic.

The annual Maple Festival is the first of five different Haudenosaunee harvest festivals (Maple, Strawberry, Bean, Green Corn, Harvest) during the year, and at that late winter festival, people thank the trees and drink maple syrup.

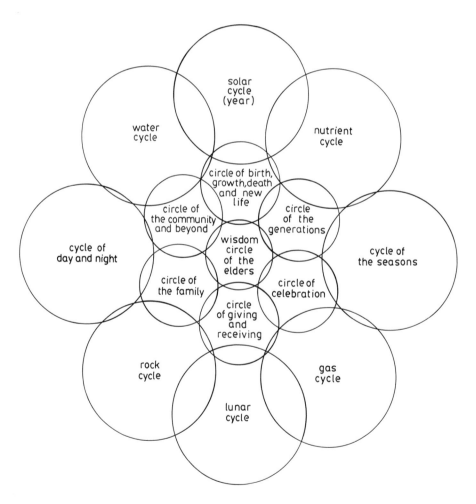

Figure 4-1. The Circles and Cycles of Life are all interconnected. Honoring these circles and cycles is essential to living in balance. As we move along the circle of birth, growth, death and new life we pass through the stages of life. When we become one of the elders near the end of the journey, we move toward the children, who are at the beginning. The seven circles in the center of this illustration represent the seven sacred directions. (Concept and design © 1994 by Michael J. Caduto.)

Thanksgiving

Thanksgiving, to Native North American cultures, is not a yearly event, it is a daily practice. Giving thanks is an integral part of *living in balance,* of maintaining the great circle of giving and receiving, one of the *circles of life* that encompass all of Earth (Figure 4-1).

> Now our minds we direct to our Mother Earth, who supports all life. We look to the shortest grasses, close to the bosom of our Mother Earth, as we put our minds together as one mind. We include all the plant life, the woodlands, all the waters of Earth, the fishes, the animal life, the bird life, and the Four Winds. As one mind our acknowledgement, respect, and thanksgiving move upward to the Sky World: the Grandmother Moon, who has a direct relationship to the females of the species of all living things; the sun and stars; and our Spiritual Beings of the Sky World. They still carry on the original Instructions in this Great Cycle of Life.[1]
>
> —Audrey Shenandoah
> *Onondaga*

Here are some seasonal ceremonies observed by the Kanienkahageh (Mohawk) people. Ceremonies remind the Haudenosaunee "to be grateful for all the things we have."[2]

- Midwinter Ceremony—starts a new cycle
- Maple Syrup Ceremony—end of spring
- Thunder Dance—early summer, to honor water life
- Moon Dance—early summer, to pay respect and give thanks to Grandmother Moon and all female life
- Strawberry Ceremony—early summer, to pay respect to the medicine plants and other healing powers
- Planting Ceremony—early summer, to acknowledge foods
- Bean Dance—midsummer, to remind The People of this main food
- Green Corn Dance—midsummer, to remind The People of this main food
- Harvest Dance—end of summer, to celebrate good fortune of the year
- Moon Dance—early fall
- End of Seasons—fall, to remind The People of the good cycle and to prepare for the next cycle

Widespread in Native North America, and around which the calendars for many thanksgiving celebrations revolve, is the recognition of the cycle of the seasons represented by the 13 large scales on Turtle's back (Figure 4-2). Each moon has a name. Some cultures name the thirteenth moon, which comes around every few years. The lunar cycle is one of the great *cycles of nature.* Observances associated with moons are a manifestation of the ways that traditional Native North American cultures share the unifying principle of living in balance.

Here, the traditional moons of the Oglala Lakota are correlated with the month of the Roman calendar to which each moon roughly corresponds. These moons tell the story of existence dependent upon hunting and foraging.

Moon of Frost in the Tepee—January
Moon of the Dark Red Calf (Bison)—February
Moon of the Snowblind—March
Moon of the Red Grass Appearing—April
Moon When the Ponies Shed—May
Moon of Making Fat—June, when the growing power of the world is strongest
Moon When the Cherries Are Ripe (red cherries)—July
Moon of Black Cherries—August
Moon When the Calves Grow Hair, or Moon of the Black Calf, or Moon When the Plums are Scarlet—September
Moon of the Changing Season—October
Moon of the Falling Leaves—November
Moon of the Popping Trees—December

Far to the east, in the land of the Western Abenaki, the "People of the Dawn," the moons reveal the importance of agriculture as well as hunting in the lives of these people.

Alamikos Kisos (New Year's Greeting Moon)—January
Piaodogos Kisos (Boughs-Shedding Moon)—February
Mozokas Kisos (Moose-Hunting Moon)—March
Sogalikas Kisos (Sugar-Making Moon)—April
Kikas Kisos (Planting Moon)—May
Nokkahiga Kisos (Hoeing Moon)—June
Temaskikos Kisos (Haying Moon)—July
Temezowas Kisos (Harvesting Moon)—August

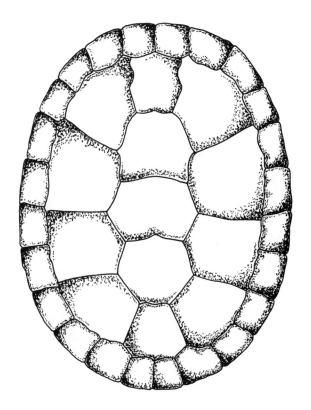

Figure 4-2. The large scales on Turtle's back represent the 13 moons and the cycle of the seasons.

Skamonkas Kisos (Indian-Corn Moon)—September
Penibagos Kisos (Leaf-Falling Moon)—October
Mzatonos Kisos (Ice-Forming Moon)—November
Pebonkas Kisos (Winter Moon)—December
Kchi Kisos (Big Moon)—for years with a thirteenth
    moon

Celebration and Appreciation

Healing Earth is not all work. It also means letting go and participating in the *circle of celebration.* Celebrations are times for enjoying and having fun, as well as honoring and appreciating someone or something. Plant celebrations honor certain plants and express appreciation for their usefulness as food that sustains life, their power as medicines that heal and their peaceful presence. Soil is appreciated as the root of all plant life and, therefore, animal life on Earth. Plants are celebrated for their aesthetic enrichment of our lives—the beauty and variety of colors among leaves, fruits and flowers; the scents of flower petals, stems, berries and leaves; the flavors in berries, nuts and other plant foods; the sounds of aspen leaves clacking or pine needles sighing in a breeze, the feel of a bark's texture or a patch of cushy moss. Plants are used for decoration and sometimes bark baskets are adorned with moose hair or porcupine quills.

Songs, games and dances are all a part of celebrating. Games are used ceremonially to give thanks, please the gods, ask for fertility, bring rain, give and prolong life, expel demons and cure illness.[3] There are thousands of Native North American games of skill, dexterity, chance and amusement. Running races and throwing contests are popular traditions, as are archery and games using sticks, balls and string.

Everyone has a song. God gives us each a song ... Our song tells us who we are.[4]

—Charlie Knight
Ute

The Continuum of Life

Many Native dances are performed in a circle or spiral, two of the essential shapes found among plants. Dances help to celebrate the *unity* and interconnectedness of all of Creation. Plants are the unifying force of life, the link between the sun's energy and all life on Earth. Many dances incorporate elements of the *four directions* or *four winds,* symbolizing the four quarters of the universe,[5] as well as Mother Earth and Father Sky—all living and inanimate parts of Earth, all environments, all peoples and cultures.

Life is a continuum. A widespread fallacy among Western cultures is the tendency to set ourselves apart from other living beings and to regard plants as less important than animals. These artificial human distinctions among forms of life, and even between living and nonliving things, are our attempt to better understand Earth. But we have come to confuse human points of view with universal reality, which they are not. As Onondaga Chief Oren Lyons once said,

"Another of the natural laws is that all life is equal."[6] Acknowledging the *equal rights of plants* as a life form is an important prelude to sharing our Earth home and its resources with plants. Just as sharing respect and acceptance are the basis for social justice and peace among human communities and cultures, so are they the foundation for an egalitarian ecological existence with life on Earth.

Connecting

Celebration is also a meeting of hearts and minds. It is about holding hands in a circle and *connecting.* Plants are masters of *empathy,* of sharing another's thoughts and feelings. Celebration brings us closer to people and plants. When we understand another person or living thing we feel for her, him or it, and we develop a sense of respect. This respect grows deeper over time as it develops into love, reverence and even awe.

My heart is filled with joy when I see you here, as the brooks fill with water when the snows melt in the spring, and I feel glad, as the ponies are when the fresh grass starts in the beginning of the year.[7]

—Ten Bears
Yamparika Comanche

Of People and Plants

Plants are sentient beings who exhibit an astounding level of awareness and interaction with their environments. No other living things are more finely attuned to the sun, moon and perhaps even the stars. Plants grow up to the sky and down into Earth at the same time. Leaves, flowers, tendrils, roots, buds and twigs are in constant slow motion: bending, plowing, searching and circling as the plant grows and reacts to the daily changes of temperature, sunlight and humidity around it. Water lily flowers are open in the morning and usually close by late afternoon (Figure 4-3). Certain tendrils, as they circle in quest of a holdfast, complete one revolution in just over an hour. When the tendril finds a place to fasten, it starts to wrap around within 20 seconds, completes the task in 1 hour and proceeds to corkscrew and pull up the vine.[8]

We do not experience plants as the lively creatures they are because they move to the beat of a different, slower drummer. *Slow,* perhaps, but *strong,* growing roots and trunks can buckle sidewalks, crack foundations and cause dams to give way. One 3-foot (.9-meter) section of root 4 inches (10.2 centimeters) in diameter exerted 50 tons (45.4 metric tons) of pressure as it grew, enough to lift 25 subcompact automobiles. Try lifting 100 gallons (378.5 liters) of water, weighing 833.7 pounds (378.2 kilograms), to treetop level: a birch tree accomplishes this feat on a dry day. Imagine holding 100,000 walnuts aloft, as some trees do prior to harvest.

It is understandable that the symbols and gifts of plants, especially flowers, are associated with many positive values, such as love, condolence and friendship, and that gardening, or a visit to a greenhouse, induces peace and serenity. Native

North Americans have known of the healing powers of certain plants, and will even stand with their backs against an old tree, arms outstretched, to absorb the tree's wisdom, peace and power, especially when out on a long, wearying journey.

In a nurturing circle of life, people have observed that plants respond positively to singing and frequent, gentle touching.[9] It has long been known that gardens and gardening induce a therapeutic "relaxation response" among people. Some controversial experiments even report that changes in the electrical potential monitored in plant cells indicate that plants may even react when they or other nearby plants or animals are harmed.[10] The boundaries of human sensory perception limit our ability to fully understand the powers of awareness and behavior among plants.

Sensory Attunement

Our bodies are the instruments we use to interact with the world around us, by which we see, hear, taste, smell, touch and intuit. *Sensory attunement* is more than merely perceiving our surroundings through our organs; it is a deeper way of connecting in a harmonious way with Earth. Plants, with their ability to elicit positive emotions in human beings, are perfect partners for establishing a sensory *circle of attunement*. When we engage plants in a loving, caring stewardship we are participating in one of the true circles of life. We are performing one of the tasks of a true human being.

* * *

Celebration and appreciation are an opening, healing beginning to attunement, connection and caring. Perhaps trees—their beauty, medicines, sweet sap, useful wood, sensory pleasures of the smells and taste of their flowers and fruits—being celebrations in themselves, would naturally find their way into traditional concerns for the future well-being of Earth. The traditional Haudenosaunee prophesies remind us that in a great circle, celebration encourages the stewardship that keeps Earth strong so future generations will have something to celebrate. These prophesies forewarn of what will happen if we do not learn how to live in balance with Earth.

Two of the old prophesies have already come to pass. It is said that the trees will begin to die from the top down. That is what the sugar maple is now doing. It was predicted that a great disease would afflict people of all kinds, and it is here. The corn, as it was foretold, no longer grows as tall as it once did. It is prophesied that the strawberries will cease to bear fruit. This has not yet come to pass and, hopefully, it never will. Perhaps we have enough time to change our behavior before it happens.[11]

—Chief Jake Swamp
Kanienkahageh (Mohawk)

Figure 4-3. Many plants show a daily cycle in response to light, dark, humidity and temperature. Blossoms of the fragrant water lily spread their petals in the morning, then close by late afternoon. (Photo by Michael J. Caduto)

QUESTIONS

1. Who decides in "The Thanks to the Trees" that there will be trees on Earth? Why?

2. Why are the trees created? How do people use these trees? How do trees bring happiness to families on Earth?

3. Which tree is chosen as a special tree? How is it special?

4. How are the maple trees thanked for maple syrup and other gifts from these trees? What does "thanksgiving" mean to you?

5. What does "thanksgiving" mean to Native North Americans? How do they celebrate Thanksgivings? How often do they give thanks? Why do they give thanks?

6. How many scales are there on Turtle's back? What do those scales represent to many Native North Americans?

7. What does *celebrate* mean? Why do we celebrate? What is a celebration for? What are the things we do to celebrate? Why would we celebrate plants?

8. What does it mean to appreciate something? How can we show our appreciation for plants?

9. What does it mean to "live in balance" with Earth, with plants and with each other? How can we keep the circles of

giving and receiving strong with plants? What does it mean to live with the next seven generations in mind?

10. What are the circles of life? What are the cycles of nature? Why are they important? Are we a part of these cycles? How can we keep them strong?

11. Why do Native North Americans believe that all life—plants, animals and people—is equal? What rights do plants and animals have? What do you believe about the equality of all life?

12. What does it mean to be connected to other living things? What is "empathy"? How do we show empathy for plants or for people?

13. How can you best use your senses to relate to other living things?

14. How do you know plants have senses? How do plants sense the world around them?

15. How can you communicate with plants? Do plants respond to human caring? Do people respond to plants?

ACTIVITIES
Round Dance of Unity and Thanksgiving[12]

ACTIVITY: List the ways we are connected to plants, animals, Earth and other people. Discuss the Native North American Thanksgivings. Perform a round dance to celebrate the unity of all things, to give thanks for all the gifts we receive from Earth, to connect with a small community of people and all people and to honor the circles and cycles of life essential for living in balance.

GOALS: Understand the true meanings and practices of Native North American Thanksgivings. Visualize the round dance as a symbol of the unity and interconnectedness of all parts of Earth, living and inanimate; the circles and cycles of nature, including the circle of giving and receiving and its importance to living in balance; and the interconnectedness among people in a small community and people and cultures throughout the world.

AGE: Younger children and older children

MATERIALS: Chalkboard and chalk or newsprint and felt-tipped markers, copy of Figure 4-4, drum with a head of rubber or leather and drum striker composed of a stick with a piece of cotton-filled felt wrapped and tied over the striking end.

PROCEDURE: Beforehand, obtain or prepare a simple, handheld drum with a striker.

Create, on the chalkboard or newsprint, headings for several columns: plants, animals, soil, rain, air (oxygen), etc., including other major parts of Earth the children think of. Ask the children to raise their hands and share ways that we are *connected* to each of these parts of the Earth. You could ask, for instance, "Where do we get what we need to live?" Then, trace food, drink and other supplies from local markets and farms

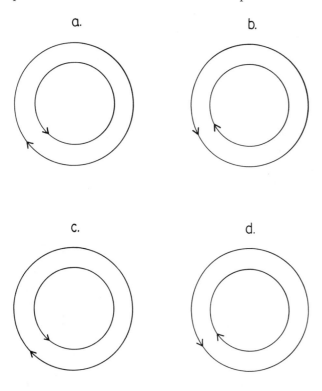

Figure 4-4. Patterns of movement for leading a group in the "Round Dance of Unity and Thanksgiving." Start the dance by having the inner and outer circles of children move in the directions indicated by the arrows in "a" above. Once the outer circle has completed one full revolution, have the two circles change direction to move as in "b". Both inner and outer circles will change direction each time the outer circle has moved around one full turn. Continue in this way for all four rounds of the dance, through step "c" and on to step "d". The dance is over when the outer circle has completed its final revolution as shown in "d".

back to their sources in nature. For instance, we eat corn; we get oxygen from plants' leaves and give plants, in turn, our carbon dioxide; corn grows in soil; and so on. Challenge the children to find *anything* that cannot be traced back to a source in nature! Once you have all created and recorded a number of connections with parts of Earth, discuss how these many connections are the glue that *unites* all parts of Earth. Explain that we are *interconnected* and that all life depends on plants for food, directly or indirectly, so plants are a unifying force on Earth. Discuss the ideas of living in balance and the circles of life and cycles of nature that are crucial to that balance (Figure 4-1). Mention the meaning of the four directions (from the "Discussion"), and that the four changes of direction in this dance represent the four directions.

Lead a brief question-and-answer session to elicit the children's beliefs about Thanksgiving. Now share, from this "Discussion," some Native North American Thanksgiving beliefs and practices, and the role of giving thanks in the circle of giving and receiving, especially the daily, ongoing aspect of Native thanksgiving. Tell the children the "Round Dance" will represent:
• unity and interconnectedness of all parts of Earth, living and inanimate, with plants as a unifying force
• Native North American Thanksgivings and the daily circle of giving and receiving
• the four directions that link us with all parts of Earth and from which all things come
• the circles of life and cycles of nature that help us to live in balance
• all people in the circle and throughout the world, all countries and cultures
• all environments of the world

Perform the dance on several occasions and have it represent just one or two of these ideas each time to keep things simple and build children's understanding over time.

Have the children stand and hold hands in one large circle. Step into the center and play a two-part drumbeat, hitting the drum alternately: hard-soft, hard-soft, hard-soft. … Demonstrate a sideways shuffle step: step sideways to your left on the hard drumbeat, then catch up with the trailing right foot, bringing it up to the left foot (on the soft drumbeat). Perform a few rounds like this as the children watch you lead with the left foot and then follow with the right foot, over and over.

Beat the drum and have the children perform the step, moving to their left (clockwise) as they hold hands around the circle. Once they have mastered the step, have them reverse directions and move to the right (counterclockwise), leading with the right foot and following with the left.

Now say, "The way we walk upon Earth shows how we respect and care for it. Let us take gentle steps to tell Earth that we want to celebrate it and keep it well. This is a silent dance so, please, no talking or making noise. Stay connected during the dance and *take careful, easy steps; no running* because someone could be pulled or pushed into a fall. Think about your steps and what the 'Round Dance' means, as we discussed earlier."

Have the children form two circles: one large one on the outside and a smaller circle inside. The two circles move in opposite directions at all times (Figure 4-4). The outer circle will begin moving clockwise, and the inner circle counter-clockwise. Tell the dancers that halfway through the dance a special drumbeat will signal that they are to change directions. Demonstrate that beat. We have found that three quick, loud beats work well. Start beating the drum to lead the dancers. The *outer* circle should travel at least one full revolution before you signal the change of direction, and should travel one full revolution in that new direction before changing again. Vary the rate of the drumbeat according to what is comfortable for that group. The dance is completed when the outer circle has traveled (alternately) four full revolutions in each direction.

Tree of Attunement

ACTIVITY: (A) Interact with trees through guided sensory awareness experiences. (B) Listen as a tree tells the story of its life. Touch a tree and create a circle of sensory attunement with it.

GOALS: (A) Exercise each of the senses through interactions with trees and parts of trees: see, touch, hear, smell, taste, intuit. (B) Understand a little about the life of a tree, its wisdom and some of its many gifts. Connect with a particular tree on an empathic level, both giving and receiving positive support and strength. Develop a sense of respect and reverence for a particular tree, as well as trees and plants in general.

AGE: Younger children and older children

MATERIALS: (A) Fragrant tree parts such as needles, cones, flowers, orange peels, cinnamon bark, etc.; knife and/or scissors to trim things to size; glass jars with lids or other containers to carry tree parts in; sample foods from trees, such as apples, nuts, cherries; enough of one kind of locally grown (if possible) tree food to give some to each child: acorns, maple seeds, beechnuts, chestnuts, pine nuts and other sample wildlife foods from trees; one blindfold for each child; a handful of acorns or other tree seeds for each child. (B) Copy of "I Am a Tree" story; stethoscope; handfuls of acorns or other tree seeds from "A" for each child; poems chosen by the children to read to their trees.

PROCEDURE A: *Sensitivi-Tree.* Beforehand, have children choose, and bring, a poem or song they want to read or sing to the tree they choose to share with outdoors. Do not require older children to do this particular aspect of the activity if they feel foolish.

Take the children to a quiet place outdoors, if possible, and have everyone sit in a circle. Ask them to identify all five physical senses. Once they have done so, pass around some fragrant parts of trees for all to smell.

Begin with mild scents, such as spruce needles or pine cones. Graduate to the scent of, perhaps, balsam fir. Finish strong with a slice of orange peel or cinnamon bark. What are their favorite scents?

Move on to flavors. Ask the children to think of as many foods as they can that come from trees. Show them some acorns, maple seeds, pine nuts or other wildlife food and discuss the kinds of animals that trees feed, and what the animals eat. Distribute a piece or two of locally grown tree food to each child if possible, such as nuts or fruit, and give children a few moments to eat them. Warn them not to eat anything they know they are allergic to.

Now take the children to a park or natural area. Have each child *choose* a tree to interact with. Have them look closely at their trees from different perspectives: far off to get a silhouette, nose up to the bark for a closeup or lying down on their back with their head up against the base of the trunk for a view into the tree's crown.

Blindfold each child and ask him or her to keep eyes closed underneath. No peeking! Place her or his hands on a prominent place along the tree's bark that can be felt and identified, such as a crack in the bark, broken off branch or oddly shaped root. Give each child a minute or so to become well acquainted with that place on the tree. Now, gently, walk him or her around the tree a few times and stop at a new place along its girth. Each child is to feel around on the bark and roots in search of the original place they felt before you moved them.

Gather the children together and give each a handful of acorns, maple seeds or other accessible tree seeds. Have the children put *all* of the seeds in their left or right hand to start with. Now, *intently* and with eyes closed, ask them to listen for sounds coming from the trees or animals living in them. Each time they hear a sound they are to transfer one seed into the hand that is empty to begin with. Listen together for about one minute. How many different sounds did they hear? What were the sounds? What was making the sounds? Did anyone hear the wind through the leaves, birds calling or squirrels giving an alarm call?

Each child is to hold onto the seeds for later use.

PROCEDURE B: *Touch of Attunement.* Have the children sit in a circle. Share with them the ideas from the sections of the "Discussion" called "The Continuum of Life," "Connecting" and "Sensory Attunement." Say that all forms of life are equally important in the natural world. Ask the children what they believe. Discuss the idea that plants, including trees, have rights just like people do. Ask, "What would these ideas mean about how we will treat trees and other plants?"

Discuss how the differences between plants and animals are just the way *people* see things, and that plants can sense their environments as well as interact with other plants,

animals and human beings. The closer we come to plants and the better we understand and respect them, the better we can become *attuned* to plants—to understand them and relate to them harmoniously.

Say, "To accomplish this, we need to learn how to understand what it would be like to *be* a plant. Let's start with our trees."

Read the following brief story, which can be adapted to apply to local trees.

I Am a Tree

I am an old _____ tree who has been growing in this forest/park since long, long before you were born. I sprouted from a seed and grew roots deep into the ground while my crown branched strong and wide.

Even though I am rooted in one place, I make a lot of movement with my leaves, branches, flowers and seeds. I move so slowly most of the time that you don't notice.

Many animals depend on me to live: birds nest in my branches, insects live on my bark and leaves and many even eat my fruit/nuts/seeds and leaves. Lichens, mosses and fungi grow on my bark and in my shade. Even when my parts fall off and die they decay and enrich the soil, which grows new plants and provides homes for animals. I have learned much and grown wise from the many years of watching, living and sharing.

I react when someone picks one of my leaves or hurts my bark. I also can sense when someone is being good to me. In that case, I give them back the support and strength I have, as well as my great wisdom.

You may not believe all of this about me at first because it is so different and new to you. But I can wait for you to grow to understand. I am very patient.

Lead the group over to a large tree. Place the stethoscope up against the tree and move the stethoscope around to a place where you can hear the flow of sap up the tree. Have each child take turns listening to the tree's flowing, living self.

Now each child is going to return to the tree she or he chose earlier. There will be two simple parts to creating the "circle of attunement." Direct the children to:

1. "Go to your tree and face it close up. Look into the bark, and then up its trunk into the branches (Figure 4-5). Share a simple greeting like, 'Hello, tree, I hope you are well today.' Reach forward and place both hands gently on the tree. *Say* some nice things to the tree or simply *think* nice things if that is more comfortable for you. Simple, positive thoughts are best, such as, 'I hope you keep growing strong and tall'; 'You are a beautiful tree'; 'You are generous to give so many things to all of the animals and people who take from you'; or 'I like you.' Now, if you would like, read your poem or sing your song to the tree."

Figure 4-5. The view up a tree's trunk into its branches is just one way of getting to know that tree by experiencing its living poetry. (Photo by Alan C. Graham)

"Place your handful of nuts on the ground at the base of the tree and say, 'Here is a gift for you to show my appreciation.' "

2. "Turn your back to the tree and gently lean up against it, standing straight so your back touches the tree's trunk. Hold your hands out in front of you and ask the tree to give you support, strength and wisdom. Stand this way, quietly, and imagine these gifts flowing into you from the tree, which is reaching deep into the ground and high into the sky to bring you the gifts. Try not to think—just let the gifts come to you. Be patient and stay still for as long as you can. When you are ready, turn and face the tree, touch it with both hands again and thank the tree in your own words. Then come gather back here with the group."

Once everyone is together again, ask the children to share their experiences. Make it clear that they do not have to share if they would rather not. Ask the children to show how what they have learned and experienced will affect the way they treat trees and other plants in the future.

Note: Have the children return to their tree each month and share something new in the circle of giving and receiving with their Tree of Attunement.

Thirteen Celebrations on Turtle's Back

ACTIVITY: Hold 13 thanksgiving celebrations to express appreciation for the gifts of plants throughout the year, in coordination with the moons and seasons. Share gifts with others and strengthen a human community.

GOALS: Understand the nature of the periodic, year-round Thanksgivings that are a strong Native North American tradition. Understand the connection between the 13 scales on Turtle's back and the celebrations of certain Native North American cultures.[13] Realize the importance of the circles of celebration and giving and receiving to show appreciation and to strengthen relationships among people and plants and within a human community. Observe how sharing is a good foundation for social harmony and connectedness.

AGE: Younger children and older children

MATERIALS: (1) A Turtle's shell or photo or illustration of a turtle's shell (Figure 4-2), list of Native North American moons found in the "Discussion," list of Native thanksgiving celebrations from the "Discussion," posterboard, pencils, markers, crayons, current year's calendar with phases of the moons marked, gifts as chosen by children. (2) Materials as needed for the activities chosen to celebrate and appreciate the gifts of plants for each of the 13 moons on Turtle's back.

PROCEDURE: Ask the children how many scales they think are found on Turtle's back. Use a turtle's shell, or an illustration (Figure 4-2) or photograph of a turtle's shell, as you point out the 13 scales on Turtle's back. Describe the way the names of each moon, and certain celebrations, are correlated with Turtle's 13 scales by many Native North Americans.

Work with the children to design a calendar/poster, in the form of a giant turtle's back, that includes 13 celebrations, one in each scale, to show appreciation for the gifts of plants. Give each celebration/moon a name corresponding to a plant being harvested in your area at that time, an event among wild plants that occurs during that moon or some other natural event. Incorporate the intent to show appreciation to plants into each of your celebrations. Another alternative is to design a calendar of celebration around the moons from a Native North American culture, preferably a people whom you live reasonably close to.

Choose specific days on which to hold your celebrations. For instance, use a calendar with the full moons marked on it and hold celebrations on, or as close as possible to, each full moon. The name of the current moon changes when each new moon arrives.

There will be two parts to each celebration:

1. Children will each bring in a natural gift from plants to give to someone else in the group on that day. Ask them to keep it simple—a small basket of fruit; a homemade appleseed necklace; something a child has made from wood; etc. Do not tell the children whom their gift is going to ahead of time. Design a simple rotating system of pairs of children to decide whom each child will give to, informing them just prior to the gift exchange. Or, you may want to put all of the names in a hat each time and have the children draw the name of the receiver of their gift. Upon receiving their gifts, children are to focus on showing appreciation, instead of judging the

gift. A strong tradition in many Native North American cultures is to appreciate every gift, whether it is or is not what you "like" or "want." The generosity of the giver and gratitude of the receiver are to be the focus of this exchange, *not* the value, quality or desirability of the gift. This focus will generate *much* discussion and will require guidance from the leader! Here is a lot of energy and opportunity to work on the skills needed for social harmony, connectedness, positive sharing and building community. Discuss these topics and dynamics with the children on a frequent basis during the gift-sharing part of the celebrations.

2. You, the leader, and the children will choose and lead appropriate activities to celebrate and show appreciation for the gifts of plants as called for by each of the 13 celebrations on Turtle's back. Appreciate particular plants, parts of plants (flowers, fruits, seeds, leaves …) and uses of plants (food, clothing, color, beauty, medicine …). Celebrate the soil that keeps plants alive! Use dances, games, songs, topical meals, crafts, the collective creation of large works of art, dioramas—anything you can imagine. Play Native North American games that use plant toys and implements: peg tops, ring and pin, buzz, cat's cradle and others.[14]

EXTENDING THE EXPERIENCE

• Hold a maple syrup celebration with pancakes and other foods sweetened by this tempting treat.

• Practice being nice to your houseplants at home: talk kindly to them, play them soothing music and take good care of them.

• Perform the *Circle Dance* in Chapter 4 of *Keepers of the Animals*.

• *Slow Motion Picture.* Create a simple time-lapse motion picture. Illustrate or photograph a plant, from the same vantage point, once every few days over several weeks or months. This sequence of images reveals the stages of growth and activities of a plant.

• Read *Thirteen Moons on Turtle's Back*, by Joseph Bruchac and Jonathan London (New York: Putnam, 1992). Celebrate and appreciate plants using ideas expressed in this book.

• Give thanks to the gifts of Native North Americans during any thanksgiving celebration.

• Practice giving thanks for each gift you receive from nature and other people each day.

• Hold a plant appreciation festival that involves everyone in your learning center in a day of festivities to celebrate plants and their many gifts.

• Find some favorite trees and other plant friends and continue to practice a circle of sensory attunement with them on an ongoing basis.

• Thank the plants around your home and learning center on a regular basis.

• Make a list of the rights of plants as being equal to all other living things, including people.

• Design your own sensory awareness activities to do with plants.

• Write and act out a story, play or puppet show in first person of your life as a tree, flower or other plant. Express how you would "feel" to be a plant and what it would be like to move as slowly as a plant and be rooted in one place. Have a bee pollinate one of your flowers. Be imaginative!

• Use a paper straw to blow soap bubbles in a glass jar and compare the way the bubbles fit together with the way the scales on a turtle's back join. The bubbles and scales join so as to minimize the surface area where they connect. This is a general rule of thumb in nature and can be seen repeatedly in many patterns, from the cells of a honeycomb to the scales on an armadillo. To make the soap-bubble liquid, stir together one part liquid soap with six to eight parts water.

NOTES

1. Harvey Arden and Steve Wall, *Wisdomkeepers: Meetings With Native American Spiritual Elders* (Hillsboro, Ore.: Beyond Words, 1990), 24.

2. Barbara (Kawenehe) Barnes, Mike (Kanentakeron) Mitchell and Joyce (Konwahwihon) Thompson, *Traditional Teachings* (Cornwall Island, Ont.: North American Indian Traveling College, 1984), 10.

3. Stewart Culin, *Games of the North American Indians* (New York: Dover, 1975), 34.

4. Arden and Wall, *Wisdomkeepers*, 16.

5. John G. Neihardt, *Black Elk Speaks: Being the Life Story of a Holy Man of the Oglala Sioux* (Lincoln, Nebr., and London: University of Nebraska Press, 1979), 2.

6. Arden and Wall, *Wisdomkeepers*, 67.

7. Kent Nerburn and Louise Mengelkoch (eds.), *Native American Wisdom* (San Rafael, Calif.: New World Library, 1991), 36.

8. Peter Tompkins and Christopher Bird, *The Secret Life of Plants* (New York: Harper & Row, 1973), xi.

9. William Bryant Logan, "The Magic Touch," *New York Times* (24 October 1993): section 9, 16.

10. Tompkins and Bird, *Secret Life of Plants,* 5–6, 13–14, 19.

11. Excerpted from a speech given at "Econiche," Gatineau Hills, Cantley, Quebec, 18 June 1992, at the 1992 Summer Institute for Environmental Values Education, conducted by the Harmony Foundation of Canada, Ottawa, Ontario.

12. Shared by Dr. Ella W. T. Sekatau, DHL, Ethnohistorian, Cultural Education Consultant, Member of the Narragansett Indian Nation, Charlestown, Rhode Island.

13. Joseph Bruchac and Jonathan London, *Thirteen Moons on Turtle's Back* (New York: Putnam, 1992), general reference.

14. Michael J. Caduto and Joseph Bruchac, *Keepers of the Night* (Golden, Colo.: Fulcrum Pub., 1994), chapter 5.

FLOWERS AND FRUITS, SEEDS AND SPORES

Then Maushop said good-bye to the People of First Light. His small friends watched him from the cliffs at Gay Head as he waded into the bay.

✦ The Circle of Life and the Clambake ✦

(Wampanoag—Eastern Woodland)

Everything in life is a circle. Everything is alive—the animals, the birds, the plants of Earth and the plants of the seas, the water, the air and the stones—and everything must be respected. All things are part of Earth, which gives us everything we need. When we take from Earth, we must give back in return. The Medicine Circle is the source of our strength.

So the Wampanoag people explain the way they have been instructed by the Creator. For untold centuries, the Wampanoag, the People of First Light, have lived along the southeastern coast of Massachusetts. And their traditions and stories relate to that circle of life which human beings must strive to maintain.

One of the heroes of the Wampanoag is a giant whose name is Maushop. Some say he lived there on the narrow land now called Cape Cod even before the Wampanoags arrived. He was not alone, for there were other beings there with him. One of his friends was a giant frog which was his closest companion.

Maushop's life was a good one. He swam in the waters of Popponesset Bay. He made great fires on the sandy beach to cook whales and other sea creatures, and when he emptied the sand into the sea from his great moccasins he made the islands of Nantucket and Martha's Vineyard.

The Wampanoag became the friends of Maushop and he enjoyed helping them. When they wanted to cook or keep themselves warm, he would carry great loads of wood on his back for their fires. When they were hungry he would drive whales onto the shore so that the people did not have to hunt for food. He was so good to the people that they became lazy.

Then Kehtean, the Great Spirit, spoke to Maushop.

"It is good that you care for your younger brothers," Kehtean said, "but it is not right that you do everything for them. They are like little children when you care for all their needs. They must take responsibility for their own lives or they will never grow. If they do not care for themselves, how can they care for the rest of Creation? Their circle will not be strong."

"It is true," Maushop said. Then he said good-bye to the People of First Light. His small friends watched him from the cliffs at Gay Head as he waded into the bay, which was greenish brown with rockweed, and swam away toward the west. As he swam, Kehtean, the Creator, transformed him into a great white whale. Maushop's friend, the giant frog, came to the cliffs, filled with sorrow at the loss of his friend. Kehtean took pity on the giant frog and changed him into a huge stone, which still sits there at Gay Head, looking out to sea. That stone reminds the Wampanoag that Kehtean cares for all things and that the decisions of the Great Mystery are made for the good of all.

Without their friend to help them, the Wampanoag wondered how they would survive. They soon found, however, that when they worked for themselves, everything that they needed was there. One of those ways of survival which makes use of all that is around them—Earth, the plants, the animals and the water—is called by them *Appanaug*. It is a word which means "seafood cooking," and, because it is a special part of the circle, it is done to honor someone or to mark the change of the seasons.

With thanks in their hearts and with care, they wade into the shallow waters of Popponesset Bay and collect some of the Rock People, old round stones which have been smoothed by the tide. They find a place in the forest which feels right, and there they make a circle and dig a shallow, round hole in the earth. The stones are then placed in that hole, and the shape of the stone and the shape of that hole remind the Wampanoag of the Medicine Circle of all life.

Dry wood is gathered from the forest. No living trees are used. That way they clear the forest floor and make use of another gift given them by Kehtean.

When the next morning comes, they gather quahog clams from the bottom of the bay and sickissuog clams from the shore when the tide is low. Then, from the shallow water, they gather great loads of a seaweed called rockweed. The rockweed is covered with chambers filled with gas, and the body of the plant contains a great deal of salt water. When the fire for the clambake has burned down to ashes and the Rock People are glowing with heat, that rockweed is piled on top of the stones. Steam begins to rise as the salt water in the plants boils, and the clams, along with lobsters and corn, are piled onto the rockweed and then covered with more armfuls of seaweed. The *Appanaug* is part of the great Medicine Circle of life, one of the gifts of the Great Spirit. So, as the food cooks, the people say prayers of thanksgiving to remember all the gifts they have been given. It is the way it was done long ago and it is still done that way today.

Note: A wonderful book about the Wampanoag tradition of the clambake has been written by Russell Peters, a Wampanoag elder whose Indian name is Fast Turtle. A former president of the Mashpee Wampanoag Tribal Council, Fast Turtle tells the story of how he and his grandson, along with other tribal members, prepare one such great feast in his book *Clambake, A Wampanoag Tradition* (Minneapolis, Minn.: Lerner, 1992). A videotape that follows every step of the clambake has also been made. It is called *Appanaug*. It was Fast Turtle who first told us the tale of Maushop and his Wampanoag friends.

DISCUSSION

Kehtean, the Great Spirit, and the giant Maushop teach the Wampanoag, the People of First Light, about the power of the Medicine Circle in "The Circle of Life and the Clambake." The Circle of Life is manifest in the many ways human beings can live within and respect the Circle. When Maushop leaves the Wampanoag and wades out into the beds of rockweed growing in the bay off the cliffs at Gay Head, the people must learn to care for themselves and keep their own circle strong. The *Appanaug*, "seafood cooking" or "clambake"—during which corn, lobsters and *sickissuogs* (clams that spit), along with potatoes, onions and sometimes other foods are steamed on seaweed heated by hot round rocks set in a circular hole in Earth—reminds the Wampanoag that the giving of work brings the gift of survival. Only dry, dead wood is gathered to make the fire; the living trees are not harmed. The round stones and cooking hole symbolize the Medicine Circle of Life. Thanksgiving prayers honor these gifts of the Great Spirit.

Algae

The rockweed growing in the shallow water that Maushop wades into, and which is used in the Appanaug, is a kind of brown algae. Microscopic algae are a principal food of the clams used in the clambake. *Algae*, along with fungi and lichens, are *thallophytes,* which comprise 100,000 of the roughly 375,000 known species of plants and plant-like organisms on Earth. The plant-like algae are often placed in the Kingdom Protoctista, along with protozoans and sponges. (See "Classifying and Identifying Plants" in Chapter 2 for a detailed description of thallophytes.)

Algae often reproduce asexually via one-celled microscopic *spores,* by cell division, vegetatively whereby pieces simply break off and grow in a new location or by some combination of these methods. (A *cell* is the basic unit of any plant or animal.) Spores are the most common form of reproduction among thallophytes. Some spores swim and some do not. *Zoospores* are powered by *flagella,* whip-like structures on the surface of the cell. Certain algae create eggs and sperm in specialized organs or cells. A number of seaweeds reproduce sexually.

BLUE-GREEN ALGAE. Blue-green algae are the most ancient of all plant-like organisms; they evolved, following bacteria, more than 2 billion years ago in the vast seas that covered Earth. Gradually, as blue-green algae emitted oxygen via photosynthesis (this is discussed later in this chapter), atmospheric levels of oxygen slowly built up. It was not until 600 to 650 million years ago that oxygen had accumulated to just 1 percent of today's levels. Aquatic environments were and still are dominated by algae and blue-green algae, while most terrestrial plants and plant-like organisms are *tracheophytes,* or vascular plants (ferns, conifers and flowering plants), *bryophytes* (mosses and liverworts) and fungi. Even though many botanists refer to algae as "primitive," algae are extremely efficient at meeting their requirements for water, sunlight and dissolved nutrients in aquatic environments, and so have existed through the ages. Over time algae evolved into increasingly

complex forms and colonized a diversity of habitats. The first land plants evolved from a group of green algae 420 million years ago. Today, the fascinating algae exhibit an astounding array of shapes, sizes, colors and patterns (Figure 5-1).

There are more than 1,500 species of *blue-green algae* that resemble the fossils of the most ancient plant-like organisms known. Blue-green algae are similar in structure to bacteria and are often called *cyanobacteria.* Although most species live in freshwater, others inhabit a wide variety of habitats ranging from the Arctic to the edges of sulphurous hot springs. A protective gelatinous coating on most blue-green algae enables them to survive in challenging environments: the ocean, mud flats, the surface of sand grains, soil, polluted water and even on moist tile. Many species of blue-green algae are *planktonic*, which means they are floating or swimming and unattached. People are most familiar with these algae in the form of the light blue scums they form in nutrient-rich waters, such as those found in many ponds and polluted habitats. Some species of planktonic blue-green algae regulate their buoyancy using tiny pockets or *vacuoles* of gas, which they cause to increase or decrease in size.

Blue-green algae are prolific, growing as single cells, in chains or in clusters (colonies). Many blue-green algae are capable of *nitrogen fixing*—they obtain nitrogen for growth

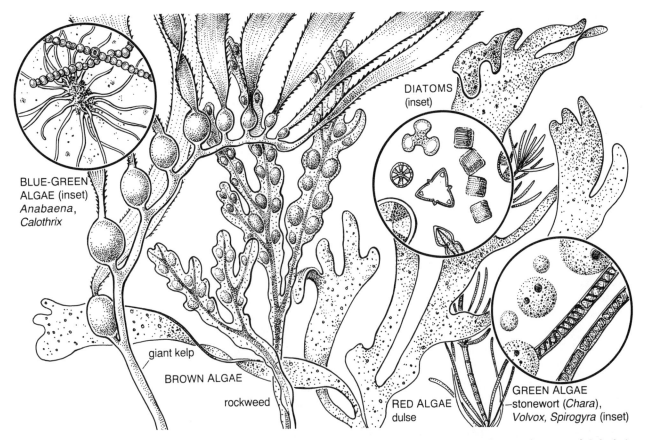

BLUE-GREEN ALGAE (inset) *Anabaena, Calothrix*

DIATOMS (inset)

giant kelp

BROWN ALGAE

rockweed

RED ALGAE dulse

GREEN ALGAE —stonewort (*Chara*), *Volvox, Spirogyra* (inset)

Figure 5-1. Samples showing the diversity found among the major groups of algae. Sizes (left to right): Anabaena *and* Calothrix, *microscopic; giant kelp, to more than 120 ft. (37 m) tall; rockweed, 4 to 20 in. (10.2 to 50.8 cm) tall; dulse, to 1 ft. (30.5 cm); diatoms, microscopic; stonewort (Chara), 6 to 8 in. (15.2 to 20.3 cm);* Volvox *and* Spirogyra, *microscopic. (Illustration by Marjorie C. Leggitt)*

directly from dissolved nitrogen gas. These kinds of blue-green algae are encouraged as a source of enrichment in rice paddies. One familiar blue-green alga is *Calothrix*, which grows in thin sheets to form a blackish zone near the high-tide mark on rocky shores, where it is periodically wet by waves and salt spray. *Calothrix* also grows as an epiphyte on the surface of other algae.

RED ALGAE. If you have ever eaten dulse or Nori (red laver), or stared into the miniature marine world of a tide pool, you have experienced red algae. *Red algae*, the *Rhodophyta*, are *benthic*—they dwell on or in the bottom substrate such as piers, rocks and on dead and discarded shells in the intertidal zone. Ninety-eight percent of the roughly 4,000 species of red algae are marine and the majority of these are seaweeds. *Seaweeds* are larger (not microscopic) forms of marine algae, most of which are benthic and grow attached to a substrate. Only a few red algae are planktonic. Because the pigments found in red algae are extremely effective at gathering light, a number of species can be found below the tideline in deep waters of up to 600 feet (182.9 meters). Red algae, which can appear red, yellow or even brown, grow at all latitudes and are most abundant in warmer subtropical or tropical waters.

BROWN ALGAE. There are more than 2,000 species of *brown algae (Phaeophyta)* that form lush growths along rocky coasts. Virtually all brown algae are marine seaweeds that include the kelps, rockweeds and several *pelagic* or open-water species of Sargassum weed floating free in the calm waters south of Bermuda.

Bladder wrack and knotted wrack are common rockweeds that dominate the rocky intertidal zone of the Atlantic coast. Ingenious air bladders provide flotation to buoy the branches of these algae up into the sunlight. The 10-foot (3-meter) sugar kelp of the Atlantic coast, which grows below the low-water mark in shallow waters along sheltered rocky shores, has ribbon-shaped leaves with crinkled edges reminiscent of a piece of lasagna. Sugar kelp is dwarfed by the giant kelp of the cold coastal waters along the West Coast that grows attached to the rocky bottom, beyond the effects of wave action. One species of giant kelp, *Macrocystis,* can reach a length of more than 120 feet (36.6 meters).

The tissue of brown algae contains a pigment called *fucoxanthin* that masks the chlorophyll and lends the familiar brown hues. The mucilaginous cell walls of brown algae, which consist partly of *alginic acid,* increase the strength and flexibility of the tissue. This helps to prevent desiccation as well as ripping and tangling as the blades are tussled by currents.

DIATOMS, GOLDEN ALGAE AND YELLOW-GREEN ALGAE. The division *Chrysophyta* contains more than 10,000 species of tiny, mostly one-celled microscopic algae, all of which live as free-floating or swimming phytoplankton. *Phytoplankton* are minute, drifting plants and plant-like organisms that are swept along by the currents. *Diatoms* are one of the most important forms of phytoplankton, which,

through photosynthesis, produce food and release oxygen. A large proportion of this production comes from diatoms. Considered to be perhaps the chief source of food energy in the sea, diatoms are consumed by *zooplankton* (tiny free-floating or swimming animals) as well as by clams, oysters and many crustaceans.

The entire cell wall of a diatom, called a *frustule,* looks like a minute hat box with a lid. Frustules, which are 96 percent silica with a thin organic skin coating, are covered with intricate symmetrical designs of which no two are alike. Diatoms require silicic acid to produce their silicate cell walls. Their tiny, decay-resistant, siliceous "skeletons" have accumulated over the eons to more than 1,000 feet (304.8 meters) deep in some places.

Golden algae and *yellow-green algae* are closely related to diatoms. Most of the 300 species of golden algae can swim and live in freshwater lakes, ponds and stagnant pools. A small number are marine. The roughly 400 species of yellow-green algae mostly inhabit bodies of freshwater, while a few species grow in felt-like mats on the surface of damp soil.

GREEN ALGAE. Wherever nutrients are plentiful in fresh water and in coastal saltwater environments, *green algae (Chlorophyta)* are likely to be found. Although many familiar seaweeds are green algae, including the well-known sea lettuce, nearly 90 percent of the roughly 6,000 species live in freshwater. Thin filaments of *Spirogyra* live in ponds and streams. One group, the *desmids,* are often the predominant algae in bogs and other acidic waters that are low in nutrients. *Cladophora* is a conspicuous algae in many freshwater streams and lakes. Many of the freshwater species are planktonic but there are only a few planktonic green algae in the sea. Planktonic green algae are either capable of swimming or not. *Volvox* lives in colonies that move through their freshwater homes using whip-like flagella for locomotion. The cell structure of green algae is similar to that of the more complex green plants: chlorophyll is contained in structures called *chloroplasts* and food is stored as starch. Whenever nutrients are abundant, green algae reproduce quickly and form large population increases called *blooms.*

There are more than 200 marine and freshwater species of *stoneworts* that are often classified as green algae. Stoneworts, such as the common freshwater muskgrass, have root-like *rhizoids* that hold fast in the mud and reproductive structures similar to those of vascular plants. Red bumps on its branches consist of sex cells surrounded by sterile cells: a unique trait among algae. Stoneworts grow in waters rich in limestone and are often encrusted with white lime.

Flagellates

Several different groups of organisms have traits of both plants and animals. Most *dinoflagellates (Pyrrophyta)* consist of single cells with two flagella (Figure 5-2) that are used for swimming. Some single-celled species are amoeba-like.

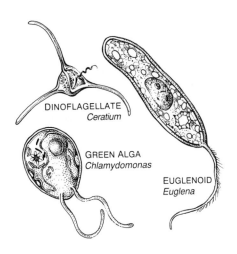

Figure 5-2. Flagellates use their whip-like flagella for swimming. Sizes: Microscopic. (Illustration by Marjorie C. Leggitt)

After the diatoms, the 1,000 species of dinoflagellates are the second most prolific producers of food in the sea. There are a few freshwater species but most dinoflagellates are marine, including some bioluminescent species. Other forms create toxic red blooms called *red tides,* which can kill fish and paralyze humans who eat infected shellfish. Many dinoflagellates have minute projectiles near the surface of the cell that they shoot whenever the cell is irritated.

Euglenoids (Euglenophyta) live in stagnant pools of water. Some have a tiny eyespot located near a flagellum to help them orient in relation to light. Some euglenoids are not photosynthetic; they are predaceous and must capture their food. Most of the 400 or so species do photosynthesize. The *cryptomonads (Cryptophyta)* are another small group of flagellates.

Algal Adaptations for Survival

Every plant stays alive because it possesses successful *adaptations*, which are particular physical structures and behavioral traits that enable it to survive and reproduce in its environment. The cells of certain green algae, for instance, are completely coated with a jelly-like covering that enables them to pass unharmed through the digestive tracts of the tiny crustaceans that eat them.

Algae occupy virtually every kind of aquatic environment. Most phytoplankton are microscopic algae that live as individual cells or as a group in chains or colonies. The largest species, which are rare, grow to only about .08 inch (2 millimeters) across. Plankton live in the open water of lakes, ponds, rivers and oceans.

FRESHWATER ALGAE. The most abundant forms of algae in streams, rivers, lakes and ponds are the diatoms, green algae, blue-green algae and, in still waters, dinoflagellates. Certain species of red and golden algae live in fast-flowing freshwaters such as streams. Diatoms thrive in the cool streams of springtime. Many stream algae are benthic, living in or on the bottom sediments, such as gravel and sand, and on rocks and logs. A common adaptation to the eroding effect of currents is to grow in low-lying clumps to avoid being washed away. Still, numerous stream algae grow quickly to replace the older generations that are carried off by the rushing waters. In addition to the speed of the current, the growth of stream algae is determined by levels of oxygen in the water (dissolved oxygen or D.O.), temperature, grazing pressures and the levels of sunlight, acidity (pH) and nutrients in the water.

Algae dwelling in the wide open channels of large rivers are similar to those found in lakes and ponds: green and blue-green algae as well as diatoms and dinoflagellates. Planktonic algae form the base of the food chain in the *limnetic zone,* which is the open water. They are most abundant during the warm seasons of spring and summer, when light, nutrient levels and water temperature are highest. The population and location of algae in a lake environment at any time are determined by movement of the algae, diseases, competition with the algae for nutrients and consumption by zooplankton. Many *filter-feeding* zooplankton possess sieve-like appendages with which they catch large volumes of phytoplankton by forcing water through strainers that remove their food. *Chlorella* is a common green alga that lives symbiotically inside of certain protozoans, sponges and hydras.

THE ESTUARY. *Estuaries* are found wherever a river flows into the sea and where freshwater and saltwater meet. Salt marshes are forms of temperate estuaries, while mangrove swamps are common in the South. In estuaries, chemical reactions occur that cause nutrients in the water to precipitate out, greatly enriching these fertile ecosystems. Nutrients, especially concentrations of nitrogen and phosphorous, have an immediate and often dramatic impact on algal populations. Levels of nitrogen in particular can cause great blooms of algae. When nutrients are scarce, so are the algae that depend upon them. During an algal bloom there is, initially, much more oxygen being created by the algae than is being consumed. During the daytime oxygen levels can become very high. When the algae die, their remains are decomposed by bacteria and fungi. This depletes the oxygen and causes a buildup of carbon dioxide.

Certain nutrients, then, are important *limiting elements* in the growth of algae. Adding these nutrients alters the balance between the population and available resources. When these nutrients are added to an ecosystem in which they are in short supply, algae grow profusely and often become overpopulated. When this happens, the stress on available space and resources, plus the accumulation of waste, tends to reduce the population. The overfertilization of aquatic ecosystems, with resulting high levels of production and decomposition, is called *eutrophication*. This process can hasten the aging of aquatic ecosystems as organic remains rapidly accumulate.

Fantastic blooms of algae in estuaries feed large numbers of the animals that live there, such as certain species of clams and mussels. Mummichogs or killifish, razor clams, flounder and sticklebacks live in the lower reaches of brackish water that mingles with saltwater tides.

SALTWATER ALGAE. Saltwater algae range from microscopic diatoms to swaying undersea forests of giant kelp. The vast biome of the oceans is the realm of billions upon billions of microscopic phytoplankton that form the base of the marine food chain. Zooplankton eat the phytoplankton, and in turn become food for larger animals such as whales, seals, birds and fish. Levels of light, temperature and oxygen affect marine algae, which must also adapt to high salinity and powerful water pressures.

Phytoplankton need to live where there is enough light and a healthy supply of nutrients in the water. The natural upward movements of ocean currents are strong enough to buoy most phytoplankton. Many algae possess spines, irregular shapes and other adaptations to cause them to move and tumble in the currents. The turbulence created by these movements slows their sinking and replenishes the nutrient-rich waters around the algae. Some marine phytoplankton can regulate buoyancy by using saltwater to change their density. Minute flagella enable some species of phytoplankton to swim. One species, *Ceratium,* can swim up to 65.6 feet (20 meters) in one day. Many *flagellates* migrate up and down near the surface in a regular, daily regimen in reaction to day and night levels of sunlight and temperature. Diatoms, which have relatively heavy cell walls made of silica, are only able to stay afloat in turbulent seas.

Ocean plants grow from the surface down to a depth of about 600 feet (182.9 meters). This is the *euphotic zone,* where sufficient sunlight penetrates to support photosynthesis in green plants and plant-like organisms. The tidal zone stretches roughly from this same lower limit to the uppermost reaches of the tides. Hard, rocky bottoms provide a habitat for seaweeds mostly, while soft bottoms are populated by certain plants and microscopic algae. In the tidal zone algae must be well adapted to an ever-changing, sometimes violent environment to survive.

The coral reefs of warm, shallow waters are home to many kinds of algae. Here, the hard bottom is composed of the accumulated, calcareous skeletons secreted by marine animals called polyps. A number of the plants and animals that live in and on the reef are found nowhere else. Remains of some tropical species of *corallinas*—a group of calcareous red algae that range from the tropics to the temperate northern Pacific and Atlantic coasts—accumulate as sediment along coral reefs. These seaweeds develop high levels of calcium carbonate in their tissues and leave behind skeletal limestone remnants when they die.

The four major groups of benthic algae are green, blue-green, brown and red. In the tidal marsh and lower reaches of tidal estuaries, dried-up seaweed washes up and provides an important source of food and shelter for small animals. Rockweed, sea lettuce and *Enteromorpha* are common types found here. Sea lettuce is often found along rocky shores, while knotted and sugar kelp inhabit sandy shores. Stare into one of the mysterious tide pools among the rocks—small worlds unto themselves—and you are likely seeing a miniature forest composed of several species of red and green algae.

The shape, size and growth habits of seaweeds are adaptations for surviving grazing by animals, competition from other organisms, wind and wave action and other environmental sources of stress. Seaweed grows in two distinct forms: *crustose,* as flat crusts hugging the bottom, and *foliose,* or upright (Figure 5-3). Crustose seaweeds, and the small reproductive stages of other seaweeds, avoid the strong forces created by water movement by growing in the *boundary layer,* a 0- to .8-inch (0- to 2-centimeter) space between flowing water and the substrate, in which water movement is less marked due to friction between the water and the bottom.[1] Other seaweeds cope with the downstream *drag* exerted by moving water with shapes that do not resist the current and with tissues that are either tough and rigid or flexible and resilient. The work necessary to break off flexible seaweed is about the same as that required to break

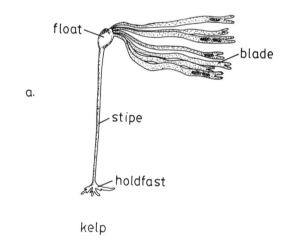

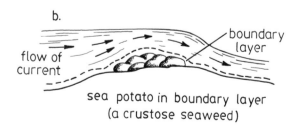

Figure 5-3. The two forms of seaweed: a. kelp, a foliose seaweed, and ***b.*** *sea potato, a crustose seaweed in the boundary layer. Friction between the water and the bottom causes the boundary layer, a thin film of slower water where plants and animals are protected from the action of waves and currents. Sizes: kelp, 24 in. (60 cm); sea potato, 4 in. (10.2 cm) across.*

wood or cast iron.[2] As water flows faster, many seaweeds bend over into the region of slower water. Giant kelp and other species that live in currents that move constantly back and forth are very pliable.

Many seaweeds have a density similar to that of seawater and so possess a natural buoyancy. *Floats* and *bladders* are common structures seaweeds possess to increase flotation. Typically, seaweeds also have a *holdfast* that anchors (but does not absorb nutrients like a root), a *stipe* or stem and *blades* to gather sunlight.

Over time, seaweeds and associated animals have evolved specific tolerances for subtle differences in ocean habitats. This is clearly seen along most rocky shores in the zonation of organisms found there. Strong, persistent winds, incessant and even violent waves, extreme exposure to air and sunlight prevail in the three major zones between the high-tide and low-tide lines. Kelp marks the lower tidal zone with its pliant stalks and rubbery blades. The middle intertidal zone is home to sea lettuce, acorn barnacles, red algae and brown algae such as knotted wrack and bladder wrack. Limpets, snails and barnacles dominate at the high-tide mark. Just above high tide grow black lichens and splotches of blue-green algae upon which periwinkles often graze. Gray and orange lichens mark the very uppermost part of the *splash zone.*

Practical Uses of Algae

The Wampanoags and other Native North Americans discovered a variety of uses for many kinds of algae. Today, algae are important edibles and essential ingredients in products ranging from beer, ice cream and infant formula to cosmetics, paints, insulation and rubber tires.

Red algae contains *carrageenan,* a thickener or stabilizer used in making chocolate milk, jelly, ice cream and infant formula. It is also the source of *agar* that is used in cosmetics, shoe polishes, hand lotions and photographic processing materials and as a bacterial culture medium for many medicines. Two kinds of red algae, *dulse* and *Nori* (red laver), are edible seaweeds. Dulse is eaten raw or is dried and used as a condiment in soups and salads. Nori has clear, thin tissue that is eaten in sandwiches and, when seasoned, with rice.

Brown algae contains *alginates*—thickeners and stabilizers used in cheese, yogurt, milkshakes and ice cream. The milkshakes sold by fast-food restaurants are, in essence, thickened with a kind of algin-based plastic. Alginates are also used in the manufacture of medicinal products, textiles, paints, automobile polishes, rubber tires and adhesives and as the base of the soft plastic used to take dental impressions. Alginates are used as jelling agents in cosmetics and as foaming agents—they provide the head of foam on beer and rootbeer. Brown algae is dried, ground up and used for poultry meal, garden mulch, agricultural fertilizers in both liquid and "seaweed meal" forms and as a pesticide to control nematodes (microscopic worms) and other pests. Kelp blades are dried, ground up and used as a salt substitute and as vitamins. Kelp is rich in potassium and iodine.

Green algae include the sea lettuce (*Ulva lactuca*), a translucent edible seaweed eaten dried, fresh as a salad green or powdered as a seasoning. *Chlorella* is grown and harvested as a crop that is used as a protein supplement—40 percent of the dried weight of *Chlorella* is protein. Its chlorophyll is added to deodorant and other products.

Diatom shells, of which thick deposits have built up over time, are used for water filters and other kinds of filters, polishes and abrasive cleansers, diatomaceous earth and insulation. The prehistoric remains of diatoms, along with the remains of ancient mosses, ferns and other plants, formed much of the fossil fuels (coal, oil and natural gas) that we use today.

Plants: Catchers of Light, Givers of Life

The sun, Earth's star, radiates heat and light so powerful that it makes life possible on our planet 93 million miles (149,670,480 kilometers) away. Green plants are the *primary producers,* because they intercept sunlight and transform it into the food energy that supports all life on Earth except for some bacteria and a few giant 10-foot-long (3-meter-long) tube worms, clams and crabs that dwell near deep-sea hot springs. All life forms that make their own food energy are called *autotrophic,* which means "self-feeding." Certain *chemosynthetic* bacteria are also autotrophic—they are able to synthesize organic compounds and get food energy from inorganic elements through chemical reactions, without the aid of sunlight.

When sunlight strikes *chlorophyll* (green pigment in plant tissues), a vital reaction occurs called *photosynthesis,* changing water (H_2O) and carbon dioxide (CO_2) into simple sugars that can be used to make starches, fats, proteins, vitamins and other nutrients that trap the sun's energy. Water is also produced and oxygen (O_2) is released, an essential gas used by plants and animals during *respiration* to metabolize their food to obtain energy for growth and maintenance. Photosynthesis is the major source of atmospheric oxygen. Oceanic phytoplankton may produce up to 85 percent of all organic material on Earth. The process of photosynthesis looks like this:

$$\text{water} + \text{carbon dioxide} + \text{sunlight} \xrightarrow{\text{chlorophyll}} \text{oxygen} +$$
$$\text{nutrients (simple sugars)} + \text{water}$$

Plants containing chlorophyll mostly appear green, and they are often referred to in this book as "green plants." In some organisms, however, such as many kinds of algae, the green chlorophyll is masked by other pigments such as red and brown.

Plants provide animals with food, shelter and oxygen. Since animals absorb oxygen and emit carbon dioxide during respiration, while plants use carbon dioxide and give off oxygen during photosynthesis, a *gas cycle* occurs as plants and animals exchange these gases. All plants use oxygen when they transpire, but, overall, green plants produce more oxygen than they consume and they take in more carbon dioxide than they produce.

Marine phytoplankton play a significant role in the atmospheric balance of oxygen and carbon dioxide. While phytoplankton produce an estimated 80 percent of all oxygen on Earth, in any given year, worldwide, the oxygen created by marine plants is balanced by the oxygen consumed by marine animals.[3] Oceans, therefore, do not have a significant effect on the levels of oxygen in the atmosphere when measured as a yearly average. However, early research has shown that, since there is 60 times more carbon contained in the oceans than in the atmosphere, oceans appear to be absorbing the carbon dioxide generated from burning coal, natural gas and oil that is not staying in the atmosphere.[4] Another estimate is that oceans absorb roughly one-half of all the carbon dioxide released into the atmosphere each year via the consumption of carbon dioxide by phytoplankton during photosynthesis.[5] Since the buildup of carbon dioxide in the atmosphere is contributing to global warming (see Chapter 7), the buffering effect oceans have on the levels of atmospheric carbon dioxide is extremely important in moderating the global temperature balance.[6]

As trappers of solar energy, green plants are regarded as the producers that support the *consumers,* which are those plants and animals that live off this energy. A periwinkle grazing on patches of blue-green algae above the high-tide mark is an *herbivore* because it eats only plants. A killer whale searching for prey in the cold waters off the West Coast is a *carnivore,* or meat eater. An American lobster is an *omnivore*— it eats both plants and animals. The lobster, along with the fiddler crab, is also a *scavenger* because it feeds on *detritus,* which is the dead remains and wastes of plants and/or animals. The *decomposers,* mostly bacteria and fungi, break down dead plant and animal remains into forms once again usable by producers. *Heterotrophs* survive by either consuming or decomposing the food energy produced by autotrophs.

When a dolphin eats a fish, roughly 90 percent of the energy stored in the fish's tissues will be expended as the energy is used by the dolphin for growth, activity, metabolic processes such as breathing and digestion and for producing heat. Thus, 100 pounds (45.4 kilograms) of fish produce about 10 pounds (4.5 kilograms) of dolphin. The 90 percent figure varies from 2 to 40 percent depending on the food energy available in the plant or animal eaten, the season and the efficiency of the consumer. *Energy flows* from sun to plants to animals and often on to other animals, creating a *food chain.* Phytoplankton are eaten by mackerel, which are in turn consumed by a bluefish that may itself fall prey to a dolphin. Bluefish also eat killifish, herring, menhaden and even smaller bluefish, and dolphins eat other kinds of fish besides bluefish. All of these food chains interlock to form an intricate *food web* (Figure 5-4). Because 90 percent of the energy is consumed when it passes from one level to the next along the way, a *food pyramid* forms with even smaller numbers of organisms living at the uppermost levels, being supported by the ones below. Since herbivores eat lower on the food pyramid and there is more food energy available to them, any given habitat usually supports a greater population of plant eaters. Conversely, carnivores feed higher up on the pyramid and are fewer because there is less energy to support them. Top carnivores are those that eat other carnivores and have no significant predators of their own, such as the killer whale and great white shark. These animals are uppermost in the food pyramid.

The *interrelationships* created by the threads connecting living things in the food web show how each organism, directly or indirectly, lives *interdependently* with all of the others. Every plant or animal in an ecosystem occupies a certain *niche* or ecological role, such as producer, consumer, decomposer, pollinator or seed disperser. Niche is defined by the relationship of a plant or animal to its habitat, food, partners and enemies. Algae are producers that are eaten by a snail, a consumer. A young sea lion is a predator that may eat a salmon, then itself fall prey to a killer whale. Plants and animals often compete for the same niche, and a single organism can fill several niches. For instance, a blue crab both stalks brackish waters for live prey (predator) and feeds on the dead remains of other organisms (scavenger).

Stewardship of Aquatic Environments

When I was a girl the sand was pearly white. Now it's covered with that green algae—from pollution they say. The pesticides and herbicides and fertilizers run down from the potato fields. Still, isn't it beautiful? This is where the Creator intended us to live.[7]
—Harriet Starleaf Gumbs
Shinnecock (eastern Long Island, New York)

Harriett Starleaf Gumbs reminds us that there is no place else to live: Earth is our home and what we do to the oceans we also do to ourselves and other forms of life. Although we use different names to refer to ocean regions around the world, the oceans and seas are, in fact, one large interconnected body of water surrounding the continents. Oceans are a global ecological link between peoples and environments. Atmospheric winds and rain connect us like an ocean in the sky, carrying the byproducts of human activities to fresh- and saltwater ecosystems lying at the far reaches of Earth, from the Arctic to Antarctica, from the Nile to the Mississippi, and from Lake Baikal to Hudson Bay.

Human threats to the well-being of aquatic life include:
• *discharge of industrial toxins* such as heavy metals
• *runoff and erosion from agricultural and forestry operations,* including pesticides and fertilizers that can cause eutrophication

- *disposal of wastes* such as solid waste, industrial waste, sewage, radioactive materials, and, from ships, both solid wastes and effluent
- *overharvesting* of fish, marine mammals and other creatures
- *urban runoff,* including lawn and garden fertilizers, pesticides and petroleum products
- *atmospheric fallout* such as acid rain
- *oil spills* and other ecological accidents
- *purposeful environmental damage* such as that sometimes used during times of war

Coastal and estuarine habitats, which are the most productive environments for fish and other forms of life, suffer the most intensive environmental damage. One study found that up to one-half million seabirds are killed each year by oil pollution in Western Europe alone.[8]

Acid rain (a commonly used catchall term for *acid precipitation*) includes rain and snow, sleet, hail, fog and dry particles that fall from the sky. It is caused by burning fossil fuels, especially gasoline and high-sulphur coal and oil. The sulphur dioxide and nitrogen oxides that are produced react with water vapor to form sulphuric and nitric acids. Carbon dioxide, a naturally occurring gas, also reacts with water vapor, resulting in carbonic acid. Normal rainwater has a pH of 5.6; most fish die when lake water reaches a pH of 5 or lower. Since the pH scale is logarithmic, a decrease in one number means a tenfold increase in acidity, and a drop of two numbers indicates rain that is 100 times more acid than normal (Figure 5-5). Measurements in the Northeast reveal that rainwater is averaging 40 times more acid than normal, often around a pH of 4.0, and readings occasionally dip into the upper 3s. Vinegar has a pH of 3.

Acid rain can leach copper, aluminum and other heavy metals out of the soil and bedrock and into runoff and drinking water. The toxicity of numerous heavy metals increases in the presence of acid rain: lead, aluminum, mercury, zinc, cadmium and copper. Copper concentrations of only 10 to 40 parts per billion (ppb) can kill fish in acid water. (One part per billion equals the volume of 1 liter placed in a lake that has the surface dimensions of a football field and a depth of 738 feet [225 meters].)[9] Copper interferes

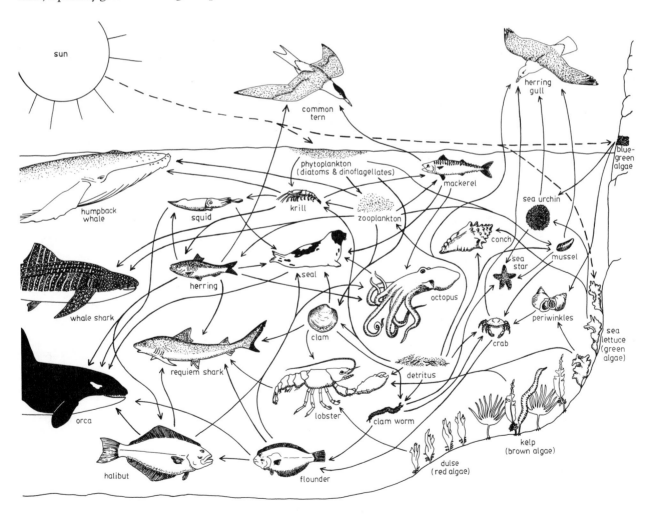

Figure 5-4. Ocean food web. Arrows point in the direction of energy flow.

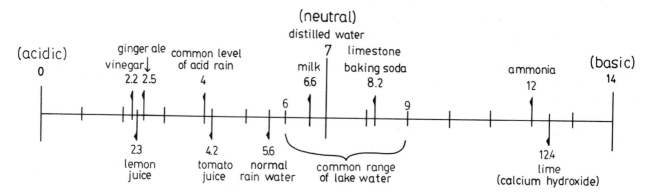

Figure 5-5. The pH scale.

with energy metabolism and enzyme function, causes a mucous covering on gills and can damage kidneys, liver and spleen. Aluminum is naturally present in the soil and lake bottoms. The increased acidity "mobilizes" this metal into solution, where it binds to fish gills and causes suffocation. Heavy metals can inhibit the hatching of fish eggs and cause deformities in the embryonic stages of many aquatic animals. If the waters become too acidic, algae are killed, eliminating the most important food for aquatic life. Fish die along with the algae. Most fish do not eat algae directly, but they feed on animals and other small creatures that need algae to live. Acid rain also dissolves the structures of buildings and cars, eroding away iron, steel, limestone and more.

Waters over hard rocks, such as granite, are most susceptible to acid rain because there is little buffering capacity. Limestone areas are more resilient because limestone acts as a buffer and is able to neutralize acidity.

Many aquatic ecosystems *are* capable, to a degree, of adapting to the changes brought about by human activities. It is when the frequency and severity of impact persists that ecological damage is done. Wise stewardship of the waters asks each of us to live so as to have a minimal environmental impact and to work toward alleviating the effects of activities that harm the air and water. We can support the creation of clean waters as well as aquatic wilderness areas where oil drilling, fishing, dumping and similar actions are prohibited. By these actions we reciprocate the multitude of gifts that these ecosystems, and the plants that live there, provide us.

QUESTIONS

1. What does it mean in the beginning of "The Circle of Life and the Clambake" where it says "Everything in life is a circle"?

2. Who are the Wampanoag? What does their name mean? Where do they live?

3. Why does Maushop leave the Wampanoag? How does his leaving help them to take care of themselves? Does anyone expect you to learn how to do something on your own? What is it?

4. To which large group of organisms does the seaweed called rockweed that the Wampanoag use in their clambake belong?

5. What is algae? How do algae feel and smell? Name some kinds of algae.

6. Where do algae live? Have you seen algae growing in the ocean before? Where? Have you seen it growing in fresh water? Where are you most likely to find algae growing near your home or learning center?

7. How do algae reproduce? What is a spore?

8. What do some algae use to swim? How do flagella work?

9. Have you ever eaten algae? In what foods are algae found? What else is algae used for?

10. What are phytoplankton? Why are they important for life on Earth?

11. What is an adaptation? What kinds of adaptations do algae have to survive?

12. How do algae and green plants grow using sunlight? What is photosynthesis? What do green plants produce during photosynthesis?

13. What is chlorophyll? Do all plants that contain chlorophyll look green?

14. What do plants provide animals to live? What is the gas cycle?

15. What is a food chain? What is a food web?

16. What is acid rain? How does it form? What causes acid rain?

17. How are people harming life in salt- and freshwater habitats? What can we do to take care of aquatic life?

ACTIVITIES

Alluring Algae

ACTIVITY: (A) Visit, observe and experience algae in the natural environments that are available to you: freshwater, ocean and estuary. Collect a few samples for close examination and for later use in an "Algae Mobile." (B) Closely observe the samples of microscopic algae collected earlier. Grow and observe microscopic algae from a small sample of pond water. **GOALS:** Understand algae and appreciate the diversity among algae. Realize that algae live in many different aquatic environments. Experience the sight, smell, feel and taste of algae. Practice growing these fascinating organisms. **AGE:** Younger children and older children

MATERIALS: (A) The "Discussion," field guides to algae and various aquatic habitats, large jar with holes punched in the lid and the sharp edges safely flattened out for use in "B," hammer, nail, foot from a pair of nylon stockings or pantyhose, rim of a lid from a preservative jar, strong string, scissors, needle, thread, small bottles for plankton samples, hand lenses, scissors to cleanly snip off algae samples in the field, small cooler with ice in it. (B) Bottle(s) containing plankton samples gathered in "A," microscope and microscope slides, eye dropper, small shallow plate, guide to using microscope, guides to algae, paper, pencils, crayons, jar of hay, jar of sterile water, sample of pond water gathered in "A," large jar and lid with air holes (made in "A").

PROCEDURE A: *Algae Afield.* Beforehand, scout out several local aquatic freshwater environments such as a pond, lake, stream, river and, if available, saltwater or brackish habitats such as a seashore or estuary. Algae can also be found in canals and ditches. Use the "Discussion" and a few field guides to freshwater and the seashore to identify and learn about the algae in your area. Try to find as many kinds of algae as possible. Some useful guides to consult are *Pond Life,* by George K. Reid and Herbert S. Zim (Golden Guide Series) (New York: Golden Press, 1967); *Seashores: A Guide to Animals and Plants Along the Beaches,* by Herbert S. Zim and Lester Ingle (Golden Guide Series) (New York: Golden Press, 1989); *The Seaside Naturalist: A Guide to Nature Study at the Seashore,* by Deborah A. Coulombe (Englewood Cliffs, N.J.: Prentice Hall, 1984); *How to Know the Freshwater Algae,* by G. W. Prescott (Dubuque, Iowa: William C. Brown, 1970); and *Pond and Brook: A Guide to Nature in Freshwater Environments,* by Michael J. Caduto (Hanover, N.H., and London: University Press of New England, 1990). Gather a jar full of hay and obtain a jar full of sterile water for use in "B," "Algae Alive." Finally, construct the plankton net (Figure 5-6) and punch holes in the lid of a jar. Be certain to pound flat the rough edges on the bottom of the jar lid to avoid injuries.

Take the children on a field trip to observe the algae you have discovered. Bring them to each site, including at least one pond, and take a small sample of the algae living there. Describe the kind of algae it is and all you have learned about it. Pass the samples around and assign someone to collect each sample when all have seen it and place it in the cooler. Encourage the children to feel, smell and, if (and only if) you have instructed them to do so, to taste a tiny piece of those algae you have stated are safe to eat. Immerse the children as

much as possible in the sensory experience of the pond, tide pool or other habitats you visit. Encourage them to use their hand lenses. Use the plankton net to gather a bottle of sample at each site: first, fill the plankton bottle halfway with water from the environment you are studying. Gently pull the plankton net through the water to gather plankton, then invert the net over the bottle and use a *little* water to back-flush the plankton free of the tip of the net into the bottle. Swish the inverted net around a little to free the plankton. Take an extra plankton sample at the pond.

Note: Because field trips can present logistical problems, and different kinds of habitats are often far apart, the leader may want to visit a few, easy-to-reach sites with the children and collect samples of algae from other sites that are more difficult to get to.

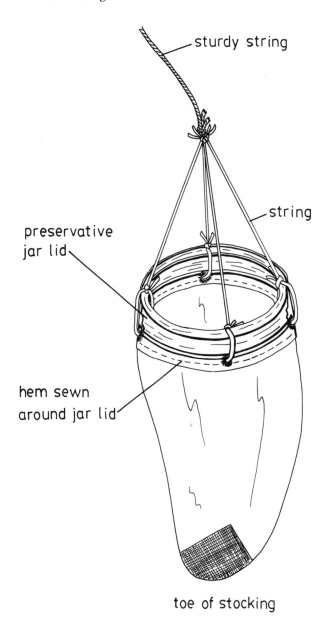

Figure 5-6. Assembly of the plankton net.

sturdy string

string

preservative jar lid

hem sewn around jar lid

toe of stocking

PROCEDURE B: *Algae Alive.* Upon returning to the home or learning center, save and refrigerate the samples of larger algae from the cooler for later use in "Algae Mobile." Gently swirl the water in the bottle containing the plankton sample so the plankton are well interspersed and not settled on the bottom. Place a bit of the water from the plankton sample onto a small glass plate and use the eye dropper to put a few drops onto a microscope slide. Focus the microscope on some algae. Good books to consult for tips here are *Discover the Invisible: A Naturalist's Guide to Using the Microscope,* by Eric V. Gravé (Englewood Cliffs, N.J.: Prentice Hall, 1984), and *How to Know the Freshwater Algae,* which is described in "A." Have the children take turns looking at the algae and using the guides to identify and read (or be read to) about each kind of algae. Pass out paper, pencils and crayons for the children to draw the algae they see as best they can, in detail, to create notebooks that record algae discoveries.

Ask the children to fill a large jar halfway with hay, and then nearly to the top with sterile water. Tell them they are going to "grow" a jar of algae, bacteria and microscopic animals (protozoans) by using the hay as a culture and a sample of the pond water to "seed" the jar. Have them add a few drops of pond water. Cap the jar using the lid with holes in it. Keep the jar in a bright spot and expose it to a few hours of direct sunlight each day, but do not let the water get too hot. Every day, over the course of the next few weeks, place a small sample of the culture under the microscope and observe it with the children. They will see the development of bacteria, flagellates, paramecia and, finally, a community of green algae, amoebas, rotifers, crustaceans and other pond organisms. Have the children illustrate each new algae as it appears.

Note: This activity leads into "Algae Mobile" in *"Algae Art."*

Algae Art

ACTIVITY: (A) Create two mobiles, one featuring microscopic algae and one presenting pieces of the large algae gathered outdoors during "Algae Afield." (B) Make giant replicas of diatoms using old boxes.
GOALS: (A) Recognize some common algae, both larger species and microscopic species. (B) Understand the basic structure of diatoms as well as the specific design of several species.
AGE: Younger children and older children
MATERIALS: (A) Illustrations of microscopic algae from "Algae Alive," newspaper strips, wheat paste, water, bucket for paste, strong thread, crayons, tempera paint, paintbrushes, water, paint containers, pipe cleaners and buttons plus other materials for crafting the "algae." Pieces of algae gathered during "Algae Afield," strong thread, models of microscopic algae made in "A," at least one dozen pieces of

very thick dowelling 1.5 feet (45.7 centimeters) long, pieces of string, screw hook. (B) Figure 5-1, Figure 5-7, one box for each child (shoebox, oval hat box, small gift box, etc.), white nontoxic glue and paste, scissors, tape, construction paper, crayons, paints and supplies as in "A," stapler and staples, guides to algae as described in "Algae Afield."
PROCEDURE A: *Algae Mobile.* Have the children use their illustrations of microscopic algae from "Algae Alive" as models to create small (hand-size) papier-mâché models of those species. These ought to be as "realistic" as possible, including shape, color and markings. For hanging, be certain that the children attach a loop of thread to the top of their algae by folding a few strips of papier-mâché through the loop. Allow these to dry.

Share with the children the algae that were gathered outdoors during *"Alluring Algae"* and that have been stored in the refrigerator. Through questions and answers, review and discuss each kind and its natural history. While the algae are still soft and pliable, work with the group to trim pieces of the algae to a reasonable size for hanging on a mobile. Make a small hole in each piece and tie a loop of thread through the hole for hanging. Carefully spread these out onto newspaper and allow to dry for several days while the papier-mâché projects are drying.

Once the drying is complete, use the dowels and thread to make two separate mobiles: one of the microscopic "algae" and one of the pieces of real algae. Use the string to hang the first dowel from something within the children's reach. Tie the algae onto the ends of the dowels using the thread—this allows them to dance and spin more easily. Use the string to tie the dowels to each other. Stagger the points of attachment and balance along the dowels to make the mobiles lively and interesting. Hang the mobile up high when it is completed.
PROCEDURE B: *Diatom Designs.* Have each child choose a box-shaped species of diatom to create from among those shown in Figure 5-1 and others found in the guides used in "Algae Afield." Help the children to fashion their boxes into a diatom shape with rounded ends as in Figure 5-7. The lid should fit snugly. Now have each child glue the lid on and decorate her or his diatom. When these are completed, have each child read (or read to younger children) about his or her

Figure 5-7. Certain diatoms are shaped like a miniature shoebox. Size: microscopic.

diatom. Children will then take turns sharing their diatoms with the rest of the group and reporting on what that diatom is called, how it lives, etc. Take time to share pictures and illustrations of other diatoms from among the incredible diversity of those that exist.

Phenomenal Photosynthesis Puzzles

ACTIVITY: Assemble two leaf-shaped puzzles: one puzzle that shows the essential elements needed for photosynthesis and a second puzzle that shows the products and byproducts of photosynthesis. Discuss photosynthesis and its vital role in supporting life on Earth through the food energy and oxygen it produces. Discover the gas cycle between plants and animals.

GOALS: Understand the basic formula for photosynthesis. Realize that photosynthesis is the life-giving process that captures the sun's energy and transforms it into a form that is usable by life on Earth. Understand the gas cycle between animals and green plants.

AGE: Younger children and older children

MATERIALS: Copy of Figure 5-8 for a master, pencils, crayons, posterboard or light card stock, scissors, large envelopes, large yellow ball or balloon for sun, string, "Discussion."

PROCEDURE: Beforehand, make an enlarged copy of Figure 5-8 to use as a master. Copy this master onto posterboard or light card stock and then cut each of the two illustrations of a leaf into puzzle pieces. Make the puzzles more or less complicated to suit the age of the children. Younger children will be challenged by a 4- to 6-piece puzzle, while older children will need, for example, a 12-piece puzzle. Label the backs of the pieces of each puzzle with all As, Bs, etc., and put them into similarly labeled envelopes to keep matching puzzle pieces together. Make a set of puzzles for each pair of children: one puzzle showing the ingredients for photosynthesis and one showing the products. Have one group triple-up if you have an odd number of children. Obtain a large yellow ball or balloon to represent the sun.

Have the children work in pairs to assemble the first puzzle (Figure 5-8a), one puzzle to each pair. Once the puzzles are put together, ask the children what they see. Tell them that they are looking at the ingredients for photosynthesis, the life-giving process by which green plants change the sun's energy into the things people and all animal life need to live. Ask the children what they think are the essential things we need to live. Describe the ingredients of photosynthesis, and the need for sunlight to make it work, but *do not tell the children the products of photosynthesis yet.*

Now hold up the yellow sphere to represent the sun and hang it in a prominent place. Hand out the second puzzles (Figure 5-8b) and have the children assemble them. Once the puzzles are assembled, review with the children the products of photosynthesis shown on the puzzles as well as the formula for photosynthesis as described in the "Discussion." Ask the children to think of specific foods and useful things plants produce via photosynthesis.

Point out that in puzzle a someone is exhaling carbon dioxide, which the plant uses during photosynthesis, and that in puzzle b someone is inhaling oxygen, which plants give off during photosynthesis. Describe how these gases pass back and forth between plants and animals in a *gas cycle*. Ask: "Have you breathed on a plant today to thank it?"

Finally, have younger children color their puzzles.

Ocean Food Web Wipe-Out

ACTIVITY: Create a simple model of an ocean ecosystem containing a food web and all things needed to sustain it. Gradually eliminate each part of the ecosystem until the food web collapses. Discuss what happened and why.

GOALS: Understand the parts of an ocean ecosystem as well as how they are interrelated and interdependent upon one another. Understand that plants are producers and animals are consumers of energy. Visualize the flow of energy in an ecosystem from plants to herbivores, carnivores and omnivores as well as decomposers. Understand food chain and food web.

AGE: Younger children and older children

MATERIALS: Old cloth sheet (blue if available); needle and spool of thread; safety pins; three dozen large, round balloons; enough different colors of posterboard and felt-tipped markers to make one card for each part of the environment; yellow ball or balloon for a sun; large pin; Figure 5-4.

PROCEDURE: Beforehand, create the ocean "ecosystem" as follows: Take an old cloth sheet from a twin bed (a bigger sheet may be needed for large groups), fold it in half and sew together the long edge and one end using big stitches. The sheet is now closed on three sides and open on one. Inflate enough large, round balloons to fill the sheet. Get help for this and take your time to avoid hyperventilating! Add one balloon for each part of the ecosystem (see following list) plus a few extras. Close the top of the "ocean" (sheet) with safety pins. Using colorful posterboard and felt-tipped markers, make one card for each part of the ecosystem, as listed below:

- sun (yellow sphere)
- saltwater
- phytoplankton (diatoms, dinoflagellates …)
- red algae
- clam
- clam worm
- common tern
- herring gull
- seal

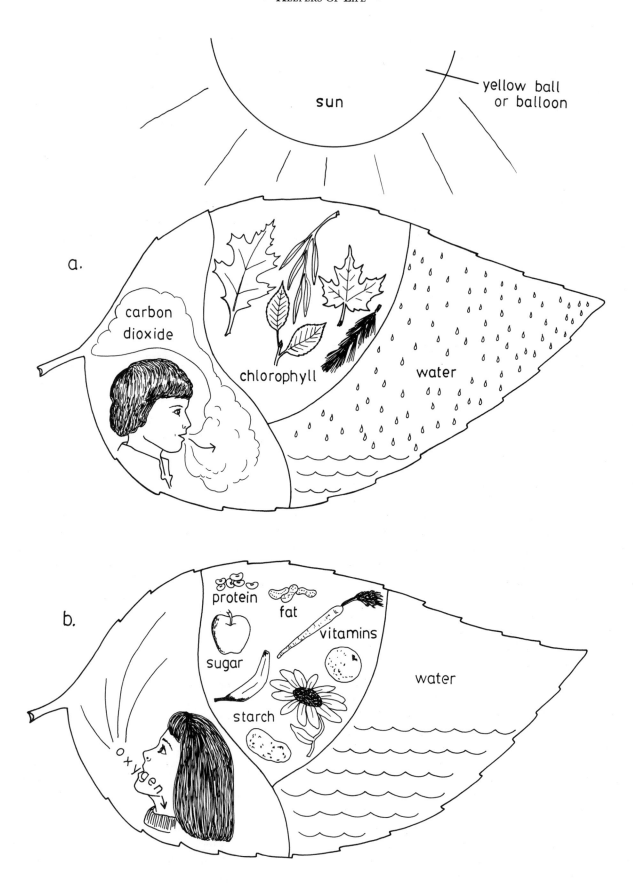

*Figure 5-8. Puzzle masters for use in "Phenomenal Photosynthesis Puzzles": **a.** the ingredients for photosynthesis, and **b.** the products of photosynthesis.*

- blue-green algae
- green algae
- brown algae
- atmosphere
- rocks
- sand
- detritus
- zooplankton
- mussel
- crab
- periwinkle
- sea star
- sea urchin

- krill
- lobster
- conch
- squid
- octopus
- requiem shark
- mackerel
- halibut
- flounder
- herring
- humpback whale
- whale shark
- orca (killer whale)

On each card, use names from this list for children old enough to read and use both the names plus simple labeled illustrations for those too young to read. Substitute different cards representing marine plants and animals local to your area if you live near the sea. On the back of each card, write down one or two things that the plant or animal needs to live, plus one or two things that need *it* to live (see Figure 5-4). A mussel, for example, needs plankton and is in turn eaten by a herring gull. Be sure there are a few more balloons in the "ocean" than there are cards. Use a yellow sphere to represent the sun.

Pass out one card to each child and give the yellow sphere to someone. If you have a small group, give several cards to each child. Introduce the children to this ocean ecosystem. Tell them, "The plants and animals listed on your cards are examples of parts of an ocean ecosystem, but would not necessarily be found together in nature. The balloons inside our 'ocean ecosystem' (sheet) represent the parts of the ecosystem described on your cards." Describe how the algae, the producers, transform sunlight into food energy through photosynthesis, and that this energy supports all life in the ocean. As the plants are eaten by herbivores and other consumers, the energy is passed along. Meat eaters are called carnivores—they eat other animals. Omnivores eat both plants and animals. In this way, all life in an ecosystem is interrelated. Ask the children to describe a *food chain* among their ocean organisms, from sun to plant to herbivore to carnivore and/or omnivore. *Energy flows* and links different food chains in a *food web,* making all plants and animals interdependent upon one another (Figure 5-4).

Ask the children representing the sun, saltwater, atmosphere, rocks and sand to stand near the "ocean" to symbolize that they are part of the environment that will be there throughout the activity. The loss of any of these would mean instant collapse of the ecosystem. These children and their cards are very important and cannot be lost.

Now ask the children, "What will happen to the ocean ecosystem if we take away any one plant or animal? If we take away two plants or animals, four or eight? What will happen if we remove the sun, saltwater, atmosphere, rocks or sand?"

Tell them that they are about to simulate removing each part of the ecosystem, one piece at a time, to see what happens. Brainstorm real-life events that would lead to the depletion and loss of parts of the ecosystem, such as an oil spill, overhunting (whales, salmon, etc.) and pollution from sewage.

Ask the other children who are holding cards to come up to the "ocean," one at a time, to present their cards and say which plant or animal that card represents. Have the children name one or two things that their plants and animals eat or need to live, as well as one or two things that need those plants or animals to live. Some ideas are written on the backs of their cards. Then, give each child a large pin to pop one balloon for each part of the "ocean" ecosystem represented by each card they hold. Ask for the pin back and hand it to the next child as she or he steps up. Help younger children to identify and describe their plants and animals and what they eat or need to eat. Gradually, the ocean ecosystem collapses as the plants and animals are wiped out. Lead a question-and-answer period afterward to discuss what happened and why. Ask children to think of human actions that could cause parts of the ecosystem to decline and disappear.

Note: There are many variations on this activity. One approach is to have the children create and color the parts of the ocean food web as links in a paper chain. Have them join these together to form a food web and hang the chain from the ceiling. See what happens when links of the chain/web are cut away! A second method is to create an ocean ecosystem on a bulletin board and have the children pin their balloons onto the board.

Acid Rain Monitoring

ACTIVITY: Measure the acidity of some common household liquids. Set up an acid rain measuring station and monitor the acidity of rainfall in your area.

GOALS: Understand the process of how acid rain forms as well as the causes of acid rain. Discover the acidity of both the rainwater in your area and some common household fluids for comparison.

AGE: Older children

MATERIALS: "Discussion"; household liquids such as lemon juice, vinegar, ginger ale, apple juice, a solution of baking soda, tomato juice, etc.; distilled water; one saucer for each liquid to be tested; litmus paper;[10] pencils, paper, note cards and file; compass for checking wind direction; sink and dish soap for cleaning the saucers; at least three wide-mouthed glass jars; enough milk crates or other props to make three supports to hold the jars roughly 3 feet (1 meter) above the ground; map on which to plot sampling locations for rainwater; calendar; Figure 5-5.

PROCEDURE: Ask the children whether they know what it means for a liquid to be "acid," and to explain "acid rain." Use the information near the end of the "Discussion" to familiarize the children with acidity, with the measurement of acidity on a pH scale and with the causes and the process of the formation of acid rain in the atmosphere. Make sure they understand that acid rain refers to all kinds of precipitation: rain, snow, sleet, hail, fog and even dry particles that settle out from the atmosphere.

Tell the children they are going to measure the acidity of several household liquids such as lemon juice, vinegar and a baking soda solution. (See Figure 5-5 for a pH scale of common substances.) Have the children clean thoroughly several small, shallow saucers and rinse with distilled water. Distilled water has a neutral pH and it rinses away any remains of dish soap, etc., which can affect pH measurements. Pour a small amount of each of the liquids to be checked for acidity into a separate saucer. To measure acidity, tear off a short (about 2-inch or 5-centimeter) piece of litmus paper and be careful *not to touch* the end that will be dipped into the liquid. Dip the untouched end into a substance and hold it there for a few seconds. When the litmus paper has reacted (in most cases it will change color), compare and match that color to the closest corresponding color on the chart (located on the package the litmus paper came in) and assess the acidity of that substance. Use a new piece of litmus for each substance. Have children make a chart as they record each pH measurement.

Now it is time for the children to test the acidity of rainwater in your area. Lead them through the following simple procedure: Clean at least three wide-mouthed glass jars thoroughly and rinse well with distilled water. Find a different place outdoors to put each jar for collecting rainwater. Locations should be under the open sky with nothing overhanging. This way the jars will not collect rainwater that runs off of leaves, rooftops, etc., all of which will throw off the pH of the rainwater collected. Place each jar upon a sturdy stack of milk crates or other support about 3 feet (1 meter) off the ground. Once a bit of rainwater has been collected, test its pH with the litmus paper and record, on a note card, the exact location, the date of your sampling along with the pH of the rainwater and the direction the wind is coming from. To measure pH of snow, gather as you would rain and then allow the snow to melt indoors before measuring the pH. Collect several inches of snow, if possible, because it melts down to a small amount of water.

Check the pH of precipitation at these same stations through several seasons, being sure to record *all* information as described above for each measurement and station. Take measurements in different locations within your region, both

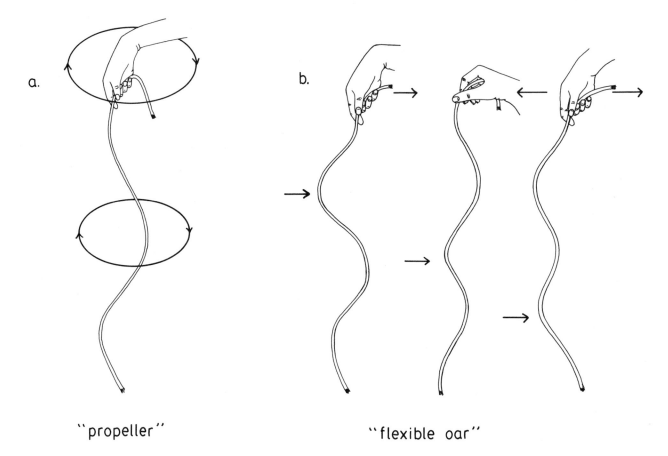

a. "propeller"

b. "flexible oar"

Figure 5-9. Using a piece of string for the "Flagellum Flail."

in an urban area and in the countryside. Keep a detailed card file of all measurements. File and sort the cards according to season, site, wind direction, etc., to study patterns of acidity.

Is your rainwater more acid than normal rainwater, which has a pH of 5.6? What kind of patterns do you notice in the acidity measured during different seasons, in different locations or in regard to wind direction when the sample is taken? Do snow and rain have similar acidity? Report your findings to the appropriate state, provincial, territorial or private environmental agency that keeps track of acid rain measurements in your region.

EXTENDING THE EXPERIENCE

• *Flagellum Flail.* Use a piece of string to mimic the two basic kinds of flagellum movements used by *Euglena*, dinoflagellates and other tiny swimmers. Figure 5-9 describes the "propeller" motion and the "flexible oar" movement. Cut a piece of string roughly 3 feet (1 meter) long, hold it in hand hanging down and make small, easy circular motions with the hand to create the "propeller" (Figure 5-9a). Mimic the flexible oar by gently moving the hand back and forth in one plane to send ripples of waves down the string (Figure 5-9b). How do these motions help a tiny organism to swim?

• *Algae Appreciation.* Hold a celebration to thank the algae for the many gifts we receive from them. Present some of the food and products made possible by algae at this celebration. The "Practical Uses of Algae" section of the "Discussion" presents a detailed description of some algae and the foods and other products that contain algae or substances derived from algae.

• Hold a clambake. An excellent book to consult is *Clambake: A Wampanoag Tradition,* by Russell M. Peters (Minneapolis, Minn.: Lerner, 1992).

• Make three-dimensional models of plankton and hang them around the learning center.

• Add to the excitement of the *"Ocean Food Web Wipe-Out"* for older children by having the children representing the parts of the ecosystem compete for available resources. Provide mates to allow populations to reproduce and add new generations as well.

• Measure the pH of a pond or lake using the same techniques as described under *"Acid Rain Monitoring."* Take at least three water samples from different places, such as near a stream or spring that feeds the pond or lake, out in the open water and along the shore. Record the pH at least once each month for a year, if possible, except when the water is frozen in winter.

• *Is It a Plant or Is It an Animal?* Create models of some microscopic organisms that have characteristics of both plants and animals: *Euglena*, dinoflagellates and certain blue-green algae. Consult the guides to algae described under "Algae Afield" in *"Alluring Algae"* to find illustrations of these organisms. What is it that makes a plant a plant, or an animal an animal? Review the classification system of living things described in Chapter 2.

• Practice giving thanks to the oceans and practice ocean stewardship with *"Circle of the Sea"* in Chapter 9 of *Keepers of the Animals.*

• Thank the sun for its many gifts with the *"Sun Circle"* in Chapter 7 of *Keepers of the Earth.*

NOTES

1. A. R. O. Chapman, *Functional Diversity of Plants in the Sea and on Land* (Boston: Jones and Bartlett, 1987), 47–48.

2. Ibid., 48.

3. Wallace S. Broecker and Jeffrey P. Severinghaus, "Diminishing Oxygen," *Nature,* vol. 358, no. 6389 (27 August 1992): 710.

4. Ibid., 711.

5. Norman Myers, *The Gaia Atlas of Future Worlds* (New York: Anchor Books Doubleday, 1990), 36.

6. See Chapter 7 for a detailed look at the role of carbon dioxide in global warming and the greenhouse effect.

7. Harvey Arden and Steve Wall, *Wisdomkeepers: Meetings With Native American Spiritual Elders* (Hillsboro, Ore: Beyond Words, 1990), 46.

8. Myers, *Gaia Atlas*, 31.

9. Michael J. Caduto, *Pond and Brook: A Guide to Nature in Freshwater Environments* (Hanover, N.H., and London: University Press of New England, 1990), 41.

10. Litmus paper can be obtained from Precision Labs, 9889 Crescent Park Drive, West Chester, OH 45069, (800) 733-0266. Chem Tech, at the same address, also offers a wide selection of biology and chemistry kits. Another source of litmus paper is Science Kit and Boreal Laboratory, which has two locations: 777 East Park Drive, Tonawanda, NY 14150-6784, and P.O. Box 5059, San Luis Obispo, CA 93403-5059, (800) 828-7777.

Fallen Star was waiting in front of the big lodge. "Creep inside," Fallen Star said to Double Face. "All is ready."

CHAPTER 6

✤ Fallen Star's Ears ✤

(Cheyenne—Plains)

Long ago, a woman married a star. She lived in Sky Land for a while, but grew homesick for her people. She made a rope and tried to lower herself and her little baby down to the ground, but her rope was not long enough and she was not strong enough to climb back up. She held on for a time and then fell. It was a long fall and the young woman was killed, but her baby survived.

The birds and animals cared for the boy, and when he was grown, he went to look for his people. Because he came from Sky Land, he became known as Fallen Star, and many things happened to him as he traveled along.

One day, Fallen Star was traveling along in the wintertime. Near dusk, as he was passing through a stand of alders, he saw smoke rising and climbed a hill. From that hilltop he could see a village. Below him, looking down into that camp, stood a very big man. Around that man's neck was a necklace made of human ears.

"I have heard of that man," Fallen Star said. "That is Double Face."

Fallen Star went back down the hill until he came to the stand of trees. He picked the bracket fungus from those trees and shaped them with his knife so that they looked just like ears. Then he strung them about his neck and walked back over the hill to the place where Double Face still stood.

As soon as Double Face saw the necklace worn by Fallen Star, he greeted him. "Friend," Double Face said, "you are welcome. Have you come to help me kill those people in that village below?"

"It will be easy to kill them and take their ears," Fallen Star said. "Do those people know how to kill men like us?"

Double Face laughed. "No," he said. "None of them know that all they have to do to kill me is to trap me so that I cannot run away. Then, if they throw buffalo grease in the fire and shake a buffalo horn rattle I will die."

"Those people are foolish," Fallen Star said, "but I will help you kill them. I will go down and see if they are asleep. If they are asleep, I will make a call like an owl. Then you can creep into that big lodge and take their ears."

"That is a good plan," said Double Face. "I will wait for you to call me."

While Double Face waited, Fallen Star went down into the village. He went into all the lodges and warned the people.

"The one who kills the people and takes their ears is here," Fallen Star whispered. "Make a fire and be ready with buffalo grease and a buffalo horn rattle."

Then Fallen Star made the sound of an owl. Double Face came creeping down into the village and found Fallen Star waiting in front of the big lodge.

"Creep inside," Fallen Star said. "All is ready."

As soon as Double Face was inside the lodge, Fallen Star closed the door flap and laced it tight. Double Face tried to get out, but Fallen Star held the door shut.

"Throw the grease into the fire! Shake the medicine rattle!" Fallen Star shouted.

The people did as he said. As soon as the grease struck the fire it flared up high. Inside the big lodge, Double Face screamed. Then they shook the medicine rattle made of buffalo horn and Double Face's screams stopped. The one who killed the people and took their ears was dead.

Then, because he had other places to go and more things to do, Fallen Star left that village. But ever since then, the fungus which grows on the trees has looked just like human ears.

DISCUSSION

Deep in the moist forests of North America, growing from dead trees or logs on the forest floor, are the reddish-brown to black, thin, rubbery-fleshed, wavy-edged fruiting bodies of tree-ear fungus (*Auricularia auricula*). At 1 to 6 inches (2.5 to 15.2 centimeters) in diameter, these mushrooms resemble the skin of the outer human ear. Throughout the continent many species of *bracket fungi* shaped like ears grow from dead trees and shrubs; this is the kind of fungus Fallen Star uses to trick Double Face in the Cheyenne story "Fallen Star's Ears." The trees do, indeed, have ears.

It is not surprising that "Fallen Star's Ears" is a story about a monster who brings death. Fungi are closely associated with dead plants and animals. Human beings, too, go back to Earth when we die. Where a tree grows in or around any burial ground, its roots are likely to be giving new life to those whose remains lie beneath the soil—a tree's version of raising the dead. As trees grow older, fungi will eventually invade their tissues and the trees, too, may fittingly grow "ears"!

Fungi

Fungi comprise one of the five kingdoms of living things and are considered by many to be unique and distinct from plants and animals. Abundant, diverse and bizarre in appearance, many species of fungi have aptly descriptive names describing appearance or edibility: Earthstar, puffball, shaggy mane, dead man's fingers, Earth tongues, witch's cap, and death cap or destroying angel. There are mushrooms that smell like fish, garlic, green corn, radishes, fruit, raw potatoes, anise, creosote, cucumbers or rotting meat. Mushroom flesh may taste bland or peppery, bitter or delicious. Through a process of genetic analysis, scientists have discovered one individual of the species known as shoestring root rot fungus (*Armillaria bulbosa*), in the hardwood forests of northern Michigan, whose total mass approaches that of an adult blue whale and that is more than 1,500 years old. This massive fungus underlies at least 37 acres (15 hectares) of woodland. As common as they are, so little is known about most North American fungi that their geographical ranges are still a mystery.

People regard fungi with fascination, curiosity, fear and, at times, joy at harvesting one or more of the edible varieties. The language we use to describe fungi expresses mixed feelings. The difference is one of *value,* as the following quote from a newspaper article reveals as it describes the discovery of poisonous strains of hitherto edible fungi in Russia and Ukraine, whose consumption killed more than 60 people: "An unidentified toxin has apparently infected at least a half-dozen types of normally edible mushrooms, turning safe-looking fungi into deadly toadstools."[1]

Fungi cause hundreds of plant diseases and dozens of others that affect animals, including people. Fungal diseases go by many names, including smut, wilt, mildew, rust, gall and late blight. Rusts and smuts infect cereal crops, such as wheat and corn, appearing as black, yellow or orange spots on stems and leaves. Blights have caused some of the most famous fungal diseases. The Irish potato famine of 1845–1846, caused by the late blight of potatoes, left more than 1 million people dead and precipitated a mass migration out of Ireland. In the early twentieth century a fungal blight was imported to New York City on chestnut wood from China. Once among the biggest and most common native trees east of the Mississippi, the American chestnut was virtually wiped out. Only a few small trees and root sprouts remain in certain areas. Mildew is seen as a whitish web on rose leaves. Black knot gall starts as a velvety black swelling on cherry tree twigs and matures in two years as a hard black "knot" up to 2 feet (.6 meter) long. Clothes, walls and paint are all susceptible to mildews. Ringworm and athlete's foot are both human fungal diseases.

However, the benefits fungi bring to human beings and the natural world far outweigh their harmful effects. Fungi:
• decompose dead plants and animals to make the nutrient cycle possible, creating the rich soil that supports plant and animal life and releasing carbon dioxide into the atmosphere.
• produce antibiotics, such as penicillin (a kind of green mold) and aureomycin.

- produce fermentation to create alcohol from sugar (yeasts).
- produce vitamins, including citric acid (vitamin C).
- leaven bread (yeast).
- provide a food source.
- are used to make cheese. Several species of *Penicillia,* which can appear blue, yellow, gray or green, are used to process blue cheese such as Roquefort and Camembert.

Fungi, along with algae and lichens, are Thallophytes (see "Classifying and Identifying Plants" in Chapter 2 for a description of Thallophytes). Unlike algae, all fungi are *heterotrophic:* they lack chlorophyll, cannot produce their own food and must rely, either directly or indirectly, on the food energy provided by green plants for their survival. Because they do not directly use sunlight for growth, most fungi can grow as well in the dark as they can in the light. Fungi live in both terrestrial and aquatic environments, carrying out the vital process of decomposition. Every species of fungus either

- is a *saprophyte* that feeds off the dead remains of plants and animals,
- is a *parasite* that consumes living tissue,
- is a *predator* that entraps microscopic animals or
- exists as *mycorrhizae.*

Mycorrhizal fungi coexist with other plants in a *symbiotic* relationship—one that is beneficial to both organisms. As these fungi grow, the *mycelium* penetrates the roots of certain trees and shrubs, expands the absorptive surface of the roots and provides the plants with nutrients derived from soil humus (see Figure 6-5, later). The fungi, in turn, obtain water and carbohydrates from the plant's sap. Certain trees, especially birches, beeches and some conifers, have co-evolved with mycorrhizal fungi and can no longer survive without their associated root fungi. Unlike mycorrhizal fungi, some *parasitic* fungi feed off the living tissue of dying trees. This hastens the tree's death but, by then, the fungus has already completed its life cycle and sent out spores to infect another host.

Reproductive fungal spores germinate into hairlike threads called *hyphae*. There are several kinds of hyphae such as *rhizoids* that anchor the fungus and *haustoria* that aid in digestion, as well as reproductive hyphae. As hyphae branch out through the soil, across an old piece of bread or other medium, they form a network called the *mycelium* that is the major growing portion and bulk of the fungus and that can be more than 50 feet (15.2 meters) across. In places along the mycelium, prompted by conditions that are not fully understood, hyphae form organized structures or fruiting bodies, usually called *mushrooms* or *toadstools*, that bear reproductive, microscopic spores.

When conditions are just right, such as following a spring or fall rain, mushrooms seem to appear magically. They form, in fact, along the mycelium hidden underground or in a tree trunk or rotting log. Mushrooms grow so swiftly because, unlike plants and fungal mycelia, which grow mostly by cell division, mushrooms develop rapidly by absorbing water into existing cells. Mushrooms are a kind of quick hydraulic cell pump that can exert pressure strong enough to crack concrete. The veil on one tropical stinkhorn fungus unfolds so quickly that photographs taken at that time are often blurred.

Fungi are more active than people realize. A certain species that inhabits animal droppings grows toward the light and shoots its spores in that direction. Animals then eat the spores that have stuck to nearby grasses, completing the life cycle. The digestive hyphae of fungi secrete enzymes that either dissolve dead organic matter or allow parasitic fungi to absorb nutrients from inside living tissues. Some fungi are *predaceous:* they consume tiny animals. Certain species hold aloft stalks bearing sticky knobs on the ends as traps. One carnivorous species has microscopic three-celled snares along its hyphal threads (Figure 6-5, later). When a worm-like soil nematode slips into the 1/1000th-inch (.03-millimeter) opening of one of these nooses, the cells of the ring swell shut in 1/10th of a second to make the catch. The filament digests its meal.

There are around 100,000 species of true fungi, including the *algal fungi* (Zygomycetes), *sac fungi* (Ascomycetes), and *club fungi* (Basidiomycetes) (Figure 6-1). In addition, there are roughly 500 species of the intriguing slime molds (Myxomycetes).

SLIME MOLDS. *Slime molds* are the true creeps of the fungus world. When growing, a slime mold consists of a slimy, streaming mass called a *plasmodium*. This animal-like mass tends to move away from light as it sends out projections called *pseudopodia* ("false feet") that engulf food of bacteria and dead organic matter. Slime molds reproduce in two ways: when the main mass divides or via a sedentary reproductive stage. In the latter case the mass forms individual cells and spore cases that grow on stalks toward the light. Brightly colored and generally less than half an inch (1.3 centimeters) across, slime molds are commonly found on dead wood.

ALGAL FUNGI. The cell structure and methods of reproduction among many *algal fungi* are similar to those of green algae. They reproduce both sexually and with asexual spores, some of which use flagella to swim. Algal fungi include some of the most common living things, such as bread mold, which, along with dung molds and vegetable molds, is a kind of *pin mold*. Spores landing on bread or old vegetables form branching threads that grow dark spore cases. These long-lived spores will grow whenever they land on a suitable food source. The spores of one parasitic pin mold, *Entomophthora*, enter the breathing tubes of flies and germinate inside their bodies, consuming tissues as the filaments branch out. Just before the fly dies it attaches its proboscis

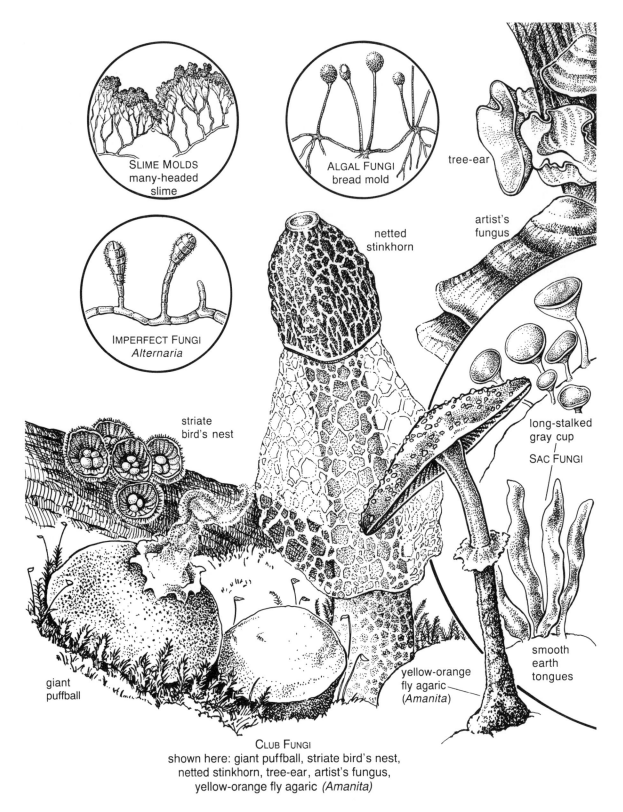

SLIME MOLDS
many-headed
slime

ALGAL FUNGI
bread mold

tree-ear

IMPERFECT FUNGI
Alternaria

netted
stinkhorn

artist's
fungus

striate
bird's nest

long-stalked
gray cup

SAC FUNGI

smooth
earth
tongues

yellow-orange
fly agaric
(Amanita)

giant
puffball

CLUB FUNGI
shown here: giant puffball, striate bird's nest,
netted stinkhorn, tree-ear, artist's fungus,
yellow-orange fly agaric *(Amanita)*

Figure 6-1. There is tremendous diversity among the representatives of the major groups of fungi: slime molds, algal fungi, sac fungi, club fungi and imperfect fungi. Sizes (from upper left): Alternaria, *microscopic; many-headed slime, .03 to .25 in. (.8 to 6 mm) high; bread mold, microscopic; tree-ear, 1 to 6 in. (2.5 to 15.2 cm) wide; artist's fungus, 8 to 24 in. (20.3 to 61 cm); long-stalked gray cup fungus, 1.25 to 1.6 in. (3.2 to 4.1 cm); smooth earth tongues, to 3 in. (7.6 cm); yellow-orange fly agaric, 2 to 6 in. (5.1 to 15.2 cm) tall; netted (collared) stinkhorn, 6 to 7 in. (15.2 to 17.8 cm); giant puffball, 8 to 20 in. (20.3 to 51 cm) wide; striate bird's nest fungus, .2 to .4 in. (.5 to 1 cm) high and wide. (Illustration by Marjorie C. Leggitt)*

to a window or another smooth surface. Gradually, the reproductive hyphae bearing spores grow out and around the dead fly, appearing like a whitish ring. *Water molds* include *Saprolegnia*, another parasite that creates whitish patches on fish, often surrounding an injury such as where a fish hook has been removed. *Saprolegnia* infections are often fatal and are one reason it is important to wet the hands before handling a fish to keep from breaking the protective mucous coating. *Blights*, such as the late blight of potato; *choke fungi*; and *downy mildews* are all algal fungi. *Mildews,* including white rust, usually form brown or white patches on plants.

SAC FUNGI. Most *sac fungi* reproduce with spores borne in small sacs called *asci*. Each ascus usually holds eight spores. Some, such as truffles and morels, also reproduce sexually with large mushrooms. *Yeast* is a well-known member of the sac fungi. In nature, yeast exists in flower nectar, in decaying fruits and other tissue containing sugars. Yeasts are microscopic, single-celled organisms that reproduce mostly by *asexual budding*, simply splitting off new yeast cells. Wine, beer and bread all owe their existence to these ubiquitous fungi. The group of molds called *Penicillia* are familiar sac fungi that appear on citrus and other foods and are grown on a medium in great vats for medicinal uses as an antibiotic. Ergot fungus parasitizes grains such as wheat and rye. Other sac fungi include cup fungi, dead man's fingers and Earth tongues.

CLUB FUNGI. *Club fungi* are a complex and diverse group that includes most of the familiar edible and poisonous mushrooms and toadstools and all of the puffballs and stinkhorns. In addition to asexual spores, all club fungi reproduce sexually, creating *basidiospores* that form in club-shaped *basidia*. Basidial spores are colorful. They may emerge from a ripe puffball or drop from the gills of a mushroom. The color and pattern of these spores is used as an aid when identifying mushrooms by gathering a *spore print*.

One large group of club fungi includes the smuts and rusts as well as the jelly and ear fungi. Wheat rust has a complex, five-stage life cycle. During one stage it parasitizes wheat cells and decreases crop yields. In another stage wheat rust inhabits American barberry. Farmers learned that wheat rust could be controlled by removing the barberry.

The second group of club fungi are the ones most people are familiar with. Within this group, the *hymenomycetes* include the gill fungi, pore fungi and the coral, leather and tooth fungi. Some common groups and species are the "horn of plenty," boletes, chanterelles, meadow mushrooms, shaggy mane, Jack-o'-lantern, bracket fungi, amanitas, tricholomas and polypores and lactarius. In these fungi the *hymenium*—the fertile, spore-producing layer—is exposed before the spores mature. Among the *gasteromycetes*, however, the fertile spore layer is covered by a tissue called the *peridium* that only breaks open once the spores have ripened. Puffballs, stinkhorns, Earthstars and bird's nest fungi are all members of the gasteromycetes.

The primary task of mushrooms is to create and spread spores, a feat that is accomplished in a variety of ingenious ways. Puffballs jet their spores through an opening at the top of the ball, while the bird's nest fungus is designed so that raindrops fall into the "nest" and splash the spores out. Many fungi, such as the stinkhorn, bear sticky spores aloft on flesh that smells of rotting meat to attract spore-spreading flies. Some spores are disseminated when animals, such as bears, eat the fungus and defecate elsewhere, or as the mushroom decays and breaks apart. In just a few days a field mushroom may produce more than 1.5 billion spores. The bracket fungus that was featured in the story "Fallen Star's Ears" can create 30 billion spores each day!

Although the structure of mushrooms varies greatly, the typical parts of a *gilled mushroom* (Figure 6-2) consist of:

- a *stalk*, which comes in all shapes and sizes. Most gilled mushrooms are stalked. The stalk may have a *ring* or *annulus*, which is a remnant of where the veil split off.

- a *cap*, that is moist or dry, sticky, domed or bell-shaped, smooth or pitted, or a combination of any number of shapes, sizes, textures, colors and odors.

- *gills* that radiate out from the stalk-like spokes attached to the underside of the cap. Spores are produced on the gills in basidia. Some mushrooms have pores instead of gills.

- a *veil,* which covered all or part of the mushroom when it first emerged but may (some mushrooms lack a veil) persist on the edge of the cap, as a ring or annulus on the stalk and as a *cup (volva)* at the base of the stalk.

Certain mushrooms that are often found on lawns form a circle called a fairy ring. Each year the hyphae grow outward from the center of the ring where the original spore germinated and, when the mushrooms form, the fairy ring

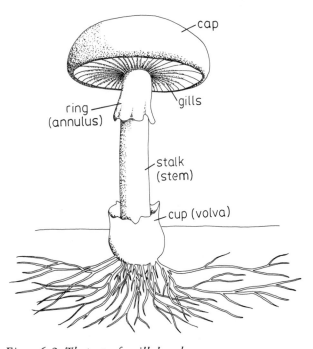

Figure 6-2. The parts of a gilled mushroom.

emerges. The center gradually dies away as the ring enlarges each year, but the mycelium can live for up to 400 years.

Several species of fungus are *bioluminescent*. The poisonous Jack-o'-lantern emits an orange glow. Once, when we were hiking after dark through a thick, fresh fall leaf drop in the Northeast, tiny bits of foxfire glowed eerily like cold greenish-yellow stars where leaves were kicked up in a certain patch along the forest floor.

Some club fungi contain deadly poisons, such as the fly agaric, death cap, destroying angel and certain other amanitas. Many others can make you extremely sick. There are, however, numerous, widely known edible varieties. ***Never*** *pick and eat mushrooms unless you have learned from an expert how to identify safe, edible varieties as well as poisonous species and are absolutely certain of the identity of the fungus. First, exhaust all means of identification such as size, shape, color, smell, habitat, look-alikes, etc. Always take and use a spore print for identification.* Additional tips are to avoid false morels and little brown mushrooms (LBMs) or large brownish mushrooms (in particular species with gills that are blackish, brownish, pinkish or purple-brown) and to *stay clear of amanitas, amanita look-alikes and other white mushrooms with bulbous bases underground.*[2]

Learn the symptoms of poisoning. Every poisonous mushroom produces unique symptoms, including nausea, vomiting, cramps, diarrhea and hallucination.

Some of the well-known edible North American species are the shaggy mane (pick when young), chanterelles, boletes, truffles and morels. The best times of year to look for mushrooms in your area are the moist periods when rain and warmth are most abundant. Autumn is a good time, when the fallen leaves provide a fresh source of food.

Several mushroom varieties are successfully cultivated, such as the common commercial species *Agaricus bisporus* and *Agaricus campestris*. Other cultivated edible mushrooms are the Shiitake, Enokitake, oyster mushrooms and the straw mushroom.

IMPERFECT FUNGI. Little is known about the life cycles of the microscopic *imperfect fungi*. Members of this group reproduce with asexual spores but not with conspicuous fruiting bodies. They cause plant blights, fruit rots, leaf spots, molds and mildew spots on clothing and walls as well as skin infections such as athlete's foot and ringworm. The spores of *Alternaria* are one cause of hay fever.

Lichens

Lichens are found from deserts to the Arctic circle. They grow in cold, dry climates, in forests and mountains and along moist coastal regions. They are the dominant form of plant-like life in many extreme northern regions, where some, growing slowly on the rocks, live to be up to 4,000 years old. Lichens are a primary winter food for caribou. They thrive in clean, unpolluted air and are rarely seen in cities except sometimes within large parks. *Lichens* are a symbiotic relationship between two organisms: an alga and

a fungus. The fungus creates the bulk of the lichen, shelters the alga and provides it with moisture and minerals. In turn, the fungus receives carbohydrates that the alga produces from sunlight. The fungus cannot live without the alga. In many cases, however, the alga can survive on its own. Research indicates that, in some cases, the fungus may actually parasitize the alga.

Some lichens produce *soredia*, which are tiny, wind-blown reproductive structures that consist of a few cells of the alga surrounded by fungal hyphae. If a piece of lichen breaks off that contains both the fungus and the alga, it, too, can land and grow anew. The fungus can also produce its own spores, but the new fungus has to connect with the correct alga once again to survive.

True *pioneer* species, lichens colonize bare soil and rock, tree trunks, sand and logs. Lichens tend to grow slowly, live long and prefer direct sunlight. As the lichen swells and shrinks over extended wet and dry periods, bits of rock are worn away. The fungus of the lichen uses acids to dissolve minerals from the rock. Over time, as the organic remains of lichens accumulate amid the small pieces of rock, soil begins to form in a process called *primary succession*.

Figure 6-3. Look for the common pyxie cup lichen on soil, rocks and rotting wood such as the tops of fence posts. Raindrops splash into the tiny cups and spores are spread by water droplets. Size: to 1 in. (2.5 cm). (Photo by Alan C. Graham)

Each lichen has a unique appearance, ranging from the large rock tripes that look like tiny elephant ears to the whimsical pink pyxie cups. Three particular forms of lichen are recognized. *Crustose lichens* slowly sprawl across the surface of rocks, stone walls, cliffs, bark and old buildings in the countryside. Their color ranges from gray and greenish to yellow, orange and black. Map lichen is a light yellow to green species of northern North America that ranges south in the mountains. Lollipop lichen has long, gray stalks with tips bearing the spores. *Foliose lichens* live on trees and rocks and on rotting logs in the forest. These include the boulder lichen and rock tripes, some of which are smooth and soft when wet; others are like a toad's skin in appearance.

The familiar old-man's-beard of the coniferous forest is a *fruticose lichen* of the genus *Usnea*. This distinctive lichen hangs from trees, forming little elfin beards. Reindeer lichen, food of the caribou, and the British soldier lichen, with its gray-green stalks and neat red fruiting caps, are well-known fruticose varieties. Pyxie cup lichen grows tiny white or pink cups on slender, tapered stalks; each cap is a spore-bearing structure called a *pycnidia* (Figure 6-3).

A traditional winter survival food of the Inuit of northern Canada is the supply of partially digested reindeer lichen removed from the stomachs of musk oxen and caribou. Some lichens are used to make antibiotics. The parula warbler makes its nest almost entirely out of lichen, while the ruby-throated hummingbird embellishes its completed nest by lining it and covering the outside with greenish-gray lichens.

The Nutrient Cycle

Soil is essential for growth of the green plants that support all life. Without fungi, there would be no soil. Fungi, along with bacteria, are the major *decomposers*, which break down *detritus*, the dead remains of plants and animals. Together, fungi and bacteria decompose roughly 80 to 90 percent of the detritus in forest soils. A teaspoon of soil can contain 2 billion bacteria and millions of fungi, algae and protozoans. Except for a few bacteria, fungi are unique in their ability to decompose persistent wood tissues such as cellulose and lignin, as well as the hard, fingernail-like outer skeletons of insects that are made of chitin. Fungi also digest the partially decomposed excrement of many other living things that consume fresh plant and animal remains including insects, mites and worms. In turn, fungi are eaten by springtails, snails, slugs (the black slugs prefer the shaggy mane), mites, nematodes, beetle larvae (grubs), flies and fly larvae (maggots).

As the decomposers work, they produce carbon dioxide while breaking organic matter down into proteins, fats, carbohydrates, ash and other compounds. In a process called *mineralization*, essential nutrients become available for plant growth as they leach from detritus, are excreted and when the decomposers die. In this way, the nature of the soil that builds up over time is partly determined by minerals found in that soil, and by the kinds of plants that grow there. This entire process of *decomposition* makes the *nutrient cycle* possible so that new life springs forth from the old in a continuing cycle of life and death on Earth.

PEOPLE AND THE NUTRIENT CYCLE. In traditional Native America, and in all indigenous cultures prior to the industrial revolution, people were a working part of the nutrient cycle. Virtually all human wastes once consisted of organic material that could reenter the nutrient cycle such as wood, flesh and excrement, as well as naturally occurring materials that did not break down or persisted for a long time such as stone, bone and seashell or metal.

Two changes have taken place since traditional cultures alone peopled Earth. First, there will be 6 billion people living on Earth by the year 2000, generating vast quantities of waste that tax the limits of the ability of Earth's nutrient cycle to assimilate this material. On the average, each household in the United States is responsible for creating several tons of waste each year, while the United States recycles only 10 percent of its waste. Second, many kinds of synthetic waste produced by people, such as plastic and other petroleum products, cannot be decomposed by fungi or bacteria; they are nonbiodegradable! The nutrient cycle has become a dead end, leading to a solid waste crisis.

We need to do everything we can to reenter the nutrient cycle at a level that Earth can assimilate. Everything we make or buy refashions and consumes natural resources, resulting in products that will, most likely, have a limited useful lifetime before they are discarded. A few of the changes we need to make are:

• *Use only what we need; avoid unnecessary goods.* Good questions to ask are, "Can I live without it?" or "Is it possible to repair the old one and keep using *it*?"

• *Purchase goods based on their "ecologic-ability."* Can you find and buy milk in a reusable glass bottle? Is a wooden (versus plastic) version of a tool or toy available? Can you find foods wrapped in paper instead of plastic? Use products that are made from renewable resources and that can reenter the nutrient cycle when their time has come.

• *Reuse whenever possible.* Compost organic waste and add it to the garden soil. Be creative and make useful things out of goods that have outlived their original purpose. Salvage anything that is usable off of a product before, if need be, recycling it. Purchase beverages that are packed in reusable containers, not just recyclable ones.

• *Recycle all materials* that have *absolutely* outlived their usefulness. Separate waste into the categories used by your local recycling center: white and colored paper, newsprint, colored and clear glass, corrugated cardboard, various categories of plastics, etc.

We live in a world that could not exist without fungi. It is up to us to strike a balance in our relationship with the soil, *giving* to continue the nutrient cycle, while *receiving* the gift of life from it. In this way we can keep the circle strong.

QUESTIONS

1. Where does Fallen Star come from in the story "Fallen Star's Ears"?
2. What is Double Face wearing around his neck?
3. What does Fallen Star use to fashion a necklace that looks like ears? How do Fallen Star and the people of the village defeat Double Face?
4. Which kind of fungus is it that, today, looks just like human ears?
5. What is a fungus? What do the fungi that you have seen look like?
6. What are some names we use for different fungi? Do you like fungi? Why or why not?
7. What is a mushroom? What is a toadstool? How do they help fungi to survive?
8. What is a lichen? Which two kinds of organisms live together in a lichen to help each other survive? What is a name for this kind of relationship in nature?
9. What role do fungi play in the soil? What do they do? What is decomposition?
10. What is the nutrient cycle? How does it work? Why is the nutrient cycle important?
11. What kinds of materials can soil fungi and bacteria decompose? Which kinds of material cannot decompose in the soil?
12. Are people part of the nutrient cycle? What do we do with our "waste"?
13. What can people do to be part of the nutrient cycle?
14. What do *you* do to keep from creating too much trash? How can you handle your waste so it is put to good use and not just "thrown away"?

ACTIVITIES

The Fungus and the Houseflies

ACTIVITY: Perform a puppet show that demonstrates some interrelationships between fungi and both plants and animals; houseflies in this case.

GOALS: Understand that fungi use different strategies to survive and reproduce. Discover that there are relationships between fungi and both plants and animals.

AGE: Younger children

MATERIALS: Paper; cardboard; crayons; felt-tipped markers; scissors; glue; tape; pictures of a housefly, honeybee and common stinkhorn mushrooms (Figures 2-2 and 6-1) for children to use as models for puppets; sticks on which to mount the puppets such as paint stirrers; table and green or brown blanket for stage; props for set (window, tree); script to *"The Fungus and the Houseflies."*

PROCEDURE: Have the children prepare puppets on a stick of two houseflies (first fly is female and second fly is male), a honeybee and common stinkhorn mushroom (Figures 2-2 and 6-1). Make a few props: one of a window with a third housefly stuck on it and surrounded by a faint white ring (pin mold) on the "glass," and a second prop of a forest tree for the second setting of the puppet show. Set up a stage using a green or brown blanket to suggest the forest floor.

Practice and then perform this puppet show with the children. Encourage the puppeteers to create and adopt voices that they think their insects would sound like.

THE FUNGUS AND THE HOUSEFLIES

First Fly (*flying around in front of the window as she tries to get out*): I just can't find a way to get outside! The sun is awfully hot on this window. Maybe there's a way out over here. (*flies to one side of window*) No, afraid not.

Second Fly: How about over here? (*flies to the other side of window*) Not here, either. If we don't find a way out soon we're going to bake.

First Fly: What's that over there? (*flies over to a third fly that is stuck on the window*) Hello, Fly. (*waits a moment for an answer*) Can't you hear me? I'm talking to you. Oh, no—it's dead!

Second Fly (*flies over near first fly*): What's that white stuff . . . wait a minute. . . it's a deadly fungus, a pin mold! Breathe in one spore and we're history!

Both (*scream*): Ahhh! (*both start buzzing around frantically*) Let us out of here! (*A child walks up and "opens" the window, then removes it from the set as flies escape outside.*)

First Fly: Wow, that was close! Nothing could have saved us if someone hadn't opened that window. I didn't breathe in any spores, did you?

Second Fly: No, just lucky. If even *one* of these spores had gotten inside of me it would sprout and the threads of fungus would have digested me from the inside out. That poor fly. What a way to go.

Honeybee: Buzzzz. Hi! Where are you two flies headed?

First Fly: No place in particular. We're just winging it. How about you?

Honeybee: Someone back in the beehive did a dance that told me there are some flowers, some pollen and nectar, out in this direction. I'm going to collect it and bring it back to the hive.

Second Fly: You bees really are well organized.

Honeybee: There are the flowers. So long!

Both Flies: Bye!

First Fly: I'm getting hungry. Let's go look for some food. I'm in the mood for something nice and rotten that really stinks. Mm . . . mm.

Second Fly: Look down there . . . a forest. I'll bet there are lots of dead, rotting things to eat. Let's go. Buzzzz . . . (*Tree and stinkhorn puppet pop up with the stinkhorn puppet at the base of the tree.*) (*Both flies fly down to the base of the tree.*)

First Fly (sniffing): Something smells good and awful!

Second Fly: It's this mushroom. It stinks! (*Both flies go over and start licking the top of the mushroom.*)

Stinkhorn: Hey, watch what you're saying! I'm a stinkhorn mushroom. I'm supposed to smell this way.

Second Fly: Don't get me wrong. I meant it in a good way. We love stinky, stenchy smells. You're pretty rotten and foul-smelling—downright rank.

First Fly: I'd say it's pleasantly putrid. Let's dig in. (*Both flies start eating spores off the top of the stinkhorn.*)

Stinkhorn: Help yourselves. There are plenty of spores for everyone, and then some. Besides, when you both fly away my spores will stick to your feet and you'll spread them around.

Second Fly: What are these *spores,* anyway?

Stinkhorn: They're like a seed but they're smaller than a speck of dust. We fungi make millions—even billions—of them. When our spores land on the right food—such as a dead tree or animal, leaves or a piece of bread—they grow new fungi. Each spore grows into its own special kind of fungus. There are all kinds of fungi. Some even glow in the dark.

First Fly: That's all very interesting, but I'm full. Thanks for everything, Stinkhorn. That meal really stunk. Well, you know what I mean. (*flies off*)

Second Fly: Yeah, it was some pretty rotten food. I loved it. You're one heck of an aromatic fungus. Thanks and goodbye! (*flies off*)

Stinkhorn: Goodbye to you both. May the spores be with you!

Familiar Fungi and Lichens

ACTIVITY: Encounter and study familiar examples of fungi from each different group: (A) Grow algal fungi on bread and in a dead fly. (B) Cultivate sac fungi by baking bread. (C) Examine and discuss the functions of the parts of a mushroom. Take a field walk to observe and record common sac fungi and imperfect fungi, slime molds and lichens.

GOALS: Understand the differences between fungi in each of the major groups: algal fungi, sac fungi, club fungi, imperfect fungi and lichens. Recognize and understand the functions of the basic parts of a mushroom. Understand slime molds and how they live.

AGE: Younger children and older children

MATERIALS: (A) Piece of organic natural bread (no fungus-inhibiting preservatives or chemicals in it), spray bottle of water, dead fly, jar of pond water, hand lenses, gloves, tweezers, Figure 6-3, containers with caps in which to incubate the bread mold. (B) Simple recipe for yeast-leavened bread, ingredients as called for in recipe, yeast, 1 tablespoon

of molasses, 1 cup of warm water, mixing bowls and utensils for bread making, nutritional yeast (optional). (C) One commercially available mushroom per child, field guides to fungi and mushrooms, hand lenses, basket, wax paper, pruning shears, pencils, crayons, paper with cardboard backing, Figure 6-2, "Discussion," Figure 6-4, camera and film (optional).

PROCEDURE A: *Gardening With Algal Fungi.* Explain to the children that they are going to grow some algal fungi and describe this group of fungi and its characteristics using the "Discussion" (Figure 6-3). Discuss spores, explaining what they are and how they enable certain organisms to reproduce, such as fungi, algae, mosses and ferns. Have the children take slices of organic natural bread and place the slices in clean containers that can be capped (later). They are to *moisten* the bread by spraying a little water from the bottle

Figure 6-4. Fungi are essential to the process of decomposition in the soil. The shaggy mane mushroom shown here is the fruiting body of a common fungus that lives in the forest floor in the wild, as well as in urban and suburban parks and lawns. Although delicate, the shaggy mane can push up through asphalt as it grows. Size: 1.6 to 6 in. (4.1 to 15.2 cm) tall. (Photo by Michael J. Caduto)

over the surface. If they keep the bread moist and exposed to the air, small particles of mold will appear in a few days. This is the time to cap the container that holds the bread and allow the mold to grow. Each spot of growing mold began from one spore of black bread mold, *Rhizopus nigricans*, one of the most common living things. Its microscopic fungal spores are so widespread that we breathe in at least a few every time we inhale. In about a week, as the mycelia of the bread mold grow, these spots will enlarge, merge and will deepen to about 1 inch (2.5 centimeters) thick. The branching hyphae of the mold can be seen under a hand lens. There are reproductive hyphae sticking up, bearing small spheres containing spores at the tip. When the spore case breaks, black spores emerge that are so light they can float on the wind for several months, only to germinate when they land on a moist, starchy food source. People are constantly breathing in these spores. Describe "saprophyte" and point out that bread mold is a saprophyte.

Caution: Do not disturb the bread mold and deliberately breathe in the spores, which can aggravate allergies.

Now gather a jar of water from a nearby pond. Take the children on a search for a dead fly. Window sills are a good place to look. Dead flies may carry disease, so pick the fly up with some gloves or tweezers and drop it into the jar of pond water, shaking the jar so the fly sinks. Within one week the spores of the water mold, *Saprolegnia*, which are in the pond water, will likely turn the fly into a slimy mass of gray or whitish filaments. On these threads will be borne either swimming asexual spores or sperms and eggs. *Saprolegnia* will also parasitize live fish and other animals, especially where a fish or animal has been wounded or has had its slimy mucous coating broken. Explain parasitism to the children and that this is why it is important to wet the hands before handling live fish to protect the fish's mucous coating.

PROCEDURE B: *Raising a Yeast Feast.* Use the "Discussion" to describe sac fungi and yeast to the children. The French scientist Louis Pasteur discovered that yeast are fungi in 1876. Yeast cells digest sugar, creating carbon dioxide gas and alcohol. The bubbles of carbon dioxide become trapped in dough, stretch the dough and cause it to "rise." Bread is just a bunch of gas bubbles held together by dough. Ask the children whether yeast is a parasite or saprophyte and why they think that is true. Explain that it is a saprophyte and that, in nature, yeast is found in sugar, such as in fruits and flower nectar.

Begin making bread by mixing the tablespoon of molasses with the yeast and about one cup of warm water in a bowl until the yeast is well dissolved. Soon, the yeast will begin to work, as bubbles of carbon dioxide float up. Continue with the recipe, having the children watch closely as the bread rises, is punched down, rises again and bakes. Enjoy your feast of homemade bread!

Note: Yeast is an excellent source of vitamins and other nutrients. Nutritional yeast is a fungus that is high in protein and B-complex vitamins and is one of the only non-animal sources of vitamin B-12. Use it as a supplement in bread recipes, mix a tablespoon into your morning glass of orange juice or sprinkle it liberally over popcorn for a nonsalt flavoring!

PROCEDURE C: *Fungi Afield.* Beforehand, scout out the area around your home or learning center for some slime molds, mushrooms and lichens—as many as you can find. *This is best done the morning after a soaking rainfall.* Obtain one store-bought mushroom per child.

Note: As a safety precaution, tell children *not to eat* anything or put their hands in their mouths while handling wild mushrooms in case any are poisonous. Hands should be washed immediately afterward, *before* eating or putting hands in the mouth.

Share with the children pictures and illustrations of slime molds, fungi and lichens from some common field guides. We suggest *The Audubon Society Field Guide to North American Mushrooms,* by Gary H. Lincoff (New York: Alfred A. Knopf, 1981); *A Field Guide to Mushrooms, North America* (Peterson Field Guide Series), by Kent H. McKnight and Vera B. McKnight (Boston: Houghton Mifflin, 1987); and *Mushrooms and Other Non-Flowering Plants* (A Golden Nature Guide), by Floyd S. Shuttleworth and Herbert S. Zim (New York: Golden Press, 1987). Discuss the life cycles of the various forms of these plants using the "Discussion." Pass out the hand lenses and one store-bought mushroom to each child. Using Figure 6-2 and the information in the "Discussion" as a guide, examine the parts of a mushroom with the children. Discuss the function of each part and the life cycle of a mushroom.

Bring along on the field trip the hand lenses and other materials listed for "C." Record each of your findings with illustrations and photographs. First, visit a bathroom or other place where mold or mildew is growing on a wall. Look at this fungus under a hand lens. Find some lichens growing on a wooden fence, rock wall or gravestone, and look at the lichens closely. Discuss symbiosis and the relationship between the alga and fungus that make up a lichen. Discuss with the children the importance of lichens in the process of *primary succession*, soil formation, and how lichens begin soil buildup on rock, sand and other places lacking soil. Review the life cycle of a lichen in the "Discussion" and the parts of a gilled mushroom shown in Figure 6-2.

Take the group into a forest or park and search for slime molds on rotting logs or dead trees, lichens on stones and tree bark, and mushrooms along the forest floor and growing from dead, standing trees and rotting logs (Figure 6-4). Discuss the life cycle and ecological importance of the fungi you discover. Is that fungus a saprophyte or a parasite or is it symbiotic, as in the case of lichens? Lichens, such as pyxie cups and rock tripe, are favorite finds. The fruiting bodies of the bracket fungi that grow from trees and logs are not poisonous and, when collected and dried, will keep well for years.

Gather a *few* gilled mushrooms, wrap them in wax paper and put them in the basket for later use in "Spore Prints" under *"Mushroom Madness."* To avoid gathering poisonous mushrooms, dig a little at the base of the mushroom stalk and look for a swollen, bulbous base—a sign of a poisonous variety. *Do not gather these!* (See the description of tips for avoiding poisonous mushrooms in the "Discussion.") Do not worry about destroying the mushroom underground, because the mycelium will produce more mushrooms.

Have the children spend some time observing the parts of each fungus found through their hand lenses and record their observations with an illustration. Use this experience as a time to discuss, in strong terms, the detailed warnings about edible and poisonous mushrooms as described in the "Discussion." Make sure everyone understands these warnings and the dangers of eating poisonous mushrooms.

Mush-Room Down Under

ACTIVITY: Create a fantastic, gargantuan world of soil fungi, roots and other organisms that live in the soil by making larger-than-life models of these creatures and props to accompany them. Use these models to turn a room into a giant diorama of life in the soil underground.

GOALS: Visualize the world of the living soil community. Understand that branching hyphae are the real bulk of each fungus. Understand the role of fungi in decomposition, the nutrient cycle and the ecological roles of fungi as saprophytes, parasites, predators and symbiotic mycorrhizae. Realize that soil is a place where the circle of life and death keeps moving to support life on Earth.

AGE: Younger children and older children

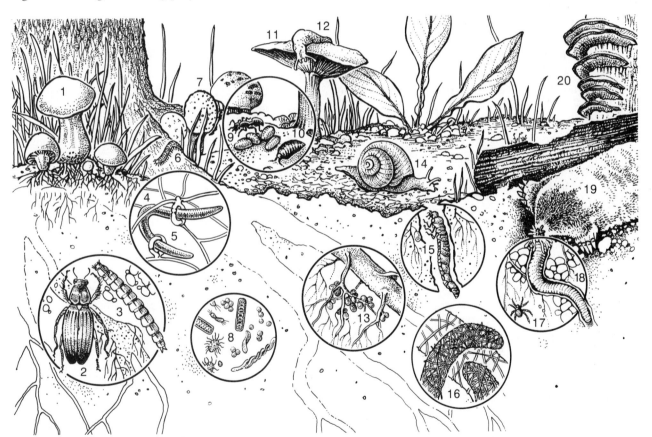

Figure 6-5. The world of soil decomposers for use in "Mush-Room Down Under." In the following list, organisms are identified by number, from left to right, and sizes are given: 1. naked tricholoma (mushroom) or wood blewit, 2 to 4 in. (5.1 to 10.2 cm) tall; 2. darkling beetle, to .8 in. (2 cm); 3. wireworm (click beetle larva), to .8 in. (2 cm); 4. nematode (roundworm), microscopic; 5. nematode caught in the snares of a predaceous fungus, microscopic; 6. centipede, .08 to 6 in. (2 mm to 15.2 cm); 7. gem-studded puffballs, 1 to 2.5 in. (2.5 to 6.4 cm) tall; 8. soil protozoans, microscopic; 9. ant, .25 in. (.6 cm); 10. sow bug, .25 to 6 in. (.6 to 1.5 cm); 11. slimy lactarius (mushroom), 1.25 to 3.5 in. (3.2 to 8.9 cm); 12. slug, to .75 in. (1.9 cm); 13. root hairs with nitrogen-fixing bacteria in nodules, microscopic; 14. common garden snail, to 1.5 in. (3.8 cm); 15. beetle larva, .6 in. (1.5 cm); 16. symbiotic mycorrhizal fungi surrounding root hairs, microscopic; 17. mite, less than .04 in. (1 mm); 18. earthworm, 3.5+ in. (9+ cm); 19. starnose mole, 7.5 to 8.5 in. (19.1 to 21.6 cm) including tail; 20. artist's fungus, 8 to 24 in. (20.3 to 61 cm). (Illustration by Marjorie C. Leggitt)

MATERIALS: Tape measure; yardstick; ruler; calculator; strong string and twine; clothesline; rope hung from side to side across the ceiling; screw-hooks twisted in or other means of hanging up creatures, roots, hyphae, etc.; wallpaper or a roll of parcel-post paper; scissors; cardboard; umbrella; balloons; newspaper strips, wheat paste and water for papier-mâché; construction paper of all colors; clay; pipe cleaners; lots of old cloth sheets; fabric shears; needles and thread and/or sewing machine; crumpled newspapers; pencils; chalk for tracing onto sheets; crayons; tempera paint, water, containers and paintbrushes; fabric paint; field guides and other books providing the correct sizes of soil organisms as well as information about their natural history; other materials as needed for original ideas; Figure 6-5; creativity, energy and time.

PROCEDURE: Create, working with the children, a soil world "down-under" where fungi and bacteria—the decomposers—work to break down plant and animal remains (Figure 6-5). Have children include *many* strands of fungal hyphae as they branch through the soil. Be sure to have children create symbiotic fungal mycorrhizae of some of the fungus branches that connect with the ends of tree roots. The roots of legumes, such as locust trees, will need nitrogen-fixing bacteria in nodules along the roots. Use whole, unground black pepper seeds to represent bacteria. Add other soil organisms that are part of the nutrient cycle: earthworms, mites, snails, slugs, nematodes, beetle larvae, fly larvae (maggots), centipedes, spiders, beetles, moles, springtails, millipedes and ants.

Inform the children as to which of the things they are creating are actually microscopic. Remind them that the living things in this soil world they are creating are not the correct sizes relative to one another. Interrelationships are the most important thing to understand here.

Your *"Mush-Room Down Under"* will be created so the ceiling represents the soil surface and the floor marks the deepest depth of soil present. Either a room or a hallway will work nicely. Fasten props to the walls, hang them from the ceiling on strong twine, rest them on the floor or paint them onto the walls or ceiling. String clothesline ropes across at ceiling level to provide additional hanging places. Use dead tree branches, hung upside down, to represent root systems of trees. Make centipedes and millipedes out of long, thin balloons with fringed construction paper for legs. Create rocks by sewing irregular shapes of sheeting together at the edges and fill the inside with crumpled newspaper. Use pipe cleaners to create small nooses along a fungal thread and show a nematode caught in several nooses (see "Discussion"). Be creative!

Once the *"Mush-Room Down Under"* is completed, discuss and demonstrate, using the props, the ecological roles of fungi: saprophytes, parasites, symbiotics (mycorrhizal) and even predators upon nematodes. Review the process of decomposition (see "Discussion") and the roles of fungi in

the nutrient cycle, soil fertility and development. Point out places where the circle of life and death is taking place in your soil world. Discuss the delicate relationship between mycorrhizal fungi and the tree roots of certain species.

Finally, have the children lead others on a guided tour of their *"Mush-Room Down Under"* as they describe all about fungi and their importance to soil life and the nutrient cycle. Have the children lead a nature walk among the plants and animals and describe all they know about these plants and animals, how they survive and why they are important to the life-giving soil.

Note: Another variation on this activity is to have children make small dioramas of a *"Mush-Room Down Under"* using shoeboxes with one side cut away and a brown piece of construction paper glued over the top to represent the soil surface. Help them to scale everything down to fit their dioramas.

Mushroom Madness

ACTIVITY: (A) Draw, create and observe spore prints of several mushrooms gathered outdoors during "Fungi Afield" in *"Familiar Fungi and Lichens."* (B) Play a game of mushroom and lichen charades. (C) Create giant mushrooms and toadstools out of papier-mâché and stools.

GOALS: Realize that there is a great variety of shapes, colors, textures and scents among mushrooms and lichens. Understand the role of mushrooms in fungal reproduction. Understand the symbiotic relationship between a fungus and an alga that creates a lichen.

AGE: Younger children (A, B, C) and older children (A, B)

MATERIALS: (A) Mushroom caps, wax paper, pruning shears, large glasses or glass jars, white sheet of paper, pencils, small glass of water, water dropper, Figure 6-6, tub of water, soap, hand towels, hair spray. (B) Photographs and/or illustrations (from field guides) of a number of different mushrooms and lichens. (C) Stools (the kind used for sitting upon), newspaper strips, construction paper of a variety of colors, water, wheat paste, bucket, scissors, crayons, tempera paints, water, containers and paintbrushes, large plastic bags (the kind that are made of recycled material and are semibiodegradable), pictures and/or illustrations of mushrooms and toadstools, pencils, paper, full sheets of newspaper.

PROCEDURE A: *Spore Prints.* Beforehand, gather several different examples of gilled mushrooms or use the ones gathered during "Fungi Afield." Trim the stalks off at the base while being careful not to disturb the fungal hyphae beneath the ground or in rotting wood. Gather the caps in a basket and wrap in wax paper (plastic bags hasten decay).

Have the children break off the stalks cleanly and gently and observe the mushroom cap and gills through a hand lens as you describe how spores form on the gills. Have the children draw in pencil, on a separate piece of paper from that on which the spore print will be gathered, the design they see in the mushroom's gills. Now, have children place the mushroom caps on the white paper with the *gill side down* (Figure 6-6). Place a drop or two of water on each cap and cover with a glass jar. In time, ranging from several hours to overnight, the spores will drop onto the white paper, creating a characteristic *spore print*. Carefully apply hair spray to the spore print to hold the spores in place. Hold the can well above the spore print and let the spray drift down so as not to blow the spores around and disturb the pattern. The mushrooms of each fungus leave spore prints with their own unique color and pattern. Spore prints are an important aid when identifying mushrooms. Have the children compare the spore print with their own illustration.

Note: Be certain to use nonpoisonous mushrooms for this activity. Caution the children to not put any fungus in their mouths and to wash their hands with soap and water after handling the mushrooms.

PROCEDURE B: *Mushroom Mimics.* Show the children the images of several different mushrooms and lichens; include at least as many different varieties as there will be groups of children. Use a few extra varieties to make the game more challenging. Photographs or illustrations (from field guides) of the mushrooms they used to make their spore prints will make a nice connection. Field guides are listed under "Fungi

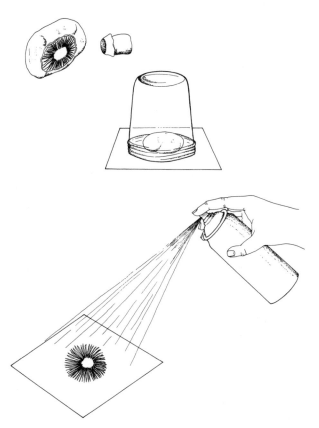

Figure 6-6. Making spore prints.

Afield" in *"Familiar Fungi and Lichens."* Point out the distinguishing characteristics of each mushroom and lichen. Now divide the children into small groups and, in secret, assign each group a certain mushroom or lichen. Each group is to go off on its own and work out a plan for using their bodies to mime their mushroom or lichen in front of the other groups. When all groups are ready, collect all images of the mushrooms and lichens and hang in a prominent place for all to see. Have groups take turns miming their mushrooms and lichens while the other groups try to decide which one they are mimicking.

PROCEDURE C: *Toad-Stools.* Tell the children they are going to use their imaginations to create toadstools of their own design. Divide them into small groups and give each group a stool and a large, biodegradable plastic bag. Have them cover the entire stool with the bag, including the feet, and tie the bag off under the feet. This will protect the stool while they work. Discuss how the use of plastic bags is to be discouraged, that this plastic bag is made out of recycled material and is, in part, biodegradable and that it can be used over again after the activity is completed.

Help the children to begin creating papier-mâché "toadstools," building up layers of the newspaper strips over time. Have them lay down the general shape of their toadstool and then let this dry for a day or two. At this point the children will decide whether they want to create a certain kind of mushroom or toadstool using the pictures or illustrations, or whether they want to design their own original version of one. Have them create a pencil sketch of their intended design and complete it in papier-mâché. If a particular group has decided to create a model of a real mushroom or toadstool, direct their attention to such features as gills, veils, texture of the cap, etc. Once their creations are finished and have dried thoroughly for several days, have the children paint them. Arrange the completed "Toad-Stools" in one area to create a giant fungus garden.

Keeping the Nutrients Cycling

ACTIVITY: (A) Analyze the products you consume for biodegradability and devise ways of conserving by working within the nutrient cycle. (B) Create new, useful things from used objects. (C) Start a recycling program.

GOALS: Realize that you can *choose* to consume goods that are biodegradable and practice doing so. Understand how objects that have outlived their intended use can be redesigned and used for other purposes. Understand that recycling can be easy and enjoyable and is wise Earth stewardship.

AGE: Younger children (C) and older children (A, B, C)

MATERIALS: (A) Products found around the learning center or home, biodegradable replacements for nonbiodegradable products that have been used up or worn out, bags of garbage. (B) Bag of recyclables or material intended to be thrown away, additional materials and tools needed to create usable items out of resources that have outlived their original uses. (C) Pencils, paper, transportation to recycling center, recycling center and list of materials that can be recycled there, recycling receptacles for everyday use (one for each kind of recyclable), larger barrels for short-term storage of recyclables, posterboard, markers, materials as needed for recycling celebrations.

PROCEDURE A: *Breaking It Down.* Begin by emphasizing the importance of *using only what you need.* Then review, with the children, the process of decomposition as described in the "Discussion." Any material that can be decomposed by fungi and bacteria is called *biodegradable.* Ask the children: "Are we natural? Are we part of the nutrient cycle?"

Tour the home or learning center, including the garbage, and ask the children which of the products they find are biodegradable and which are not: plastic bottles, pencils, furniture, glass containers, pens, paper, white glue, etc. Ask the question, "Can fungi and bacteria decompose this material?" Separate out those things that *are* biodegradable and think of biodegradable alternatives for those things that are not. For instance, paper, wood, cellophane "plastic" (which is composed of cellulose from trees) and pure soap are biodegradable, while plastic (made from oil), certain detergents, glass, aluminum foil, and plastic-coated paper are not biodegradable. Make two lists: one of the biodegradable materials found and one of those that are not biodegradable.

Experiment with the biodegradability of different materials. Outline an outdoor plot in which to bury pieces of wood, plastic, cellophane, glass, paper, aluminum, steel, etc. Mark the location of each in the plot. Return once each month and check to see which materials are decomposing.

Brainstorm, with the children, alternatives to nonbiodegradable products. For instance, use plain wooden pencils (the kind without erasers attached) and put rubber erasers on the end for a biodegradable writing tool. Use cellophane bags or airtight containers instead of conventional plastic bags. Use plain soap instead of soap containing lots of additives. Now, once a week or so, replace a nonbiodegradable product with a biodegradable one. Do not waste the products, but simply wait until the old ones have been used up or worn out before replacing them.

PROCEDURE B: *Keeping It Going.* Collect a bag of material that was intended to be thrown away or recycled. Identify those items that can be recycled or composted and put them aside for later use. Hold up each of the remaining items and ask the children to think of as many things as possible that each one can be used for, either as is or with modifications. For example, newspaper can be rolled up tightly and burned as logs in a fireplace; plastic bottles can be reused as canteens or filled and stacked in a greenhouse to store heat during the day, which will moderate nighttime temperatures; old tires

can be neatly stacked and filled to make a retaining wall; plastic containers can be used to store pencils, pens, marbles and other things; cans of the same size can be opened on one end and pushed into sand close together to create a simple, nonskid walkway; and plastic or metal containers can be cut open, flattened and used as shingles on a dog house or other small structure. Be careful of sharp metal edges and use sandpaper to dull these edges. Have the children make a habit of reusing as many things as they can think of.

PROCEDURE C: *Re-Cycling.* It is best to use deposit containers in states and provinces where these are available. Wherever such containers are *not* available, and for containers and materials not covered by returnable bottle laws, recycling helps to reduce the mass of solid waste we produce. There are four basic steps to creating a recycling program. *First,* identify the nearest recycling center and research the categories they use to recycle used materials, such as clear glass, green glass, brown glass, newspaper, magazines, aluminum cans, corrugated cardboard, "bi-metal" cans (most soup cans), etc. Have the children call the local solid waste or public works department to obtain information about local recycling programs. *Second,* arrange transportation for getting collected recyclables to the recycling center. This is a good place to get parents involved in the children's projects. *Third,* set up appropriate containers to receive each kind of recyclable. Waste baskets, boxes, bushel baskets and other neat receptacles work well. Set up larger barrels in a storage area into which to empty the smaller receptacles, which will fill up regularly. *Fourth,* demonstrate to the children how to recycle using the receptacles by showing examples of each kind of recyclable as well as the proper method of preparing recyclables (i.e., removing paper labels from soup cans). Set up a rotating schedule by which children will take turns wrapping newspapers and emptying the smaller receptacles into the large barrels in the storage area.

Keep track of the volume of material you recycle as a positive reinforcement to show what the children are accomplishing. Set up a system of rewards, such as a small outing or a special dance or party to mark and celebrate attaining certain recycling (volume) targets and positive habits.

EXTENDING THE EXPERIENCE

• Establish a compost heap and recycle the organic waste from the activity *"Keeping the Nutrients Cycling."* A good reference describing how to compost is *Let It Rot! The Gardener's Guide to Composting,* by Stuart Campbell (Pownal, Vt.: Storey Publications, 1990). Additional references are described in the Teacher's Guide.

• Obtain some red worms and use them to enrich the compost. Consult the *Earthworm Buyer's Guide 1994–1995: A Directory of Earthworm Hatcheries in the U.S.A. and Canada,* available from Shields Publications, P.O. Box 669, Eagle River, WI 54521, (715) 479-4810.

• *Litter-Watch.* Take turns working in pairs picking up litter from around the home or learning center. Sort the litter and recycle all that you can. Regular cleanups help to beautify an area, make it safer to play there and put waste in its appropriate place.

• Send for these two catalogs that advertise a variety of materials for studying, growing and collecting fungi: (1) *Fungi Perfecti,* P.O. Box 7634, Olympia, WA 98507, (206) 426-9292; (2) *Mushroompeople,* P.O. Box 220, Summertown, TN 38483-0220, (615) 964-2200.

• Read stories that have mushrooms in them, such as *Alice in Wonderland.* Is there any truth to how the mushroom changes Alice? How are mushrooms and other fungi portrayed in stories?

• Hold a mushroom meal featuring mushroom recipes such as stuffed mushrooms and fried mushrooms. Use commercially grown mushrooms to be safe.

• *Mushroom Giant.* Take out a map of the area surrounding the home or learning center. Mark off an area of 37 acres (15 hectares), which is equal to a square that is 1,270 feet (387 meters) on each side. Show this area to the children and tell them that the fungus called shoestring root rot (*Armillaria bulbosa*), a kind of mushroom-producer, spreads out as it grows into an area at least as big as the one you have marked off! Hold up a photograph or illustration of a blue whale and tell the children this giant fungus weighs almost as much as a full-grown adult blue whale! Now mark off the 37-acre (15-hectare) space outdoors around the home or learning center.

• Branch out into an extensive program of environmentally sound management of "waste" using the curriculum *Waste Away: Information and Activities for Investigating Trash Problems and Solutions for Upper Elementary and Junior High Students,* Bonnie Ross, Project Director (Woodstock, Vt.: Vermont Institute of Natural Science, 1989). Available from Vermont Institute of Natural Science, P.O. Box 86, Woodstock, VT 05091.

• For more information and fun on the nutrient cycle, play the *"Nutrient Cyclers"* game in Chapter 16 of *Keepers of the Earth* and *"Cycle Says"* in Chapter 6 of *Keepers of the Animals.*

NOTES

1. Stephanie Simon, "Mysterious Poison Mushrooms Kill Dozens in Russia," *Valley News* (10 August 1992): 7.

2. Gary H. Lincoff, *The Audubon Society Field Guide to North American Mushrooms* (New York: Alfred A. Knopf, 1981), 871.

The earth in Koluskap's hand twisted and fell to the ground. There stood an animal unlike any of the others.

CHAPTER 7

✦ Koluskap and Malsom ✦

(Passamaquoddy—Eastern Woodland)

Long ago, before there were human beings, Koluskap and his brother Malsom lived together on the island of Oktomkuk. They were giants and both of them had great power. Because of his nature, Koluskap always tried to do things which would make life better for others. And because of his nature, Malsom always did things which made life difficult for everyone.

When Koluskap made the rivers, he made them so that one bank flowed downstream and the other flowed upstream. That way, the people yet to come would find it easy to travel. But Malsom threw stones into the rivers, twisted their courses, and made them all flow downstream.

Next Koluskap made all kinds of flowering and fruiting plants. He made beds of moss which would be soft places for people to sleep. But Malsom followed behind him and made plants which had thorns and plants which were poisonous, and he made the moss so moist that the people would grow cold if they tried to use it as a bed.

Then Koluskap began to make the fish. He took great care with them and the last one he made he tried to make the best of all. But Malsom came along, stepped on that last fish and flattened it out so that it was no longer so beautiful. Today that fish is the flounder.

One day, as Koluskap was walking around, he decided to make animals. He picked up some earth and shaped it in his hands and spoke the names of the animals as he shaped each one.

"Moose," Koluskap said, and the first moose stood there.

"Mooin," he said, and Mooin, the Bear, was made.

So he continued, shaping the deer, the squirrel, the rabbit and many others. But as he did this, hidden among the tall ferns, Malsom watched him. Malsom did not have the power to shape things, but he did have the power to twist Koluskap's creation.

As Koluskap began to shape the last handful of earth, Malsom whispered a word from his hiding place before Koluskap could speak.

"Lahks," Malsom whispered. And as he whispered that word, the earth in Koluskap's hand twisted and fell to the ground. There stood an animal unlike any of the others. It was smaller than Mooin, yet it was fiercer than the bear and had great strength. It was shaped a bit like the beaver, but its teeth were pointed and sharp and its eyes gleamed in a way unlike any other animal. It was Lahks, the wolverine.

As soon as he had been made, Lahks began to try to make things difficult. He went to Moose and spoke to him. "If you meet a human being," he said, "you must pick him up with your sharp horns and throw him high in the air."

Moose listened and went along his way until he came to Koluskap. "Koluskap," said Moose, "I know what I must do. If I meet a human being, I must pick him up with my long sharp horns and throw him up into the air."

Koluskap shook his head. "Nda," Koluskap said, "you must not do that. If you meet a human being, you must run away."

Then Koluskap reached out his hands and made Moose smaller and then flattened its horns so they would no longer be so sharp and dangerous.

One after another, Lahks went to the animals, telling them what they should do. In those days, Squirrel was as large as the bear is today.

"You must grab the human beings and tear them apart," Lahks said to Squirrel.

But Koluskap was following behind Wolverine. When Koluskap came to Squirrel, he picked Squirrel up and stroked him until Squirrel became as small as all squirrels are to this day.

Next Lahks went to Bear, who was twice as large as bears are today. "When you see a human being, you must swallow him," Lahks said.

But Koluskap followed behind the wolverine. He made the bear smaller and closed his throat tighter so that Mooin's food would be small things and not human beings.

Malsom watched all this from his hiding place among the ferns, and he was not pleased. So he went to Koluskap.

"Older Brother," Malsom said, "I know that you have great power. But is there not something which can kill you?"

"Younger Brother, it seems that I might be killed by an owl feather," Koluskap said.

That night, while Koluskap slept, Malsom crept off and found an owl feather. He came back and struck Koluskap on the head with it. But all that it did was to wake Koluskap.

"Younger Brother," Koluskap said, "why are you tickling me?"

"Older Brother," Malsom said, "you were having a bad dream and so I decided to wake you."

The next day, Malsom asked Koluskap again. "Older Brother," he said, "is there nothing that can kill you?"

"Younger Brother," Koluskap answered, "it seems that I might be killed by a cattail."

That night, as Koluskap slept, Malsom crept up to him with a large cattail in his hand. He struck Koluskap on the head with it and the fluff of the cattail scattered as he struck.

"Ah-ha!" Malsom said, "I have broken his head."

But then Koluskap sat up. "Younger Brother," he said, "what is wrong?"

"Older Brother," Malsom said, "you cried out in your sleep and so I decided to wake you."

So it went on, with Malsom trying to find the way to destroy his brother and Koluskap never telling him how to do it. One day, however, as Koluskap sat by the river which ran through the hills, he thought he was alone.

"My brother does not know," Koluskap said, speaking to the sky, "that I can only be killed by a blow from a flowering rush."

But Koluskap was not alone. Lahks, the wolverine, was hiding in the tall ferns, and he crept to the place on the other side of the hills where Malsom sat.

Malsom, too, thought he was alone. "Ah," Malsom said, speaking to the sky, "I have tried and tried to find what will destroy my brother. But he does not know that the only thing which can destroy me is a blow from the root of a fern."

Then Lahks came out of his hiding place. "Malsom," he said, "will you give me whatever I ask for if I tell you the one thing which can defeat your brother?"

"I will give you whatever you ask," Malsom said, leaping to his feet. "Now tell me quickly."

"Koluskap can be destroyed by striking him with a flowering rush," Lahks said. "And now you must give me what I want. I want to have wings so that I can fly like the hawk."

But Malsom laughed at Lahks. "What need do you have for wings?" he said. Then he went off to find a flowering rush.

Lahks was angry. He went as quickly as he could to Koluskap. "I have told your brother what can defeat you. He is looking now for a flowering rush," the wolverine said. "But the one thing which can destroy him is the root of a fern like those all around us!"

Then Koluskap reached down and pulled out a fern root. As he did so, Malsom came running down the hill with a flowering rush in his hand, ready to strike his brother and destroy him. But Koluskap struck first with the fern root. As soon as it struck Malsom, he was defeated. Malsom fell and was changed into a long mountain range.

So it happened long ago. And though Malsom has gone from the world, wolverine still goes about making things difficult for everyone. And those mountains, which are called the Long Range, are still there in northwestern Newfoundland.

DISCUSSION

In this Passamaquoddy story, the giant Koluskap is a creative force, shaping the plants and animals, including soft beds of moss. However, Koluskap's brother, Malsom, and the wolverine, Lahks, twist Koluskap's work around to make life difficult. Malsom makes the beds of moss too moist for people to sleep on without growing cold. When Koluskap undoes Lahks' bad deeds and makes things right again, Malsom becomes frustrated and tries to discover how to kill Koluskap. Lahks first overhears Koluskap telling the sky that he can only be killed by a blow from a flowering rush, and then Lahks listens to Malsom say to the sky that only the blow from a fern root can destroy him. When Lahks tells each of the brothers what it is that can kill the other, they engage in battle until Koluskap strikes Malsom with a fern root and defeats him, changing Malsom into the Long Range Mountains in northwestern Newfoundland.

This chapter presents two groups of plants that are introduced in this story: the bryophytes (mosses, liverworts and hornworts) and the pteridophytes (ferns and their allies). These two plant groups, along with the spermatophytes (conifers, flowering plants and related plants), comprise the *embryophytes*. Among other characteristics, embryophytes reproduce sexually: an embryo is produced when sperm fertilize a separate egg. Mosses and ferns produce spores, whereas conifers and flowering plants create seeds.

Adaptations for Life on Land

The first land plants evolved from a group of aquatic green algae about 420 million years ago. Prehistoric seed ferns, horsetails, ginkgoes and clubmosses were gigantic, tree-size plants. Tree ferns grew to about about 26 feet (8 meters)! Even though they are now mostly terrestrial, ferns and mosses are largely restricted to moist environments such as wetlands and shaded forests because their sperm need to swim through a thin film of water to reach and fertilize an egg.

The transition from water to land required a number of adaptations. Aquatic plants are immersed in an abundant supply of water that provides buoyancy, so their tissues need little support. Water also allows aquatic plants to multiply without the danger that reproductive structures will dry out. Reproduction is only possible on land if there is enough moisture present for sperm to swim, or if fertilization takes place in an enclosed structure. Swimming sperm is found in the bryophytes, ferns and related plants and in the cycads and ginkgoes, which are both related to conifers. Sperm lack flagella in pines and flowering plants; they are conveyed to the egg by pollen tubes that develop from pollen grains.

While most aquatic plants take up minerals from the soil, some are capable of absorbing nutrients directly from the water. Land plants need a supply of water and a means of obtaining water and minerals from the soil. Many land plants have *vascular tissue* that both provides support and transports water from the soil to the aboveground parts of the plant. A water-resistant layer of cells on the outside of land plants called the *cuticle* helps to prevent evaporation and drying out. Another water-retaining adaptation is the *stomata*, which consists of a tiny pore ringed by *guard cells* that open and close the pore to control gas exchange and moisture loss.

Land plants must also deal with gravity, providing their own support to remain upright. The cell walls of terrestrial plants contain *cellulose* fibers that are stronger than silk, steel or nylon. Cell walls are flexible, yet incredibly strong for their weight. Water confined inside cell walls provides *turgor*—it presses outward, causing cells to push against their neighbors, and so lends rigidity to plant tissues. Wilting plants experience a loss of turgor and the tissues droop. Turgor is important for maintaining the delicate structure of nonvascular plants, such as mosses, and plant parts that do not contain woody tissue such as those of flower petals and leaves. Algae, fungi, lichens, mosses, liverworts and hornworts do not produce vascular tissue. *Vascular plants* include the ferns, conifers, flowering plants and related groups (see also Chapters 8 and 9) that produce vascular tissue and, therefore, are able to grow to great heights and conduct fluids from the roots and leaves to the rest of the plant. Lacking this tissue and these abilities, mosses are limited to a much smaller size. Vascular tissue consists of *xylem*, which transports water and minerals from the roots upward, and *phloem*, which moves the organic nutrients produced in the leaves downward to the rest of the plant. Xylem tissues are composed of a strengthening substance called *lignin* in which layers of cellulose fibers are embedded at angles to one another, much like the rubber of a radial tire contains steel belts.

✹ Bryophytes: Mosses, Liverworts and Hornworts

From the rubbery green liverworts growing along the edge of a cool waterfall to the soft cushion of moss that covers an old stump in a moist woodland, *bryophytes* are an intriguing group of around 25,000 species of plants that live in damp environments. These minute plants fascinate us even though they exist along the edge of most people's awareness. Bryophytes do not produce vascular tissue and they lack true roots, stems or leaves. The *gametophytic* generation—the one that forms the male and female sex cells—is the most visible stage.

It is a challenge to distinguish the three groups of bryophytes in the field (Figure 7-1). Many mosses grow an erect shoot, bearing leaves arranged in a spiral pattern. Feathery mosses grow more prone. Liverworts, which tend to grow in dim light, may be either short, flat, ribbon-like lobes or prostrate stems with two or three rows of flattened leaves that never occur in a spiral pattern. The least abundant bryophytes, called hornworts, form flat lobes that are not leafy.

Each of the many different growth forms of bryophytes is designed to help the plant retain water, from the dense mats of moss to the short, flat lobes and tiny leaves of many liverworts.

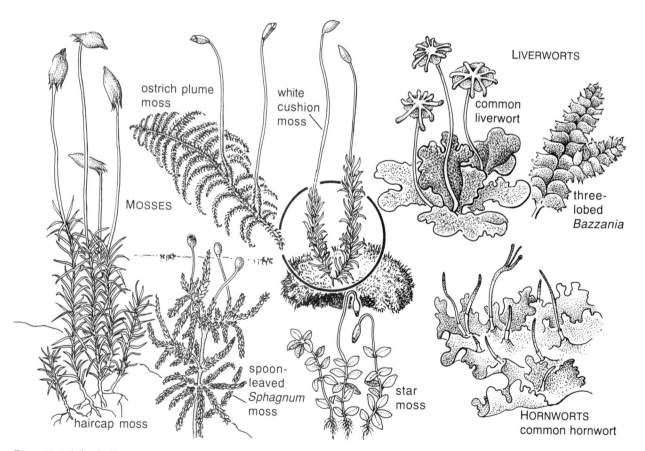

Figure 7-1. The challenging bryophytes: mosses, liverworts and hornworts. Sizes (from left to right): haircap moss, 6 in. (15.2 cm) tall; ostrich plume moss, to 4 in. (10.2 cm); spoon-leaved Sphagnum *moss, to 1 ft. (30.5 cm) tall in mounds; white cushion moss, to 4 in. (10.2 cm); star moss, 1 in. (2.5 cm); common liverwort, thallus 2 to 5 in. (5.1 to 12.7 cm) long; common hornwort, to 1 in. (2.5 cm) high and wide; three-lobed* Bazzania, .5 in. (1.3 cm) wide. (Illustration by Marjorie C. Leggitt)

When water is plentiful, as much as 90 percent of a plant's tissue may be water. During a drought the water content may drop to as little as 5 percent. Certain bog mosses (*Sphagnum*) will absorb up to 25 times their dry weight in water. In tropical cloud forests, where water is abundant and ever-present, some bryophytes grow as long pendants. Some bryophytes absorb water from the soil using root-like *rhizoids* and then conduct the water to the tissues. Evaporation from the surface of the plant drives this process, much like a sponge wicks water up when placed in a pool of water. Some bryophytes absorb water over the entire surface of the plant.

REPRODUCTION. When we look at a moss, liverwort or hornwort, we see the gametophytic generation of the plant (Figure 7-2). Reproductive structures form on top of this plant: the female *archegonia* and the male *antheridia*. Water is always necessary for the sperm to reach the archegonia. On some plants, sperm spreads via the passive movement of rainwater, while other plants have splash cups in which sperm is transported by splash droplets and runoff. When the egg is fertilized it grows into an embryo that becomes the tiny *sporophyte* generation, bearing a spore capsule that either is on a *seta* or stalk (mosses and liverworts) or is stalkless (hornworts). When spores land on a suitable substrate and environmental conditions are right, they germinate and produce a new gametophyte.

Spores are spread by some remarkable mechanisms. Most liverworts and some hornworts actually throw their spores into the air. Some mosses produce a capsule that bends over when it ripens and sprinkles the spores along the ground. One of our favorite things to observe on *Sphagnum* mosses is the ripe capsules atop their whorls of leaves as they explode and discharge an impressive cloud of spores with a barely audible "pop"! Just prior to exploding, pressure in these capsules ranges from 4 to 6 atmospheres.

MOSSES. More than 14,500 species of moss grow in many different environments, from saturated bog soil to rocks, from damp forest humus to tree bark and from seashore to mountaintop. Hardy and widespread, mosses live on every continent, from the Arctic to the tropics. *Mosses* are often divided into three groups: bog mosses, rock mosses and true mosses.

Take a walk in any moist environment and you are likely to find an array of mosses that seem to create a miniature, elfin world of their own. Haircap moss, with its four-sided capsule that sprinkles ripened spores like a tiny salt shaker, is widespread. Look for the barely visible, green to reddish-brown, tall elf-cap moss growing on moist soil or rotting wood as it holds its spore capsules aloft on half-inch (1.3-centimeter) stalks. Bright green ostrich plume moss may also be growing nearby, forming a thick carpet of minute, feather-like branches. Other common mosses are the dark green, 1-inch (2.5-centimeter) star moss that grows in damp soil and decaying wood and the white cushion moss, which is whitish-gray when dry and blue-green when wet. The aquatic water mosses grow completely submerged.

LIVERWORTS AND HORNWORTS. About one-fifth of the roughly 8,500 species of *liverworts* form lobes in the shape of a tiny human liver, thus their name of "liver plant" (*wort* means "plant"). Most liverworts, like the three-lobed *Bazzania,* are tiny, green, leafy plants that never grow taller than 1 to 2 inches (2.5 to 5.1 centimeters). Some of the most beautiful gardens of liverworts, mosses and lichens are found in shady, dripping wet grottos along the banks of cool streams. Liverworts also grow on tree trunks and rocks.

One species, the common liverwort *Marchantia,* looks like small pieces of green seaweed. The erect male branches grow plate-like structures on which antheridia are produced. The female plants bear stalks that look like minute, lotus-shaped umbrellas on whose undersides the archegonia form. Raindrops spread sperm from the male to the female branches below. *Marchantia* also grows minute cups with *gemmae* inside that allow the plant to reproduce asexually. These structures look like minute bird nests with eggs inside. Raindrops splash the gemmae from the cup. Each gemma produces a new liverwort plant.

Common hornwort is one of only about 300 species in the world. The structure of *hornworts* is similar to that of some liverworts. Hornworts have a gametophyte that is flat with tiny rhizoids growing from the bottom that attach to the soil. The sporophyte is a long, thin capsule that looks like a blade of grass.

Ferns and Related Plants

This group of vascular plants includes the ferns, whisk ferns, horsetails, clubmosses, spikemosses and quillworts. Worldwide, there are more than 11,000 species in this group, many of which are tropical and subtropical.

REPRODUCTION. Each of these different plant groups, and the species within them, have their own individual variations in reproductive life cycles. The life cycle of a fern represents the general strategy used by many of these plants to produce and distribute spores (Figure 7-2).

Among ferns the sporophyte is the dominant generation. The fern leaves, called *fronds,* have vascular tissue and bear spores in cases called *sporangia*. The sporangia occur in brownish clusters called *sori* (Greek for "heaps") located either on the underside of the frond, upon a separate stalk or in small sacs. The sporangia have a thin layer of food to nourish the developing spores. When the spores are mature, a specialized series of cells in the wall of the sporangium actually shoot the spores into the air to disperse them. Spores landing on a place that provides enough light and moisture grow into the gametophyte—a tiny, often heart-shaped structure called the *prothallus*. The female, egg-bearing archegonia, as well as the male, sperm-producing antheridia, are produced on the underside of the gametophyte. If there is sufficient moisture present, the sperm swim to the eggs. No matter how many eggs are fertilized on any particular gametophyte, only one forms an embryo and develops into a new sporophyte. Ferns, whisk ferns and horsetails are *homosporous,* meaning they produce only one kind of

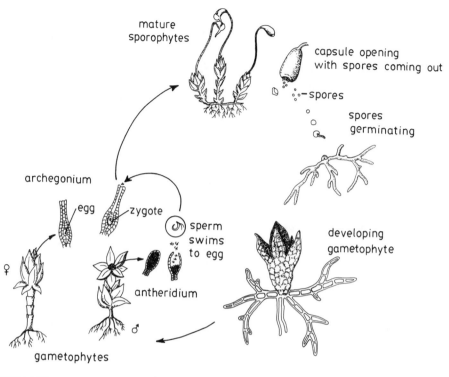

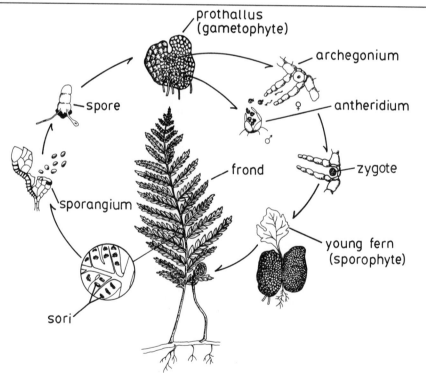

Figure 7-2. **Top:** *The life cycle of a moss. Water-borne sperm from the male gametophyte swim to and fertilize the egg on the female gametophyte. The fertilized egg develops into the sporophyte. The sporophyte often consists of a capsule borne on the end of a stalk growing from the female gametophyte. Spores mature in the capsule and, when released into a suitable environment, the spores produce the next generation of gametophytes and the cycle begins again.*

    Bottom: *The life cycle of a fern. Spores are clustered in sori on the underside of the frond (the sporophyte generation). Thrown from the sporangium, each successful spore germinates into a heart-shaped prothallus (the gametophyte), which contains the male and female reproductive organs. Only one fertilized egg on each prothallus forms an embryo. This embryo develops into a frond, completing the life cycle.*

spore. *Heterosporous* plants, such as the spikemosses, gymnosperms and flowering plants, produce separate male and female spores.

FERNS. *Ferns* are an amazingly diverse group of plants, from the 1/4 inch (.6-centimeter) water ferns of North America to the 60-foot (18-meter) tall Tahitian tree ferns, and from the delicate, lacy fronds of maidenhair fern to the thick, evergreen Christmas fern on which each leaflet is shaped like a miniature Christmas stocking (Figure 7-3). Damp, moist, shady habitat is a good place to search for ferns, but they can also be found in fields and on the edges of cliffs.

Some ferns, as well as lichens, mosses and flowering plants, are *epiphytes*. Epiphytic plants grow on other plants for support (they are not parasites); they use roots for anchorage and, with other structures, obtain their water from rain and dew. Nutrients are absorbed from leaves and other plant matter that accumulates around the roots of epiphytes. Spores of epiphytic ferns are spread by wind and rain. A number of epiphytic ferns, including the resurrection fern and strap fern, can be found in the Everglades.

Ferns possess true stems, leaves and roots. They spread using horizontal underground stems called *rhizomes*. The entire fern leaf is called the frond, and leaflets are known as *pinnae* (Figure 7-4). New leaves appear as a tight roll called a *fiddlehead*, which gradually unfurls into a frond. The fiddleheads of ostrich fern and some other species are favorite springtime wild edibles.

Many temperate wetland ferns grow to impressive heights. Cinnamon fern, with its woolly coat at the base of each stem, can reach a height of more than 6 feet (1.8 meters), and ostrich fern commonly grows to 5 feet (1.5 meters) or more. Sensitive fern is so named because it is particularly susceptible to late spring frosts, which kill the new growth and cause the plant to start over. Rattlesnake fern is widespread throughout North America. Common bracken, with its three-part frond, is a worldwide species that grows in dry upland forests, fields, meadows and waste areas atypical of the habitat preferred by most ferns. Dense, evergreen colonies of polypody are a welcome sight during the months when most plants have lost their leaves. Other widespread ferns include the lady fern, adder's tongue fern, woodsias, spinulose woodfern, hay-scented fern and the small water ferns, some of which are rooted and others free-floating.

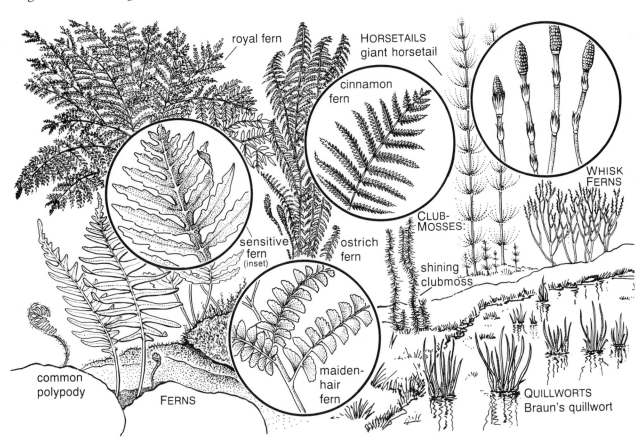

Figure 7-3. A sampling of some of the beautiful ferns and related plants that are commonly encountered, including whisk ferns, horsetails, clubmosses and quillworts. Sizes (from left to right): royal fern, to 6 ft. (1.8 m); common polypody, 6 to 12 in. (15.2 to 30.5 cm); sensitive fern, 1.5 to 2 ft. (45.7 to 61 cm); maidenhair fern, 10 to over 20 in. (25.4 to over 51 cm); ostrich fern, 5 ft. (1.5 m); cinnamon fern, 3 to 4 ft. (.9 to 1.2 m); shining clubmoss, 6 in. (15.2 cm); Braun's quillwort, 9 in. (22.9 cm); giant horsetail, sterile stems of 4 to 6 ft. (1.2 to 1.8 m), fertile stems (inset) of 1 to 2 ft. (30.5 to 61 cm); whisk ferns, 6 to 18 in. (15.2 to 45.7 cm). (Illustration by Marjorie C. Leggitt)

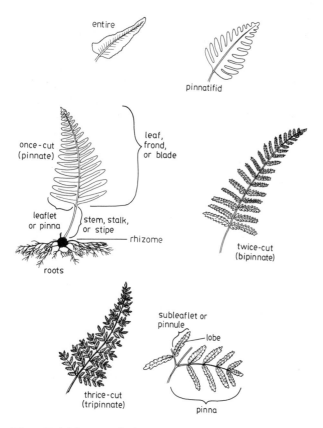

Figure 7-4. The parts of a fern and the different forms of fern fronds.

WHISK FERNS. Primitive and simple-looking, *whisk ferns (psilopsids)* do not possess true leaves or roots but they do have vascular tissue. The broom-like branches of these 6- to 18-inch (15- to 46-centimeter) tropical and subtropical plants have small scales instead of leaves and are found on moist soil and logs. Descendants of the first terrestrial vascular plants that ever developed, whisk ferns resemble in many ways plants that lived 420 million years ago.

HORSETAILS. *Horsetails* are known to many people as "scouring rushes." They have tough, hollow, ridged stems that Native Americans have taught others to use to scour pots blackened by cooking fires. The cell walls of horsetails contain a high amount of silica, which gives the stems their toughness. Horsetails have true roots and stems that are interrupted at intervals by whorls of tiny leaves, giving the plant a bamboo-like appearance. Ancient plants that look very similar to their 40-foot (12.2-meter) tall ancestors that lived during the Devonian period 390 million years ago, there are only about 16 species in the genus *Equisetum* that have survived. Rough horsetail is a dark evergreen that grows throughout North America on gravel and sand along streams, wet banks and waste areas. It has a simple spike-like stem up to 5 feet (1.5 meters) tall that bears a spore-bearing "cone" or *strobilus* on top. The tannish fertile spike stems of field horsetail emerge in spring where they grow in damp places to about 6 inches (15 centimeters) tall. Sterile stems

are finer, with a whorl of many fine branches growing from each joint.

CLUBMOSSES. Despite their name, *clubmosses* are more closely related to ferns and are not true mosses. The ancient relatives of clubmosses lived from 300 to 345 million years ago and grew to be more than 50 feet (15.2 meters) tall. Many people are familiar with clubmosses such as the evergreen ground pine and the deep green leaves of shining clubmoss. Princess pine tends to grow in acid soil and is used for making Christmas wreaths. Even though many evergreen clubmosses look like miniature relatives to pines, they are not related. Clubmoss spores, which are like tiny specks of dust, burn with an explosive flash when ignited. They have been collected in great quantities and used for photographic flash powder as well as fireworks, and they produce the magician's loud bright flash. Clubmosses are homosporous. Spores form, depending on the species, either on specialized leaves or on a cone-like *strobilus*. All clubmosses have simple leaves. Clubmosses grow from underground rhizomes that live for many years and survive even when the visible plant dies back aboveground.

There are more than 100 species of clubmoss in existence. One fascinating variety is the 3-inch (7.6-centimeter) resurrection spikemoss of the arid Southwest. It curls up tight and becomes dormant during dry periods, and then unfurls its leaves and grows once again when the rains come.

QUILLWORTS. "Merlin's grass," or *quillworts,* are rarely more than 12 inches (30.5 centimeters) tall and look like a bunch of wild scallions. They grow in fresh or somewhat brackish water and are mostly found completely submerged or as an *emergent* that is rooted underwater but grows up past the water's surface. Sometimes they are simply growing on damp soil.

Wetlands

While the array of plants just described are not confined to aquatic environments, they are common plants of the wetlands. Wetlands are fascinating and exciting environments that teem with a stunning diversity of plant and animal life. A *wetland* is an area that is intermediate in wetness between upland or "dry" habitats and the deep water of rivers, lakes or oceans. Saturation with water largely determines the nature of soil development and the plant and animal communities living in the soil and on its surface. The water table in wetlands is near, at or above ground level and the area may be flooded constantly, seasonally or only occasionally. In the saturated soils found in wetlands, water displaces air, which inhibits the decomposers, such as bacteria and fungi, from breaking down plant and animal remains. Over time, the organic remains of dead plants build up and create dark mucky or peaty soils. The plants that grow here, known as *hydrophytes,* can tolerate saturated soils and low levels of oxygen. The deepest water in which most emergent plants can grow, about 6.6 feet (2 meters), represents the lower limit of wetlands, beyond which are found *deep-water habitats*. All aquatic environments shallower than this depth, including ponds, streams, seashores and shallow zones along lakeshores and riverbanks, are wetlands. *Marsh, wet meadow, bog* and *swamp* are some terms that we commonly use to describe freshwater wetlands, although ecologists have devised a more technical, accurate system for classifying wetlands (Figure 7-5). Saltwater and brackish wetlands, which are discussed in more detail in Chapter 5, include rocky and sandy shores, marshes, mangrove swamps, beds of seaweed and reefs.

In Canada and the northern United States, most wetland basins were formed by glaciers. Wetland basins are still being formed by rivers, landslide dams, beavers and other animals such as alligators, wind, permafrost, people, *tectonic* forces (movements of Earth's crust), volcanic action and sinkholes that appear when soluble bedrock such as limestone is dissolved underground.

MARSH. A freshwater *marsh* can be as productive as a tropical rainforest, growing 4.4 pounds (2 kilograms) of plant material or biomass per 11 square feet (1 square meter) each year. A shallow, productive marsh in a temperate region can give off 90 cubic feet (2.6 cubic meters) per acre each day of highly combustible *marsh gas* or methane, a byproduct of anaerobic bacterial decomposition.[1] The denizens of the marsh range from many forms of plankton to cattails, reeds, rushes and water lilies, and from aquatic insects to muskrats, beavers and bullfrogs. Algae and green plants form the base of the wetland food chain. The black mucky soil of the marsh underlies areas that are known by many different regional names. There are the prairie potholes of Saskatchewan, Alberta, Minnesota, Montana and North and South Dakota that serve in the spring and summer as nesting areas for waterfowl and that provide resting and feeding areas during migration. The vast, 680-square-mile (1,761-square-kilometer) marshes of the Okefenokee Swamp in southern

Georgia are also known as "prairies." Large floating mats of peat in these marshes are called "batteries." Salt marshes grow in coastal waters. These habitats are extremely important for supporting life in the sea: they provide breeding grounds, nursery areas and food for many of the fish that live in the open water. The algae of coastal wetlands such as tidal pools and rocky shores are discussed in detail in Chapter 5.

WET MEADOW. Grasses, rushes and sedges are the dominant plants in the *wet meadows,* areas that are often covered by shallow standing water at some time during the fall, winter or early spring. Water may be below the surface during the summer, and some meadows that are not flooded simply have saturated soil with a water table that is near the surface. Smartweed, blue flag, bedstraw, St. Johnswort and marsh marigold or cowslips are common plants here.

SWAMP. More than one-half of all wetlands in the United States are *swamps*. Trees and shrubs predominate in the wooded swamp and shrub swamp, respectively, where the mucky black soils are saturated and often flooded. In some northern swamps the peat is found to be up to 20 feet (6 meters) thick. The mangrove trees of saline and brackish tropical coasts and the bald cypress of inland freshwater swamps possess some remarkable adaptations to deal with wetland conditions. Mangrove trees have prop roots that give the plant stability in tidal waters, and bald cypress trees possess "knees" that protrude up above the water. These structures absorb oxygen and transport it to submerged roots. Mangrove forests outline the edge of the extensive wetlands complex that comprises the more than 2 million acres (810,000 hectares) of Everglades National Park in southwestern Florida. Other plants of the southern swamps include loblolly bay and tupelo gum. Evergreen shrub swamps and forested wetlands of North Carolina are called "pocosins." Dominant plants in swamps farther north include red maple, black gum, larch, Atlantic white cedar, willow, alder, dogwood, azalea, jewelweed, royal fern, cinnamon fern and sensitive fern.

BOG. A visit to a bog is a journey to another world unlike any other natural area, inspiring feelings of reverence, awe and mystery. *Bogs* are unique and fragile environments harboring many rare and often threatened plants that are restricted only to bogs, especially in southern states. Bogs are so sensitive that simply walking over a bog mat several times leaves a deep path that can last for many years. Many bog plants, such as Labrador tea, normally occur in the boreal and Arctic regions and in alpine areas. A bog often begins forming at the edge of a poorly drained body of water where *Sphagnum* moss and sedges create a floating mat. Sedges and cotton grass, along with the white-fringed orchis, can tolerate the wet, acid conditions of the bog mat. Bogs are home to many delicate orchis: the white-colored lady's tresses, rose *Pogonia*, yellow lady's slipper and both *Calopogon* and *Arethusa,* with their flowers ranging from pink to magenta.

Common Wetland Type	Technical Class Name
Open Water	Aquatic Bed
Marsh	Emergent Wetland
Wet Meadow	Emergent Wetland
Bog*	Moss-Lichen Wetland
	Emergent Wetland
	Scrub-Shrub Wetland
	Forested Wetland
Swamp*	Scrub-Shrub Wetland
	Forested Wetland

*Technical names for bogs and swamps depend upon the type of vegetation that dominates the wetland.

Figure 7-5. Common and technical names for freshwater wetlands.

Figure 7-6. Tollund Man. (Photo courtesy P. V. Glob, Director, Danish National Museum, Denmark)

The conditions that make bogs such a challenging environment in which to grow are low soil and water temperature, low oxygen levels and low mineral nutrients in a highly acidic soil. *Sphagnum* contributes to the highly acidic growing conditions. Fungi, bacteria and other decomposer organisms that are found in upland soils find life difficult in bogs, so dead plants accumulate into a fibrous, spongy soil that, in some bogs, fills the basin more than 40 feet (12.2 meters) deep. Any animals that happen to fall into a bog are also preserved. In May 1950, two Danish men were harvesting bog peat when they discovered, buried in the peat, the body of a man with a noose around his neck. The body, now known as Tollund Man, was dated back to the Iron Age, 2,000 years ago.[2] Tollund Man was perfectly preserved; his beard clearly showed several days' growth (Figure 7-6). Archaeologists believe that Tollund Man had been a criminal who was buried in the bog as a sacrifice to Nerthus, the goddess of fertility who is also known as Earth Mother. Bogs were believed to be sacred places, and a criminal who was condemned to death could appease the anger of the gods if he or she volunteered to be sacrificed. These deaths brought good luck and fertility to the peasant community.

Paleolimnology is a fascinating science that has taught us much of what we know about past climatic changes and accompanying responses among natural communities. The remains of living things have been found where decomposition is poor in the ancient strata of bogs, marshes and lakes: diatom frustules, pollen grains, insects and other animal remains. By dating and studying these remains, scientists are able to draw a chronological picture of life on Earth, particularly plant growth, as well as climatic changes over time.

Slow decomposition is not the only attribute of bog soils. Absorption of minerals by plant roots is decreased in anaerobic, acidic bog conditions, and these soils can be depleted of important minerals. Some bog trees that have trunks the diameter of the large end of a baseball bat have been dated to more than 150 years old. Toxic concentrations of aluminum are sometimes found in bogs.

To supplement nutrient-poor diets, some carnivorous plants consume insects and other tiny animals: horned bladderwort, pitcher plants and sundews are widespread, but the Venus' flytrap is limited to the southeastern United States (Figure 7-9, later). Worldwide, there are more than 500 species of carnivorous plants. While the *Venus' flytrap* quickly and dramatically snaps shut to trap unwary insects, the *bladderwort* has tiny insect-trapping sacs on underwater leaves that deflate when at rest. When a small animal, such as a nematode, swims near a bladder and touches one of the trigger hairs near its opening, the sac suddenly inflates. The creature is sucked inside by the rushing water, held tight by a trapdoor and digested. The *pitcher plant* has red veins and a scent that guide insects into the opening. The hairs on the inner lip of the hood point down, making it difficult for insects to travel out of the "pitcher." Once trapped in the pitcher's fluid, the insects are slowly digested by enzymes. Nevertheless, the female of one species of mosquito (*Wyeomyia smithii*) lays eggs in the fluid of the pitcher and the larvae develop there, somehow immune to the digestive juices. *Sundews* possess drops of clear, sticky fluid on the ends of hairs in which small insects founder. The sundew's Latin name, *Drosera*, comes from the Greek *droseros*, meaning "dewy." Slowly, the hairs, and the sticky pads to which they are attached, fold inward and entrap the insect meal. Once the insect is digested, the hairs gradually unfold, ready to trap once again.

Buckbean and water willow commonly grow at the edge of the bog mat, along with sedges and *Sphagnum* moss. Cranberry creeps over the bog. Its roots, along with those of leatherleaf, bind the moss. Other common shrubs include sweet gale, sheep laurel, bog laurel, bog rosemary and Labrador tea. Bacteria located in nodules on the roots of sweet gale improve this plant's diet in the nutrient-poor soils by obtaining or *fixing* nitrogen directly from the air. Eventually, as peat builds up and consolidates, taller shrubs and trees take root in the bog mat: black spruce and larch in the Canadian muskegs and Atlantic white cedar in eastern and southern coastal bogs. Deciduous trees such as red maple do not grow well in the bog until the peat is firm and has begun to decompose. This aging process of the bog, during which the open water gradually fills in with accumulating silt and dead plant remains, is an example of the process called *ecological succession* or *primary succession* (where no soil had been present) (Figure 7-7). (See

Chapter 6 about soil formation or *primary succession.*) During ecological succession, plants and other organisms change as their environment (soil, water level, soil chemistry) changes. Many of today's bogs were open bodies of water 10,000 years ago when the glaciers melted back. Wetlands persist as advanced stages of succession, such as swamps. The rate of succession depends upon the kind of plants growing, water chemistry and depth, water level fluctuation, local climate, geology and drainage. People frequently cause succession to speed up by draining a wetland or by polluting it with fertilizers and causing eutrophication. Succession may be slowed down by dredging the wetland or raising its water level.

Since the process by which peatlands form takes thousands of years, peatlands are nonrenewable resources. The largest peatlands occur in the spruce-fir forest and tundra belt of North America, northern Europe and Siberia, where they cover 2 million square miles (5,180,000 square kilometers), an area

seven times the size of Texas. Canada and the former Soviet Union harbor 75 percent of the world's peatlands, the United States contains about 7 percent and the rest are concentrated in Finland, Sweden, Indonesia and the United Kingdom. The removal of peat on a commercial scale has a severe impact on bogs and other *peatlands* (fens, mores and mires), particularly the harvest of peat for fuel and peat moss. Peatlands are disappearing rapidly in parts of the former Soviet Union, Finland, Ireland and Canada.

WETLAND VALUES. Wetlands possess many important ecological and cultural values:

• *Fish and Wildlife Values:* Wetlands provide abundant food, water and plant cover for many animals. U.S. wetlands and deep-water habitats comprise only 9 percent of U.S. land area but support 28 percent (29) of the plants and 50 percent (94) of the animals listed as threatened or endangered under

Figure 7-7. Ecological succession in a bog. (**a**) *The basin is mostly open water where drainage is congested.* (**b**) *Some sedges and* Sphagnum *moss are beginning to grow out from the edges.* (**c**) *Peat accumulates and the area of open water begins to shrink as the bog mat develops further. Older sections of the bog are supporting growth of some low shrubs. The edge of the young bog mat is floating or "quaking." As peat builds up and becomes more consolidated with the accumulation of plant remains, the soil becomes better aerated and is capable of supporting decomposition by aerobic fungi and bacteria. Nutrients are more available than in the young bog mat where peat is saturated and growing conditions are anaerobic or nearly so. Eventually, large shrubs and young trees grow in the oldest sections of the bog* (**d**), *and the open water becomes closed off completely* (**e**). *The bog continues to develop toward a swamp.*

the U.S. Endangered Species Act.[3] The prairie potholes constitute 10 percent of North America's waterfowl breeding habitat, yet they produce 50 percent of the waterfowl on this continent. The sedges and lichens of Canadian peatlands are a staple food for woodland caribou.

• *Environmental Quality:* The microbes, plant litter and living plants of wetland habitats filter out toxins and the nutrients in fertilizer runoff: they maintain the quality of both surface water and ground water. Plants add oxygen to the water and cause sediment to settle out as they decrease the rate of water flow. By adding nutrients and organic detritus to open water, wetlands support other aquatic life. Wetlands moderate local climate by acting as a heat sink. Evaporation from water surfaces and leaves has a cooling effect.

• *Socioeconomic Values:* Wetlands located along floodplains store high waters and release them slowly into the river channel, which diminishes flooding downstream, slows the flow of water and decreases wave damage to property. Plant roots hold the soil in place and reduce erosion. Wetlands protect and provide water supplies for drinking and irrigation. Wetlands provide us with many foods (blueberry, cranberry, wild rice, fish, shellfish) and materials, such as wood. Peat moss is used as a soil supplement and as fuel for heating homes and powering electrical generating plants, particularly in northern Europe. The traditional Netsilik, an Inuit people, use peatland mosses to line the bottom of sled runners, for insulation and as diapers. Peat mosses are naturally antiseptic: bacteria and fungi cannot live in them. Much of our scientific field research and outdoor educational studies would not be possible without wetlands. The contributions of wetlands to such recreational pursuits as boating, swimming, skating, fishing, birdwatching, wilderness excursions and canoeing are immeasurable. Wetlands are a place to visit when seeking recreation, to renew a close relationship with nature and to replenish the human spirit.

How well are we protecting our wetlands? There were 215 million acres (87 million hectares) of wetlands in the United States when it was first settled by Europeans. Less than one-half of the original wetlands found in the lower 48 states remain; the rest have been drained, filled, polluted, dredged or altered so that their natural values no longer exist.[4] More than half of the original acreage of prairie potholes in Canada and the United States has been destroyed. Draining for agriculture accounts for 87 percent of the wetlands destroyed from the mid-1950s through the mid-1970s.[5] An area of wetlands the size of Delaware is being decimated every three years in the United States.

Our provident wetlands need to be protected and managed. Many ecologists now advocate managing entire drainage basins of rivers or *watersheds,* as opposed to individual wetlands. After many years of decline and neglect, the preservation of the ecological integrity of wetlands remain-

ing in Everglades National Park and adjoining wild areas is now a priority. In many places, protecting the only remaining wetlands in urban environments offers a last chance to create sanctuaries. In the countryside, wetlands offer the last vestiges of wilderness.

Fossil Fuels and the Greenhouse Effect

The fossilized remains of the prehistoric ancestors of ferns, horsetails, ginkgoes, clubmosses and other plants that accumulated during the coal age (280 to 345 million years ago) have been transformed over millions of years into *fossil fuels*—deposits of coal, oil and natural gas. By burning gasoline and other forms of fossil fuels we create many kinds of air pollution, including carbon dioxide and ozone. Synthetic fertilizers are a significant source of nitrous oxide, another pollutant. All three of these gases, as well as CFCs (chlorofluorocarbons), contribute to the problem of global warming. CFCs also deplete the ozone in the upper atmosphere. (See "Discussion" in Chapter 14.) CFCs are the byproducts of a number of industrial processes and they are emitted by refrigerants used in refrigerators, freezers and air conditioners (in buildings and automobiles). These chemicals are now banned in the manufacture of aerosols in the United States and Canada.

GREENHOUSE EFFECT. The *greenhouse effect* occurs as the sun's radiation penetrates the atmospheric gases and reaches Earth's surface. Earth then reflects this energy back as heat (infrared), which is again reflected back to Earth by atmospheric gases that act much like the window panes of a greenhouse. Carbon dioxide causes nearly 50 percent of the greenhouse effect. Most carbon dioxide comes from two sources: (1) the burning of fossil fuels in power plants, factories and vehicles and (2) the burning of tropical forests. There are smaller volumes of methane, nitrous oxide, ozone and CFCs being emitted, but these gases are far more potent at trapping heat. CFCs trap 10,000 times more heat than carbon dioxide does. Methane, of which cattle and rice production are major producers, reflects back 27 times more of the sun's heat than carbon dioxide. The anaerobic bacteria that live in peatlands produce about 40 percent of Earth's methane. Conversely, peatlands store 15 to 20 percent of the world's terrestrial carbon, which helps to moderate global warming. Widespread burning of peat would release this carbon as carbon dioxide and contribute to the greenhouse effect. Clearly, we need to know more about the important dynamic between peatlands and global climate.

At the current rate of increase of these gases and advancement of the greenhouse effect, global temperature will rise by an estimated 5.4 to 9°F (3 to 5°C) by the mid 2000s.[6] Most *global warming* will occur in the polar regions, as temperatures rise 10.8 to 21.6°F (6 to 12°C), and in the temperate climates, which may warm up by 9 to 12.6°F (5 to 7°C). These climatic changes would require plants to adapt by shifting their ranges, "migrating" 10 times faster than they ever have. The predicted sea rise of from 1.6 to 4.9 feet (.5 to 1.5 meters), due to the warming and expansion of the upper layers of ocean water and the melting of glaciers and polar ice caps, would inundate major coastal regions and cities such as New York City, Calcutta, London and Tokyo, as well as one-fourth the land area of Florida. This would create roughly 400 million environmental refugees.[7] Although the tropics would experience a smaller increase in temperature, they would experience flooding, disruption of local economies and the possibility that semi-arid lands could become deserts. Tropical diseases would migrate farther north. North America's grain belt would decline while the former Soviet Union could become the world's bread basket.

The eruption of the Mount Pinatubo volcano in the Philippines in June 1991 only slowed the advancement of the greenhouse effect. Sulphur dioxide emitted by the volcano reacted in the atmosphere to create a layer of sulphuric acid droplets that have blocked a significant amount of solar energy from reaching Earth's surface. This cooling effect should last for about five years. Sulphur dioxide emissions from coal burning have also had a cooling effect.

There are many different ways to slow the greenhouse effect, including:

• *Conserving energy* by using mass transportation, car pooling, insulating homes and businesses and installing energy-efficient heating systems and electrical appliances, auditing energy use in the home and workplace to discover new ways to conserve and using alternative, renewable sources of energy such as wind, wave and solar power.

• *Halting and reversing tropical deforestation* by shifting to sustainable harvests of wood and other crops such as rubber, nuts and other foods and medicines. By planting new trees we increase the amount of carbon being absorbed as well as the amount of oxygen being given off by photosynthesis.

• *Reducing our use of beef and beef byproducts* to decrease the methane produced by cattle.

• *Reducing the application of commercial fertilizers* in agriculture because the manufacturing process creates large volumes of nitrous oxides.

In addition to the greenhouse effect and other forms of atmospheric pollution, the consumption of fossil fuels causes other environmental problems. The recent decrease in atmospheric oxygen is directly related to burning fossil fuels. Strip mining for coal is a major source of large-scale habitat destruction as well as water pollution in the forms of erosion and siltation in waterways and acid leachate in runoff from mine tailings. Oil spills cause tremendous ecological destruction. In recent times, oil spills and the burning of oil wells have become weapons of war. Oil refineries are significant sources of both particulate and toxic air pollution. Global competition for fossil fuel reserves also continues to be the source of political tension and conflict.

QUESTIONS

1. In the story "Koluskap and Malsom," why do you think it is Koluskap's nature to try to make things better for others? Why does Malsom do things to make life difficult for everyone? Do you know any other stories in which someone who is of good character fights with one who is bad?

2. Koluskap creates soft beds of moss for people to sleep on. What does Malsom do to the moss? Describe a time when you sat in or laid down on moss. How did it feel?

3. During their battle, what plant, and which part of that plant, does Koluskap use to destroy Malsom? Which plant does Lahks say that Malsom can use to kill Koluskap? Why do you think the root of a fern can defeat Malsom? What does Malsom turn into when Koluskap defeats him?

4. What type of plant is a moss? Describe a moss. What is a liverwort? What is a hornwort? How are these plants related to mosses? What does *wort* mean?

5. How is a moss different from a fern? What is it about a plant that tells you it is a fern? In what kind of habitat do mosses and ferns grow?

6. What type of plant is a fern? Describe a fern. Have you ever heard of a horsetail, clubmoss or quillwort? How are these plants related to ferns?

7. What is an epiphyte? Where and how do these plants grow?

8. What is a spore? How do mosses and ferns use spores to reproduce?

9. Describe a time when you visited a marsh, swamp, bog, meadow, salt marsh, mangrove swamp or rocky ocean shore. What is it like in these wet places? What characteristics make these environments wetlands?

10. How is a bog different from other wetlands? What are the conditions in a bog that prevent dead plants and animals from decomposing? Have you ever visited a bog? What does it smell, feel and look like as you walk around the bog?

11. Why do some bog plants consume insects, spiders, mites and other small creatures? How do these plants catch their prey? What are the names of some of these plants?

12. If you could stand on the shore of a bog, marsh or other wetland and watch it for a thousand years, what would you see happening to the wetland? How is this ecological succession?

13. Why are wetlands important? What kinds of useful things do people receive from wetlands and the plants and animals that live in these habitats? Give an example of how people treat wetlands. What do we need to do to make sure that wetlands are cared for?

14. Coal, oil and natural gas formed from the remains of what kinds of prehistoric plants? Why do we call these "fossil fuels"? How and when do we use fossil fuels?

15. What kinds of environmental problems does the use of fossil fuels cause? Why do we keep using these fuels when they are harming the environment?

16. What could you do to help reduce the problems caused by using fossil fuels?

17. What is the greenhouse effect and what causes it? How does the greenhouse effect affect Earth's climate, especially temperature? What can we do to slow the greenhouse effect?

ACTIVITIES
Moss and Fern Foray

ACTIVITY: (A) Follow a trail of clues while exploring mosses and ferns outdoors. (B) Use rubbings to create impressions of fern fronds.

GOALS: Understand the basic characteristics of mosses, ferns and some related plants. Understand what an epiphyte is and how it lives. Discover the intricate beauty of fern fronds and the amazing variety of branching patterns and venation among ferns. Understand what a wetland is and discover some of the plants and animals that live in wetlands.

AGE: Younger children (A, B) and older children (A)

MATERIALS: (A) Field guides to ferns and mosses as described in "A"; hand lenses; "Discussion"; wetland area to work in; boots, old sneakers or other footwear for a wet area plus a change of dry footwear; towels for drying feet; pencils; paper with cardboard backing; (for each pair of older children) one copy of the "Moss and Fern Detectives Trail" you create; pruning shears; newspaper; materials as required for the activities the children will conduct at each station along the trail. (B) One fern frond for each child, newsprint, crayons, pencils, tape or tacks, enlarged copy of Figure 7-4.

PROCEDURE A: *Moss and Fern Detectives Trail.* Beforehand, take some field guides to ferns and mosses to an accessible wetland near the home or learning center. Some recommended guides are *Mushrooms and Other Non-Flowering Plants,* by Floyd S. Shuttleworth and Herbert S. Zim (Golden Guide Series) (New York: Golden Press, 1987); *A Field Guide to the Ferns,* by Boughton Cobb (Peterson Field Guide Series) (Boston: Houghton Mifflin, 1963); and *Fern Finder,* by Anne C. Hallowell and Barbara G. Hallowell (Berkeley, Calif.: Nature Study Guild, 1981). Identify and learn about the natural history of about one dozen or so of the many ferns, mosses and related plants living in a specific part of that wetland and its environs, including at least one epiphytic moss (preferably). Locate and learn about some common lichens. See the "Discussion" for information about epiphytes as well as the ferns, mosses and related plants. Focus on some basic information about these plants such as life cycles, means of reproduction, unique adaptations, etc. Be sure to include the characteristics that distinguish mosses, ferns and the related plants in these two groups. Choose an area that the children will be able to walk around in—one that is not too wet and that has a variety of habitats to visit. Record the details of your findings about each plant and write down a *simple* activity for the children to do at each

plant that is fun and informative and will guide their observations. You may have the children use their hand lenses to observe the pattern of the veins on a fern frond, count the parts of a fern fond, shake the spores off a clubmoss, draw a picture, describe the feeling of some moss, put their noses to the ground and smell the soil, listen to the sounds or search for particular colors or shades of one color. Collect a variety of fern fronds to use in "B," making sure that each child will have a frond of her or his own. Store the fronds flat between some pieces of newspaper.

Now, set up an interesting trail that the children, working in pairs, will follow by using clues to get from one station to the next. Be certain to include an epiphytic moss (preferably) or lichen as one of the stations along the trail. Plan the route carefully so the children's foot traffic from station to station will have a minimal impact on that habitat. Give especially wide berth to any rare or fragile plants or animals you encounter while scouting out the trip. Younger children should be able to easily spot the next station from the one they are standing at. Older children could be clued in to a landmark or two between stations to make the trail more challenging. For instance, a clue might say: "From this moss you can see a large rock that looks a little bit like a frog. Walk over to it. From the frog's head, go to the big forked tree that has a patch of moss growing near its base. The next clue is in the fork of the tree." A simple map to accompany the clues is also helpful. Create enough stations on the trail so that each pair will get to lead the group at least once during the field trip. Once you have designed a trail that is appropriate for the age of your children, make one copy of the trail clues, map and activities for each pair of children.

Take the children out to the site and introduce them to their excursion using tips from "Taking Your Children Outdoors" in Chapter 2. Emphasize that this is a visit to the homes of plants and animals and that the children should behave respectfully while visiting. The quieter and more observant they are, the more they will see. Tell the children that, when moving from one station to the next, the group is to follow the leaders in single file to minimize impact on the habitat. Ask them not to run at any time. This is a cooperative activity.

Ask the children what they think a wetland is. Share some information from the "Discussion" on what makes an area a wetland, and on the kinds of plants and animals that are found in local wetlands. What other kinds of wetlands are there?

Begin at the first station. If you are working with older children, let them conduct the entire journey, with occasional tips from you if they get confused along the way. If your children have not yet learned to read, simply read the information, activity and directions to the next site for the leaders at each stop. Ask the children to keep eyes, ears and noses alert for any exciting and unexpected adventures en route. Take time to explore the interesting discoveries that will present themselves.

PROCEDURE B: *Fern Frond Rubbings.* Once back indoors, remove the fern fronds collected while scouting out for "A" and distribute one frond to each child. Have the children place a sheet of newsprint over their frond and use crayons or pencils to make a rubbing. Ask them to look closely at the branching patterns of the fern fronds and group those that look similar. Why did they put the rubbings of those fronds together? What is similar about those branching patterns? Use the enlarged copy of Figure 7-4 to elaborate on the different kinds of fern fronds and have the children compare the categories in Figure 7-4 with the fern frond groupings they created. Now have the children match the branching patterns of their fern fronds to those in Figure 7-4. Help the children to hang their rubbings on the wall. You may want them to hang the rubbings in groups according to branching pattern, or you may ask them to simply arrange the rubbings artistically.

Note: A variation on this activity, which works better with older children, is to have them make "fossils" by carefully rubbing aluminum foil over fern fronds to create detailed impressions.

Wetland Wonders

ACTIVITY: (A) Immerse yourself in the rich sensory experience of a wetland. (B) Create a story, illustration or a group poem (older children) using some words that describe the wetland and your experience of it. Through this expression, show your appreciation for the gifts we, and all living things, receive from wetlands.

GOALS: Discover the beauty and wonder of a wetland by using your senses of touch, taste, smell, hearing and sight. Realize how an experience can be recorded and deepened through written and visual arts. Realize that there are different kinds of wetlands and that wetlands are valuable to people, plants and animals. Practice showing appreciation for the gifts of wetlands.

AGE: Younger children and older children

MATERIALS: (A) Waterproof mats to sit on, earth-toned clothes, accessible wetland. (B) "Discussion," pencils, crayons, paper, cardboard backing, Earth-friendly insect repellent.

PROCEDURE A: *Naturalizing.* Naturalizing is an exciting way to experience a natural area from the perspective of being a part of the environment, and not apart from it (Figure 7-8). This technique brings children closer to nature in understanding and empathy, enhances and deepens their experiences in the out-of-doors (Figure 7-8).

Have the children wear inconspicuous, muted earth colors. Choose a wetland you want the children to visit and have each child find a spot where he or she can be comfortable for an extended period of time—next to a tree, in the soft moss, in the sun or shade. If possible, situate the children downwind from the area so their scent will not spook the animals.

Tell the children: "Settle into your place and look around you at the plants, rocks, water and animals while getting to know your spot—this will help you to focus your attention. Sit *quietly* and patiently. Try not to move at all, and if you must, move very slowly and smoothly so that an animal could not see your motion." Have them practice a few simple motions as slowly as they can move. "As you sit, you will notice much about the plants that you did not see at first. The animals will begin to accept you as part of their surroundings. Anything can happen. While you (older children) are sitting still, think of two adjectives to describe your spot, such as 'green' and 'alive.' Remember these words. Return to the spot we are now sitting in when you hear me make this sound." (Demonstrate a bird call or other sound from nature.)

Have younger children sit still for about 10 to 15 minutes depending on their tolerance level for this kind of activity. Older children can handle longer periods of time, perhaps 20 minutes. You may want to conduct this activity at different times with the children seated in these same spots or in different environments. Begin with shorter periods of time and, as children build up a tolerance for sitting perfectly still, increase the length by a few minutes during each subsequent visit. As they improve, the children will see insects, birds and other animals come in close to them, as well as many other things they otherwise would have missed. We have had deer come to within several feet of us and a turtle swim to within 6 inches (15 centimeters) of where we were sitting on a rock wall near a marsh!

PROCEDURE B: *Art of Appreciation.* Ask the children: "What did you like about your visit to the wetland? Do you think wetlands are important to plants and animals and to people? What kinds of things do we use that come from wetlands?" Share the names and descriptions of the different kinds of wetlands, and the values and gifts of wetlands from the "Discussion."

Tell the children they are going to express their appreciation for wetlands by saying thank you in their own, unique way. Have younger children do so by drawing a picture of something they saw while sitting quietly (very young children) or by writing a story (younger children) about an event that happened as they sat at their spot.

Divide the group (older children) into groups of about four children each. Have the children in each group recall, share and record on paper the two words they remember that describe their wetland places. Working in these groups, have the children create a poem using these descriptive words. They may create a poem using just these eight words, or a longer poem using additional words, as long as the original eight words are included. When all poems are

Figure 7-8. Ponds and marshes are beautiful, accessible environments alive with plant and animal life. These places are perfect for sitting quietly and becoming part of one's surroundings. (Photo by Michael J. Caduto)

finished, have someone from each group read their poem to the rest of the group. Remind children that these poems are a showing of appreciation to wetlands. The children can best show their appreciation for the poetry of others by listening and appreciating the poems quietly, without comment.

Butterfly's Choice: Adapt and Survive

ACTIVITY: Play a game of choices to see whether you can adapt to survive the carnivorous plants of the bog.

GOALS: Understand that the individuals that can adapt successfully to the threats found in their environment will survive. Understand the ecology of a bog and that a bog is one kind of wetland. Discover the adaptations of some carnivorous bog plants.

AGE: Younger children and older children

MATERIALS: "Discussion"; copy or copies of *"Butterfly's Choice: Adapt and Survive"*; other materials as needed depending upon the format you use for this activity, such as a game for each child to play individually (each child will need one copy of this activity) or a course that children will walk

through while making the decisions (you will need index cards, each with one of these numbered situations set up as separate stations and any props you may want to add to create a more life-like course for the children to experience); Figure 7-9; "Discussion" from Chapter 6.

PROCEDURE: Use information from the "Discussion" section to review with the children the adaptations of carnivorous bog plants and the reasons that insects are attracted to them (Figure 7-9). Explain what a bog is, what the growing conditions are like in a bog, why bogs contain such nutrient-poor soils for plants, and how some plants have adapted to supplement their diets by taking (fixing) nitrogen directly from the air, by consuming insects and other small animals such as spiders or by existing symbiotically with mycorrhizal fungi (as in the case of the shrub called sweet gale). (See the description of mycorrhizal fungi in the "Discussion" from Chapter 6.)

Insects, including butterflies, are constantly flying around the bog searching for pollen and nectar. The showy petals, colors, patterns and attractive scents of bog flowers and other parts of bog plants serve to attract insects while ensuring that the plants are pollinated to set seeds and reproduce. A few bog plants have developed extraordinary mechanisms that draw insects in and then trap and consume them. Insects are constantly adapting to the bog environ-

Figure 7-9. Three carnivorous bog plants that supplement their nutrient-poor diets with insects and other tiny animals. From left: sundew, Venus' flytrap and pitcher plant. (Photo of the sundew by Alan C. Graham. Photos of the pitcher plant and Venus' flytrap by Michael J. Caduto.)

ment by either landing or not landing on these dangerous plants. Although insects do not "choose" in the same way that human beings do, in order to simplify, this activity refers to the action taken by an insect as a "choice." Sometimes insects make the right choice, adapt successfully and survive, and sometimes they make the wrong choice and perish. Also, the colors described in this story are the colors a human being would see. A butterfly would not necessarily see these flowers as being the same colors, and would actually see many colors and patterns that the human eye would miss.

Have each child read the following story, making choices along the way as he or she thinks a small butterfly might make. Even if a child makes the wrong survival choice at a certain point in the story, he or she is to continue to the next station, and so on, until reaching the end of the story. When all of the children are through, have them share their choices, adaptations and experiences. How many of them *honestly* made *all* of the right choices and were able to make the necessary changes to survive each time? Which choices made it most difficult to make the right survival decisions? Which choices were the easiest?

Note: This activity can also be set up as a fun series of stations in which the initial situation is described and illustrated and children must choose one course or another by turning over a card or lifting up a flap to reveal the consequences of their decision. Then they can move on to the next station to test their wits there.

BUTTERFLY'S CHOICE: ADAPT AND SURVIVE

1. You are a tiny butterfly called a skipper and you are flying around a bog searching for flower nectar to eat. There, below you, growing from the moss is a plant that has pitcher-shaped green leaves with deep purple veins that look like nectar guides *inviting* you to enter for a meal. You flutter down for a closer look, and then you
   a. fly off in another direction to look elsewhere for a meal.
   b. follow the veins guiding you into the opening where there might be some nectar.

If you chose (a) you survived. If you chose (b) you landed on a pitcher plant and found there really was no nectar. You tried to turn around but could not get out of the pitcher because stiff hairs were everywhere, forcing you to go deeper. Sticky cells from the inside walls of the pitcher kept sticking to your feet, making it even harder to escape. You finally fell into the water at the bottom of the pitcher, drowned and became a meal yourself.

2. Now you spot a small pinkish-magenta flower that looks like it is a delicious source of sweet nectar. You feel a very strong desire to visit this flower, and you decide to
   a. drop in for a sip of sweet nectar.
   b. keep flying to look for a bigger flower to feed on.

If you chose (a) you had a pick-me-up sip of nectar from the *Calopogon* orchid and gathered more energy for your journey. You survived. If you chose (b) you missed out on a small meal. You survived but are beginning to tire and need some energy soon.

3. Flying low, you spot a flat green platform that looks like a good place to rest for a while in the sunlight before continuing your search for nectar. Then you

a. land on the flat place because you have not eaten in a while and are tired.

b. keep going because the meal you just had gave you plenty of energy to fly on.

If you chose (a) you found out, too late, that the flat green plant is really the open leaf of a Venus' flytrap. Before you can escape, the two sides of the leaf quickly snap shut around you in a tooth-edged trap. You are consumed by the plant and do not survive. If you chose (b) you survived.

4. It is getting late in the afternoon and you are searching for a few last sips of nectar before nightfall. You see the red glow of sunset reflecting off some beads of liquid stuck on the ends of the hairs of a small plant growing close to the ground up ahead. The beads look like round drops of dew or nectar waiting to be sipped up by your long mouth. You decide to

a. stop off for a sip of that irresistible nectar.

b. keep going because you do not see any place to land on while sipping the nectar.

If you chose (a) you became hopelessly stuck on the sticky drops of a sundew plant. Slowly, as you struggled to get free, the hairs bent over and pulled you in to be digested. You are a goner. If you chose (b) you survived.

5. Suddenly, a small bird with a golden cap darts out from a bush and heads straight for you. You react very quickly by

a. dropping quickly and landing on the petal of a flower.

b. flying very fast and darting to get away from the bird.

If you chose (a) you managed to camouflage yourself and the bird flies away. You survived. If you chose (b) you could not possibly outfly a golden-crowned kinglet, which brought you back to its nest to feed its young. You did not survive.

6. If you have successfully survived by making all of the right choices so far, you will mate with another butterfly and a new generation will be born when your eggs hatch.

Greenhouse Effect

ACTIVITY: (A) Conduct a demonstration of the greenhouse effect. (B) Discuss, choose and practice conservation measures needed to reduce the creation of greenhouse gases that contribute to global warming and to reduce the consumption of fossil fuels.

GOALS: Understand the process by which increased concentration of certain atmospheric "greenhouse" gases is causing global warming. Discover and practice conservation measures by which the rate of increase in atmospheric levels of greenhouse gases can be slowed down, and that will reduce the consumption of fossil fuels. Understand that sacrifices need to be made to be good Earth stewards.

AGE: Younger children and older children

MATERIALS: (A) "Discussion" from this chapter; sunny window sill; clock or watch; chalkboard and chalk or newsprint and markers; and for each small group of children, one wide-mouthed glass jar, two identical thermometers capable of fitting inside the glass jar and a piece of natural-colored cardboard. (B) Chalkboard and chalk or newsprint and marker, "Discussion," pencils, journals, materials as needed for specific conservation measures chosen by the children.

PROCEDURE A: *Greenhouse Glasses.* Use the "Discussion" to describe the greenhouse effect. Ask some questions: What is the greenhouse effect? What causes it? How does it contribute to global warming, and what are the consequences if global warming continues at the rate that it now seems to be going? Lead a brief question-and-answer period to find out what the children know about fossil fuels and the environmental problems associated with their use. Share the information from the "Discussion" about the ancient origins of fossil fuels from diatoms and giant prehistoric ancestors of ferns, clubmosses and horsetails.

Tell the children they are going to demonstrate how the increased levels of atmospheric greenhouse gases act like a greenhouse to increase global temperature. Pass out to each small group one wide-mouthed gallon glass jar and two identical thermometers that show the same reading at room temperature. The thermometers must be small enough so one of them can fit completely inside the glass jar. Explain that, in this experiment, the glass jar will represent the increasing levels of greenhouse gases that are causing global warming.

Have the children take and record an initial reading from the thermometers. Each group will then place a piece of cardboard on a window sill that is directly exposed to bright sunlight. The cardboard will ensure that both thermometers are resting on a background of similar color and composition so the temperature readings are not affected by differing backgrounds. Now instruct children to place the glass jar over one of the thermometers, which will stand right-side-up inside the jar and facing the sun. Have the children place the other thermometer right-side-up on the cardboard. *At this time children find it interesting to predict the temperature change that will occur during the experiment.*

After about 15 minutes have elapsed, have the children take readings from both of the thermometers they set out. Each group will now share these two readings as you record them where all can see the figures. Take an overall average of the two readings. How do the findings compare with the children's predictions?

If the uncovered thermometer represents Earth's temperature without the effect of global warming from high levels of greenhouse gases, and the jar represents these gases we are creating, then what does this experiment tell the children? Point out to the group that this is just a simulation and that the temperature difference between the two readings is extreme as compared to what is happening in the atmosphere. Share with the group the information from the "Discussion" regarding the predictions for the rate of global warming between now and the mid-2000s.

PROCEDURE B: *Taking the Heat Off.* Ask the children to think of specific things they can do to reduce their personal contribution to greenhouse gases and global warming, as well as to cut back on their consumption of fossil fuels. List these suggestions up front for all to see. Now review the conservation measures listed at the end of the "Discussion." Add any of the "Discussion" ideas that the children missed to their own list. Praise them for the ideas they thought of that are not listed in the "Discussion."

Have each child pick two things she or he is willing to do from the complete list of conservation measures: one that will help to slow global warming and one that will reduce the use of fossil fuels. A number of things on the list will accomplish both of these objectives at once, but, for the sake of focusing on these two related but separate problems, the children will make a commitment to take two conservation measures. Instruct the children to practice these two conservation measures conscientiously for one week, keeping a log of notes and/or illustrations describing what the experience is like. At the end of the week, have each child, in words and/or pictures, tell the story of how his or her life was affected by making some sacrifices to reduce the greenhouse effect and the use of fossil fuels. Ask them to describe in the story how it is challenging to take these conservation measures as well as how it makes them feel to know they are doing something to take care of Earth.

EXTENDING THE EXPERIENCE

• Grow your own ferns and mosses. Moisten and fill a clay pot with damp peat moss, and then place it upside-down under a glass jar in a window. Gather spores from familiar ferns and mosses in your area and sprinkle them over the surface of the inverted clay pot. In a few weeks the spores will begin to germinate. Soon the young ferns and mosses can be transplanted into terraria or pots with soil, whichever habitat best approximates the plant's natural home.

• Hold a wetland festival: serve meals and feature things around the home or learning center that came from wetlands. Include products from wetland plants such as blueberries, cranberries and wild rice. Celebrate the things we do in wetlands, for example swimming, canoeing, skating and fishing, as well as the values of wetlands, such as their role in flood control and as nursery areas for fish. Brainstorm the children's ideas of other wetland gifts. Additional gifts from wetlands are listed at the end of the "Discussion." Have children think of and practice ways to say "thank you" to wetlands.

• Send for *CO₂ Diet for a Greenhouse Planet: A Citizen's Guide for Slowing Global Warming* from the National Audubon Society, 700 Broadway, New York, NY 10003-9562.

• Set up a terrarium of mosses and small ferns to observe.

• Adapt the activity *"Birth of a Forest"* in Chapter 8 to look at ecological succession in a wetland.

• Obtain some magician's dust from a supply store or catalog. This dust is made of the spores of clubmosses. Use a candle and a small sprinkling of this dust hidden in your hand to create the dramatic flash that magicians use to make things "appear" and "disappear."

• Conduct a role-playing, conflict resolution activity focusing on whether to preserve or develop a wetland. Find a local wetland for which this is a real, ongoing conflict in your community. Take on the roles of the developer, town and state or provincial environmental and regulatory officials, members of a few local conservation groups, expert wetland ecologists, abutting property owners, etc. Each group will research the issues, pro and con; organize their ideas on paper; and make a presentation at a mock public hearing designed to decide whether or not to develop this wetland. Assign several members of the group to be the moderators and legal representatives of the state or province who will conduct the meeting and, when it has concluded, decide whether or not to issue a permit to develop.

• Map the wetlands near your home from topographic maps. Take some field trips to explore the wetlands you find on the maps.

• Design and create your own giant carnivorous bog plants out of papier-mâché!

• See the information and activities on energy in Chapter 6 of *Keepers of the Earth.*

NOTES

1. Michael J. Caduto, *Pond and Brook: A Guide to Nature in Freshwater Environments* (Hanover, N.H., and London: University Press of New England), 217.

2. P. V. Glob, *The Bog People* (London: Paladin, 1971), 142.

3. William A. Niering, "Endangered, Threatened and Rare Wetland Plants and Animals of the Continental United States," *National Wetlands Newsletter* (May–June 1987): 16–19.

4. Ralph W. Tiner, Jr., *Wetlands of the United States: Current Status and Recent Trends* (Washington, D.C.: U.S. Government Printing Office, 1984).

5. Ibid.

6. Norman Myers, *The Gaia Atlas of Future Worlds* (New York: Anchor, 1990), 72.

7. Ibid.

The first night passed and all of the animals and plants stayed awake.

CHAPTER 8

✤ Why Some Trees Are Always Green ✤

(Cherokee—Southeast)

When the plants and animals were first made, they were told to watch and stay awake for seven nights. All of the animals and plants wished to do this. They knew if they did not sleep, they would be given some special sort of power.

The first night passed and all of the animals and plants stayed awake. It did not seem hard to them and some of the animals and plants even began to boast about how easy it was.

When the second night came, it no longer seemed so easy for all of them and some found it very hard not to fall asleep. When the next night came, some of them could stay awake no longer, and by the fourth night, nearly all of them slept.

When the seventh night ended, only a few had stayed awake. Among the animals, only the panther and the owl had not slept. So they were given the power to see in the dark. From then on, the panther and the owl would be able to prey on those animals which had failed to remain awake and watchful and now must sleep each night.

Among the plants, only the pine, the spruce, the hemlock, the cedar, the laurel and the holly had remained awake and watchful. Because they were faithful, they were given the power to remain green all year around, and their leaves would hold great medicine. But all of the other plants would have to lose their leaves each winter because they did not endure the test. Not only that, but they would also have to fall asleep until the warmth of spring came again.

So it is that to this day when young men go out to fast on a hill and pray for their medicine, they remind themselves they must stay awake like the cedar and the spruce and the pine. They must look into the dark with the vigilant eyes of the panther and the owl. For great medicine never comes to those who are not watchful.

DISCUSSION

Evergreen plants become an example of wakefulness and vigilance in the Cherokee story "Why Some Trees Are Always Green." As a reward for remaining watchful for seven nights, the leaves of the pine, spruce, hemlock, cedar, laurel and holly are made to be green year-round and to contain powerful medicine. In Native North American cultures, medicine means more than merely a substance that can help to cure a physical ailment. *Medicine* refers to a person's source of power and healing—physical, emotional and spiritual—and is often symbolized by a particular plant or animal. When the now evergreen leaves of these plants, along with the panther and the owl, receive "great medicine," they are given a great gift indeed.

In addition to their place in the oral tradition of the Cherokee, whose traditional name, *Aniyunwiya*, means "real people," evergreens have long held a position of great honor among many Native North American cultures. Among the nations of the Haudenosaunee (Iroquois), a great white pine was planted long ago to safeguard the League of Peace. This Tree of Peace is known by the Onondaga as Tsioneratisekowa. Many a person has sought solace and healing in the midst of the calming quiet of a grove of pine, spruce, hemlock or cedar. In the quiet, there is great strength to be found.

Silence is the absolute poise or balance of body, mind and spirit … Silence is the cornerstone of character.[1]
—Ohiyesa (Charles Alexander Eastman)
Santee Dakota (Sioux)

Often in the presence of evergreens, the only sound is the wind through the boughs of needles. Here a person can seek a deeper level of attunement with nature and, in so doing, come to a greater clarity of mind.

Gymnosperms

With the exception of a few species, gymnosperms (conifers and related woody plants) appear to be "ever green." Evergreen *needles,* which are special kinds of leaves, do eventually fall off, but they remain on the tree for two to four growing seasons in most cases. There are always some green leaves present on these plants because only the oldest ones fall off each year. The needles of bristlecone pines may last for up to 20 years.

Gymnosperms ("naked seeds") include the ginkgoes (only one species survives), cycads, gnetophytes and conifers. Conifers—members of the pine and spruce families—are the earliest seed plants whose descendants are still alive today. The first gymnosperms evolved more than 300 million years ago, and this group of plants dominated the landscape around 250 to 270 million years ago. Modern gymnosperms have changed little since they first evolved.

REPRODUCTION. Earlier plants relied on water to moderate their habitat, to provide a means of protecting eggs and keeping sperm from drying out and to allow sperm to swim to the egg. Without an abundance of water, algae, mosses and ferns could not reproduce. Gymnosperms, however, developed internal fertilization as well as seeds that are better suited to the extremes of temperature and moisture found on dry land. Seeds liberated gymnosperms from the need for an aquatic environment or damp earth to reproduce. *Seeds* are more successful than the spores described in earlier chapters because they contain a source of nourishment, an embryo and a protective *seed coat.* All gymnosperms and flowering plants (see Chapter 9) produce seeds.

GINKGOES. The *ginkgo* or *maidenhair tree* has the oldest fossil record of all living plants and is the only surviving species in this group. Individual ginkgo trees are either male or female. Ginkgoes have fan-shaped, deciduous leaves in which the veins radiate out from the leaf stalk. These trees are famous for their habit of losing their entire crown of leaves within 24 hours following the first hard frost of the year. Be careful when sampling these colorful ginkgo leaves, however, as the yellow, fleshy seeds that lay among the leaves give off a foul odor when squashed. Ginkgoes are often planted in urban and suburban parks and other green pockets.

CYCADS. Primitive in appearance, the *cycads* bear large, fern-like leaves in a whorl atop the trunk reminiscent of the branching of a palm tree. Cycad trees, which are either male or female, along with ginkgoes, are the only seed plants in which the sperm actually swims toward the egg during fertilization. Most species of cycad are tropical.

GNETOPHYTES. Although these unusual plants may not share a common ancestry with other gymnosperms, they are often grouped in with them. *Gnetophytes* produce cones bearing sterile, leaf-like *bracts.* This combination of fertile and sterile structures is characteristic of flowering plants. One species from this group, *Ephedra,* is found in deserts of the world, including those in southwestern North America.

CONIFERS. Distinctive needle-like leaves and bold profiles formed by profuse branching distinguish the well-known *conifers* such as pine, spruce, redwood, fir, cedar and hemlock. Some individual conifers are among the oldest and largest living things on Earth. Massive giant sequoias growing on the western slopes of California's Sierra Nevada are up to 3,500 years old. The largest of these gargantuans tops off at more than 275 feet (83.8 meters) tall and exceeds 40 feet (12.2 meters) in diameter! At up to 2 feet (.6 meter) thick, sequoia bark is nearly fireproof. Heavy resins that permeate the bark make it virtually immune to insects. These magnificent trees, which were named for the Cherokee Chief Sequoia, who invented the Cherokee alphabet, do not start to produce their tiny, pinhead-size seeds until at least 70 years old and are not mature until they have lived for 300 years. Also a kind of sequoia, the California redwoods of the Pacific coastal fog-belt forests, at up to 367 feet (112 meters) in height, are the tallest trees in existence. From Death

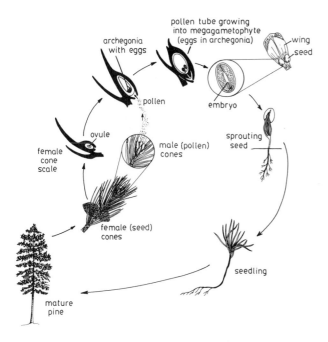

Figure 8-1. The life cycle of a pine. Male pollen cones *produce billions of* pollen grains, *which are carried by the wind to female* seed cones. *Each scale on the female seed cones bears two* ovules. *At the time of pollination, the scales on the female cones open slightly and pollen sticks to drops of sap found on the tips of the ovules. Pollen is pulled into the ovules when the pollination drops dry out. Then the scales close tight. Over the course of the summer and fall* pollen tubes *digest their way toward the developing female cells. Sperm cells fertilize the eggs the following spring. During the second summer the fertile eggs grow into* embryos, *each of which is surrounded by nutritive tissue enclosed in a seed coat. By late summer, when the cones open up, two mature, winged seeds are shed by each cone scale and dispersed by the wind.*

Valley to the high elevations of nearby mountain ranges and the slopes of California's White Mountains grow the bristlecone pines, among the oldest living things in the world. Some individuals have been catching the sun's energy for more than 4,000 years. Through *dendrochronology,* the study of the annual rings of ancient trees, variations of growth in these ancients record climatic fluctuations of temperature and rainfall over several millennia.

Each group and species within the conifers exhibits its own, unique variation on the process of **reproduction.** The life cycle of a pine is one example (Figure 8-1). Pines have separate male and female cones. A *cone* is a reproductive structure made of specialized, closely fitting *scales* arranged in a spiral pattern. Cones come in many different shapes and sizes. Pinecones take two growing seasons to mature and produce seeds.

When most people are asked to say what defines a conifer, they refer to cones and needles. Virtually all conifers are evergreen except for the larch (tamarack) and bald cypress, which are *deciduous*—they lose their leaves every autumn and grow new ones in the spring. *Needles* are true

leaves that possess the same adaptations for saving water as broad leaves: a water-retaining *cuticle* covering and *stomata* ("little mouths") or pores on the underside of the leaf that control the loss of water and exchange of gases (carbon dioxide and oxygen). A wax-coated, lacquer-like, virtually waterproof layer forms the covering of needles. Even during the winter months, when deciduous trees have dropped their leaves, as long as the temperature is above freezing needles continue to photosynthesize and transpire at a reduced rate. At a few degrees below freezing this activity ceases.

One of the most intriguing and universal patterns in nature can be found in the arrangement of scales on a cone. Scales form in spiral patterns around the stem with particular numbers of scales contained in each spiral (Figure 8-2). Similar patterns and numbers can be observed throughout the natural world in spirals found among the seedheads of sunflowers and daisies, flower-bud scales, flower-petal arrangements, artichoke leaves, the growth patterns among palm-tree leaves and pineapple fruits; in the geometric patterns of snowflakes, spider webs, horns of wild sheep, the

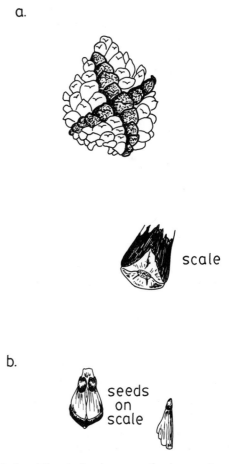

Figure 8-2. **a.** *The spiral arrangement of scales on a pine cone is one example of the Fibonacci sequence. The vertical shading marks 1 of 13 parallel rows of scales spiraling steeply around the cone. The mostly horizontal shading shows 1 of 8 parallel rows of scales spiraling gradually.* **b.** *Some cone seeds.*

shell of the chambered nautilus and in countless other examples.[2] All of these numbers, it turns out, are part of the *Fibonacci sequence* discovered by a mathematician living in Pisa, Italy, 800 years ago. Fibonacci numbers are based on similar patterns of helical growth.[3] Calculating Fibonacci numbers is accomplished by starting with the number 1 and arriving at each subsequent number by adding the value of the last number in the sequence to the one that precedes it. The sequence is 1, 1, 2, 3, 5, 8, 13, 21, 34, 55 and so on. Pine needles always occur in bundles or *fassicles* of 2, 3 or 5—more Fibonacci numbers. These numbers also show up repeatedly in art, architecture, poetic verse, music, science and technology. The pentagon is a common Fibonacci number in nature, appearing in the number of arms on a sea star, the pattern found on a sand dollar and in the flowers and fruits of plants in the rose family, such as apples. Slice an apple in half horizontally to see the star-shaped arrangement of seed chambers.

Trees

There are about 750 species of trees in North America, ranging from the tiny pawpaw to giant redwoods. Although each kind of tree has a certain appearance, trees are individuals: there is a tremendous variety within and among species. Tree watching is one of our favorite pastimes; looking closely at such characteristics as silhouette, bark texture, growing site, branching pattern and the appearance of flowers, leaves and buds. Whether pine, maple, cedar, aspen or fir, every species of tree has a branching pattern that creates a distinct *silhouette*. Tree profiles are beautiful to observe and they provide a strong clue for identifying each species.

PARTS OF A TREE. Here is a look at the parts of a tree (Figure 8-3) and how they function to move the sap and keep the tree alive, growing and healthy:

• *Roots* anchor the tree in addition to absorbing water and minerals from the soil. A growing root that is 4 inches (10.2 centimeters) in diameter and 3 feet (.9 meter) long can exert 50 tons (45.4 metric tons) of pressure.

• *Leaves* (broad leaves and needles) use sunlight to create food for the tree via photosynthesis (see "Discussion" in Chapter 5 for details about photosynthesis).

• *Branches* hold the leaves aloft in patterns that allow them to intercept sunlight efficiently. Branches also bear flowers and fruit and aid in seed dispersal.

• *Trunks* provide support and act as pipelines to carry water and nutrients to the parts of the tree. Figure 8-3 shows the major trunk layers, whose functions are described below, moving from the outside to the inside:

　＊ *Outer bark* is what we see covering the trunk and branches. It protects the tree from disease, fire and injury.

　＊ *Inner bark,* or *phloem,* carries sap—which is rich in sugars made in the leaves as well as minerals—down from the leaves to the branches, trunk and roots. Phloem can also bring stored sugar up from the roots when it is needed.

　＊ *Cambium* is a layer that is one cell thick. Each year it produces new phloem to the outside, sapwood to the inside and new cambium. Branches, trunks and roots grow in thickness as a result of cambium growth.

　＊ *Xylem,* or *wood,* makes up the bulk of the tree and provides mechanical support for the trunk, roots and branches. Just inside the cambium is the new xylem called *sapwood,* which carries minerals and water up from the roots to the rest of the tree. To the inside of sapwood is old xylem, called *heartwood,* which mainly provides support for the tree. Heartwood is older, dead sapwood that is usually darker and can no longer carry minerals and water up from the roots. Since it is dead, heartwood can rot away to leave a hollow tree with only a sleeve of living wood on the outside. Many conifers contain *resin* in their tissues, which makes the wood resistant to insect damage, moisture and decay.

The yearly cycle of tree growth forms distinct layers of xylem that appear in cross-section as *annual rings.* The inner, lighter-colored part of each annual ring, called *springwood,* forms during the spring when water is usually abundant and thus growth is rapid. Springwood has larger cells and is less dense than the darker *summerwood,* which forms later in the growing season when water is often in short supply, causing the tree to grow more slowly. Annual rings can be counted to determine the approximate age of a tree.

A common question is, "How can a tree move water up the great length and height of its trunk?" In some trees water can rise 150 feet (45.7 meters) per hour, and in coast redwoods water travels more than 450 feet (137 meters) from root tips to the highest leaves. While the movement of water to the tops of trees is not fully understood, it is thought that water absorbed by roots is drawn up the tree by two forces. 1. Evaporation from leaf surfaces, called *transpiration,* draws water upward in the vessels of the wood. Water evaporates at the top and more water replaces it from below. Since there is a strong *cohesion* among water molecules—they have a strong attraction for one another—a pull at the top of the column of water in a tree moves the entire column upward. 2. *Capillary action*—which can be observed by how water moves up the end of a thin straw—also plays a role in transporting water up the conducting vessels found in wood. These forces, working together, can exert an upward pull of 100 times the force of the atmospheric pressure, or 1,470 pounds per square inch (103.4 kilograms per square centimeter).

Because the leaves of trees do not absorb moisture, water must be obtained by roots from the soil. Transpiration accounts for the loss of up to 99 percent of the water absorbed by roots. On a hot day, the roots of one birch tree can take in up to 400 quarts (378.8 liters) of water. Miles of thin

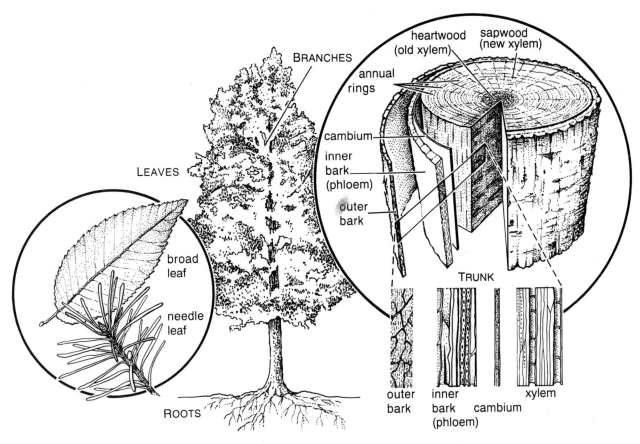

Figure 8-3. The parts of a tree: leaves, branches, trunk and roots. (Illustration by Marjorie C. Leggitt)

rootlets branch off the main roots, which are in turn covered by numerous *root hairs* that take up minerals and water from the soil. One rye plant was found to have 14 billion root hairs in its rootlets, totaling 6,600 miles (10,621.7 kilometers) in length, nearly enough to reach across Earth from pole to pole. Rootlets grow toward soils that are moist and rich in nutrients.

The following true story provides a good example of a root seeking and using nutrients in the soil. During the 1800s, when the State of Rhode Island was moving the remains of its founder, Roger Williams, to place the remains in a new commemorative park overlooking the city, workers found that the root of a nearby apple tree had grown down and followed the exact location of where the body had been. The root reached the place where the head was, made a 90-degree turn along the axis of the body (long since decomposed), forked at the hips along the path of each leg (one branch formed a crook at a knee) and turned up at each heel to follow the axis of the feet.[4]

The Coniferous Forests

A boreal chickadee calls from a balsam fir, filling the northern forest with bright song. Looking for the singer, you notice tufts of old-man's-beard lichen hanging from the branches of a black spruce, each growth looking like a tiny set of elfin whiskers. In the branches of a larch a red crossbill cracks open some cones in search of a seed meal. Farther along, the trail is flooded by water backed up behind a freshly constructed beaver dam. Several of the quaking aspens and American white (paper) birches surrounding the newly formed pond have been toppled into the water by these industrious rodents. The notes of a flock of gray jays ring out from a grove of white pines on a rise nearby. You hold a handful of bread scraps left over from lunch out at arm's length and a gray jay fleetly swoops down and picks one off; the weight of the bird is surprising in your outstretched hand. Working your way over the beaver dam and then through a mucky section of trail covered with *Sphagnum* moss, you continue up the trail past some white spruce and into a dry clearing where a stand of balsam poplar fills the air with a spicy, aromatic scent.

This, the *boreal coniferous forest* biome located south of the tundra, stretches like a 400- to 800-mile- (644- to 1,287-kilometer-) wide belt across Canada and Alaska, dipping its fingers south along the high mountain ridges. Some other trees of the boreal forest are the willow, hemlock and cedar. Moose and woodland caribou inhabit much of this range, with mule deer found in the western states, provinces and territories. The cold-resistant evergreens growing here are well adapted to the available levels of light, temperature, water and soil minerals. Trees require at least 14 consecutive frost-free weeks and 15 to 20 inches (38.1 to 50.8 centimeters) of rain each year.

There are other, magnificent coniferous forests found in North America. The *Pacific coast forest* stretches from the west coast of Alaska south to California. In some parts of these forests, where the moisture-laden coastal air rises, cools and drops its moisture, more than 12 feet (3.7 meters) of rain and snow fall each year. Spruce, hemlock and cedar forests abound in northern British Columbia. Farther south are stands of Douglas fir, western red cedar and western hemlock, with Sitka spruce and hemlock growing along the coast in the frequently foggy air. Douglas fir is the dominant tree in Oregon's Willamette Valley, stretching from the coast to the ridges of the Cascades. Along the California–Oregon border is a *mixed evergreen forest* in the Siskiyou and Klamath mountains. Nowhere else in the world is there a more diverse coniferous forest. Here can be found Pacific yew and Douglas fir, Port-Orford cedar, incense cedar and sugar pine. Broadleaf trees in this forest include the Oregon oak, madrone and tanoak. Redwoods tower farther south in the *coastal fog-belt forests* of California. Each year in the *redwood forests* of northern California (see Figure 8–5), especially during the dry summer months, 7 to 12 inches (17.8 to 30.5 centimeters) of fog condenses onto the needles of tall trees and falls to the forest floor, adding significantly to the annual rainfall. This *fog drip* was found to account for 35 percent of the total rainfall in one region of Oregon's forest. Finally, in California's Sierra Nevada amid the mixed forest of cedars, pines and firs are small patches of the giant sequoias, sentinels of time.

About 800 miles (1,287 kilometers) to the east, in the *Rocky Mountains* ranging from Canada to Mexico, much of the coniferous forest consists of ponderosa pine, Englemann spruce, white fir and larch. Farthest east, the *boreal forest of Canada* runs through New England and farther south along the spine of the Appalachian Mountains: spruce, fir, larch, pine, hemlock and northern white cedar. At one time, before they were cut down, the crowns of giant white pine trees vaulted more than 200 feet (61 meters) above the forest floor. Southern pines, including longleaf, loblolly, shortleaf, pitch and slash pines, inhabit the sandy soils of the *Atlantic coastal plain.*

The changes in forest type found while traveling from south to north can be experienced moving from the lower to higher elevations in mountain ranges. A climb of 1,000 feet in altitude is roughly equivalent to traveling 300 miles closer to the nearest pole or every 300-meter climb in altitude is roughly equivalent to traveling 475 kilometers toward the nearest pole. Vegetation in the foothills of the Rocky Mountains, for example, up to about 4,000 feet (1,219 meters) where there is little rain, consists of grasses, flowers and sagebrush. Farther up the slope, through piñon pine, alder and willow, the *transition zone* begins at about

6,000 feet (1,829 meters). Here, ponderosa pine and juniper grow where rain is more plentiful. The *montane zone* starts at about 8,000 feet (2,438 meters), where Douglas fir forms dense crowns with narrow tops that afford less resistance to strong winds. Englemann spruce and alpine fir are the dominant trees at roughly 10,000 feet (3,048 meters) in the *subalpine zone.* Due to high winds, cold temperatures and the effects of snow and rain, growing conditions are so extreme in the *alpine zone* at 11,500 feet (3,505 meters) that short, stunted, twisted trees of fir, spruce and willow, which may be only several inches tall, are actually hundreds of years old. Only a few rock-hugging lichens and snow-dwelling algae can survive on the very tops of the mountains.

FOREST ECOLOGY. Spruce and fir are the dominant trees in the mature boreal forest community—the association of plants and animals that tend to establish and perpetuate themselves over time. But change is part of the natural order (Figure 8-4). If this community is disturbed by fire, logging or damage from insects or diseases, wildflowers and other herbs soon begin to grow in the new clearing. Brambles and shrubs follow, and then quaking aspen and balsam poplar frequently appear. Where the clearing was once sunny and the top layer of soil warm and often fairly dry, the new plants provide increasing shade, humidity and cooler temperatures. The soil becomes more aerated and drainage improves. Humus and plant remains lend a sponginess to the soil. The nature of soil microorganisms changes along with soil conditions. Soils created by the remains of coniferous trees tend to be acid and support a community of fungi, herbs (ferns, mosses and wildflowers), vines and shrubs that tolerate these conditions. Insects, birds and other kinds of animals can be found here that are associated with each stage of community development and, finally, the mature forest itself. During the process of ecological succession, where soil is present, which is sometimes called *secondary succession,*

Figure 8-4. From clearing to forest: ecological or secondary succession. This illustration shows that over time (from left to right), a forest clearing grows through a series of stages to become a mature forest. The development of a boreal forest is shown here. Natural or human disturbances can create new forest clearings and succession will begin again.

plants and other organisms change as their environment changes. (See the "Discussion" in Chapter 7 for a definition of and detailed look at ecological succession.)

Lightning is the major cause of natural fires that set back the forest community to an earlier stage of succession. The destruction caused by a forest fire is not as dire as it may seem at first glance. Even during a raging blaze, soil temperatures will not exceed 212°F (100°C) until all of the water has evaporated, so the underground parts of many plants survive the fire. Fire makes nutrients more available to surviving plants and those that soon sprout amid the ashes. Many plants that inhabit grasslands, as well as certain trees, *need* fire to germinate. The cones of jack pine will not release their seeds until a fire has heated them to at least 150°F (65.6°C). In addition, the seedlings require a ground fire to burn away all needles, which contain an oil that kills the young plants. Ground fires also open up the cones and release the seeds of the lodgepole pine.

Just as environmental conditions such as soil type, rainfall, sunlight intensity and slope determine which plants will grow in a particular location, so do plants alter their environment as they grow. Gradually the forest develops distinct layers, including the soil, forest floor, herbs, shrubs, young trees, old trees and the air over the forest canopy. The roots of fallen trees thrust large piles of rock and soil upward, leaving behind a hole where the tree was rooted. Over the years, as the roots decompose, a pile of soil and rock remains next to the hole, forming hummocks and hollows on the forest floor. Animals live in every forest niche, such as leaves, trunks, bark, branches and soil, and share the available space, water and food in the web of forest life.

State of the Coniferous Forests

Most of the old-growth or virgin forest has been cut throughout North America, but a look at the state of the old-growth forest of the Pacific Northwest, which is still being cut, is revealing. Sixty percent of British Columbia's old-growth forest is gone. At present rates of cutting—1.5 square miles (3.9 square kilometers) per day—it will be nearly wiped out by the year 2020. Less than 10 percent of the original old-growth forest is left in Oregon and Washington, and half of this is so fragmented and ecologically bereft that it cannot support the characteristic plant and animal communities of the old-growth forest. Ninety-two percent of California's coastal redwoods have been cleared to date. The 16.9-million-acre (6.8-million-hectare) Tongass National Forest of the Alaska panhandle is one of the few wild areas that still contains large tracts of unbroken old-growth forest. It is home to grizzly bears, Sitka black-tailed deer and salmon. Yet only 10 percent of this wilderness is protected and the rest is quickly being cut in an operation that is heavily subsidized by the federal government.

THREATS TO THE FOREST. *Clear-cutting,* during which all trees in an area are cut down, is the most common commercial forestry practice. Large clear-cut areas do not allow for adequate natural reseeding because few or no seed trees are left to produce and disperse seeds and because the open areas are too large for successful reseeding from neighboring tracts of forest. In 1988 about 2.5 million acres (1 million hectares) of forests were clear-cut in Canada. Roughly 40 percent of these clear-cut areas were replanted; the remaining clearings were left to regenerate naturally. Twenty percent—about half a million acres (200,000 hectares)—did not regenerate successfully. Clear-cuts are usually replanted to a few species of trees, usually pines, spruces and fir, creating areas that are of a lower species diversity than a natural forest. Clear-cutting also removes the best trees and leaves behind those that are of lesser quality, physically and genetically. Because clear-cutting so completely removes the vegetative cover from an area, other environmental problems result, including erosion and pollution of waterways. Silt that washes into streams and rivers covers the gills of fish as well as fish eggs, suffocating both. With shade removed from riverbanks, water temperature increases above that tolerable by many cold-water species of insects and the fish that feed on them, such as trout and salmon. The nutrients that wash into waterways with the soil can overfertilize ecosystems and cause eutrophication. (See the "Discussion" in Chapter 5 for a description of eutrophication.)

On a larger scale, forests play a major role in moderating global climate because they cover such a large percentage of Earth's surface. Forest vegetation absorbs a tremendous amount of the sun's radiant energy. When forests are cut down, more solar radiation is reflected back into the atmosphere. Plants and plant roots intercept significant amounts of rainfall and green leaves release much water into the air. Removing the trees decreases atmospheric humidity in an area.

Logging operations are not the only threats to forest health. Fires caused by both lightning and arson destroy vast regions of forest every year. Because of the devastation caused by fires, a debate rages among ecologists and foresters as to whether it is ecologically in the best interest of forested areas to allow natural fires to burn periodically or to extinguish fires as they occur.

Native and introduced diseases and insects have virtually eliminated entire species of trees from North America, such as the Dutch elm disease that infects the American elm, the chestnut blight on American chestnut and the gypsy moth caterpillar that defoliates entire regions of oak forest. Native insects and diseases also take their toll. Millions of acres of boreal forest across North America experience massive periodic outbreaks of the spruce budworm, a small caterpillar that defoliates evergreens such as balsam fir, white spruce and black spruce. The budworm also damages the Douglas fir forests of British Columbia and the western United States. Frequently, loggers move in directly behind the budworm and remove the dead trees as quickly as possible while the wood is still sound. Insecticides have been heavily used to control the budworm in many areas.

Air pollution continues to threaten the survival and well-being of many large tracts of forest. Acid precipitation turns rainwater into a powerful leaching agent. It can leach nutrients from leaves and can damage the waxy coating on evergreen needles, causing them to lose water and wither. Botanists at the University of Vermont in Burlington concluded that acid rain is implicated in the death of 50 percent of the spruce trees on Camel's Hump, a picturesque peak in the Green Mountains of Vermont, since 1965. The growth of living spruces has been stunted by one-half.[5,6] Acid rain also leaches toxic metals, such as aluminum, out of soils and into solution, where they are absorbed by roots and cause damage to trees. In addition, rime ice deposits toxic heavy metals such as cadmium, copper, lead and zinc.[7] Ozone pollution, a byproduct of exhaust emitted by trucks, planes and automobiles, especially those with high-compression engines, is causing decline and death among the trees in the San Gabriel Mountains outside Los Angeles.[8] As a result of this smog, among the ponderosa pines and Jeffrey pines of the San Bernardino National Forest, needles are dying back, growth is decreasing, vigor is declining and tree crowns are becoming thin and yellowish. Ironically, the thinning of the ozone layer in the upper atmosphere caused by CFCs and other chemicals (see Chapter 14), which allows more of the sun's harmful ultraviolet radiation to reach Earth's surface, is also decreasing the natural vigor of both plants and animals. Many ecologists believe that drought cycles, native insects and diseases have, in recent years, had a far more negative impact on forest trees than in earlier times because the trees' resistance is already weakened by air pollution such as acid rain as well as by the effects of ozone depletion in the upper atmosphere. The combination of these factors may well be *synergistic*, which means the overall effect is greater than the sum of the impact of each individual factor. Other kinds of air pollution that cause harm to forests include those generated by smelting operations, industrial emissions, fire (arson) and warfare.

Development in mountainous regions, such as ski slopes and accompanying resort communities, is also having large-scale impacts. Ski areas disrupt fragile alpine environments, impinge on scenic views and, through extensive snow-making operations, degrade aquatic ecosystems. Winter water levels in nearby waterways are often significantly reduced when water is siphoned off for snow-making. Spring runoff from ski slopes also frequently creates siltation problems in aquatic ecosystems downstream.

Forest Stewardship

If managed properly, forests are a renewable resource that will allow us to live off of the sustainable growth they generate while not cutting into the essential stock of growing trees themselves. There are many alternatives to clear-cutting.

Selective cutting removes certain individual trees for harvest while leaving plenty of seed trees as well as a mixed-age stand of trees to perpetuate the forest. Cable systems of logging, by which the trees are cut and removed from the forest while suspended by steel cables, greatly decrease the impact of equipment and logs on the forest floor. Leaving the forest untouched for at least several hundred feet (100 meters) along all streams, riverbanks and other bodies of water further helps to control runoff, erosion and pollution of waterways while maintaining shade along the banks and creating a *greenway* for wildlife. In many large-scale operations, cutting is being done in the form of relatively small, circular plots in which all trees are brought to a central point for loading onto equipment. These clearings are small enough for the seed trees found along the edges to be able to reseed the area.

From conserving resources manufactured out of wood products to reducing the levels of air pollution we generate, every ecologically sound act we take as individuals or as a society will, either directly or indirectly, help to preserve our trees and forests. We share an intimate relationship with all plants through the air we share in common and the soil that supports all life. An important aspect of long-term forest stewardship involves identifying and protecting the wilderness areas that remain. We need to establish environmentally sensitive and sustainable ways of maintaining the forests that we harvest. Once a stand of old-growth forest is cut from the slopes of the Cascades in Washington State, it takes at least 200 years before the forest that replaces it even begins to possess the ecological characteristics and appearance of an old-growth stand once again. Forests are not simply tree farms created and presented to us by nature. They provide open space and wilderness—places where people can seek the kind of recreation and peace of mind that can only be found in communion with the wild. Beyond their utility to human beings, forests are of value in themselves, as homes to the myriad plants and animals that dwell within, simply because they exist.

QUESTIONS

1.   What instructions were given to the plants and animals when they were first made? Which ones were able to follow the instructions?

2.   What was the reward that the pine, spruce, hemlock, cedar, laurel and holly received for staying awake and watchful? What happened to those plants that fell asleep?

3.   What does the story mean when it says, "For great medicine never comes to those who are not watchful"? Why is silence an important part of being watchful and learning about the world around you?

4.   What kinds of trees are evergreen? Do these trees ever lose their leaves? When?

5.   What is a conifer? How many kinds of conifers can you think of? What kinds of trees are related to conifers?

6.   What does a conifer use its needles for? Are needles any different than other leaves?

7. Why do conifers have cones? What do cones produce?

8. Why do trees have roots, bark, leaves and wood? How do trees move water and minerals?

9. When you visit a forest, what do you find there, both alive and not alive? How do these parts work together to form the forest community? How do trees help to keep the forest community alive?

10. In what ways are trees valuable to people?

11. Why do people cut down trees? How is the wood used once the trees are cut? What things do you use that come from trees?

12. What happens to the forest community when the trees are all cut down? Are there ways to cut trees that help to take care of the forests for the future?

13. How are trees important to people when the trees are alive and growing? What kinds of gifts do living trees give to people and the rest of nature?

14. How does air pollution hurt trees? What kinds of other things are people doing that hurt trees?

15. What can we all do to be kind to trees and to help preserve our forests? How would you like to help trees in your neighborhood?

ACTIVITIES

Concentrating on Conifers

ACTIVITY: (A) Play some matching games to closely observe cones, needles and the kinds of trees they grow on. (B) Mark off and walk along a distance equal to the heights of the largest living trees on Earth. (C) Closely observe the numerical spirals found in the scales on cones and the numbers of needles found in bunches on conifers. Calculate the first 10 numbers in the Fibonacci sequence and relate these to the numbers found in cones and needles.

GOALS: Understand that conifers are gymnosperms and that there are other kinds of plants in this group. Realize that every kind of conifer tree grows its own unique cones, seeds and needles. Understand the function of cones and needles. Discover the size of the largest living trees in the world. Understand the Fibonacci sequence and how Fibonacci numbers are arrived at. Discover how these numbers are found in the arrangements of scales on cones and bunches of needles.

AGE: Younger children (A, B) and older children (A, B, C)

MATERIALS: (A) Enough cones and needles for each child to have one of each, plus a few extras (roughly equal numbers of both cones and needles from at least four different kinds of conifers); a few seeds from each kind of conifer cone in the collection; one piece of yarn for each child; tacks; large pieces of cardboard; crayons; tape; "Discussion"; photographs and/or illustrations of some plants from each group of gymnosperms; hand lenses; pruning shears. (B) Large open space at

least 375 feet (114 meters) long, "Discussion," photographs or illustrations of California redwoods and sequoias, tape measures, Figure 8-5. (C) One cone and one cluster of conifer needles for each group of children, gathered from different trees, if possible, on which clusters grow in twos, threes and fives; "Discussion"; Figure 8-2; chalkboard and chalk or newsprint and markers; apple; knife; pruning shears.

PROCEDURE A: *Cone and Needle Match Game.* Beforehand, scout out and identify at least four different species of conifers growing within the general vicinity of the home or learning center—the more the better. Collect enough cones and needles for each child to have one of each, plus a few extras. There should be roughly equal numbers of both cones and needles from each tree in the collection. Look around on the top inside edge of cone scales, and in the leaf litter around the base of the trees, to gather a few examples of seeds from each type of conifer. If you are working with older children and plan to conduct "C" afterward, be sure to gather enough clusters of pine needles to give one cluster to each small group of children. If possible, gather from different trees on which the needles grow in clusters of two, three and five needles per bunch. Tie a piece of yarn around the bottom whorl of scales on each cone and make a small loop by which to hang the cone. Make a simple field sketch of the silhouette of each tree from which the cones and needles come and record which cones and needles match which silhouettes. Have some children help as you use large pieces of cardboard and crayons to create a 4-foot (1.2-meter) silhouette of each of these conifer trees. Hang the silhouettes on an easily accessible wall. Tack one cone, and tape several needles, above each silhouette that represents the tree that each cone and cluster of needles comes from.

Hold up a cone and ask the children what kind of tree it is from. Lead a question-and-answer period about conifers and bring out the basic characteristics of conifers as described in the "Discussion." Discuss gymnosperms ("naked seeds") and the other trees besides conifers (ginkgoes, cycads and gnetophytes) that are found in this group of plants. Hold up some photographs or illustrations of these trees as you speak.

Pass out one cone to each child and instruct the children to study their cones very carefully, using hand lenses to look for small details. Have the children look for anything special that will help them to recognize this as *their* cone when compared to all the others. Once they are ready, have them gently *place* their cones in a pile in the center of the group. Carefully mix up the pile of cones and have the children take turns picking out their cone from all the others. Ask them to point out what characteristics helped them to identify their cones. Now give each child a tack and have him or her attach the cone to a branch of the appropriate tree silhouette, using the cones you have hung above each tree as a guide. When all cones are hung, ask the children to describe the silhouettes and what makes them distinctive. Ask: "Have you ever seen a tree that looks like one of these silhouettes?

Figure 8-5. The magnificent coast redwood is the tallest tree in the world. It can reach a height of up to 325 ft. (99 m) and a diameter of 15 ft. (4.6 m). (Photo by Alexander Lowry)

Where is it growing? Why does each kind of tree have its own special shape?" Allow the children to observe the seeds you gathered from each conifer.

Pass out one evergreen needle to each child and have them observe the needles closely with hand lenses. The two bluish-white lines on the bottom of hemlock and fir needles, for instance, are rows of stomata through which the needles "breathe." Now tell the children, "Look around for people who have the same kind of needle as you do and form groups in which everyone is holding that kind of needle." Once the children have formed into the appropriate number of small groups (depending on the number of different kinds of needles you passed out), ask them: "What makes your needle the same as others in your group? How is it different from needles in other groups?" Have each child match the needle in hand with one of the needles you taped above the tree silhouettes. Once the correct silhouette is found, have the children tape their needle onto a branch of that tree.

PROCEDURE B: *Evergreen Giants.* Take the children outdoors to a large open area, such as a park or athletic field. Discuss the immense size and old age of California's sequoias and redwoods (another kind of sequoia) using the information from the description of conifers in the "Discussion."

Hold up a photograph of each of these trees as you discuss it (Figure 8-5).

Demonstrate to the children how to cooperate while using a tape measure to measure the distances equal to the heights of the tallest sequoia (275 feet or 83.8 meters) and the tallest redwood (367 feet or 112 meters). Have children take turns working in pairs using the tape measures to mark the heights of these trees as distances on the ground. Once they are finished, have the pairs of children stand at opposite ends of their distances to create visual images of the trees' heights. Now have them walk the entire distance of a redwood's and sequoia's height from one end, up around the far end and back to the starting point. Ask the children for their reactions. An excellent picture of a giant sequoia can be found on pages 66 and 67 of *The Forest,* by Peter Farb and the Editors of Time-Life Books (Alexandria, Va.: Time-Life Books, 1978).

Note: A fun variation on this activity is to measure the height of a giant tree from the ground end of a kite string. Tie off a colorful cloth marker at the point that marks the treetop. When the kite flies, the marker will show the approximate height of the tree. Actually, the angle of the kite string will cut off some of the height, but this gets the point across.

PROCEDURE C: *Finding Fibonaccis.* Describe the Fibonacci sequence and how Fibonacci numbers are arrived at as presented in the "Discussion" under "Conifers." Have each child calculate the first 10 Fibonacci numbers starting with the number 1.

Now tell the children they are going to search for Fibonacci patterns and associated numbers among the cones and needles of conifers. Pass out one cone and one cluster of pine needles to each child (gathered in "A" above). Share Figure 8-2 and have the children search for the patterns of cone scales. Have them count the number of cone scales in a spiral row moving from the bottom of the cone to the top. How many scales do they count? Record these numbers for all to see. Now ask them to count the number of needles in their cluster. Record these numbers as well. Look at all of the numbers you have recorded. Except for those cases where someone was missing a needle from their cluster, or cone scales were broken off or miscounted, the numbers you have recorded will be Fibonacci numbers.

Ask the children: "Can you think of other places in nature that Fibonacci patterns and numbers might show up? Why do plants and animals develop these numbers in their patterns of growth?" Plants and animals grow so as to make the most efficient use of space. Fibonacci numbers develop over and over in nature as the scales of a cone, the clusters of needles and other plant and animal parts. Now share and show some additional examples of Fibonacci patterns and numbers in nature from the "Discussion," including an apple core cut cleanly in half horizontally, revealing the pentagonal seed chamber. An excellent book on this subject is *Fascinating Fibonaccis: Mystery and Magic in Numbers*, by Trudi Hammel Garland (Palo Alto, Calif.: Dale Seymour, 1987).

Parts of a Tree

ACTIVITY: (A) As a group, turn a person into a tree to demonstrate the parts of a tree and their functions. (B) Create a history of a particular tree and its environment by reading the annual growth rings.

GOALS: Recognize the various parts of a tree and understand the function of each part. Understand that annual growth rings form on trees each year in response to growing conditions at that time, and that these rings form a record of those conditions.

AGE: Younger children and older children

MATERIALS: (A) Construction paper, large pieces of newsprint, two branches with leaves on them, pruning shears, cardboard, glue, tape, string, pencils, crayons, scissors, markers, pipe cleaners and other material as needed to make the parts of the tree; "Discussion"; Figure 8-3; note cards. (B) Stump or large cross-section of a tree trunk on which the annual growth rings can be clearly seen, hand lenses, paper and pencils, newsprint and marker.

PROCEDURE A: *Personalitree.* Beforehand, copy the descriptions and functions of the "Parts of a Tree" as found in the "Discussion" onto eight separate note cards; one description to each card. The eight descriptions are roots, leaves (including broadleaves and needles), outer bark, inner bark or phloem, cambium, sapwood (xylem), heartwood (xylem) and branches. Make an enlarged version of the illustration of the "Parts of a Tree" (Figure 8-3) and hang it in a prominent place.

Ask for a volunteer to come up front. Do the children think that this child could live if she or he were brought outside and had her or his feet planted in the ground? Now say that the children are going to turn the volunteer into a tree by making tree parts and putting them on the child. Divide the children into eight small groups and pass out one note card to each group (one card for each of the eight parts of the tree). If you are working with just a few children, have each child work on several tree parts so that all eight are completed. Include the person who will be made into a tree as a member of one of these groups.

Move around among the groups and answer any questions they have. Show them where their tree parts are located on the enlarged illustration you hung up earlier (Figure 8-3). Have them learn about their tree parts and how each part works to keep the tree alive. They are to use the materials to create versions of their tree parts that are to be measured so that they will fit onto the child who will be made into a tree.

When all groups have completed their tree parts, have the groups come up, one at a time, to attach their tree part to the Personalitree and explain to the rest of the group what that part is and how it works to keep the tree alive. Once the Personalitree is completed, review, with leading questions, the many parts of a tree and their functions, starting with the tree roots and tracing the path of water and minerals up the xylem (wood) of the tree until it reaches the crown. Have the child hold one branch up in each hand and place the hat of leaves on his or her head. Talk about the process of photosynthesis in leaves (see "Discussion" in Chapter 5) and trace the pathway of sugars, starches and other nutrients down into the tree through the phloem or inner bark. Discuss the growth of the tree via the cambium.

Note: As a variation on this activity, have children make their friends into trees. Or, have each child combine the "Materials" to make a small model of a tree. Another way to demonstrate the layers of a tree trunk is to have the child's body represent the heartwood (old xylem) and skin represent the sapwood (new xylem). Now add more layers to demonstrate other parts of the tree moving outward: shirt (cambium), sweater (phloem or inner bark) and jacket (outer bark).

PROCEDURE B: *Story Written in Wood.* Beforehand, find a nearby stump or obtain a large cross-section of a trunk on which the annual rings are clearly visible.

Use a question-and-answer period to review the parts of a tree trunk described in the "Discussion" and how the yearly cycle of tree growth creates annual rings. Now ask the children: "Why do you think some annual rings are wider than others? Do you see any scars in the tree's trunk? Are there any signs of fire or insect damage? What does the width of the rings from the various years tell you about the rainfall in those years?" Encourage the children to use their hand lenses and take a close look at the annual rings. Record the children's answers on the newsprint as pieces of the story about this particular tree. Once you are all satisfied that you have the essential parts of the story recorded, have each child put those pieces together to write or illustrate his or her own version of the life of that tree in first person, starting with, "Once I was a seed …" Point out that the original story was recorded in wood, and that the stories they are now writing are recorded on paper made from wood. Have the children take turns sharing their stories when completed.

Note: A good visual aid for this activity is Figure 17-1 in Chapter 17 of *Keepers of the Earth,* which shows a cross-section of a tree.

Conifer Forest Alive

ACTIVITY: (A) Listen to the sounds of a conifer forest and spend some time in quiet solitude. (B) Go on a scavenger hunt in the conifer forest.
GOALS: Discover both the sounds and the silence of a conifer forest. Understand how silence and solitude can help us to better know ourselves and to develop a deeper empathy for the life of the forest. Realize that the coniferous forest is a place of interesting plants, animals and other discoveries awaiting.
AGE: Younger children and older children
MATERIALS: (A) Access to a quiet conifer forest, pencils, paper with cardboard backing or clipboards. (B) Copies of "Conifer Forest Excursion" (Figure 8-6), pencils, cardboard backing or clipboards to write on, hand lenses, index cards, Figure 9-4.
PROCEDURE A: *The Sounds of Silence.* Lead the children to a quiet conifer forest where the ground is dry enough to sit upon. Have the group sit down in a circle. Explain: "Conifer forests are a special place where people from many Native North American cultures go to seek to be close to Earth and to better know their own self. Quiet is very important for hearing well. Let's see how well you can listen." Have each child pick up a small amount of whatever kind of needles (leaves) are on the forest floor and place them in one hand *or* the other. Then say: "Close your eyes and keep them closed until I ask you to open them. Be absolutely quiet. Every time you hear a sound, move one of the needles from the hand you're holding them in to the other hand. Listen for the different kinds of songs the wind creates when it blows

through the leaves on different kinds of trees." Allow about two minutes to elapse and ask them to open their eyes. Inquire: "What did you hear? Did you have any idea there were that many sounds here when you first sat down? Did you hear any bird sounds? Can you imitate them? How many different tree songs did you hear? Why do the leaves on different trees sing a unique tune when the wind blows through them? Which sounds were made by people?"

Give each child a pencil and some paper with cardboard backing. Have each child either write a story or draw a picture that tells something about herself or himself. The story or illustration should complete a thought that begins with, for instance, "I am …, I hear …, I see …, I feel …" Instruct the children to come back from their places when you make a bird sound or give some other signal. Assign each a separate place to sit down that is far enough from their nearest neighbors to allow some solitude, but close enough for you to be able to keep an eye on them. Leave younger children in their spots for about 10 minutes and older children for about 20 minutes. Make the call and gather the children together. Ask the children to say what it felt like to be alone for a time. "Did you like it or not? Why or why not?" Invite them to share their illustrations or stories. Make it clear that this is a request and they are not required to share if they do not want to.
PROCEDURE B: *Conifer Forest Excursion.* Beforehand, scout out the area where you will lead this activity and look for some specific plants and animals or signs of animals that children may be expected to find. Add these to the "Conifer Forest Excursion." It is also a good idea to delete things that you are sure the children will not be able to find in that area so they do not get frustrated searching for them.

Arrange the children into pairs and pass out one copy of Figure 8-6, "Conifer Forest Excursion," to each pair, along with pencils, backing to write against, hand lenses and index cards. Ask the children some questions about the plants and animals they may expect to find in the forest: "What kinds of plants live here? What kinds of animals make their homes in this forest? Where do they live and what do they eat?"

Lead the group over to a young conifer. Most conifers—particularly pine, hemlock, spruce and fir—grow a new *whorl* of branches each year that emerge from one place around the stem (Figure 9-4). By counting the number of these whorls from the ground to the top of the tree, and adding two more years for the time it took the tree to sprout and send out its first whorl, you can make a close estimate of the age of the tree. Find a tree and demonstrate its age by having the children help you count the age of the tree. The children will be doing this during their excursion.

Once you have oriented the children to this activity, emphasize that the goal is to observe and leave the plants and animals in their own homes. Now send the groups off on their excursions. Gather the small groups together in about 20 minutes and have them take turns sharing their findings with the entire group. Have the small groups lead everyone

Conifer Forest Excursion

Directions: Place a mark next to each of the plants, animals and other things you find. Do not try to see everything. Take time to observe each discovery and have fun. Draw pictures of your discoveries on the index cards. Look for:

____ a tree that has needles in bunches of two

____ a tree that has needles in bunches of three

____ a tree that has needles in bunches of five

____ needles that feel sharp

____ needles that feel soft

____ a tree as old as you (count the whorls of branches and add two)

____ a plant with insects living in its leaves

____ insects living on the bark of a tree

____ insects living in the wood of a tree

____ a bird nest close to the ground

____ a bird nest high up in a tree

____ a squirrel nest (a ball of leaves and needles in the branches)

____ a squirrel

____ the chewed core of a cone that a squirrel has eaten

____ a pile of cone scales that have been chewed off by a squirrel looking for seeds (this is called a "midden")

____ bark that feels smooth

____ bark that feels rough

____ roots that are tall enough to trip over

____ a rotting log with a tree growing out of it

____ a cool, damp, dark place

____ a warm, dry, sunny place

____ a place where a woodpecker has made a hole in a tree

____ a hollow tree that is still alive

____ at least three layers of the forest, from the soil to the treetops

____ something growing on a rock

____ three different kinds of cones

____ four different kinds of seeds

____ flowers that are red, blue and yellow

____ a spider's web with something caught in it

____ a plant that is as tall as your shoe

____ something that smells old

____ something that smells fresh and new

____ something that smells sweet

____ some sticky sap coming out of a tree

____ four different kinds of animal homes

____ two different mushrooms or other kinds of fungi

____ new soil forming from an old tree

Figure 8-6. "Conifer Forest Excursion."

over to see any particularly exciting findings, such as an interesting mushroom, an animal's home or a bird nest.

Birth of a Forest

ACTIVITY: (A) Take a blindfold walk from a forest to a field and use your senses to notice the changes that occur on the way, and then return to observe the area you just walked through. (B) Make observations and take measurements of plants, animals and their environments in areas at different stages of ecological succession.

GOALS: Understand that change is a natural part of the environment. Understand the environmental changes that occur during ecological succession and some of the plants and animals associated with the different stages of succession.

AGE: Younger children (A) and older children (A, B)

MATERIALS: (A) Outdoor area with plant growth representing stages of ecological succession from open field to forest, pruning shears, enough clothesline rope to cover 200 feet (61 meters), branches or other tall wooden stakes as needed, hammer, one blindfold for each child (younger children) or enough blindfolds for one-half the class (older children), 30-foot (9-meter) rope, "Discussion." (B) Thermometers (with a loop of string tied on for hanging); yard or meter sticks; large, identical, one-quart (one-liter) juice cans opened cleanly at both ends (be careful to not leave metal burrs that children could get cut on); quart or liter containers of water; watches on which seconds can be read; hand lenses; copies of Figure 8-7 ("Succession Sleuths"); pencils; clipboard or cardboard backing; field guides.

PROCEDURE A: *A Walk Through Time.* Beforehand, locate an area where there is a good sequence of successional growth that spans in a short distance (200 feet [61 meters] or less) from mature forest to open field. Find a pathway from the mature forest to the open field that is *clear* of roots and rocks that children might trip on as well as branches and brambles that could cut them or brush them in the face. You may need to prune away some branches and brambles. Be especially careful that all is clear at eye level. Now, for younger children, tie the clothesline rope onto a tree in the forest and lead it through the cleared pathway into the open field. There may be enough trees along the way to tie the rope at about waist level, or you may need to drive a few tall wooden stakes or branches into the ground on which to anchor the rope.

Omit the guide rope when working on this activity with older children. Instead, pair children up and have one partner lead the other blindfolded along the "Walk Through Time" trail. Then have them switch roles so each child has a turn at being led blindfolded. Use the directions that follow but adapt them for partners who lead themselves along the trail.

On a sunny day, lead the children into the forest. Once at the beginning of the trail, have the children look around and describe the conditions of light, heat, moisture levels and the density and kinds of plants growing in that place. What kinds of sounds do they hear? Now line them up along one side of the rope trail facing the field and help them to put blindfolds on. Tell them they are about to walk back in time to a habitat that looks like what the place they are now standing in looked like long ago before the forest grew up. Lead them slowly from forest to field as they hold onto the rope trail with one hand. Stop every so often and ask them to describe in what ways it feels and sounds different at each location. Once they reach the end of their rope, ask them to remove the blindfolds and look around. Say: "This is what the forest once looked like. How do you think it got to be a forest? What kinds of changes occurred to cause the forest to develop? How does the growing forest affect the kinds of animals that live in the new habitats that develop? How do you think the soil changes over time? *Change* is an important reality in the natural world. Look back down the trail at the changes you just walked through. Do you think the forest changes once it matures? What might cause it to change?" Facilitate a brief discussion about the idea of a mature forest as described in the "Forest Ecology" section of the "Discussion" from this chapter and mention the agents of change that can set the forest back to an earlier stage of succession. Finally, lead the group back along the trail so the children may see where they just passed through. Stop back at the forest end of the trail and gather the group together. This is the time for older children to switch roles so the partner who was the leader can now be led blindfolded.

PROCEDURE B: *Succession Sleuths.* Divide the group into small groups and brief them on how to use the equipment to take measurements of temperature, estimated plant heights, density of stems and soil water percolation rates. The method for measuring soil water percolation is simple. Each group has a quart or liter of water and an identical, large juice can opened cleanly at both ends. (To prevent cuts, be sure no metal burrs are left around the rims where the lids were removed.) One open end of the juice can is worked into the top of the soil by pushing down and turning through the uppermost inch (few centimeters) or so until there is a seal that will not allow water to leak out along the rim. Then, one child fills the juice can with water while another uses the watch to time how long it takes for the water to completely drain out of the can into the soil. Air temperature is to be measured at about shoulder height by finding a branch to hang the thermometer from. Soil surface temperature is measured by placing the thermometer face down on the soil. Be careful not to step on the thermometer! Thermometers should be left in each place about 10 minutes before a reading is taken. Measure plant heights with the measuring sticks wherever possible, and by estimating where the plants are too tall to measure directly. Density of plant stems is measured by marking out a square with a measuring stick and counting all of the stems of plants growing within that square. Show children how to estimate the overall amount

Succession Sleuths

Start by setting the thermometer out to begin recording temperature. Continue exploring and measuring, then answer the following questions:

1. How much of the ground is covered by shade?
    ___ almost all or all of it
    ___ about 3/4's
    ___ about 1/2
    ___ about 1/4
    ___ almost none or none of it

2. What is the temperature
    ___ of the air?
    ___ at the soil surface?

3. How long, in minutes and seconds, does it take one quart (liter) to percolate into the soil?
    ___ minutes and ___ seconds

4. How tall are most of the plants in your habitat?
    ___ less than 1 foot (30.5 centimeters)
    ___ 1 foot (30.5 centimeters) to about 3 feet 4 inches (1 meter)
    ___ 3 feet 4 inches (1 meter) to about 10 feet (3 meters)
    ___ 10 feet (3 meters) to about 20 feet (6 meters)
    ___ over 20 feet (6 meters)

5. How many plant stems are growing in 1 square yard (1 square meter)?
    ___ stems per square yard (square meter)

6. How many different kinds of plants are growing in your habitat?
    ___ kinds of plants
    Describe some ways that these plants are adapted to survive in that habitat (seed dispersal, kinds of leaves, types of flowers, etc.).

    _____

    _____

    _____

7. What kinds of animals and signs of animals do you see? How are they adapted to living in their
    habitat (foods, homes, etc.)?_____

    _____

    _____

Figure 8-7. "Succession Sleuths."

of shade that is cast on the ground in their habitat. Pass out the following equipment to each group: thermometer, juice can, quart or liter of water, yard or meter stick, field guides, hand lenses, copy of Figure 8-7 ("Succession Sleuths"), pencil and clipboard or cardboard backing.

Assign each small group to one of four habitats to study along the rope timeline: mature forest, young forest, old field and young field. Have the children take measurements and observe the animals (mammals, birds, insects, etc.) and signs of animals (such as homes, droppings, browse) in their assigned habitat as they record their findings on paper with words and illustrations. In about a half hour, or when the children are finished, gather them together so they may explain and demonstrate their findings. Have the children describe the adaptations among the plants and animals found (seed dispersal mechanisms, food preferences, etc.) that make those organisms well suited to live in their environments. How are conditions different in the four habitats? How do you explain these differences and how they affect the animals living there?

EXTENDING THE EXPERIENCE

• Draw on a large piece of cardboard a gargantuan cross-section and timeline about the events that occurred during the life of the giant sequoia tree known as General Grant. This tree is more than 40 feet (12.2 meters) in diameter, greater than 267 feet (81.4 meters) tall and more than 3,500 years old! Research interesting events that happened over the course of this tree's life, write these events down on small pieces of paper and place the pieces of paper like small flags along the timeline. Be sure to include important events in the history of the Cherokee, whose story "Why Some Trees Are Always Green" opens this chapter. Now give guided tours of this tree's ancient history.

• Plant and nurture a tree: do the activity *"Seventh-Generation Stewardship"* in Chapter 15. Refer to the section called "Planting Trees and Shrubs" in Chapter 2.

• Take a hike up a tall mountain and study the changes in vegetation as you climb. Read over the description of mountain plant zones found under "The Coniferous Forests" in the "Discussion." Use this information to calculate how far north you would have to travel to equal the climatic changes experienced over the height you are climbing.

• Interview some senior citizens in your area to learn stories about what the forests were like when they were growing up. Ask their permission to record their stories and do so if that is acceptable. Visit some of the old sites they remember and take photographs or make illustrations of what you see. Put these stories and images together to create your own book of forest history.

• Next springtime, catch conifer pollen on sticky paper to see just how much is produced by the trees. Look at the pollen under a hand lens.

• *Root Power.* A growing root that is 4 inches (10.2 centimeters) in diameter and 3 feet (.9 meter) long can raise 50 tons

(45.4 metric tons). Calculate how many pounds (kilograms) this is. Divide this figure by the average weight of the people in your group. The answer tells the number of people having the weight of those in your group that a growing root could raise. A subcompact car weighs about 2,000 pounds (907 kilograms). How many of these cars could the root lift?

• Use a living Christmas tree that you can replant after the holidays are over. This requires planning ahead. Before the ground freezes, dig the hole outdoors that you will plant the tree in later. Gather, and keep thawed, sufficient soil for planting the tree. Be sure to get a good ball of roots on your tree. Acclimate the tree gradually to the warmth of indoors by placing it in a cool spot indoors before bringing it fully inside. Do not bring the tree indoors until the ball of roots is completely thawed or the needles may brown off, possibly killing the tree. Place the ball of soil in a large, waterproof bucket while inside and keep the ball moist. Gradually acclimate the tree to the outdoors once again before planting.

• Figure out how much paper waste you generate every week by saving it and weighing it. There are 52 weeks in a year, so how much waste do you generate every year? If you lived to be 70 years old, how much waste would you create in your lifetime?

• Visit a local sawmill and lumber yard to see how trees are milled, to look at the inner parts of logs and to find out what kinds of wood are being used for lumber and where those trees are coming from. Ask about the kinds of forestry practices used by those who supply the sawmill.

• Conduct the acid rain activities found in Chapter 5.

NOTES

1. Kent Nerburn and Louise Mengelkoch, *Native American Wisdom* (San Rafael, Calif.: New World Library, 1991), 7–8.

2. Trudi Hammel Garland, *Fascinating Fibonaccis* (Palo Alto, Calif.: Dale Seymour, 1987), 6–18.

3. Peter S. Stevens, *Patterns in Nature* (Boston and Toronto: Little, Brown, 1974), 159.

4. Jean O. Kriebs and Albert Schatz, "Who Ate Roger Williams?" *American Biology Teacher,* vol. 35, no. 3 (March 1973): 155.

5. Hubert W. Vogelmann, "Catastrophe on Camel's Hump," *Natural History,* vol. 91, no. 11 (November 1982): 8–14.

6. Hubert W. Vogelmann, G. J. Badger, M. Bliss and R. M. Klein, "Forest Decline on Camel's Hump," *Vermont Bulletin of the Torrey Botany Club,* vol. 112 (1985): 274–287.

7. Tim Scherbatskoy and M. Bliss, "Occurrence of Acidic Rain and Cloud Water in High Elevation Ecosystems in the Green Mountains of Vermont," *Transactions of The Meteorology of Acidic Deposition,* Hartford, Conn., 16–19 October 1983 (1984). Air Pollution Control Association, P.O. Box 2861, Pittsburgh, PA 15230.

8. Charles E. Little, "The California X-Disease," *American Forests,* vol. 98, no. 7/8 (July/August 1992): 32–34, 55–56.

Chapter 9

✦ The Bitterroot ✦

(Salish—Plateau)

It was the time just after winter in the valley in the mountains. There was no food and the people were starving. The fish had not yet returned to the streams and the game animals had moved far away into the mountains. The men had gone out to seek game and they had been gone a long time. It was not yet time for berries to ripen, and the women had gathered what plants they could find that could be eaten, but the ones that were left from the winter were tough and stringy.

In one of the lodges, an old woman was grieving because there was no food for her grandchildren. She could no longer bear to look at their thin, sad faces and she went out before sunrise, to sing her death song beside the little stream which ran through the valley.

"I am old," she sang, "but my grandchildren are young. It is a hard time that has come, when children must die with their grandmothers."

As she knelt by the stream, singing and weeping, the Sun came over the mountains. It heard her death song and it spoke to that old woman's spirit helper.

"My daughter is crying for her children who are starving," Sun said. "Go now and help her and her people. Give them food."

Then the spirit helper took the form of a redbird and flew down into the valley. It perched on a limb above the old woman's head and began to sing. When she lifted her eyes to look at it, the bird spoke to her.

"My friend," the redbird said, "your tears have gone into Earth. They have formed a new plant there, one which will help you and your people to live. See it come now from Earth, its leaves close to the ground. When its blossoms form, they will have the red color of my wings and the white of your hair."

The old woman looked and it was as the bird said. All around her, in the moist soil, the leaves of a new plant had lifted from Earth. As the sun touched it, a red blossom began to open.

"How can we use this plant?" said the old woman.

"You will dig this plant up by the roots with a digging stick," the redbird said. "Its taste will be bitter, like your tears, but it will be a food to help the people live. Each year it will always come at this time when no other food can be found."

And so it has been to this day. That stream where the old woman wept is called Little Bitterroot and the valley is also named Bitterroot after that plant, which still comes each year after the snows have left the land. Its flowers, which come only when touched by the sun, are as red as the wings of a red spirit bird and as silver as the hair of an old woman. And its taste is still as bitter as the tears of that old woman whose death song turned into a song of survival.

*The old woman looked and it was as the redbird said. All around her, in the moist soil,
the leaves of a new plant had lifted from Earth.*

Indian Summer

(Penobscot—Eastern Woodland)

Here lives my story. It happened long ago that there was a man named Zimo who was a good planter. He cared well for his crops and he gave thanks to Ketci Niweskwe. But when the time came for him to do his planting, he became sick. The other people of his village planted their crops and harvested them and dried them for the winter, but Zimo remained sick all through that time. The other people of the village and their families had plenty of vegetables, but Zimo had none. The first cold winds of late autumn were blowing and he knew it would be hard to survive the winter without the food he always got from his fields.

So Zimo went to Gluskabe.

"Master," Zimo said, "I have been sick. The time came to plant and then the time to harvest and now I have no food for the winter. I have always been thankful, and I have worked hard in the past. Help me."

"Go back to your field," Gluskabe said. "Plant your seeds."

Zimo did as Gluskabe said. The people of Zimo's village thought he was crazy as he began to plant his corn and squash and beans. But as soon as he put the seeds in the earth, the weather changed and it became as warm as summer. The seeds sprouted and grew tall overnight. By the time seven days had passed, Zimo had gathered a whole season's crop. Then winter came.

Since then, though the seeds no longer grow as quickly as Zimo's seeds did with the help of Gluskabe, there is always a time of warm weather just before the snows. That is the time the Penobscot people call "A Person's Summer." It is known to most as "Indian Summer," even though few seem to remember that it is a time given as a reminder to us all to be thankful for the gifts from Earth and the Creator.

DISCUSSION

A flowering plant is no less than the source of life that saves the Salish people in the story "The Bitterroot." Sun answers an old woman's prayer and sends a redbird to help. The old woman's tears grow into a plant bearing a red flower. Even though this plant has a bitter root, it is survival food for the people. As we have found often in Native North American stories, a strong element of natural history fact is hidden in the plot. Birds can see the color red and are attracted to it, but red falls outside the visible range of color for most insects. Hummingbirds play a role in the life cycle of certain plants by pollinating the plants' red flowers. Many birds that eat red berries spread the seeds of those plants in their droppings. The deep and intimate knowledge of nature found among Native North American cultures reminds us, once again, of the educational value of close *observation*.

Knowledge was inherent in all things. The world was a library and its books were the stones, leaves, grass, brooks, and the birds and animals that shared alike with us, the storms and blessings of Earth. ... Observation was certain to have its rewards. Interest, wonder, admiration grew, and the fact was appreciated that life was more than mere human manifestation: it was expressed in a multitude of forms.[1]

—Chief Luther Standing Bear
Oglala Lakota (Sioux)

In the Penobscot story "Indian Summer," the failure of Zimo's crops reminds us of how dependent we all are on flowering plants for our survival. All of the seeds Zimo plants—corn, beans and squash—are seeds of flowering plants. In fact, leaves, roots, fruits (including grains) and other parts of

"Master," Zimo said to Gluskabe, "I have been sick. The time came to plant and then the time to harvest and now I have no food for the winter."

flowering plants comprise 80 percent of the food human beings have eaten over the millennia. Gluskabe saves Zimo by creating a special time of year that is as warm as summer, which the Penobscot call "A Person's Summer," and which is known to many as "Indian Summer." In the story, A Person's Summer lasts seven days, a powerful number that appears often in Native North American stories.

Flowering Plants

While it is generally believed that flowering plants evolved around 136 million years ago and have been the dominant plant life on Earth for 130 million years, some fossil evidence indicates that flowering plants may have evolved about 100 million years earlier.[2,3] With their seemingly infinite variety of forms and flowers creating a landscape awash in all colors of the rainbow, the more than 250,000 species of flowering plants alive today make up more than one-half of all living plants and are the most widespread of all life on Earth. *Angiosperms*, "enclosed seeds," have become so successful because of the flower, a remarkable structure that co-evolved with insects, birds, bats and other animals.

The many subtle relationships between specific flowers and animals are all variations on a basic theme: insects and other animals obtain food energy (pollen, nectar, seeds and other plant parts) and sometimes shelter, while plants get their pollen transferred through pollination and cross-pollination, and have their seeds dispersed in droppings, carried by fur and spread by other means. As flowering plants developed over millions of years, the major groups of pollinating insects emerged in this order: beetles, flies, wasps and bees, and finally moths and butterflies about 40 to 50 million years ago. Over time, insects and other animals were attracted to flowers and seeds that possessed certain shapes, scents, colors, sizes and quantities of food energy. The flowers that were found most attractive became more successful at setting seeds and so began to dominate. This evolutionary process is called *natural selection*. Irises, orchids, snapdragons and other flowers that evolved later have intricate color patterns, strong scents, complex structures and fewer numbers of petals and sepals and are symmetrical from side to side.

Flowers possess a tremendous variety of shapes and structures designed to attract and manipulate insects into performing the act of pollination: disks, funnels, lips, traps, tubes and bells are among them. When a bee enters the moccasin flower (lady's slipper), one of about 140 species of North American orchids, it cannot escape without passing both the pollen and the *stigma*, the female structure that receives the pollen. The colors of flower petals, which create some of the most beautiful forms of art in nature, consist of dots, lines, spots, veins and other patterns that guide insects to sources of pollen and nectar. *Nectar*, a sweet liquid, is formed in structures called *nectaries*. Many nectar-bearing flowers have petals that are fused to form a protective *corolla*. Insects use pollen and nectar as food and for nourishing their young.

Three major groups of pigments, in various combinations, create the amazing hues found in flowers and other plant tissues. *Chlorophyll* imparts the basic green color in plants and is essential for the process of photosynthesis (see "Discussion" in Chapter 5). More than 60 varieties of *carotenoid* pigments color flowers, fruits and other parts of plants. The two main groups of carotenoids are *carotenes* and *xanthophylls*, which range in color from red to yellow. The hues of a third major group of plant pigments, the *anthocyanins*, vary from red to blue, and they form shades of pink, red and purple. These pigments are dissolved in plant sap and are sensitive to changes in acidity and alkalinity, which is why the flower color varies in many species of plants. Morning glory flowers, for instance, can appear to be pale pink with the acid sap of morning, but they gradually take on blue tints as the sap becomes mildly alkaline by afternoon. Certain plants produce flowers of different colors depending on whether they are grown in soils that are acid or alkaline. Hydrangea produces red flowers in neutral soil and blue blooms in alkaline soil.

MONOCOTS. *Monocotyledons* (monocots), one of the two major groups of flowering plants, include grasses, orchids, lilies and a variety of *herbaceous* plants, those that are relatively small and nonwoody. The aquatic duckweeds, such as the .08-inch (2-millimeter) "small duckweed," are among the tiniest flowering plants in the world. Of the roughly 50,000 species of monocots, only those in the palm family are not herbs. Monocots possess:
- one seedling leaf or *cotyledon*, which is used for photosynthesis food storage and/or food storage
- leaves that have parallel veins, are *entire* (lack lobes or teeth) and often appear grass-like
- flower parts (petals and sepals) that occur mostly in 3s or multiples of 3
- bundles of vascular tissue distributed throughout the stem

The flowers of many monocots tend to be simpler, more highly evolved and possess fewer parts than those of dicots (see below). While orchids and other insect-pollinated monocot flowers are among the most beautiful and delicate on Earth, wind-pollinated flowers, such as corn and other grasses, do not produce nectar, are not colorful (are often green), grow in clusters and produce prodigious amounts of pollen. Monocot stems are usually soft and less complex than dicot stems. Many monocots produce fibrous roots that frequently form underground structures for food storage and reproduction, such as rhizomes, bulbs and tubers.

DICOTS. There are about 200,000 species of *dicotyledons* (dicots), all of which possess two seedling leaves. This diverse and widespread group of plants includes most flowering trees, shrubs and many herbaceous plants. Dicot blooms range from complicated flowers with numerous parts, such as sedum, columbine and red maple, to flowers that have fewer, simpler parts, such as cardinal flower and violet. The fundamental traits of dicots are:

- two seedling leaves.
- leaves in which veins form an intricate network and that may be entire, lobed, toothed and divided in a variety of ways.
- flower parts (petals and sepals) that occur mostly in 4s or 5s or multiples of 4 and 5.
- stems that, in cross-section, show a ring of *vascular bundles* (which transport water and nutrients) surrounding a *pith* in the center in which food is usually stored. To the outside of vascular tissues is the *cortex* covered by protective bark.

The composite family, which includes sunflowers, daisies, thistles, goldenrods, hawkweeds, asters, black-eyed Susans and dandelions, is the largest family of flowering plants. The typical structure of a "flower" in the composite family is actually an outer ring of large, colorful, sterile *ray flowers* that attract insects, surrounding a cluster of many fertile flowers.

REPRODUCTION. From the fuzzy immature flowers of pussy willow, harbingers of spring, to the elegantly ornate blooms of many orchids, flowers are ingenious natural sculptures that accomplish a vital task: they produce seeds to ensure the birth of the next generation. During *pollination*, sperm-bearing *pollen*, which is produced by male *stamens*, is transferred to the female *pistil* (Figure 9-1). Each stamen is composed of a pollen-bearing *anther* held aloft on a stalk-like *filament*. The pistil consists of a swelling (*stigma*) that receives the pollen, perched on a stalk (*style*) that leads down to the egg-bearing *ovary*. The green *sepals* and colorful *petals,* both of which attract insects, are really a form of specialized leaves. When a pollen grain alights and sticks to a stigma,

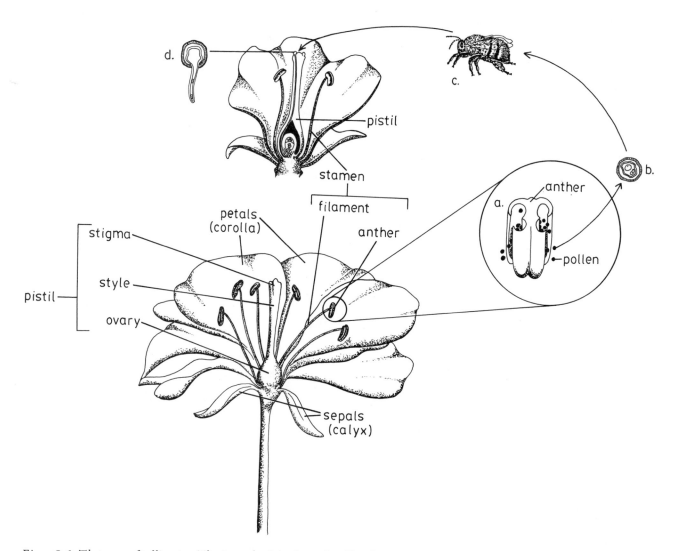

*Figure 9-1. The process of pollination. The ripe anther (**a**) releases the pollen (**b**). An insect, such as the bumblebee shown here (**c**), transports the pollen to the stigma of another flower of the same species. Once it arrives on the correct stigma (**d**), the pollen grain germinates; the pollen tube grows down to the ovary, where the ovum is produced and fertilized.*

it grows a *pollen tube* down the style and into the ovary (only seed plants have a pollen tube). An *embryo* forms when one sperm cell fertilizes the egg. The surrounding tissue or *endosperm,* which provides food and protection for the embryo, forms when another sperm fertilizes the endosperm nucleus.

The shapes and structures of flowers help to determine how reproduction occurs. *Pollination* takes place when the pollen from any flower lands on the stigma of another flower, but *fertilization* occurs only if the sperm from that pollen unites with the egg of that flower. If the pollen is from the same plant, *self-pollination* can result in *self-fertilization.* The designs of many flowers discourage self-fertilization because it stunts the process of evolution and the development of new traits that increase the plant's chances of survival. *Cross-pollination* occurs when pollen comes from a different plant and can result in *cross-fertilization.* An entirely new combination of genetic traits results from cross-fertilization, which is the basis for evolution among plants. For example, a new plant may result that has a slightly different color pattern on its petals that is more successful at attracting insects. This new plant is more likely to become pollinated and set seeds than the flowers of the plants that produced it. In time, the offspring of the new plant will increase in number. One study found that flowers with larger, showier blooms and a greater number of flowers are more apt to be pollinated by insects.

A number of strategies are used by flowers to increase the likelihood of cross-fertilization.

- In the case of *monoecious* plants, which produce both male and female flowers on each plant, pistils and stamens are often located on different flowers.
- Among *dioecious* plants, on which each plant bears either male or female flowers only, pistils and stamens are located on different plants. Holly is one example.
- Plants produce similar flowers but the pistils and stamens ripen at different times. Usually, pollen is dispersed on any given tree before the pistils are ready.
- Flowers, such as orchids, produce pistils and stamens that are located in separate places on the flower.
- Flowers are produced, as in the case of bluets (Quaker ladies) and primrose, on which the lengths of the pistils and stamens on any given flower are different to prevent self-fertilization.

Pollen is spread mostly by wind, water, insects and other animals. Since wind-pollinated flowers do not need to attract insects, they are usually small and green and lack attractive scents. Most wind-pollinated flowers are single-sexed and produce tiny, dry pollen grains in great quantities. This pollen can drift for hundreds of miles (kilometers) but may fall anywhere, so pollination is more reliable on plants growing close together. Water-pollinated flowers simply drop their pollen on the water, or they produce it underwater, and the pollen is carried away.

The relatively large, odd-shaped, sticky pollen grains produced by animal-pollinated flowers attach to visiting animals, primarily insects, birds and bats. Animals are attracted to flowers for food (nectar, pollen, flower parts and wax), because of the bright colors and scents or because they think a flower is something else. Certain flowers that mimic both the appearance and smell of the mates of particular insects get pollinated when the insect actually tries to copulate with the bloom! The four main groups of pollinating insects are the beetles, flies, bees and wasps, and the butterflies and moths. Animal-pollinated flowering plants do not have to produce large quantities of pollen because insects and other animals are selective and accurate at finding and pollinating the flowers they find attractive. For this reason, animal-pollinated plants can often grow far apart and are capable of forming highly diverse communities, such as tropical rainforests.

The seeds that are produced by successful pollination are the genetic result of millions of years of interaction and evolution between plants and animals. *Seeds* are composed of an embryo surrounded by nourishment and encased in a hard *seed coat.* Dormant seeds will only sprout when they encounter the right conditions of moisture, temperature and light. Some seeds are astoundingly long-lived. Several 2,000-year-old lotus seeds were discovered in 1951 inside a Neolithic canoe that was buried under 18 feet (5.5 meters) of peat in a bog close to Tokyo. These seeds were successfully sprouted and their offspring are now growing in botanical gardens around the world.

The seeds of flowering plants, in the forms of grains, pits, nuts and beans, constitute more than half of the food humankind eats every day (Figure 1-1). Seeds and roots of the American lotus are some traditional wild edibles of Native North Americans.

Seeds are dispersed by many different forces, including the action of wind, water and animals and the active, mechanical forces of the seed pod itself. Witch hazel, jewelweed (touch-me-not) and Virginia knotweed seed pods forcefully eject their mature seeds. Many people are familiar with the dandelion's seeds borne upon wispy parachutes. Cottonwood and aspen seeds are carried on the breeze by tufts of whitish "cotton," and one orchid can produce millions of seeds that are so tiny they are swept up by the wind and carried great distances. Hooks and barbs are among the most effective means by which seeds, such as those of beggar's ticks and cocklebur, hitchhike on the fur and feathers of animals.

Fruit provides a special form of seed dispersal. A *fruit* is a ripened ovary of a plant surrounded by other fused flower parts, such as stigma, sepals and petals. Slice an apple in half horizontally and you will see the star-shaped, five-part seed chamber formed by the original flower that contained the same number of parts. Once an animal has eaten and digested a fruit, the seeds are deposited in its droppings, which provide a strong dose of natural fertilizer. Trees and shrubs frequently grow in fields beneath powerlines and other structures, where birds have dropped the seeds while roosting. The seeds of many fruits require *scarification* before they can germinate—the physical and chemical weakening of the seed coat as it passes through the digestive tract of an animal.

When a seed germinates, the root, which grows down toward Earth's force of gravity and anchors the young plant, is the first to appear. It is soon followed by the sprout, and later the leaves, growing up against the force of gravity.

PARTS OF A FLOWERING PLANT. The parts of flowering plants and their functions are similar to those described under "Parts of a Tree" in the "Discussion" in Chapter 8. Roots anchor the plant, absorb and transport water and minerals from the soil and store nourishment. Some plants, such as corn, have aboveground *prop roots* that impart additional support.

The variety of stems found among flowering plants all serve the same functions: they support and elevate the flowers and leaves; transport water, minerals and sugar; store food; and, in many cases, provide a means of vegetative reproduction. Growth occurs via *meristem* tissue—cells that continually divide at the tips of branches and roots (*apical meristem*) and along the sides of trunks and stems (*cambium*). Branches only grow in length by adding new cells at their tips—a nail driven into the side of a tree always remains at the same height from the ground. *Annuals* are plants that die each year after producing seeds, while *perennials* live on to grow another year. *Biennials* require two growing seasons to complete their life cycle.

Epiphytic flowering plants, including many orchids and bromeliads, have stems, leaves and roots that allow them to

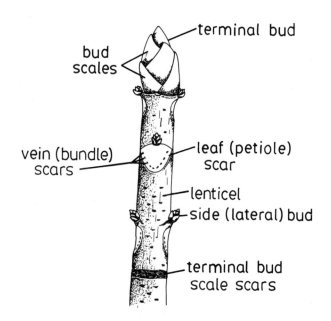

Figure 9-3. The parts of a twig.

sprout and grow in the crowns of trees where, in most cases, the roots never touch the ground. Water and nutrients are absorbed from those available in the tree crowns. Many epiphytes are succulent and can store water. The swollen leaf bases of bromeliads form water basins that catch the rain and fog drip. Certain amphibians and insects use these tiny treetop ponds to breed in, and some aquatic insects in tropical rainforests live nowhere else but in bromeliad basins. The Florida butterfly orchid (Figure 9-2) is found in the Everglades, as is Spanish moss, another common southeastern epiphyte that also grows in Mexico. Spanish moss is a bromeliad—a flowering plant related to pineapple—that grows in great hanging plumes on the branches of live oaks and other trees of the U.S. Southeast.

A look at the parts of a twig reveals that they are not as simple as would seem at first glance (Figure 9-3). *Terminal buds* and *lateral buds* are covered with protective *bud scales,* which are a specialized form of leaves. Winter buds, of which there can be millions on a single large tree, contain embryonic leaves and/or flowers, cells for growth, sugars and other nutrients and bud scales to protect from dry winter winds. Usually, when two sizes of lateral buds are present, the larger are flower buds and the smaller are leaf buds. Every year twigs grow in length and they form and shed leaves, leaving *bud-scale scars* at the juncture of different growing seasons and *leaf* and *petiole scars* where each leaf falls off. Inside each leaf scar are smaller dots—*vein* or *bundle scars*—that mark the places where conductive tissue entered the twig at the base of the old leaf. Many twigs, especially those of birches and cherries, have pronounced spots or striped markings called *lenticels* that mark pores that provide for gas exchange. When a leaf bud swells, it either grows into a *simple leaf* with a single blade or it forms a *compound leaf* on which the leaf blade is

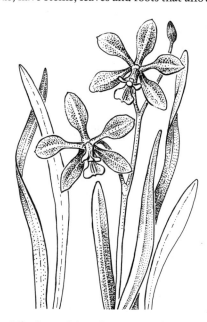

Figure 9-2. This beautiful epiphyte, the Florida butterfly orchid, is found in the Everglades. Size: to 31.5 in. (80 cm). (Illustration by Marjorie C. Leggitt)

divided into numerous distinct *leaflets,* each of which could be mistaken for an individual leaf.

Growing plants are sensitive beings that interact with their environments. A tendril will react and begin to coil around a piece of silk thread weighing nine-millionths of an ounce (.00025 gram) that is laid carefully across it.[4] Once a tendril finds a place of attachment, it coils up tighter and actually pulls the plant up. Stems and leaves move in response to sunlight and the leaves of one species of sunflower of the North American prairies, *Silphium laciniatum,*

alternate

opposite

whorled

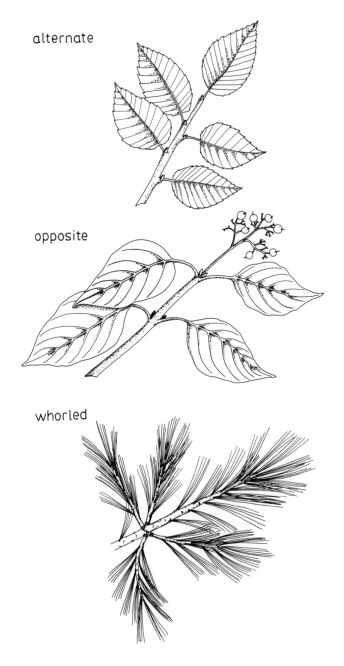

Figure 9-4. Three basic kinds of branching patterns: alternate, opposite and whorled.

orient to the points of the compass. Most stems reach toward the sun and most leaves grow at right angles to sunlight to capture the maximum amount of solar energy available. Leaves of the mallow face toward the sun and follow its progress during the day; then, after sunset, they turn back to the east to prepare to catch the rays of the rising sun once again!

In early plants, leaves and branching patterns arose as a way of increasing the surface area over which photosynthesis occurs. Prior to the appearance of leaves photosynthesis took place in stems. Much photosynthesis still does occur in the green stems of plants. Leaves and branches form one of three primary branching patterns: *opposite, alternate* and *whorled* (Figure 9-4). Most plants possess an alternate branching pattern. The majority of the trees and shrubs that exhibit opposite branching are either **m**aples, **a**shes, **d**ogwoods or belong to the **cap**rifoliaceae family, which includes the honeysuckles, viburnums and elderberries. The **buck**eyes also branch opposite, along with the related **horse**chestnut, which was imported to North America from Europe. One way to remember these opposite-branching woody plants is the mnemonic "**madcap bucking horse.**"

The two main parts of a leaf are the stalk, or *petiole,* and the thin *blade.* Leaves are covered by a protective *cuticle.* Most photosynthesis occurs within the leaf blade, but a small amount does take place in the petiole. Primarily, the petiole is a pipeline through which water and minerals enter the leaf and the products of photosynthesis (sugars, starches, proteins, etc.) exit. Numerous veins run throughout the leaf. Gas exchange takes place through *stomata,* openings that are usually located on the bottoms of leaves on land plants. Among some aquatic plants, such as the water lily, stomata are located on top because the bottoms of the floating leaves are in contact with the water. The upper surfaces of water lily leaves possess a waxy coating that repels water to keep the leaves dry. Many aquatic plants channel air from the leaf stomata on the surface down through tubes to the submerged roots.

Upon going outdoors during the morning hours, many people have noticed small droplets of water that have formed on the margins of some leaves, particularly those of strawberry plants. This is not dew, but is actually excreted from special pores and contains sugars, minerals and salts.

DORMANCY, DECIDUOUS LEAVES AND AUTUMN COLORS. Deciduous trees and bulbs *require* a dormant period consisting of a certain number of days below a particular temperature before they can leaf out again. This adaptation prevents them from resuming growth during any of the many winter thaws that come each year and so protects them from winter injury that could prove fatal. Another safeguard is provided by the fact that many dormant plants will not start growing until the amount of daylight reaches a certain minimum during the lengthening days of spring.

Some evergreen leaves, like those of the rhododendron, respond to extreme cold, and the dry conditions cold creates, by drooping and rolling up lengthwise to reduce surface area and moisture loss. *Deciduous* (from the Latin word for "to fall off") trees and shrubs shed their leaves during the cold season in part because freezing would destroy delicate cell walls. Also, while the ground is frozen roots cannot absorb water, so plants cannot afford to lose water through their leaves or they would dry out and die. Similarly, scarce water is the reason that deciduous desert trees and shrubs lose their leaves during the dry season.

Among deciduous trees and shrubs, cold or dry periods, depending on the habitat, cause a layer to form across the base of each leaf stem. The decreasing day length of autumn also prompts the formation of this layer, called the *abscission layer,* which cuts the leaf off from sap flow and protects the stem from the environment and desiccation where the leaf was attached. Soon, the leaves die and fall off. A few trees, such as oaks and beeches, tend to hold onto many of their leaves throughout the winter and lose them when the buds and twigs flush with new spring growth. Up to 10 million autumn leaves may fall in 1 acre of deciduous temperate woodland!

Few spectacles in nature are as dramatic as that of the intense autumn leaf colors that adorn many trees such as maples, birches, aspens, elms, oaks, basswoods, larches, cottonwoods and willows as well as some shrubs and vines such as Virginia creeper. When the abscission layer forms at the base of each leaf in the fall and cuts off the flow of sap, green chlorophyll breaks down, revealing the yellow, gold and orange hues of the carotenoid pigments (carotenes and xanthophylls) that were already present but masked by the green chlorophyll. Sugar becomes trapped in the leaves and, therefore, more concentrated. Meanwhile, the bright sunlight, cool nights and high sugar content in leaves cause anthocyanin pigments to form, creating the scarlets, reds and purples that adorn red oak, red and sugar maple, Virginia creeper, sumac and both sweet and black gums.

The Deciduous Forest

"Going UP—COMING down, going UP—COMING down" calls a red-eyed vireo incessantly from among the crowns of yellow birch and buckeye. This, the most common songbird of the deciduous woodland canopy, is not alone as a blackburnian warbler is feeding in the tops of a hemlock while a redstart tends its nest in a nearby sugar maple. In the lower hemlock branches a magnolia warbler is calling "weeta-weeta with you," while the ovenbird's "teacher teacher teacher" rings out from the forest floor. The hairy woodpecker that taps out its mating call shares the forest canopy with the striking red-headed woodpecker. Several white-tailed deer browse in a lush patch of shrubs and young trees growing where some large windfalls opened up the forest floor to bright sunlight. The thickets in this clearing have attracted the chestnut-sided warbler, which sings out "please please pleased to meet'cha."

This, the Great Smoky Mountains National Park in North Carolina and Tennessee, which covers more than 500,000 acres (202,500 hectares), holds the largest stand of virgin forest in the eastern United States. One-third of the woodland in the Smokies is *virgin forest:* that is, it has never been cut. Other dominant trees include basswood and yellow poplar or tulip tree. More than 100 species of native trees live in this forest region, and the tops of some individual trees soar 100 to 150 feet (30.5 to 45.7 meters) above the forest floor. The canopy may contain more than one dozen tree species and the understory as many as 40 or 50 species. Holly and magnolia create a lower layer in this rich woodland, with rhododendron, hydrangea and viburnum forming a shorter layer still. More than 100 species of herbaceous plants, including many ferns, grow on the forest floor.

Worldwide, temperate deciduous forests comprise 21 percent of Earth's total mass of living things, or 193 billion tons (175 billion metric tons).[5] Although they are called "temperate," these forests experience widespread fluctuations of temperature and humidity during the year. Even today, forest patterns in the northern temperate regions are greatly affected by the scouring action of the most recent glacier, which melted back some 10,000 years ago. This glacier covered the land as far south as New Jersey and Nebraska. Northern forests have not developed the diversity of species that is found in the forested areas south of the glacier's reach, such as in the Great Smoky Mountains National Park.

The temperate deciduous forest of North America once stretched in a continuous, nearly unbroken swath of green from southern Canada, as far north as Hudson Bay, south through the eastern United States to northern Florida, then from the Atlantic coast west past the Mississippi River, deep into the prairies and reaching as fingers along riverbanks wending their way nearly to the Rocky Mountains. Yellow birch, American beech and sugar maple are the dominant trees in northern parts of the hardwood forest, interspersed with ash, hemlock, white pine and patches of spruce and fir. Oak and hickory, mixed with white pine and hemlock, predominate in southern New England and south through the mid-Atlantic states down toward the Great Smokies. South of the Great Smokies, in southern states, are forests of pecan, hickory, magnolia, cypress, persimmon, live oak and, in sandy soils, long-leafed pine and palmetto. Along the lower Missouri River grow ash, hickory, cottonwood, cedar, oak, willow and walnut. Giant sycamores can still be found in isolated patches in the Ohio Valley, along with yellow poplar, walnut and cottonwood. Only a few, intermittent groves of old-growth or virgin forest remain in much of the East. These stands are mostly limited to preserves and inaccessible sites.

A variety of shrubs and vines is found throughout the deciduous forest. Some common shrubs, depending on the habitat, are the willow, sweet fern, hazelnut, alder, spice-bush, ninebark, witch hazel, greenbriar, spiraea, shadbush, rose, sumac, holly, dogwood, rhododendron, azalea, laurel, blueberry, elderberry, viburnum and the many species of brambles such as blackberry and raspberry. Vines can frequently be seen spiraling up and seeking support amid the tree crowns and forming dense mats in clearings. Adhesive disks, tendrils and special *adventitious roots* are used for attachment by various species. Each species of vine spirals either clockwise or counterclockwise as it grows. Bittersweet, grape, Virginia creeper, trumpet vine, honeysuckle, wild cucumber, wild pea, moonseed and nightshade are species of vines familiar to many. There are also a few poisonous plants: the familiar poison ivy, poison oak and poison sumac, which lives in wet areas.

Deciduous woodlands are rich environments full of surprises and natural wonders to reward the observant eye. Insects can be found munching on leaves, sipping nectar, decomposing wood and using plants for egg-laying. Leaf miners eat the layers of leaf tissue that lie in between the upper and lower epidermis, leaving a visible brown trail through the leaves. Larvae of a tiny moth called the maple leaf cutter live as a leaf miner when young. When older, the larvae cut two, circular, roughly .25-inch (.6-centimeter) pieces from a maple leaf, which are joined together at the edges to create a small, disk-shaped case. In late summer and early fall, wherever the maple leaf cutter is abundant, maple leaves that are still attached to the tree become riddled with tiny round holes and the forest floor is littered with the round, turtle-like pupal cases of the larvae. Dead trees are the apartment complexes of the forest, providing homes, nesting sites and food sources for insects, birds, mammals and other wildlife.

The forest floor is a fascinating environment that receives an average of 6 percent of the sunlight striking the tops of tree crowns and in which wind speed can be as low as 1 to 2 percent of that blowing over the woodland. Many woodland wildflowers bloom before the trees leaf out so they can take advantage of the few warm days when bright sunlight still reaches the forest floor. Although the forest, from soil to treetop, is a complex layering of habitats, most plants and animals live in just one or two levels throughout their lives. Nearly three-quarters of all arthropods (insects and their relatives) inhabit only one forest layer throughout their lifetimes, and 95 percent of all insects dwell in the soil for at least part of their life cycle. Up to 1,350 creatures can be seen with a hand lens or the naked eye in a patch of forest measuring 1 square foot (.1 square meter) that is 1 inch (2.5 centimeters) deep.

Figure 9-5. An idyllic scene in the Great Smoky Mountains National Park belies the unseen threats to the well-being of the forest. The health and vigor of trees in southeastern forests are being diminished by air pollution that, in some cases, originates hundreds and even thousands of miles away. (Photo by William S. Lea)

State of the Deciduous Forest

Signs of damage to trees by insects, fungi, viruses and other diseases are evident on any walk in the deciduous woods. The white pine weevil kills the terminal bud on the tallest branch of this common associate of deciduous trees. Side branches then take over as the lead growing branches: crowns become bushy and trunks crooked. Gypsy moths, insect pests that were accidentally introduced from France by would-be silk producers, periodically defoliate vast acreages of deciduous trees. Walking about the forest during a bad Gypsy moth infestation, we have heard caterpillar droppings so numerous that they sounded like a light rain.

The mixed, mesophytic forest of the U.S. Southeast is the richest, oldest and most diverse in North America. It covers an area larger than New England, including southwestern Pennsylvania, southeastern Ohio, parts of Maryland and Virginia, much of West Virginia, a piece of Kentucky and portions of Tennessee and Alabama (Figure 9-5). Since this habitat was never glaciated and never flooded by seas, its origins reach back 60 million years ago to the Cretaceous period. Abundant rainfall and warm weather create optimal growing conditions.

But the actions of humankind, especially the production of air pollutants such as acid rain (primarily from coal-burning industries) and ozone (from vehicular exhausts), are causing decline and death among the remaining trees of the mesophytic forest.[6] Ozone causes leaf growth to decline, which in turn diminishes the supply of nourishment flowing to the rest of the tree. Root growth drops off and reduces water and mineral uptake, sending less of life's essentials up to the leaves. This action-reaction response to stress becomes a downward spiral in the health, vigor and natural resistance of the tree. The excessive amounts of nitrogen oxides being absorbed by trees from polluted air are causing a complex nutritional and chemical imbalance in the trees, creating another source of increased stress and loss of resistance to fungi, insects and diseases. In affected areas, such as the Coal River Valley west of Beckley, West Virginia, among other locales, this combination of root loss and increased susceptibility to natural enemies causes large numbers of trees to fall over and snap off at rates much higher than those that normally occur in nature.[7]

An overall decline in the health, vigor and natural resistance of sugar maples is also occurring in the forests of the northeastern United States and southeastern Canada due to the effects of the same air pollutants affecting the southeastern woodlands: ozone and acid precipitation. Acid precipitation destroys the protective waxy coating on leaves and leaches toxic aluminum as well as heavy metals from soils, which increases absorption of these metals by tree roots. Trees absorb aluminum and build it into their cell walls. In addition, polluted air is causing the accumulation of the heavy metals lead, cadmium, copper and zinc in northeastern forest soils. Symptoms of the decline include:[8]

- the growth of smaller than usual, pale leaves that are often brown around the margins

- thinning and dieback of terminal twigs and branches in tree crowns from the top down
- decreased rates of growth
- the growth of buds that normally are dormant on healthy trees
- leaves turning color and dropping off early in autumn
- bark peeling off large branches and trunks

Most of the original virgin deciduous forest was cleared long ago. Many eastern forests have been cut over and grown back two or more times—the trees in these stands are young and lack the diversity and height associated with older stands. There are still numerous problems associated with the forestry practices used in many operations. Clear-cutting remains the preferred method of harvesting among loggers, bringing with it a host of environmental problems. A detailed review of these problems is found in "State of the Coniferous Forests" in Chapter 8.

Ironically, the increasing popularity of many forms of outdoor recreation is having a negative impact on forest environments in some areas: erosion along hiking trails and degradation of habitat in heavily used camping areas where firewood is cleared from underbrush and stripped from trees, as well as disruption of wildlife. The picking of plants for recreational purposes, transplanting into home gardens and commercial uses is depleting many areas of attractive flower species that are often rare or endangered.

Forest Stewardship

Many of the same principles apply to stewardship of the deciduous forests as are discussed in Chapter 8 for coniferous forests. We need to preserve the wild woodlands that remain and practice better forestry management, relying on sustainable, low-impact cutting in mixed-age stands in place of clear-cuts. In some regions, such as the immense tract of remaining forest located in northern New Hampshire, Vermont and southern Quebec, specific regions need to be identified and preserved before the forests are gone or their ecological values are compromised by poor management. Wise use of wood and wood products, as well as energy conservation, will help to reduce the demands placed on forest ecosystems and alleviate the air pollution that is stressing and, in some cases, killing trees throughout eastern North America. Deciduous forests are a green jewel that has survived hundreds of years of use and abuse. Their continued existence is a testimony to the ecological resilience that is inherent to many environments: a resilience that will be seriously compromised if the general quality of the environment does not soon improve.

QUESTIONS

1. In the Salish story "The Bitterroot," why does the old woman go down to the stream to sing and weep? Who comes to help her find food for her grandchildren?
2. What happens when the old woman's tears fall into

Earth? What color is the flower that grows all around her?

3. Why do you think the food plant that is given to the old woman and her people tastes so bitter?

4. Why is Zimo not able to plant his crops in the Penobscot story "Indian Summer"? Who comes to Zimo and tells him to plant his seeds? What would you have done in Zimo's place?

5. Where does the special warm weather for Zimo's seeds come from? Why do you think Gluskabe helps Zimo? How many days does it take for Zimo's seeds to sprout and bear a crop?

6. What do the Penobscot people call the warm time of year that comes just before the snow falls? What is this time of year meant to remind us of? What do we call this time of year today?

7. What is a flowering plant? Why do plants bear flowers? What do flowers produce?

8. What is pollination? How does pollen spread from one flower to another?

9. Why are insects and other animals important for pollination to take place? What attracts insects and animals to the flowers, and what do they take when they get there? Name some animals that pollinate flowers.

10. What is a seed and why are seeds important to flowers? What is inside a seed, and how is a seed fed and protected? How do flowers produce seeds?

11. How does a fruit help a plant to spread its seeds? What are some other ways that plants spread their seeds?

12. What kinds of patterns do branches form on plants? What are the markings on the twigs of trees and shrubs and how do they form?

13. What is a bud? What parts of plants grow from buds?

14. Why are leaves important to plants? What do leaves do? Can you name some parts of leaves? What is a simple leaf? What is a compound leaf?

15. Why do many plants lose their leaves every year? How many different colors have you seen leaves turn in autumn?

16. What does *deciduous* mean? Where does the deciduous forest grow? What kinds of plants and animals live in the deciduous forest?

17. Why is it important to observe nature closely? How do your senses help you to do this? What are those senses?

18. What is happening to the plants and animals that live in deciduous forests today? How can you help to take care of deciduous forests and the things that live there?

ACTIVITIES

Flower Fantasy

ACTIVITY: Take a fantasy journey from seed to flower and back to seed.

GOALS: Understand the life cycle of a flowering plant.
AGE: Younger children and older children
MATERIALS: Copy of *"Flower Fantasy"*; picture and/or illustration of sunflowers; enough of both kinds of sunflower seeds for each child to have a handful: whole birdseed sunflower seeds and *edible* sunflower seeds (not birdseed) for the children to eat; dried sunflower seedhead (optional and often available where birdseed is sold).
PROCEDURE: Beforehand, obtain enough sunflower seeds, both hulled and whole (with the hulls on), to give each child a handful of each.

Note: To surprise the children, do not tell them ahead of time what kind of flower they are going to become. As a variation on this activity, have younger children act out the fantasy, going through the movements as you read.

Tell the children to hold out an open hand during the fantasy when they hear you say, "You have formed a beautiful head of seeds to grow the next generation." Now have the children close their eyes and take a few deep breaths. Ask them to relax their bodies and to let their imaginations lead them as you read the following story out loud.

FLOWER FANTASY
You are a tiny seed buried in a field of rich, dark soil. It is springtime and each day the soil surrounding you grows a little warmer in the sun and wetter with spring rain. Soon you are about to sprout. First, your root splits out of your seed coat and reaches down into the soil. Then, two small seed leaves push their way through the soil into the bright sunlight. As each day grows a little longer, and the sun travels higher in its arc across the sky, you grow a strong, straight stem and large wide leaves that catch the sun's energy and make the food that feeds you. Leaves appear along your stem. Near the top, your main stem begins to form a few side branches, each with a flower bud on top. The blustery wind bends you at times, but the roots that anchor you are strong and nourishing as they bring water and minerals from the soil to grow on.

One day, the large bud on the very top of your stem begins to open. In a few short weeks you are holding up to the sun a large, round, yellow flower with a circle of long petals ringing hundreds of small flowers in the center. Buzzing bees and other insects visit your flowers every day. Each time an insect visits, it gathers some of your nectar and pollen. The pollen the insects bring from other flowers brushes off onto your pistils and fertilizes them. Tiny seeds form where the flowers once grew. By the time the days of summer are getting shorter, **you have formed a beautiful head of seeds to grow the next generation.** (*Go around to the children and place a handful of whole sunflower seeds in each outstretched hand.*)

Birds are landing on you now to eat your seeds. Some of the seeds are dropped by the birds far from where you are growing. The days are getting colder and soon the first frost causes your leaves and flowers to droop. Some of your seeds begin to fall out and land on the ground. A squirrel comes and gathers those seeds and buries them in shallow holes for winter food. The squirrel eats some seeds, but forgets others. These forgotten seeds, and the ones dropped by birds, will grow into new plants next year. By the time the first snow falls, your stems, leaves and flowers are brown and withered. But your seeds, in and on the soil, are waiting for the moist rains and warm sunlight of spring to return.

Ask the children to open their eyes. Inquire: "What kind of flower did you become? Do you recognize the kinds of seeds you are holding in your hand?" Once someone identifies the flower and seeds as those of a sunflower, hold up a photograph or illustration of a sunflower, or a sunflower seedhead (optional), and pass out some edible sunflower seeds for everyone to munch on. Ask: "What kind of gifts do sunflowers give us?" Have the children thank the sunflowers for the gift of their seeds, their bright, cheery flowers and their food for people, insects, birds, squirrels, mice and other animals. Have the children show their appreciation for the gifts of sunflowers by planting some seeds around the grounds of the home or learning center.

Color the World With Flowers

ACTIVITY: Observe flowers carefully using all your senses. Illustrate many kinds of flowers and color them in. Research and report on the natural history of these flowers. Create booklets out of these illustrations and reports.

GOALS: Experience the rich sensory world of flowers. Recognize the appearances of some different kinds of flowers, including monocots and dicots. Understand the basic natural history of these flowering plants.

AGE: Younger children

MATERIALS: Tracing paper or thin typing paper for tracing, pencils, paper, photocopies of masters (optional), staples (optional), crayons, tempera paints, brushes, containers of water for paints, cardboard backing or clipboards, hand lenses, copies of Figure 9-6, children's and adult's books and other resources that teach the basic natural history of flowering plants, cut flowers.

PROCEDURE: Tell the children that they are about to use their senses to discover the world of flowers. Take a walk outside to see some flowers growing outdoors nearby, or visit a botanical garden or a greenhouse. Cut flowers can be observed in the learning center for several days. Use hand lenses to look closely at venation in leaves and flower parts. Have the children smell the flowers and guide the children as they gently feel the texture of flower petals and other plant parts. Where appropriate and *safe,* have the children taste some leaves, seeds or nuts or berries. Divide the group into

pairs and pass out some paper, backing and a box of crayons to each pair. Ask the children to take some time to look very carefully at the flowers while recording on the paper, with splotches of crayon coloring, as many different colors they can find on the flowers and other plant parts. Have them use crayon that is the best match for the plant colors, even if it is not exactly the same. Try shading with several colors of crayons or paints to create original colors as needed. Also, have them trace in pencil as many patterns of leaf venation as they can find.

During this walk, and when looking at the color splotches, leaf vein patterns and pictures and illustrations of other flowers later, review with the children the differences between monocots and dicots, such as the number of seedling leaves. Key in on leaf and flower characteristics as well. Now have each child choose a flower and sit carefully and quietly while drawing and coloring that flower as accurately as possible.

Once back indoors, gather pictures or illustrations of flowers and flowering plants from both dicots and monocots (see "Discussion"). Have the children draw free-hand *or* use thin typing paper to trace or even enlarge a number of flowers from each group, with one flower per sheet of paper. If the children are very young, you may want to create some masters and staple some books together out of photocopies of the masters. Figure 9-6, which can be enlarged, provides some flowers for tracing and for using as masters.

Have the children color their flowers and flowering plants. When the "coloring books" are completed, allow time for the children to research and share what they have learned about their flowering plants. Compile these illustrations and reports into booklets and publish them.

Pollination Time Machine

ACTIVITY: Discuss the life cycle of a flower, especially pollination, the means by which plants are pollinated and the structures they possess to ensure pollination. Create a flower of your own design that has all the parts of a real flower. Construct a pollination time machine that will produce seeds in one "growing season" before your very eyes.

GOALS: Understand the parts of a flower and how these parts function during the process of pollination to create seeds and complete the reproductive life cycle of a flower. Realize the many structures that flowers possess for wind pollination, and for attracting pollinating insects and other animals. Understand the kinds of animals that pollinate flowers.

AGE: Younger children and older children

MATERIALS: Cardboard; scissors; markers; one spreading paper clasp for clock; bed sheets; tacks; desk or table; string to tie back the sheets for stage area; Figure 9-1; materials as needed for making flowers such as cardboard tubes (empty paper-towel tubes), pencils, tape, construction paper, glue or paste, crayons, watercolor paints, brushes, water and containers to put it in, string, balloons, pipe cleaners, clay, chalk dust or flour for pollen, straws, etc.

PROCEDURE: Beforehand, create a large cardboard clock with one hand on it that points to a clock face divided into the four seasons of winter, spring, summer and autumn. Hang sheets to set up an enclosed space behind which children can work to make their flowers produce seeds. Design this space so that when the sheets are rolled up or drawn back everyone can see what is inside, and when the sheets are rolled down no one can observe the inside of the time machine. Start with the sheets rolled up. Set up a table or desk inside.

Use Figure 9-1 as a guide as you discuss with the children the parts of a flower and how they function during reproduction to create seeds and complete the life cycle of a flowering plant. Now ask them: "How does pollen get from one flower to another? What moves it? What kinds of structures do flowers have that help them to become pollinated?" Review the many means by which pollen is transferred: wind, birds, bats and insects (beetles, flies, bees, wasps, butterflies and moths). "Flowers, insects and other animals," you continue, "have developed over millions of years so that they each get what they need to survive—flowers become pollinated while animals receive food of nectar and pollen."

Divide the children into small groups and have each group choose to make a flower that is pollinated by either wind, birds, bats or one of the insects listed in the preceding paragraph. Each of these means of pollination must be represented by at least one group. Now, have each group create a giant flower of their own design that contains all of the parts of a flower shown in Figure 9-1. They will also need to design pollen grains to go with that flower and means of pollination, as well as seeds that the flower produces. The children need to create the seeds in private so they can surprise the other children when those seeds are revealed later in the activity. Each flower they create must have a particular strategy to become pollinated. Ask the children to be creative and use their imaginations to make original flower designs: their flowers do not have to look like real flowers.

Once the flowers are completed, have each group practice their *"Pollination Time Machine"* presentation and then perform it for the other groups. Each group will take turns bringing their flowers up and placing them on the table or desk inside the pollination time machine. Have someone from each group describe what pollinates their flower, and how the structure of the flower works during pollination. This will be done in the following way: someone will stand off to the side and hold up the clock with seasons marked on it for all to see. As the clock hand is slowly turned to point to each season in succession (winter, spring, summer, fall

and back to winter), the children showing their flower will explain what is happening during each season (dormancy, pollination, seed growth, etc.). When the clock hand points to autumn, the sheets will be rolled down or drawn together and the children will attach their seeds to the flower. Then, the sheets will be raised for everyone to see the seeds.

Note: A fun extension to this activity is to have the children redesign the seeds they've created, and their plants, so that they possess a means of seed dispersal. Seeds can be dispersed by wind, water, animals or by a structure that throws the seeds away from the plant. Hold a contest to see who, using the same materials as everyone else, can design a structure to throw a particular seed the farthest, such as a bean seed.

Seed Dispersal Scatter

ACTIVITY: (A) Play a matching game to pair seeds with descriptions of how the seeds are dispersed. (B) Walk through an old field and gather seed "hitchhikers" on your clothes. Sort these out to see which seeds are most successful and which plants they come from. (C) Hold a brief seed release ceremony and thank seeds for their gifts of life.

GOALS: Understand the various means by which seeds are dispersed. Realize, and show gratitude for, the fact that seeds give human beings the gift of life.

AGE: Younger children and older children

MATERIALS: (A) One copy of Figure 9-7 for each child, pencils, examples and sample photographs and/or illustrations of flowers and their seeds. (B) Old field with seed-bearing plants, pair of old pants for each person, old white sheet, pencil, paper and cardboard backing or clipboard, hand lenses. (C) Sufficient milkweed seeds, or some other kind of windblown seed, to give one to each child.

PROCEDURE A: *Seed Dispersal Match-Up.* Ask the children, "How many ways can you think of that seeds are spread or dispersed by plants?" Hold a question-and-answer discussion of seed dispersal and the ways plants disperse their seeds. Present some examples and/or photographs or illustrations of plants and their seeds, showing how the seeds are dispersed. Ask the children to try to name other plants and how those plants disperse their seeds. List their answers up front for all to see in four columns according to dispersal by wind, water, animals and mechanical structures on plants, but do not label the columns. When the children are finished sharing their ideas, ask them what kind of dispersal the plants listed in each column have in common.

Pass out one copy of "Seed Dispersal Match-Up" (Figure 9-7) to each child and ask the children to match each seed in the left-hand column with the corresponding description on the right of how that seed is dispersed. With younger

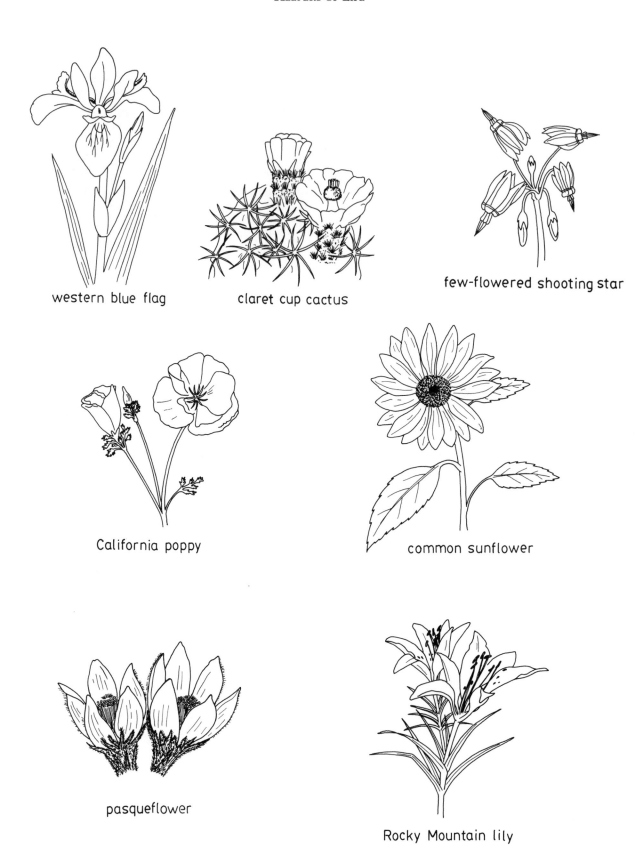

western blue flag

claret cup cactus

few-flowered shooting star

California poppy

common sunflower

pasqueflower

Rocky Mountain lily

Figure 9-6. Flower outlines for "Color the World With Flowers." These flowers are from western and central North America. A key to the color of each flower: western blue flag, blue to violet; claret cup cactus, scarlet; few-flowered shooting star, deep pink with a yellowish ring near the ends of petals and a purplish tip; California poppy, orange; common sunflower, yellow rays with a maroon center; pasqueflower, blue, purple or lavender petals with a yellow center; Rocky Mountain lily, red petals that are yellowish with purple spots near the center.

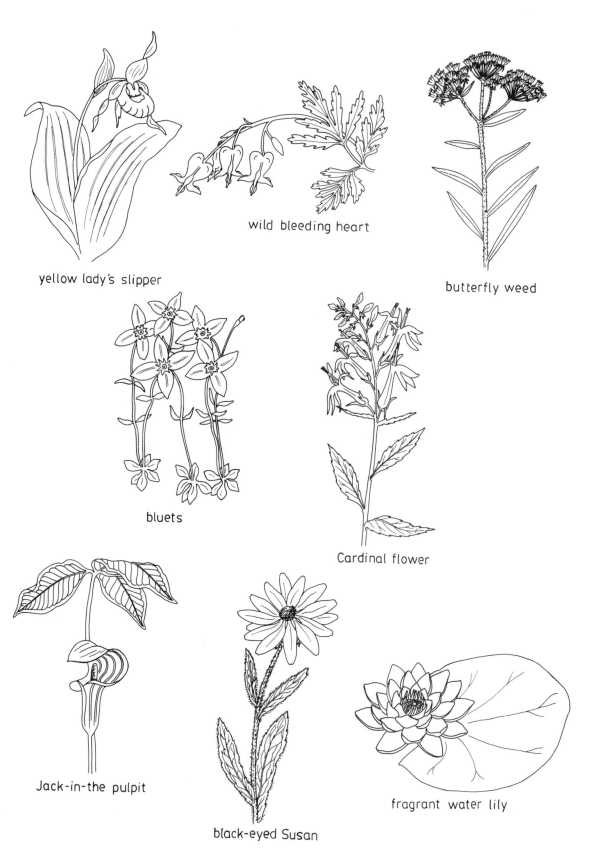

yellow lady's slipper

wild bleeding heart

butterfly weed

bluets

Cardinal flower

Jack-in-the pulpit

black-eyed Susan

fragrant water lily

These flowers are from eastern and central North America. A key to the color of each flower: yellow lady's slipper, yellow; wild bleeding heart, deep pink to red; butterfly weed, orange; bluets, pale blue with a golden yellow center; Cardinal flower, red; Jack-in-the-pulpit, green to purplish-brown, streaked; black-eyed Susan, golden-yellow rays with a brown center; fragrant water lily, white or pink petals with a yellow center.

children, read the words on the worksheets together as a vocabulary lesson, but have the children make their own matches. Once the children are finished, have them explain the matches they made, and then share the correct answers.

PROCEDURE B: *Hitchhikers.* Beforehand, scout out an old field near the home or learning center in which there are a number of seed-bearing plants that are knee-high or better, but that is free of brambles. Test the area by walking through it and making sure a good number of seeds stick to your clothes. Ask the children to come dressed for this activity wearing sneakers and a pair of older pants: seeds will stick to both. Take an old sheet with you on this trip.

Take the children out to the old field and tell them, "You are going to pick up some hitchhikers in this field." Ask them, "What do you think I might mean by 'hitchhikers'?" Have the children slowly walk across the field and back to the place they started from. Have they found the hitchhikers? Which strategy for dispersal are the seeds using that are stuck on the children?

Have the children help each other to pick all of the seeds off of their clothing. Ask them to look closely at the seeds under their hand lenses. Then have the children place the seeds in separate piles on the sheet, with one kind of seed per pile. Once they have picked all of the seeds off of themselves, help them to count the number of each kind of seed. Which seeds are most numerous? Which ones are the most successful hitchhikers? Take the children on a walk through the part of the field they crossed and search for the plants that their seeds came from.

PROCEDURE C: *Returning the Gift.* Beforehand, gather enough milkweed seeds, or another kind of seed dispersed by the wind, for each child to have one seed.

Ask the children, "What kinds of gifts do seeds give to human beings and other animals?" Mention that half of all the food people eat all over the world each day, in the forms of grains, nuts, beans and pits, comes from the seeds of flowering plants.

Pass out one windblown seed to each child. As the children release their seeds into the wind, have them thank the seeds, and the plants that produce seeds, for a particular gift of life.

Mind-Growing Seed Game

ACTIVITY: Play a concentration matching game using different kinds of seeds.

GOALS: Develop observation skills and hone the skills of concentration and memory. Discover the great variety of seeds and learn how to recognize them.

AGE: Younger children and older children

MATERIALS: One pair of seeds from each of 5 (younger children) to 20 (older children) different varieties of seeds;

white glue or paste; enough small, identical paper cups to supply two cups per seed for this activity.

PROCEDURE: *Note:* It is a good idea to have an alternative activity going during the *"Mind-Growing Seed Game"* so children are not standing around as others play the game.

Beforehand, obtain pairs of seeds representing from 5 to 20 varieties of interesting seeds, using a greater number for older children. Your collection will include two of each kind of seed. Varieties of dried beans, peas, rice, nuts, etc., work well, as long as they are small enough to fit completely inside the paper cups without sticking out. Double-up two small paper cups, gluing one inside the other, to make one cup for each individual seed. Double cups are necessary so children cannot see through the cup to what is inside. Make sure the cups all look alike so children cannot use differences in outward appearance to form matches during the game. Glue each seed in your collection to the bottom, inside of a cup. You will have an even number of seeds glued into the cups. After the glue has dried, mix the cups up, turn them upside-down and arrange them in rows and columns on a desk or table.

Have the children work in small groups to play this game while others are involved in an alternative activity. *Only the children actually playing are allowed to talk during the game so that no one else is giving them clues.* This is a variation of the game called Memory or Concentration. To take a turn, a child turns over one cup (leaving it turned over in its place) and then tries to turn over the cup that has the matching bean in it. If *no* match is made the cups are turned back over to hide the seeds and are kept in the same row and column where they were found. That child's turn is completed. If a match *is* made, those two cups are left turned over but are kept in place on the playing surface. The child who made the match takes another round to make another match. When a match is not made, someone else takes a turn. The object of the game is to observe the seeds carefully as the cups are turned over and to remember where the matching seeds are beneath the cups. The game is over when all matches have been made. Now lead a question-and-answer period about the kinds of seeds that are in the cups and which plants they come from.

Winter Tree Trilogy

ACTIVITY: (A) Create bark rubbings from certain trees and have others use the rubbings to find the trees the rubbings were made from. (B) Play a game of charades and try to guess which tree's silhouette people are miming. (C) Observe a twig closely and match it with the tree it came from.

GOALS: Understand that every tree has its own unique, characteristic bark, twigs, branching pattern, growth habit and silhouette. Recognize the parts of a twig and understand their functions.

Seed Dispersal Match-Up

Connect each illustration with the matching description of how those seeds are dispersed.

- Feathery plumes attached to these seeds cause them to glide through the air.

- The two hooks on these seeds get caught in fur and on clothing.

- Miniature, delicate parasols carry these seeds aloft on the breeze.

- Deer and other animals bite into this sweet fruit and spread the seeds in their droppings.

- Some people say these seeds flutter away from the tree like tiny helicopters.

- The thousands of tiny bars on these seeds stick like Velcro® to clothes and fur.

- Strong winds cause the seeds to drop out of this capsule like a tiny salt shaker.

- When the heavy seeds fall from this tree onto water they may float far away.

Figure 9-7. "Seed Dispersal Match-Up."

AGE: Younger children and older children
MATERIALS: (A) Woodland or park where a variety of trees grow, strips of cloth to mark each tree, field guide to identifying trees and shrubs, newsprint, crayons, name tags for trees, marker. (B) Trees as described and marked in "A." (C) Area in which there are as many trees and shrubs growing that have branches close to the ground as there are children in the group, Figure 9-3, Figure 9-4, strips of cloth to mark each tree and shrub, pruning shears, field guide to trees and shrubs, name tag for each tree and shrub, marker.
PROCEDURE A: *Rubbing Trees the Right Way.* Beforehand, find a woodland or park near the home or learning center where a good variety of trees is growing. Choose about one dozen trees (including several species) that have bark that can be easily distinguished from the others in this group. Mark each tree by tying a strip of cloth to a low branch or around the trunk. Use a field guide to identify each tree and place a name tag hidden up high so you can use it later on.

Pair the children up and give a piece of newsprint and a crayon to each child. One child in each pair will begin by making a bark rubbing of one of the trees you have marked, while the other child, who is not making a rubbing at that particular time, will remain out of sight of the tree so he or she cannot see which tree the rubbing is being made from. When the rubbing is complete, have the child who made it give it to her or his partner. This partner now has to locate the tree from which the rubbing was made from among those you marked. Now have the children switch roles and repeat the entire sequence. After all children have had a chance to both make a rubbing and find a tree, go around to each tree and look carefully at its bark, asking the children: "What kinds of patterns do you see in this bark? How is it different from bark on the other marked trees?" Have the children give each tree a name according to the appearance of its bark. Then share the common name of each tree with the children. Do not go inside yet! It is time to play "Silhouette Charades."
PROCEDURE B: *Silhouette Charades.* Observe, with the children, the marked trees and discuss how their distinctive silhouettes form because of the particular branching habit and growth pattern of each tree. Choose several of the trees that have distinct silhouettes that are easily distinguished from one another. Divide the children into small groups and secretly whisper to each group which tree they are going to mime for the game of charades. They must keep it a secret so the others will have to guess later on. Give the groups 10 to 15 minutes to go off on their own and cooperate to create a group imitation of the branching pattern of their tree. They could do this standing, or by arranging themselves in a pattern on the ground. When all groups are ready, have them take turns miming their trees while the rest of the group tries to guess which tree they are miming. Since there will be more marked trees than small groups, it will be a challenge to guess the right tree.

PROCEDURE C: *Winter Twig Detectives.* Beforehand, find an area near the home or learning center where a number of trees and shrubs have branches close to the ground. You will need as many trees and shrubs as there are children in your group. Carefully mark each tree or shrub with a piece of cloth and prune one representative twig from each tree or shrub, being careful that the branching habit can be determined from the sample. Prune back to the living wood that the branch splits off of. Try to obtain twigs that demonstrate each of the most common branching patterns: opposite, alternate and whorled. Use a field guide to identify these plants and place a name tag up high and hidden so you can read it later.

Pass out one twig to each child, and then discuss the origins and functions of the parts of a twig (Figure 9-3), as well as twig branching patterns (Figure 9-4). Have the children find the parts on their twig, and its branching pattern, as you discuss them. Not all twigs have all of the parts in Figure 9-3, such as lenticels, so children may or may not find these present.

Take the children out to where you collected the twigs and marked the trees and shrubs the twigs came from. Ask children to match their twig with the appropriate tree or shrub. When all of the children have found their plants, have each child take the group on a brief visit to her or his plant to explain the characteristics of its twigs and branching pattern. Have the children give each tree or shrub a name describing its twigs and branching. Try to find leaves still clinging to the branches, or lying on the ground near the plant. Share the common names of these plants with the children.

EXTENDING THE EXPERIENCE

• Sprout seeds by keeping them in between moist layers of paper towel in a jar in a warm space. Bean and citrus seeds sprout well, especially those from grapefruit and oranges.
• *Seeds of Stewardship.* Create a pile of stewardship seeds by adding one seed every time you do something to conserve and care for plants.
• *Flowering Plant Feast.* Hold a feast of dishes and snacks made from flowering plants, such as nuts, grains, fruits, vegetables, popcorn, maple syrup, etc.
• *Autumn Leaf Mosaic.* Read the "Discussion" to learn how and why leaves turn color every autumn. Gather bags of colorful autumn leaves and have fun jumping in leaf piles. *Make sure there is nothing to get hurt on in the piles before jumping in.* Press leaves flat between pieces of newspaper and allow to dry for a few weeks. Use leaves to create a giant, colorful mosaic mural.
• *Seeing Red.* Experiment with anthocyanins, which are red plant pigments. Peel off and boil the skins of several deep red apples in two cups of water in a light-bottomed pan. Starting at the edges and moving toward the center, the apple skins will turn from red to purple, and then their color

will disappear. As cell walls break down, pigment leaves the cells and dissolves in the water, which appears clear or pale pink. Once the color is boiled out of the apple skins, strain the water and pour into a white, heat-resistant container. Add a few teaspoons of clear (white) vinegar to the water and it will turn deep pink! The more acid, the deeper the color. Anthocyanins are pink in the presence of acid.

• Make some dried fruit. Thinly slice some apples, pears or other fruit, and dry the pieces on a clean tray placed in the sunlight in a warm, dry space.

• Make a seed collection. Seeds have beautiful designs, colors and interesting shapes. Research the seeds in the collection and learn about the plants that produce them.

• Invent your own seed art: mosaics, necklaces and other creations.

• Find some spotted touch-me-not plants on which the seed pods are ripe (late summer) and have fun pinching the bottoms of the pods and causing them to explode and throw their seeds.

• Adapt the activity *Conifer Forest Alive* in Chapter 8 for use in a deciduous forest.

NOTES

1. Kent Nerburn and Louise Mengelkoch (eds.), *Native American Wisdom* (San Rafael, Calif.: New World Library, 1991), 19.

2. Bruce Cornet, "Dicot-Like Leaf and Flowers From the Late Triassic Tropical Newark Supergroup Rift Zone, U.S.A.," *Modern Geology*, vol. 19, no. 1 (August 1993): 81–99.

3. Nicholas C. Fraser, "Cascade: A Triassic Treasure Trove," *Virginia Explorer,* vol. 9, no. 1 (Winter/Spring 1993): 15–18.

4. Peter Tompkins and Christopher Bird, *The Secret Life of Plants* (New York: Harper & Row, 1973), xii–xiii.

5. Norman Myers, *The Gaia Atlas of Future Worlds* (New York: Anchor Doubleday, 1990), 29.

6. Charles E. Little, "Report From Lucy's Woods," *American Forests,* vol. 96, nos. 3–4 (March/April 1992): 25–27, 68–69.

7. Ibid.

8. Brent Mitchell, "Air Pollution and Maple Decline," *Nexus,* vol. 9, no. 3 (Summer 1987): 1–13.

When the women of the village saw the woman's basket carrying her load, it filled them with wonder.

CHAPTER 10

✤ The First Basket ✤

(Mandan—Plains)

In the old days, it was hard work for the women when they went to gather food on the prairie. Not only did they have to walk far from their villages to dig for roots, but they also found it hard to carry the food they found back to their earth-lodges. One day, long ago, a woman sat down to rest under a cedar tree. She leaned back against its trunk, and the sound of the wind in its branches was so peaceful that she fell asleep. And as she slept, the cedar tree spoke to her.

"Sister," the cedar tree said, "I see that you are tired and I want to help you. Do as I say and good will come to you and to all the women of your people. Dig down into the earth beneath you. Take my slender roots and weave them together. They will help you carry your load."

When the woman woke, she did as the tree had told her. She uncovered the long, thin roots with her digging stick and cut them free with her flint knife. Then, remembering that she should show her own thanks because she had been given a gift, she placed some tobacco and then filled the hole back in with dirt. Then she took the roots and wove them together as she had been shown in her dream. When she was finished, she had the first cedar basket, and she saw that it would be good to carry things. It was light and strong.

The woman had been digging tipsin roots before she rested and now she went back out onto the prairie and loaded all of the tipsin into her cedar basket. But when she tried to lift the basket, she began to weep.

"This basket is so heavy," she said, "and I am so tired now."

Then the cedar basket spoke to her.

"Sister," said the basket, "do you not remember the words my mother spoke to you? Did she not say that good would come to you? Did she not say that I would help you? If you will sing as you walk back to your lodge, then I will carry this load."

The woman stood and began to sing as she walked back to her lodge. The basket came with her, carrying her load.

When the women of the village heard that song coming from the prairie, they came out of the village to see why someone was so happy after a day of hard work. When they saw the woman's basket carrying her load, it filled them with wonder.

"Where did you get this basket?" they asked her.

"The cedar tree showed me how to make it," the woman answered.

Then all the women begged her to show them how to do the same. Soon, every woman in the village had her own basket made of cedar roots, and at the end of each day the voices of singing women could be heard as they returned from the prairie with their baskets beside them, carrying the loads.

One day, though, a woman took her basket out on the prairie, and as she dug, she found there a granary of the Mouse People. The Mouse People gather the beans and seeds of the prairie plants and store them underground for their winter food. It was the practice of the Mandan people, when they found one of these granaries, to always leave some behind so that the Mouse People would not starve. This woman was greedy, however, and filled her cedar basket to the top, taking all of the beans and seeds which the Mouse People had worked so hard to gather. In the tall grass, the Mouse People were crying, but this woman paid no attention.

However, when she stood up from filling her basket, this greedy woman found that she could not remember the song to sing to make the basket carry her load. She ordered the basket to carry her load, but the basket did not move. Even when she struck it, the basket remained on the ground.

"It is your job to carry my load," the woman said.

But the basket did not answer her. That woman, in her greed and anger, had forgotten that what the cedar baskets did for the people was done out of kindness. Because of the way she acted, the basket became resentful. It refused to carry her load. Because the load was too heavy for her to carry, she had to pour out most of the beans and seeds she had taken from the Mouse People. After that woman had gone, the Mouse People took those beans and seeds to a new and better hiding place.

And from that time on, no basket ever again carried a load on its own for the people again.

DISCUSSION

Mandan people are agriculturalists who live in the heart of the North American prairie. Like the stories of other Native peoples of the grasslands, including the Winnebago, Iowa, Illinois and Lakota, the stories of the Mandan reveal a relationship with the local environment. The message conveyed in the story "The First Basket" shows that the Mandan value the virtues of sharing and generosity. The woman who listens to the cedar tree expresses gratitude, reciprocates the gift given her and returns the earth back to the hole it came from. She, in turn, learns how to make the first cedar basket: a basket that carries the woman's loads as she sings her way back to the lodge. This woman shares knowledge of these new gifts with the other women in the village. However, when another woman is greedy and does not leave some beans and seeds behind in the winter cache of the Mouse People, all baskets stop carrying loads for the women. The Mandan believe that the necessities of life and comfort are to be shared by all of Creation.

Prairies and Other Grasslands

In prehistoric times, much more of North America was forested than today, and many Native cultures lived in the zones of transition between forests and other kinds of habitats. Lightning fires were common and fire was used throughout North America as a Native management tool.[1] Fire reduced the extent of forests in many areas and maintained ecological communities of grassland plants and animals. As forests disappeared, humidity decreased and so did the land's ability to retain soil moisture. The steady, dry grassland winds fan the fires that start and quickly evaporate rainwater down to the thick, spongy mulch layer of the prairie grasses. But fire only burns off the parts of prairie plants that are above ground. Roots survive to sprout anew using the nutrients released in the ensuing ash. Seeds of some grassland species *need* fire to germinate.

Prairie grasses were burned to control the spreading of forest and the migration of the American bison (buffalo), to create new growth and increase the amount of grazing land and habitat for bison and pronghorn antelope, to control biting insects and to facilitate travel through the tall grasses. Frequent, systematic burning also reduces the danger that wildfires will be ignited by lightning. Native North Americans later taught Europeans the practice of creating controlled back-fires to contain larger fires. Because fire was used as a weapon, and since enemies could hide in tall grasses, burning also decreased the chance that fire could be used against a village and minimized the likelihood of an ambush. As open land drew grazing herds in closer to villages, hunting became easier and more time was left for farming. The extensive burning of prairie in the Missouri and Mississippi basins extended the plains bison's range eastward until, by A.D. 1000, some herds had crossed the Mississippi River and adapted to life in the eastern forests.[2]

In conjunction with the aforementioned effects of *fire,* grasslands also persist because of *low rainfall* and the effects

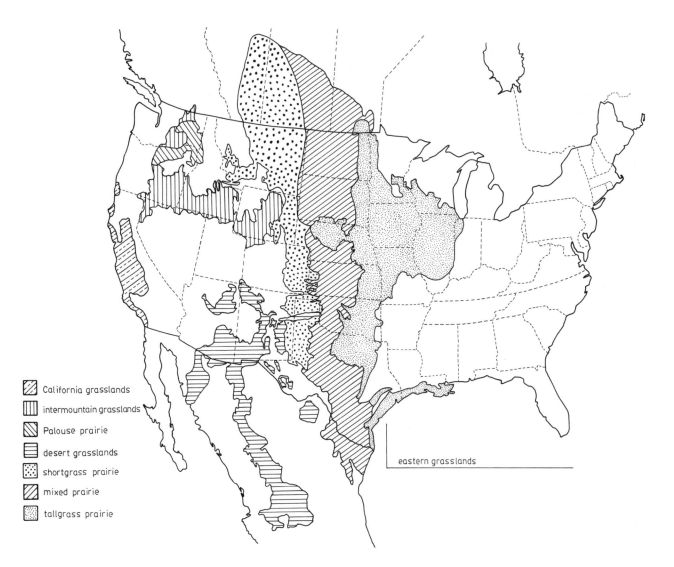

California grasslands

intermountain grasslands

Palouse prairie

desert grasslands

shortgrass prairie

mixed prairie

tallgrass prairie

eastern grasslands

Figure 10-1. Map showing the major kinds and ranges of North American grasslands. There is much intermixing of plant communities within the ranges shown here for each type of grassland. In the range shown for intermountain grasslands, for example, prairie is found in the uplands while desert occupies the lower elevations in many areas.

of *grazing animals* and *burrowers* such as the prairie dog. All of these factors inhibit the growth of forest trees and shrubs. Grazing animals help maintain the prairies by cropping plants, exposing bare soil with their hooves and leaving ample fertilizer. In addition, rainfall is moderate to marginal in the grasslands. Moist air flowing in from the Pacific Ocean drops most of its moisture as it rises and cools while passing east over the Sierra Nevadas, Cascades and Rocky Mountains. This creates dry zones known as *rain shadows* on the leeward, eastern side of the mountains. Rainfall is about 10 inches (25.4 centimeters) in the dryer grasslands to the south and west that border on desert lands, and gradually increases to a maximum of around 39 inches (1 meter) at the eastern edge of the tallgrass prairie. Much moisture flows into the Midwest in weather fronts moving north from the Gulf of Mexico. There *is* sufficient rainfall in the tallgrass prairie region to support forest growth, but fire and grazing

and burrowing animals have, historically, maintained the prairie and inhibited the growth of woody plants.

The greater height and diversity of grassland plant species moving east correspond with increasing amounts of rainfall. But there are long dry periods between the rains. Moving from west to east, the major kinds of North American grasslands are California grassland, intermountain grassland, shortgrass prairie, mixed prairie and tallgrass prairie (Figure 10-1). Desert plains grasslands are located in parts of New Mexico, Arizona, Texas and northern Mexico. Smaller grasslands are found throughout North America within forest biomes, including freshwater marshes and salt marshes, meadows, old fields, agricultural croplands, pastures and lawns.

Grasslands blanket one of the largest areas of any biome in North America. In Canada alone, grasslands cover around 193,050 square miles (500,000 square kilometers) in southern Alberta, Saskatchewan and Manitoba. Except for some grasslands in the East, in California and in the intermountain zone, most grasslands are on fairly flat ground. Unlike the complex layering of forests, prairies generally have three main layers, from top to bottom: the herbaceous, ground and root zones. A thick mulch covers the soil surface, where shade and shelter from the wind create a cooler, moister environment. Each winter, prairie plants are bent over and matted down by wind, rain and snow. As the growing season progresses, the short plants bloom first, then those of medium height and finally the tall grasses and large herbs in late summer and autumn.

Prairie soils are extremely fertile—they are thick and rich in humus, especially in eastern tallgrass prairies where big bluestem grass sometimes grows up to 10 feet (3 meters). The fibrous, moisture-retaining roots of prairie plants anchor, aerate and enrich the soil. In general, plant roots account for two-thirds of a plant's total mass. Some plant roots reach down more than 15 feet (4.6 meters) and can live for decades and, perhaps, for more than a century. These extensive root systems help grassland plants to survive drought, fire, grazing, winter weather and dry summer heat and wind. Other plants are discouraged from taking root by the thick mat of roots, heavy leaf litter and dense, shade-casting greenery.

A rich variety of grasses, flowers and other plants is found in the grasslands, creating hues of blue, purple, orange, yellow and white amid the heat and rustle of green leaves and singing insects. The feathery fruits of pasque-flower and "prairie smoke" look like puffs of smoke in the tallgrass prairie. Trees and shrubs grow along waterways and in unburned and undisturbed places. Cacti and other desert plants are interspersed in grasslands that border desert country. Most, if not all, grasses are pollinated by wind and a small number of species sometimes cover large areas. Insects are important to the prairie ecosystem because of their role in flower pollination, as the base of the food chain, as decomposers and in maintaining soil tilth.

GRASSES. *Grasses,* which are monocots, dominate the prairies. They comprise the third largest family of flowering plants in terms of number of species. Nearly one-third of Earth's land mass is covered with grasses. Bamboo is a grass, as are 10 of the 15 major food crops that feed the world's people, including wheat, oats, rye, corn, barley and sugarcane.

Many people think of grasses as mostly tall leaves that eventually form seeds on top of a stalk. Grasses do, however, have small, delicate, inconspicuous flowers whose beauty we can learn to appreciate (Figure 10-2). Grass leaves are narrow with parallel veins. The stems are usually round and have *joints,* or *nodes,* along their lengths where the leaves are attached to the stem by a loose-fitting *sheath.* Instead of growing from the tip of the stem or leaf as most plants do, grasses grow from the base of the leaf or stem. When grass is burned or cropped it grows back from the base. Up to 90 percent of a grass plant's weight is contained in the roots.

One young rye plant produced 387 miles (623 kilometers) of roots and rootlets in its four-month lifetime.[3]

It is tricky to differentiate among grasses and two other families of plants, the rushes and sedges. In addition, the common names for plants in these three families are confusing: a few grasses are called sedges, some sedges are called grasses and many sedges are called rushes. Round stems are not a way to distinguish grasses, rushes and sedges since any one of the three can have a round stem. Here are a few additional pointers to distinguish among the three families:
- The flowers of rushes have three sepals and three petals that are much less conspicuous than the petals of familiar flowers.
- There is more than one seed in *each* capsule on the seedhead of a rush. Grasses and sedges contain only one seed in each scale, but there may be many scales in a seedhead.
- Plants with triangular stems are sedges ("sedges have edges"). Yet most, but not all, sedges have triangular stems. Sedges are *three-ranked*—when viewed from the top of the stems, sedge leaves are seen to emerge in three distinct rows.
- Grasses are two-ranked. The flowers and leaves are arranged on the stems in two rows growing opposite one another down the stem.
- When distinguishing between grasses and sedges:
   - Grasses usually have hollow stems; sedge stems are usually solid.
   - Grasses usually have open sheaths; sedge sheaths are usually closed.

CALIFORNIA GRASSLANDS. Native *California grasslands* once covered about one-fourth of California, primarily along the coast and in the central valley. Brilliant spring displays of native wildflowers adorned the central valley of

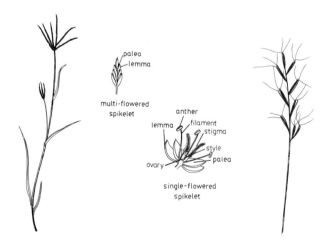

Figure 10-2. The parts of a typical grass flower (center) and some flowers of prairie grasses (sides). Flowers are arranged in two rows. The stamens and pistil—the male and female flower parts—are located between each lemma and palea. See also Figure 9-1 for greater detail in flower structure. Sizes: big bluestem (left), 2.5 to 5 ft. (76 cm to 1.5 m); prairie three-awn (right), 1 to 2 ft. (30.5 to 61 cm).

California each spring with a tapestry of color: Indian paintbrush, owl's clover, lupines, nemophilas, gilias, California poppies and vast carpets of yellow-flowered tarweed. The once-dominant native grasses included purple needlegrass (a bunchgrass) in the central valley and, along the coast, red fescue, Idaho fescue and California oatgrass. *Bunchgrasses* of dry grasslands grow in clumps with space in between rather than as a continuous mat. Rainfall varies from 6 to 29 inches (15.2 to 73.7 centimeters) and is generally heaviest in the coastal grasslands. Temperatures in the valley region can exceed 100°F (37.8°C) and most of the rain comes in the fall, winter and spring. The rain-fed greens of fall and winter alternate with the golds of spring and summer, which are caused by introduced species of grass.

Today's California grasslands are different from those encountered by European migrants in the 1800s—they are greatly reduced and consist mostly of alien species. In place of native perennial bunchgrasses, annual grasses such as wild oats predominate that die back each year. Cattle grazing, crop growing, draining of vernal pools, urbanization and the introduction of alien species have changed these habitats. With the removal of predators, such as the coyote and badger, rodent populations that feed intensively on seeds and greens increased dramatically. The use of fire has brought back small areas of native wildflowers and perennial grasses in recent years, but for these intensive management techniques to be successful requires constant vigilance.

INTERMOUNTAIN GRASSLANDS. The *intermountain grasslands* found between the Rockies to the east and the Cascades and Sierra Nevadas to the west encompass the Great Basin, which borders on desert to the south and includes the northern fringe of Utah and Nevada, eastern Oregon and Washington and part of southern Idaho. Intermountain grassland is also found in parts of Colorado, Wyoming, Montana and British Columbia. Sagebrush and bunchgrasses dominate here where the 10 to 15 inches (25.4 to 38.1 centimeters) of annual rainfall comes mostly during the fall and winter. Bluebunch wheatgrass, Idaho fescue and bottlebrush squirreltail are the dominant grasses, and sagebrush has increased due to grazing. An introduced species, cheatgrass brome, now covers significant areas. Wildflowers include scarlet gilia, desert plume, sweet fennel, fiddleneck, cream cup and mule's ears. Big sagebrush, greasewood, single-leaf piñon pine, desert sage, iodine bush, Utah juniper and shadscale are some of the trees and shrubs of the intermountain grasslands.

The fertile Palouse prairie in southeastern Washington, northeastern Oregon and northwestern Idaho also lies within the range of the intermountain grasslands. Fairly pure stands of grasses once covered much of the Palouse, but cultivation has overrun this native grassland. The remaining wild vegetation closely resembles that of the intermountain grasslands.

DESERT PLAINS GRASSLANDS. Lying between desert in the lowlands and forest in higher elevations, roughly from about 4,000 to 8,000 feet (1,219 to 2,438 meters), the *desert plains grasslands* cover parts of western Texas, New Mexico, Arizona and northern Mexico. A variety of habitats are found in this spectacular basin and range landscape. Plants have formed a patchwork quilt of cover types in response to elevation and slope. Desert grasslands are interspersed with piñon, oak and juniper forest as well as plants of the true desert (Chapter 12). Although about 11 to 17 inches (28 to 43.2 centimeters) of rain falls annually, this is the most arid of the grasslands because of steady, intense sunlight and strong drying winds. With little rain to leach these pale soils, a hard layer of salts called *caliche* has built up below the surface. Bunchgrasses dominate here, especially grama grasses, such as the perennial hairy grama, black grama, blue grama and slender grama. Annuals include the six-weeks grass and six-weeks needlegrass. Tobosa grass grows in the lowlands. The soil compaction, runoff and erosion caused by grazing have lowered the water table in desert plains grasslands and promoted the invasion of shrubs including creosote bush, mesquite, ocotillo and Mormon tea. Fire has been used to restore these grasslands, but the burning has proved harmful to animals.

SHORTGRASS PRAIRIE. Many plants of the western reaches of dry *shortgrass prairie*, which receive as little as 10 inches (25.4 centimeters) of rain each year, have water-conserving adaptations similar to those of desert species. Rain falls intermittently, with long periods of dry winds in between. Most growth occurs in the spring, and plants are dormant during the dry summer months. Buffalo grass and blue grama grass are two dominant species. In season, many colorful wildflowers can be seen: candelabra cactus, buffalo gourd, curlycup gumweed, Rocky Mountain bee plant, locoweed, yellow bell, arrowleaf balsamwood, cowpen daisy, plains prickly pear and plains yucca. Shrubs and trees include rabbit brush, winter fat, snakeweed, fringed sage and Rocky Mountain juniper. Shortgrass prairies are largely unaffected by cultivation because of the severe climate and dry soils. Livestock overgrazing, however, has denuded many areas of plant cover and greatly increased wind erosion. Grazing also encourages exotic species of grass, such as cheatgrass brome and Kentucky bluegrass, that are better adapted to grazing.

MIXED PRAIRIE. The 14 to 23 inches (35.6 to 58.4 centimeters) of rain that falls on the *mixed prairie* is not enough to support the growth of trees except along streambeds, around springs and in other low, moist places where some willows, cottonwoods, ashes and a handful of other species are found. Big bluestem grass is also found in wet areas. A few trees and shrubs, such as osage orange and prairie acacia, grow in the eastern reaches bordering the tallgrass prairie. The western extreme of the mixed prairie roughly marks the edge of the Great Plains. Dominant grasses include little bluestem, June grass, needlegrass and, to the north, western wheatgrass. Buffalo grass and blue grama occur in the higher, dryer places. Many of the same wildflowers grow here as in the tallgrass prairie, plus Mexican hat, mouse-ear chickweed, crazy weed, blue salvia, snow-on-the-mountain, pasqueflower, prairie rose, sego lily and prairie mimosa (Figure 10-3).

TALLGRASS PRAIRIE. Sufficient rain, about 25 to 39 inches (63.5 centimeters to 1 meter), falls each year over parts of the *tallgrass prairie* to allow the growth of trees and shrubs wherever fire, grazing and cultivation do not prevent them from developing. In many places trees and shrubs, including cottonwood, green ash, box elder, American elm and shrubby cinquefoil, are confined to wet habitats. Trees and shrubs also grow in dry soil, such as bur oak, pasture rose, common chokecherry, gray dogwood, quaking aspen, paper birch, eastern red cedar, common prickly-ash and leadplant. A variety of grasses grow in the diverse plant communities of the tallgrass prairie. Native grasses include big bluestem, prairie cordgrass, little bluestem, prairie dropseed grass and Indian grass. Redtop, Kentucky bluegrass, and foxtail barley are common exotic species. The sea of prairie plants forms waves of rainbow hues created by the flower petals of prairie blazing star, various anemones, plains larkspur, pale spiked lobelia, prairie coreopsis, compass plant, pasqueflower, bird-foot violet, purple prairie clover, spiderwort, various milkweeds, butterfly weed, goldenrods, numerous asters, spotted Joe-Pye weed, northern bedstraw, Indian paintbrush, dogbanes and prairie lilies.

Fate of the Grasslands

The once rich grasslands of North America controlled erosion, maintained fertile soils and supported biologically diverse ecosystems. Even today, when used as landscape plants, locally native species require little maintenance because they are well adapted to their native climate, soils

Figure 10-3. Large-bracted wild indigo is one of many beautiful prairie flowers. (Photo by Kenneth W. Wood)

and other growing conditions. But the introduction of the self-cleaning steel plow by John Deere in 1837 at Grand DeTour, Illinois, was the portent of a momentous change in the ecological annals of North American grasslands. Over time, the native grassland plants that are a valuable part of our natural heritage have been all but wiped out in many areas due to cultivation, cattle grazing, forest growth, urbanization and the introduction of species from other continents that out-compete many native flowers and grasses. Today, tallgrass prairies have been planted to corn, soybeans and other crops. Vast areas of shortgrass prairie have been overgrazed, which destroys the native grasses, compacts the soil, decreases water percolation and results in areas dominated by sagebrush, cactus, mesquite and other species. Contemporary remnants of prairies and other grasslands, including the tallgrass prairie that at one time spanned 400,000 square miles (1,036,000 square kilometers) in 12 states, are relegated to preserves and overlooked or inaccessible places. These remaining grasslands are places that people go to reconnect with these and other wild species, and to seek recreation, renewal and aesthetic enjoyment.

Grasslands are home to many rare, threatened and endangered North American plants. The prairie white-fringed orchid is rare in Canada and threatened in the United States. Soapweed and western silver-leaf aster are also rare in Canada. Gattinger's and Skinner's purple false foxgloves are endangered in the prairie remnants of southwestern Ontario and are rare in the United States. Once abundant in low, open prairies, the small white lady's slipper is now endangered in Canada, surviving in only six places in southern Ontario and Manitoba. The delicate, moccasin-shaped flowers of this beautiful plant can take up to 12 years to appear and set seed.

Grassland Stewardship

Activity is strong among organizations contributing to the preservation, well-being and restoration of native grasslands. (See the list of midwestern and California sources in the activity *"Growing Grasslands."*) The University of Wisconsin at Madison Arboretum conducts research on the restoration and management of the major ecological communities of Wisconsin and the upper Midwest, including prairies, forests and wetlands. This arboretum has established a living outdoor "museum" of habitats covering nearly 1,300 acres (526.5 hectares) demonstrating the ecology of presettlement Wisconsin. The museum is open to the public and used for educational programs on restoration for children and adults. Walnut Creek National Wildlife Refuge, which lies east of Des Moines, Iowa, consists of 5,000 acres (2,025 hectares) of prairie being restored where bison and elk will eventually be reintroduced. The Society for Ecological Restoration promotes ecological restoration and management research, networks with other groups involved in restoration and the promotion of policy, educates for and supports restoration of urban and rural wilderness areas and recognizes individuals and organizations for exceptional work in restoration. Grassland education and restoration also take place in Illinois, Minnesota and other states.

Numerous organizations are doing valuable work that enables individuals to become involved in learning about and growing native grassland species. In the Midwest, seeds and information on the planting and maintenance of native prairie grasses and wildflowers are available from many nurseries that specialize in them. In California, which is home to some of North America's richest, most diverse native grasslands, native seeds, seedlings and guides to growing them are available from several sources. This is a hopeful and exciting time to become involved in assuring a future for North America's native grasslands and the beautiful, diverse communities of plants and animals that have survived here against great odds.

QUESTIONS

1. Why does the cedar tree offer to help the woman when she leans against it and falls asleep in the Mandan story "The First Basket"? What does the tree tell her to make the basket out of?

2. Why does the woman take such care when digging up the cedar roots to make the basket? In what way is she later rewarded by the basket for expressing her gratitude?

3. What happens when one of the women becomes greedy and takes all of the beans and seeds from the Mouse People? Why do people have to carry their own loads in baskets today?

4. What is a prairie? Are all grasslands prairies?

5. What are the different kinds of North American prairies and other grasslands? Where are they located in North America? Where are there grasslands growing nearby?

6. What kinds of plants grow on the prairies? Can you name any flowers or grasses from native grasslands? Describe an experience you have had in a grassland.

7. Why do grasslands stay grasslands instead of growing up to forests?

8. What kind of plant is a grass? How are grasses different from other kinds of plants?

9. What kinds of foods do we eat that come from plants that are grasses? In what other ways are grasses important? How can we show our appreciation for the gifts of grasses?

10. What has happened to the grasslands that were here a few hundred years ago? Where are there prairies and other grasslands left?

11. What have people done to cause grasslands to disappear over the past few hundred years? Why did they do these things?

12. What are people doing to conserve and restore grasslands and the plants that grow there? Why is it important to save these plants and native grasslands?

13. What are some things that you can do to help grasslands?

ACTIVITIES

Into a Grassland

ACTIVITY: Take a fantasy journey to experience a grassland community. Go on a scavenger hunt to a nearby grassland environment.

GOALS: Understand what a grassland is. Discover the ecology of a grassland and the plant and animal communities found there.

AGE: Younger children and older children

MATERIALS: Paper, pencils, crayons, cardboard backing to write against, copy of the fantasy *"Into a Grassland,"* hand lenses, supplies as needed for the scavenger hunt, Figure 10-4.

PROCEDURE: Beforehand, scout out a grassland area near the home or learning center and create a simple scavenger hunt to focus the children's attention on the plant and animal communities in that particular environment. Be sure to include observations that involve the children's senses. Make the hunt fun and interesting. For an example of a scavenger hunt to use as a model, see the activity "Conifer Forest Excursion" in *"Conifer Forest Alive"* in Chapter 8.

Note: Some leaders prefer to conduct the outdoor portion of this activity before presenting the guided fantasy.

Lead the children on the following fantasy journey. Ask the children: "How would it feel to walk into a grassland of native grasses and wildflowers? What would you hear, see, smell and feel?" Have them close their eyes and take a few deep breaths. Tell them to relax their bodies and to let their imaginations go as you read the following story out loud.

INTO A GRASSLAND

A warm, dry wind is blowing steadily and softly against your face, mussing your hair and whooshing by your ears. You walk over a round swell in the ground and look before you into a beautiful valley covered with green grasses and flowers shimmering blue, white, yellow and red in the hot sun. A gust of wind blows downslope and bends the stalks of the plants, moving them like giant waves across the land. You want to sit down, but the grasses are tall and you cannot see over them from the ground.

Quietly, you look out over the land. There, moving up from the middle of the valley, is a small herd of animals that look like deer or elk. The large animal out in front of the herd munches on some grass, looks up to make sure everything is still safe, takes a few steps, then swishes its tail back and forth and munches on some more grass.

You realize that it is not very quiet out in the grassland. A high, pleasant sound is coming from the grasses and wildflowers. Insects are making their songs to attract mates. There are so many insects that their songs join to make a beautiful chorus. The sound of the wind keeps humming in your ears.

A sudden movement catches your eye. You look just in time to see a gray jackrabbit dart into the open and back into a clump of grass. You know the jackrabbit is right in front of you, but no matter how long you stare at the clump of grass you cannot see it.

Slowly, you inch your way toward the spot where you think the jackrabbit is hiding. Nothing moves. Finally when you are standing right next to its hiding place, the jackrabbit bolts away into the tall grasses. You are so startled you almost fall down.

There is a beautiful deep blue flower where the jackrabbit had been hiding. You bend over and carefully smell its petals. With your nose close to the ground, you notice that the leaves of one of the plants you stepped on are giving off a spicy scent. The leaves feel soft and fuzzy as you run your fingers over them. You sit down near these flowers and close your eyes, smelling the crushed leaves as the sun washes over your skin and the insects sing in your ears.

Have the children open their eyes when they are ready, and ask: "How did you like visiting the grassland? What was your favorite thing that happened during the journey? Would you like to have stayed around longer to explore the grassland? What else would you have discovered there?" Share the illustration of a mixed prairie grassland with the children (Figure 10-4).

Take the children outdoors and introduced them to the scavenger hunt you designed specifically for the grassland community near the home or learning center. Bring hand lenses along for the children to make close observations. Ask them to observe carefully and to try to see as much as they can while outdoors. Once the children have had 20 to 30 minutes to explore the grassland on their scavenger hunt, call them all together and have them share their findings. Visit the sites of special discoveries that the children made in the grassland. Finally, have the children write and/or illustrate a story about their experience visiting the grassland.

Note: Take the children to a deeper level of understanding of grasslands by having them create a grassland food web made up of the plants, animals and other parts of the environment they find in the grassland you visited. Emphasize how all of the parts of the grassland work together to create a living ecosystem. A grassland food web and activity can be conducted by adapting *"Ocean Food Web Wipe-Out"* found in Chapter 5.

Getting a Grip on Grasses

ACTIVITY: Solve a grass riddle. Play a matching and observation game with grasses. Make a grass mural. Visit and observe grasses outdoors.

GOALS: Discover grasses in the local environment. Understand the characteristics of grasses.

AGE: Younger children and older children

MATERIALS: Small cooler with ice in it, pruning shears, samples of different kinds of grasses as described below, copy of the grass riddle, "Discussion," Figure 10-2, hand lenses, paper, pencils, construction paper, crayons, markers, paste, scissors, stapler and staples, tape, other materials you decide to use for the mural, newspaper and some heavy books.

PROCEDURE: Beforehand, take a small cooler (with some ice in it) and some pruning shears outside to use for collecting samples of grasses in the immediate vicinity of the home or learning center. Gather samples from a variety of grasses and place them in the cooler to keep them fresh. You will need at least *two* samples from each kind of grass—enough so every child will have one sample. The children will be given a sample of grass and will have to find the person who has the matching sample. If possible, gather enough different kinds of grasses so none is repeated. If this is not possible, gather three or four samples from each kind of grass.

Read the following riddle to the children and ask whether they can identify the kind of plant it describes. Tell them to listen to the entire list of clues without saying a word, and then to raise their hands if they think they know what kind of plant this riddle describes:

- You often step on me when walking outdoors.
- Much more of me is below ground than you see above.
- I have small, beautiful flowers that you have probably never noticed.
- My leaves are long and thin.
- You probably ate one of my kind when you last had cereal for breakfast.
- My stems are usually round and they have joints.
- I grow from the base of my leaves instead of from the tip of my stem.
- People have said that I am "always greener on the other side."
  I am a (grass).

Once someone has guessed that this riddle describes *grass,* hand out one sample of the grasses you collected earlier to each child. As children observe their grasses, share with them the information on grass from Figure 10-2 and the "Discussion," including the characteristics that make a grass a grass. Every child needs to have a grass sample that matches at least one other sample in the group. Encourage the children to closely observe their grass by having them draw a picture of it. Once the illustrations are completed, have the children mill around and look at others' samples until they have found someone with a sample that matches their own. Each small group with the same kind of grass will now take turns holding their samples up for all to see as they describe their grass to the rest of the group. This continues until all have shared. Help the children to find the distinguishing characteristics that identify their samples as grasses.

Pass out hand lenses to all and take the children (still holding their samples) outdoors on a brief walk to look at

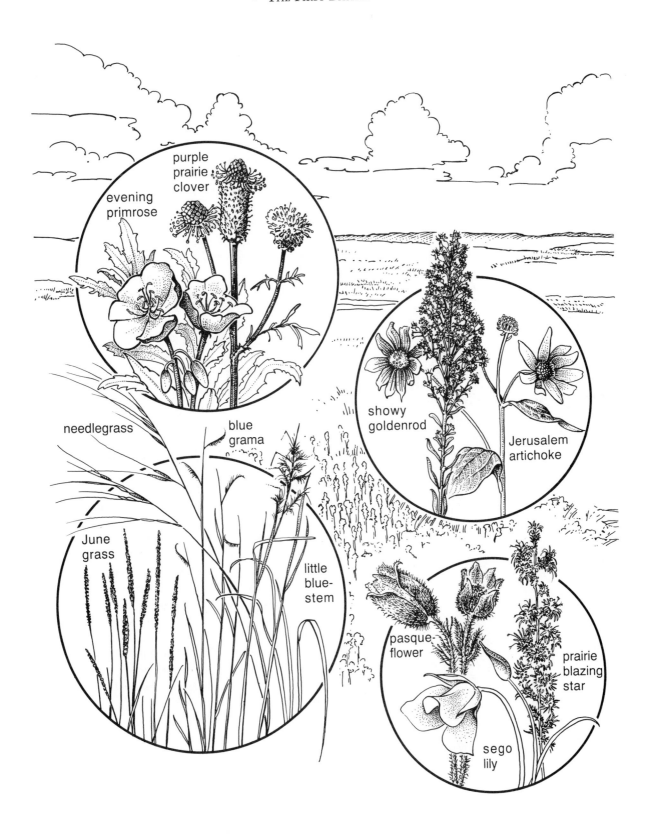

Figure 10-4. Some flowers and grasses of the mixed prairie. Sizes (clockwise from upper left): evening primrose, 1 to 6 ft. (30.5 cm to 1.8 m); purple prairie clover, 1 to 3 ft. (30.5 to 91.4 cm); showy goldenrod, 2 to 7 ft. (61cm to 2.1m); Jerusalem artichoke, 5 to 10 ft. (1.5 to 3 m); prairie blazing star, 2 to 5 ft. (61 to 1.5 m); sego lily, 6 to 18 in. (15.2 to 45.7 cm); pasqueflower, 6 to 16 in. (15.2 to 40.6 cm); little bluestem, 1.5 to 5 ft. (45.7 cm to 1.5 m); June grass, 1 to 2 ft. (30.5 to 61 cm); needlegrass, 1.75 to 7 ft. (53.3 cm to 2.1 m); blue grama, 6 to 20 in. (15.2 to 50.8 cm). (Illustration by Marjorie C. Leggitt)

local grasses. Emphasize that they are to observe but not pick any plants. Look at and share a number of different kinds of grasses, and then have the children search the area for a grass that matches the sample they received indoors. When they have found the grasses in their habitats, walk around with the group and figure out what is unique about the place where each particular grass is growing: shade, sunlight, temperature, moisture, wind, etc.

Finally, work with the children to help them arrange the grasses nicely and press the grasses in between pieces of newspaper. Weight the newspaper with some heavy books and wait a week or so for the grasses to dry flat. Then have the children create a habitat mural on which they will attach their dried grasses. Have them draw in other plants, insects and other animals to emphasize that grasses are the basis for life in the grassland community.

Growing Grasslands

ACTIVITY: Discuss the kinds of North American grasslands, plant a small community of your native grassland plants and get involved with grassland preservation and restoration.

GOALS: Discover the different kinds of North American grasslands and how we must help to preserve and restore those grasslands that remain. Realize that traditional Native North Americans are actively involved in maintaining grasslands and taking care of grassland plants.

AGE: Younger children and older children

MATERIALS: References and native seeds and/or plants from the sources listed in this activity, curriculum materials and project ideas on grassland ecological restoration from the sources listed, references describing your local grassland ecosystem, Figure 10-1, Figure 10-4, "Discussion," native seeds and/or plants, shovels, hoes, stakes, string, garden plot, identification tags, indelible marker, garden cart or wheelbarrow, other garden tools, water, additional materials as needed for specific projects chosen, "Discussion" from Chapter 14.

PROCEDURE: Beforehand, send requests to the following organizations for information on how to become involved with education and action around current prairie restoration efforts:

United States
• Society for Ecological Restoration (SER), 1207 Seminole Highway, Madison, WI 53711, (608) 262-9547. SER publishes a list of individuals and organizations in midwestern states with expertise in prairie restoration.
• Prairie Restoration Education Coordinator, University of Wisconsin–Madison, Arboretum, 1207 Seminole Highway, Madison, WI 53711, (608) 262-5522. Order a copy of *Prairie Restoration for Schools*, by Molly Fifield Murray.

• Project WILD, which is run through your state's or province's Department of Natural Resources or Environmental Management. Ask for "WILD Site Development" information.

Canada
• Manitoba Naturalist Society, Suite 401, 63 Albert St., Winnipeg, Manitoba R3B 1G4, (204) 943-9029. Order a copy of their book called *Manitoba's Tallgrass Prairie: A Guide to an Endangered Space*, by Tom Reaumel (1993).
• Mixed Grass Restoration Project, Last Mountain Lake National Wildlife Area, Box 280, Simpson, Saskatchewan S0G 4M0, (306) 836-2022.
• Nature Saskatchewan, Box 4348, Regina, Saskatchewan S4P 3W6, (306) 780-9273.
• Grasslands National Park, Box 150, Val Marie, Saskatchewan S0N 2T0, (306) 298-2257. This site features a visitors' interpretive center and naturalist-guided educational tours.

Also, the following groups offer information on ordering seeds and seedlings of native grassland plants from your region and references on how to plant and care for native grasses and wildflowers.

Midwest
• A list of native plant nurseries that are sources of seeds and/or plants native to Wisconsin and the Midwest is available. For a copy of the list "Native Plant Nurseries," contact the Bureau of Endangered Resources, Wisconsin Department of Natural Resources, P.O. Box 7921, Madison, WI 53707. Also contact the appropriate environmental agency from your state to find out whether they publish a similar list.
• Wehr Nature Center, 9701 West College Ave., Franklin, WI 53132, (414) 425-8550. Ask for ordering information for the *Prairie Propagation Handbook*, the seed mix of native prairie species and referrals to other sources of native grassland seeds.
• Prairie Seed Source, P.O. Box 83, North Lake, WI 53064. Request information on obtaining seeds and on how to order the book *Prairie Restoration for the Beginner*, by Robert Ahrenhoerster and Trelen Wilson.

Canada
• Prairie Habitat, Box 1, Argyle, Manitoba R0C 0B0, (204) 467-9371. Prairie Habitat specializes in the seeds of tallgrass prairie plants and other native species.
• Prairie Originals, Box 83, Group 6, RR 1B, Winnipeg, Manitoba R3C 4A3, (204) 338-7517. Prairie Originals is a good source of native plant *seedlings*.
• Mixed Grass Prairie Habitat Restoration Project, Box 280, Simpson, Saskatchewan S0G 4M0, (306) 836-2022. This project is a good source of small quantities of native mixed grass prairie seeds for use in educational projects only.

California

• Theodore Payne Foundation, 10459 Tuxford St., Sun Valley, CA 91352, (818) 768-1802. Inquire about their catalog for seeds of wildflowers and native plants, as well as ordering information for *Gardener's Guide to California's Wildflowers,* by Kevin Connelly (Sun Valley, Calif.: Theodore Payne Foundation, 1991).

• California Conservation Corps Napa Nursery, P.O. Box 7199, Napa, CA 94558, (707) 253-7783. Ask how to obtain young *plants* from their native plant nursery. These plants are only available to schools, scout groups and other organizations in California.

Once you have the necessary information and materials from these sources, discuss with the children the kinds of grasslands found in North America, using the information from the "Discussion," the grasslands map (Figure 10-1), the illustration of a grassland (Figure 10-4) and references describing your local grassland ecosystem. Few people are aware that grasslands covered such a large part of North America. Ask the children to say why they think grasslands remain grasslands rather than growing into forests. Explain the basic ecology of grasslands from west to east across North America using the "Discussion," and mention the names of some of the flowers, grasses and other plants that grow in various grasslands. Share the information at the beginning of the "Discussion" from this chapter of how and why Native North Americans have worked to maintain the grasslands. Read to the children from the beginning of the "Discussion" in Chapter 14 about Anishinabe stewardship toward the wild rice in marshes of the midwestern prairies and forests. What do Native North Americans do to take care of the plants of the prairies? What can we do?

Work with the children to use the information, seeds, plants and other resources you gathered earlier to plan a local native grassland/wildflower garden. This activity is meant as a small-scale group effort at planting and nurturing some nursery-bred native species of plants, many of which may be quite rare because of the destruction of their habitats over the past few centuries. There is no substitute for the kinds of connections that grow between the children and plants as their own native plant garden develops. Have the children find out as much as they can about, and give reports on, the specific native species they are planting and tending.

Use the curriculum materials and other project ideas that you collected about prairie restoration to involve the children in that aspect of habitat stewardship. This is a great way to get the children involved in actual conservation work that is reestablishing rare plants and habitats that have become virtually wiped out over much of their original natural range.

EXTENDING THE EXPERIENCE

• Eat grass! Prepare a feast of foods whose main ingredients are plants in the grass family, such as wheat, rye, oats, corn, barley, sugarcane and millet.

• Visit a prairie or other natural grassland area.

• Create a grassland food web using the mural of grasses, other plants and animals you prepared in *"Getting a Grip on Grasses."*

• Conduct some of the activities from Chapter 9 on flowering plants in a local grassland.

• Conduct *"Exploring Flowers of City and Suburb"* from Chapter 11 in a nearby grassland.

NOTES

1. Jack Weatherford, *Native Roots: How the Indians Enriched America* (New York: Crown, 1991), 41.

2. Ibid., 42.

3. Lauren Brown, *Grasses: An Identification Guide* (Peterson Nature Library) (Boston: Houghton Mifflin, 1979), 6.

As they sang the first words, they rolled the Ma-koor hoop. As they did this,
Blue Dawn became human from the top of his head to his neck.

CHAPTER 11

✦ Blue Dawn ✦

(Isleta Pueblo—Southwest)

In a house, they say, lived Black Cane Old Man; Old Corn Woman, his wife; their daughter, Yellow Corn Girl; and their small son, Blue Dawn. Black Cane Old Man was the one in the pueblo whose work it was to bring the rain.

Each day, although Old Corn Woman was blind, she would work at her loom. While her mother worked, Yellow Corn Girl ground corn and her little brother, Blue Dawn, played *huib*, a game where you run and kick a stick ahead of you as you go. Blue Dawn's uncle, Nachuruchu, was a great *huib* player and Blue Dawn wanted to be as good as his uncle at running. Each day, as Blue Dawn played his game, an eagle watched him and wanted the boy for her own.

To make sure she knew where her small son was, Old Corn Woman always kept him tied to the end of the long belt she was weaving. One day, though, she no longer heard the sound of his running. She pulled the belt back in and Blue Dawn was gone. The eagle had come and stolen her child.

"Come here," she called to Yellow Corn Girl. "Hurry! I don't know where my little child is."

Yellow Corn Girl came out and searched for her brother but she could not find him. She asked all the people of the pueblo, but no one had seen him. The village crier went about telling all the people to look for Blue Dawn. But the little boy was nowhere to be found.

All the people were sorry. Black Cane Old Man no longer was able to work to bring the rain. Now the rain did not come. Now the corn all got dry. Now all the people knew they would be hungry, for without the rain they would have no crops.

One day, Nachuruchu, the uncle of Blue Dawn, rose at dawn and began to play *huib*. He kicked the stick ahead of him as he ran. He ran far from the pueblo. He ran up high into the mesas. Then, sometime in the middle day, as he ran he heard a song being sung by a child. It came from high on the top of a cliff which no one could climb.

> Che-e mah-weh, mah-weh
> Che-e mah-weh, mah-weh
> I am the little son of Black Cane
> I am the little son of Black Cane

When Nachuruchu heard this he stopped to listen.

"That is no other but my little nephew," he said.

Back to the pueblo Nachuruchu ran.

"My nephew was carried away by the eagle. I heard him singing from the top of the high place where no one can reach. That is why we have not been able to see him."

"Go back again at dawn," Nachuruchu was told by the old men, the fathers of wisdom. "See if you hear the same song again."

Nachuruchu did as the people said. He went again to that mesa at dawn, and again he heard the voice of his nephew singing.

Now the people knew where Blue Dawn had gone. The young men were sent out. They tried to climb that cliff to reach him, but the cliff was too steep.

As they tried, the Stone-Layers, the swallows who make their nests out of clay, were flying around them.

"Bird-Masons," the young people called to the swallows, "what payment do you want to help us bring our small child down from the cliffs up there?"

But the swallows were flying and calling out, "Chee-Chee," and did not hear the people. Up and down the swallows went, calling out, "Chee-Chee! Chee-Chee!"

The people kept calling to them and at last one swallow heard the people. "Listen," he said. "Someone is talking."

Then the swallows listened and heard the people asking them what payment they would ask to bring the human child down from the cliffs.

"We will take pine nuts," the swallows said. "You can give us pine nuts to bring down your child."

All the swallows flew up and tried to lift Blue Dawn down from the eagle's nest. But the boy was too heavy.

"We are sorry," they said, flying back to the people. "We tried but we could not lift your child."

But because the swallows had tried their best, the young men still gave pine nuts to the swallows.

Then the birds spoke among themselves. "Let us go to Grandmother Spider," they said.

When they came to her house, Grandmother Spider was waiting. She said to them, "What is it that you want?"

The swallow told her about Blue Dawn. Grandmother Spider listened closely.

"So it is?" she said. "My poor grandson is crying? Grandsons, let us eat first and then we will see what I can do."

With that, Grandmother Spider served up atole and acorn mush for the swallows in dishes made of acorn shells. Together, Grandmother Spider and the swallows ate. Then, when they had thanked her for the food, Grandmother Spider took one of her baskets.

"Now," she said, "I will go to see what I can do."

Soon they came to the mesa where the young men were waiting at the bottom of the cliff. As soon as they saw Grandmother Spider, they called to her.

"Our Grandmother, will you help us? Will you bring our child down from way up there?"

"Yes," Grandmother Spider said. "I will do this. But take care not to look up."

Then Grandmother Spider went up the cliff with her basket. She found Blue Dawn and put him into her basket.

"Here he is!" she called and began to lower him.

But, as soon as she said that, the young men looked up. When they looked up, a wind began to blow and it lifted the basket back up into the air.

"Do not do that!" Grandmother Spider called down.

"Grandmother," the young men called back, "we will not look up again."

Now Grandmother Spider hung the basket down. She lowered the basket down to the young men. But when the young men looked into the basket, they did not see a little boy. Instead, they saw only a young eagle.

The young men carried the eagle child back to the pueblo. The fathers of wisdom came and looked at the eagle child.

"This is Blue Dawn," they said. "We must make him a human being again."

For four days the fathers of wisdom went without food. Then they began to work wisdom. They set the eagle child down. They sang. As they sang the first words, they rolled the Ma-koor hoop. As they did so, Blue Dawn became human from the top of his head to his neck. They sang a second time and rolled the Ma-koor hoop. Now Blue Dawn became human down to his waist. They sang a third time and rolled the Ma-koor hoop. Now Blue Dawn was human down to his knees. A fourth time they sang and rolled the Ma-koor hoop and Blue Dawn was human down to his ankles. A fifth time they sang and rolled the Ma-koor hoop and it was done. It was finished.

They warmed water then and made Blue Dawn drink. After drinking the water he began to cough. Each time he coughed, the food he had eaten as an eagle child came from his mouth. He coughed and lizards came out, snakes came out, rabbits came out, mice came out. All that the eagles had fed him came from his mouth as he coughed. When this was done, the fathers of wisdom gave Blue Dawn back to his parents.

Black Cane Old Man came and picked up his son and embraced him. Old Corn Woman and Yellow Corn Girl embraced Blue Dawn. They carried him back to their home. Now Black Cane Old Man could work again to bring the rain. Rain began to fall. In the fields, the corn came up. The corn blossomed and it ripened.

Now the *Cacique*, the chosen leader of the people, told them it was time to pick the corn. The village crier proclaimed that it was time to pick the corn. The people went out into the fields and picked. They brought the corn into the house of the Cacique. The house was filled and there was still more corn left over.

"Go to the east," the Cacique said. "Go to the north. Take the corn through the streets. From northwest to west, from west to south, from south to east, take this corn through the streets and give it to all the people."

So it was that the people of Isleta were glad and lived well. *Ta-kee-whee kay-ee.*

DISCUSSION

Pueblo peoples were among the first Native North Americans to build and live in small, city-like villages. They are highly social and used to living, as they have for thousands of years, in large, adobe-brick complexes of apartments with a central plaza for gatherings. The largest pueblo, in Chaco Canyon, New Mexico, has 800 rooms. These peoples are among the world's greatest dry-land farmers, growing corn, beans and squash in near-desert conditions.

When living in a community, *cooperation* is essential to accomplish important tasks. The Isleta Pueblo, in the story "Blue Dawn," cooperate with each other and the animals to get Blue Dawn down from the steep cliff that no one can climb where the eagle, after stealing the boy, has placed him. A series of events transpire in which each group or individual plays an essential role: the people, the swallows, Grandmother Spider, the young men, the fathers of wisdom, Old Corn Woman and Yellow Corn Girl. Then, Black Cane Old Man works to bring the rains back: the corn grows, blossoms and ripens again in the fields. The Cacique, chosen leader of the people, tells all that the time to pick the corn has arrived. At last, the corn is taken through the streets in all directions and given to the people, who are glad and live well.

Urban and Suburban Environments

By the year 2000, more than half of the world's population will live in cities and many others will dwell in the surrounding suburbs. The presence of buildings, people, vehicles and pavement has a dramatic impact on urban environments. Overall, when compared to their rural surroundings, city climates are warmer, drier and have less sunlight. Wind speeds are generally less, except for gusty places where, due to a process called the *Venturi effect,* wind is funnelled between buildings and other tall structures and generates strong gusts. City temperatures are several degrees warmer than those of surrounding areas and cities have more frost-free days. Buildings, roads and parking lots, made of stone, brick, cement and asphalt, absorb and store the sun's heat, then re-radiate it back into the air, increasing both daytime and nighttime temperatures. Many people notice crocuses and other early spring flowers sprouting first along the sunny south sides of buildings. Not only do plants bloom earlier in these *microclimates* but also species of plants that normally grow farther south can often be successfully cultivated. Urban temperatures are also increased by the warmth from heating systems in buildings, air conditioners, motor vehicle engines and body heat. One automobile engine creates as much heat as a home furnace.

Large areas of hard pavement and rooftop affect the urban water cycle. Instead of soaking in, rainwater quickly runs off of impermeable surfaces into drainage systems and sewers. This increases the chance of flooding downstream along streams and rivers by up to six times that found in natural areas. Urban runoff washes many pollutants, such as oil, salt, fertilizer, pesticides and asbestos dust, out of the air, off roadways and other surfaces and into wetlands and open water. More pesticides are used in urban and suburban areas, particularly on lawns treated for strictly aesthetic reasons, than are used on any other land area in the United States.

A significant amount of urban sunlight is blocked by air pollution in the form of particles from exhausts and industrial plants. Clouds form more frequently as water vapor condenses on these tiny particles, further reducing levels of sunlight reaching the ground.

GROWING CONDITIONS IN CITY AND SUBURB.
A tree may seem timeless, even poetic, as you pass by on your daily business, but for any plant, survival in a city or suburb is a continual struggle. Most urban plants are adapted to high levels of disturbance and stress.

Urban plants are exposed to many of the same *diseases* as the rural forest. *Dutch elm disease* infects the American elm. Around 1930 a fungus and a European elm-bark beetle were imported from the Netherlands in veneer logs. The disease first showed up in Ohio and spread throughout this region, killing many American elms. The beetle inadvertently carries the fungus to a new tree where, each springtime, it feeds and lays eggs in the smaller branches. As the fungus spreads, it blocks the flow of sap and branches die from lack of water. Burning the dead wood of a fallen elm kills the fungus and beetle larvae and slows the spread of the disease.

White birch trees are attacked by several insects. The larvae of the *bronze borer* eat through the outer bark, encircle the upper branches, devour the inner bark and kill the branches. *Leaf miners* munch on the inner tissue of birch leaves, leaving distinctive signs or *galleries*. *Tent caterpillars* erect tent-like homes of woven silk in the crotches of wild cherry trees. These leaf-eating larvae pose no real threat unless they defoliate a tree for two or three years in a row. The *white pine weevil,* described in Chapter 9, is another common bark-eating insect.

In addition to their natural enemies, trees and other plants must grapple with the *environmental conditions* of a densely populated built environment. Although tree roots can buckle sidewalks, and some herbaceous plants are able to sprout right through sun-softened asphalt, the *poor quality of air, water and soil*—a plant's most basic needs—presents a daunting challenge for urban plants: air is contaminated with automobile exhaust and smokestack emissions; water is polluted with salt,

gasoline and oil before it reaches plant roots; and soil is almost completely paved over and compacted, impeding the penetration of air, water, nutrients and roots. *Drainage* is so poor in city soils that many plants are rooted in wet soil. Many trees that are adapted to wet soils with low levels of oxygen, and which normally grow in wetlands, such as swamp white oak, sycamore and pin oak, survive well in the city. Plants must also tolerate *intense reflected heat* from buildings and sidewalks; *mechanical damage* from cars, bicycles and people; *road salt;* and *herbicide exposure* from lawn treatment. The *poor handling* of urban plants, and the *use of the wrong plants* for existing growing conditions, are common problems.

An observant eye can easily find *symptoms* of plant reactions to urban stresses. Many *leaves* are smaller than usual, have brown margins or are a pale yellow-green. *Sparse tree crowns* with top branches that are dead or dying are common. Few trees have escaped without a number of *wounds* on branch and bark where someone has chained up a bicycle, bumped with a car, carved a name or snapped off a branch. The tiniest break in the inner bark opens a tree to invading fungi, bacteria and viruses that can seriously impair a tree's growth or contribute to its death.

Plants: Keepers of Urban and Suburban Environments

Tucked amid the buildings and parking lots of any urban or suburban neighborhood are green pockets that enrich the experience of even the most hectic urbanite. From their tangible *value* as windbreaks on a winter day to the spiritual lift they give us when looking at free-flowing patterns of branch against sky, trees and other plants are some of our most provident neighbors. Plant communities are found in many locations:

parks	wetlands (ponds, marshes,
backyards	rivers, swamps)
school grounds	street shoulders and medians—
vacant lots	"tree lawns"
gardens	botanical gardens
riverbanks	fairgrounds
railroad shoulders	lawns
fields	embankments
meadows	construction sites

Many people equate value with money. In fact, *home and property values* are increased by even a small grove of urban forest. The U.S. Forest Service finds that trees increase property values by up to 20 percent, with an average of 5 to 10 percent. Even the Internal Revenue Service recognizes the values of trees and shrubs: loss of property value due to damaged or stolen plants is a tax deduction. Economics, however, is just one of a multitude of green values.

Our urban *greenery* provides many of the same values of plants found in the countryside. The leaves, trunks and limbs of urban trees are like sprawling townhouses, providing *shelter* for many forms of life, such as squirrels. Large, round, leaf nests provide squirrels with a summer home. Bird songs and nests are plentiful: robins, starlings, woodpeckers and more. English house sparrows often nest in ivy and lend their bustle and chatter to the scene. Many insects winter in and around plants, such as the basal rosettes of mullein or a hole at the base of a tree where a colony of ladybird beetles (ladybugs) may spend the winter.

On many summer evenings the buzzing of locusts, the clicking wings of grasshoppers or the incessant calls of their close relative the katydid ring out overhead. These and other insects, especially moths and caterpillars, are abundant *food* for mammals, birds and bats. Hickories, oaks, chestnuts, black walnuts and other nut-bearing trees drop a feast of nuts. Squirrels can be seen and heard throughout the city in autumn as they gorge themselves to store fat for the long winter months. One squirrel may hide 20 or more bushels of nuts in one winter's cache. People, too, collect nuts from trees that were planted generations ago.

In the heat of the next hot summer day, try walking barefoot from a cement or asphalt sidewalk to a patch of green grass. Or walk from a scalding parking lot into the relative cool of a nearby park. Water evaporating from leaf surfaces cools the environment and *increases humidity.* More than 300 gallons (1,136 liters) of water can evaporate from the leaves of one large tree in a single day. Urban plants provide a measure of the *natural cooling* that occurs in the countryside when water evaporates off of soil, lakes, wetlands, rivers, fields, forests and farmland. Green leaves afford shelter and *shade* from a scorching sun, or temporary respite from a cloudburst.

Trees help *improve air quality* in their immediate surroundings. Leaves actively filter out pollution and cleanse the air (Figure 11-1). They produce oxygen and absorb carbon dioxide during photosynthesis, thus replenishing the oxygen needed by all animal life and decreasing carbon dioxide in city air. As moving air slows down amid the tree crowns, a significant amount of particulate pollution settles onto leaf surfaces, further cleansing the air. In areas where there are many trees and few sources of pollution, such as in large cemeteries, this cleansing action creates small pockets of relatively clean air. Lichens are especially sensitive to the hydrocarbons from engine exhausts, which can stunt or completely inhibit their growth. Colonies of lichens growing on rocks, headstones or tree trunks indicate that the air in that locale is relatively clean.

Urban trees *mask undesirable sights and sounds.* Shrubs and evergreens provide a visual screen blocking the view of a parking lot from sidewalk, road or house. When planted on a median or along the shoulders of a roadway, shrubs and evergreens protect drivers from the glare of oncoming headlights and serve as sound insulation for neighboring homes. Even if the din of cars and trucks is not greatly reduced, trees planted between roads and bordering houses can make the noise more bearable. In addition, the rustling

Figure 11-1. *Trees add beauty and grace to the urban scene. Animals find food and shelter amid the branches and trunks. Leaves mask undesirable sights and sounds, filter pollution from the air and release oxygen. Leaves cool the hot summer air by providing shade and moisture. Parks provide places for recreation, relaxation and social gatherings surrounded by the ever-changing seasonal interplay of plant shapes, colors and textures. (Photo by Michael J. Caduto)*

leaves of trees and the sounds of wind through evergreen boughs provide a soothing background sound screen.

Trees *provide a more comfortable, smaller human scale* in contrast to tall buildings. What would cities be like without the *recreational areas* and collective *gathering places* found in parks, gardens and wetlands? These *green spaces* allow urbanites to maintain physical well-being and they build a sense of community. Parks and playgrounds, the gathering places of people both young and old, are often located near one another. In addition to the recreational value of wetlands, when they are left undeveloped along riverbanks they also help to *control and moderate flood waters, filter pollution* from runoff, *prevent erosion, protect and provide water supplies* for drinking and irrigation and serve as natural areas for *educational pursuits.*

People who live in a city or suburb depend on plants to provide green open spaces and the kind of *soft influences* that make these environments more pleasant and livable. By increasing the *aesthetic beauty* of city and suburb, trees and other plants afford us small corners of quiet amid the rush and roar. They inspire us and preserve our peace of mind. The *shape, color and texture* of plants provide a contrast to other city sights. The diverse and *pleasingly changing appearance* of trees and other plants, such as the fluttering leaves of ivy greening the side of a wall, soften the sharp lines of buildings, streets and signs, much as the shrubs in front of homes alter harsh architectural angles. *Seasonal change* offers variety to the unchanging faces of buildings. Buds bursting in springtime, sparkling summer greens, fiery fall colors and the grace of naked winter branches each offer their own visual feast. Evergreens provide greenery year-round. Fungi, lichens and mosses splash color along tree bark on the bleakest days. The mere presence of green in our surroundings has a *soothing effect* on our temperament. Blowing leaves and swaying branches are welcome sights in a scene where most structures are rigid.

BOTANICAL GARDENS. Botanical gardens are special kinds of habitats for plants. Historically, this is where wild plants were collected, studied and assessed for economic usefulness in agriculture, medicine and as ornamentals. In recent times, botanists have also focused on studying and classifying plants from threatened habitats, such as tropical rainforests, as well as learning how to save endangered plants. Some groups have created seed banks as repositories to help ensure species survival. Another trend has been to study the reasons for degradation of entire ecosystems. Botanical gardens are using this knowledge to create elaborate rainforest exhibits for education, public visitation and aesthetic appreciation, and to promote ecological stewardship. Certain organizations, such as the New York Botanical Garden and the Jardin Botanique de Montréal (Montreal Botanical Garden), conduct research in urban horticulture and how to better grow urban plants and develop new varieties, discover new ways of using plants in cities, teach people about the values and need for urban plants and coordinate people and organizations working on urban plant issues and projects.[1]

FIELDS AND VACANT LOTS: ACCESSIBLE GREEN COMMUNITIES. Most people live within minutes of an old field or a vacant lot covered with a mixture of wildflowers, both native and introduced from distant lands. When allowed to grow wild, lawns are soon covered with plantains, dandelions, violets, red and white clover, hawkweeds, wild strawberries and bluets. Fungi occasionally sprout their fruiting mushroom caps. Cool, damp habitats beneath a hedgerow or even on the bark of a tree are good places to search for mosses. Any of the urban and suburban plant communities discussed earlier are likely places to look for wildflowers. Even during the cold winter months the intricate shapes and patterns of hardy winter weeds persist.

Insects and Flowers

Some of the most fascinating and easily observed relationships in the oft-forgotten wildflower gardens of city and suburb are those between flowers and insects. Many of these interactions center around the acts of *plant pollination* and *insect foraging*. Some insects are active during the day: bumblebees, honeybees, butterflies and certain moths, such as the hummingbird moth, which hovers and gathers nectar

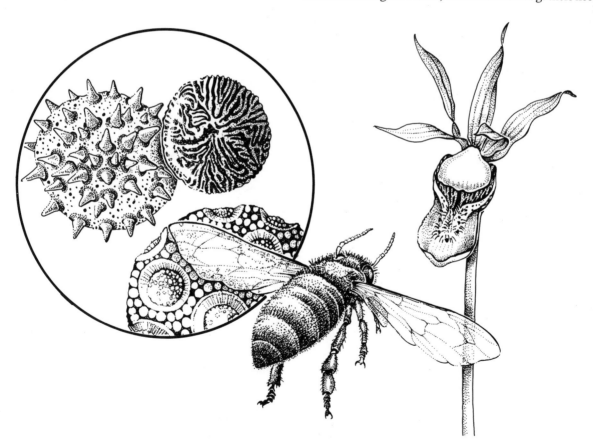

Figure 11-2. When foraging for nectar and pollen, insects are attracted to flower scents as well as colors and patterns that are invisible to the human eye. Nectar guides are drawing this honeybee in to the petals of this orchid called the calypso or fairy slipper. Even the most common pollen grains reveal beautiful, intricate patterns and shapes when magnified. Shown here, clockwise from the upper right (inset), are the microscopic pollen grains of phlox, geranium and plants in the genus Polygonum, *which includes smartweeds and knotweeds. Size: honeybee, .6 in. (1.5 cm); calypso, flowers are 1.5 to 2 in. (3.8 to 5.1 cm), height is 3 to 8 in. (7.6 to 20.3 cm). (Illustration by Marjorie C. Leggitt)*

just like its namesake. Most hawk moths or sphinxes, however, are active at twilight and night. Butterflies and moths use a long, curled, tube-like *proboscis* to feed on nectar, which is eaten on the spot and not gathered. Solitary bees collect the sticky pollen that forms on willows blooming in wet places early each spring. Although most people know the social bees that live in colonies, such as honeybees and bumblebees, more than 99 percent of the roughly 20,000 species of bees in the world are solitary—they live alone.

Insects are equipped with an array of sensory structures that enable them to forage for pollen and nectar. Bees and other insects detect odors with sensory organs located on their antennae as well as others scattered over their exoskeleton. Sensory hairs located on an insect's feet enable the insect to taste. This sense informs the insect whether or not to extend its proboscis. Bees, wasps and most other insects detect many of the colors that human beings can see, except red. These insects also can detect colors in the ultraviolet range, which are not visible to people.

The *nectar* that attracts insects is mostly water that contains about 40 percent sugar on the average. Nectar, which is produced in gland-like *nectaries,* also contains vitamins, protein, enzymes and other nutrients. In some flowers insects locate their sweet food via *nectar guides.* These markings on the flower petals or *corolla* usually consist of veins, spots or other patterns that direct insects toward the source of nectar (Figure 11-2).

Insects use a variety of proboscises for gathering nectar. Butterflies and moths—the *Lepidopterans*—sip nectar with a unique proboscis that, when relaxed, is curled under in a spiral. To extend the proboscis the insect flexes muscles that alter the shape of the tube, create hydraulic pressure and cause the tube to unfurl. The proboscis works much like the way a partly inflated bicycle tube becomes rigid and straightens out when squeezed. The natural coiled shape of the proboscis is maintained by an elastic protein substance called *resilin.* There is a tremendous variation in the length of proboscises in insects. In honeybees the proboscis is about .26 inch (6.5 millimeters), in one species of bumblebee it is .55 to .63 inch (14 to 16 millimeters), in the cabbage white butterfly it is .63 inch (16 millimeters) and, in the hummingbird hawk moth, the proboscis can grow to 1.1 inches (28 millimeters).[2] The length of the hummingbird hawk moth's proboscis is equivalent to a human being 5 feet 6 inches (1.7 meters) tall having a tongue that is nearly 4 feet (1.2 meters) long! When a drop of nectar is large enough, a bee sucks it up directly. Smaller drops of nectar are licked up first before being sucked with the proboscis. Nectar is stored in the bees' *honey crop.*

The *honeybee,* which was brought to North America from Europe, is the most productive among those bees that create *honey,* including the bumblebee. A honeybee can gather nectar from 1,000 to 1,500 clover blossoms before its stomach is full. It requires 20 million visits to flowers to create 2.2 pounds (1 kilogram) of honey, yet a colony of bees produces this much

honey in about a day. A strong summer colony of honeybees may contain more than 50,000 bees. In one spring day the *queen* can lay up to 2,000 eggs. Altogether, these eggs weigh about as much as the queen who laid them.[3] The honey-making process consists of several distinct steps:

• The bee empties nectar stored in its honey crop into waiting cells.
• Other bees in the hive drink the nectar again, mixing it with enzymes in their honey crops, and then regurgitate the nectar.
• Bees fan the open cells with their wings to increase evaporation.
• The nectar becomes thicker as water gradually evaporates in the warmth of the hive.
• Open cells are used to store the honey.
• Wax is used to cap the ripe honey in the cells of the honeycomb.

Enzymes contained in bee secretions mix with the nectar and transform sucrose into glucose and fructose. Besides nectar, another source of raw material for honey is the sweet drops, or *honeydew,* that are excreted onto needles and other tree leaves by aphids and scale insects.[4]

It is not uncommon, in the early morning chill, to find a bumblebee still sitting on a flower, where it was caught in the evening chill while gathering nectar and pollen. Close relatives of the honeybee, our native *bumblebees* also live on nectar and pollen—foods that are used to feed their brood. Bumblebees have a longer proboscis than honeybees and can, therefore, obtain nectar from flowers where the sweet fluid is found deeper than the honeybee can reach. Bumblebees are also heavier and more aggressive when foraging, enabling them to work their way into some flowers that are inaccessible to honeybees. There are only a few hundred bumblebees in a hive and they do not collect winter food because the colony dies in autumn. Only the fertilized female queens overwinter. Rather than building hexagonal comb cells like honeybees, bumblebees store honey and pollen in little wax "pots." In early spring the large queens, who have emerged from winter dormancy, begin to search for nest sites, such as abandoned mouse nests or other holes in the ground.

Most pollen-gathering insects are covered with dense *hairs.* When a bumblebee visits a flower, which may be up to a mile from the hive, its hairs become coated with pollen. On the way to another flower the bumblebee uses tiny *brushes* on its hind legs to clean the pollen from the hairs. Minute *combs* are used to remove pollen from the brushes. This pollen is packed into *pollen baskets,* which are hollows on the outsides of the hind legs. Nectar moistens the pollen as it is packed into the baskets. Up to a million grains of pollen at a time are stored in each pollen basket. Back inside the hive, the bee unloads the pollen into a storage cell and *workers* push the pollen into the cells. *Nurse bees* then consume the pollen and use it to make *"mother's milk"* with which to nourish the *larvae.* Since the male *drones* do not collect pollen, they lack the brushes, combs and pollen baskets of workers.

Stewardship of Urban and Suburban Plant Communities

It takes constant *planting, vigilance* and *maintenance* to ensure that the plant communities of the built environment, and the animals that live interdependently with them such as the insects just described, are able to survive. Competition for space and resources is high in the city. It is important to match the biological needs and character of each plant to the nature of its site and to use proper planting and maintenance practices. Should a tree that will grow tall be planted under a powerline even though the crown will have to be severely pruned as it grows, or should it be offset or located on the other side of a street to allow its foliage to develop unimpeded? A variety such as the small-crowned globe maple or the tall, thin columnar maple can be planted wherever growing space is limited. The London plane tree, an Asian and European hybrid related to the American sycamore, can tolerate heavily compacted soil with poor air penetration and drainage.

City governments provide some essential services, such as tree planting, pruning, inspection and disease control. More and more cities now have urban foresters and forestry departments to care for their trees. With proper training and knowledge, individuals can help by pruning where needed, preventing injuries to plants, watering, fertilizing and protecting from insects and diseases. These efforts can be coordinated with the local city forester and department of parks and recreation, who offer information, advice and services. Because many trees and other city plants have been around for generations and will live long after we are gone, the city belongs as much to the plants as it does to us. We are their caretakers during our short life spans.

A number of communities are reaping the benefits of treating their urban plant communities wisely while they enjoy their pleasures. Some people are calling these communities "new pueblos." Quebec City and Ottawa are excellent examples in which greenery is an integral part of the urban fabric. *Urban Renewal Initiatives* (URIs), of which environmental restoration is an integral part, are springing up all over North America and beyond, in cities such as San Francisco, Portland, Toronto, Detroit, New Haven, New York City and Baltimore.[5] The town plan for Bamberton, British Columbia, is based on ecological principles and a strong intent to make little use of cars. Portland, Oregon, is planning an extensive "urban wilderness system" within the city limits that will connect to outlying open spaces. Urban Ecology, in Berkeley, California, has drawn up the Ten-Point International Ecological Rebuilding Program for cities. Baltimore has reorganized its Recreation and Parks Department into districts that conform to the boundaries of the city's three natural watersheds. This city has also established the *tree stewards* volunteer program as well as a youth program that integrates environmental

education and adventure challenges such as those used by the Outward Bound program. In Detroit, some of the 60,000 vacant lots that are maintained by the city are being converted, with the help of city youth, into Christmas-tree farms. Toronto's "Bring Back the Don" program aims to clean up and restore a heavily polluted river that feeds Lake Ontario, reestablishing delta marsh grasses and soils that cleanse the water. Ninety-five percent of Boston's 192 parks and playgrounds, including Frederick Law Olmstead's "emerald necklace" parks in Back Bay, have been refurbished and improved as part of a $120 million investment over the past eight years. Olmstead's Central Park in New York City remains an inspiring example of what can be created with vision and persistence. Gardens are now springing up in the Bronx and many other New York neighborhoods. Foresters in both New Haven and Baltimore are involving inner-city children in the creation of urban parks.

The kinds of urban greening projects that can be undertaken seem to be endless, bounded only by the imagination and energy it takes to make things happen:

• establishing urban gardens and tree farms
• planting trees and wildflowers in vacant lots and other "waste" places
• creating new parks in unused lots
• setting up and carrying out environmental monitoring and cleanup projects
• managing lawns and other green areas as a diverse ecosystem without the use of pesticides and herbicides
• creating mini-gardens and other plantings on terraces and rooftops

Growing a garden is akin to building a community and providing young people with some essential skills for growing successfully into adulthood. Planting trees and gardens educates, enriches and gives direction to young lives while providing social, environmental and economic values to the community. A sense of involvement and meaning come to those who cooperate on community gardens and other greening projects. To create an urban garden people must choose a site that has plenty of sunlight and is sheltered from the wind, dust and air pollution. Then, the gardeners must remove the trash from a site, enrich the soil, obtain a supply of water and begin planting. In many places, where the community is at first as decrepit and littered as a neglected vacant lot, gardening projects gradually provide a focal point for what cohesiveness and collective effort can produce. Just as the fears of a forest and the animals that live there decrease over time as people get to know those environments, so do the fears held toward other members of the community diminish as people come to know one another working side by side. A new urban garden is often vandalized despite the best efforts to prevent it, such as fence building and community watches. Yet, over time, as the garden becomes recognized as an important part of community life, the vandalism declines. The best fence is community spirit.

QUESTIONS

1. Who is watching Blue Dawn each day as he plays the game of *huib*? Why do you think the eagle takes the boy? Where does she take him?

2. Why are the young men not able to save Blue Dawn when he is found?

3. Whom do the young men ask for help? Whom do the Stone-Layers, the swallows, ask for help? Whom does Grandmother Spider ask for help? How does she get Blue Dawn down from the cliff?

4. Can you name everyone who helps to get Blue Dawn back home? What does it mean to cooperate to get something done?

5. How do the fathers of wisdom turn Blue Dawn from an eagle back into a young boy?

6. What kind of houses do the Isleta Pueblo people, who bring us the story "Blue Dawn," live in? What is a city? What is a suburb? Where do you live?

7. How are the city and suburb different from the countryside? What is the weather like in the city?

8. Where do plants grow in the city and suburb? What kinds of things make it hard for plants to grow in these habitats?

9. How do trees and other plants change the city and suburb? What do you like about spending time in a park? How do plants make parks and other green spaces nice places to be?

10. Where would you look for wildflowers growing in the city or suburb? What kinds of insects would you see on these flowers? Why do these insects visit the flowers?

11. In what ways do plants in the city need our help? What can you do to take care of these trees and other plants?

12. What can you do by working with other people to take care of plants that you could not accomplish alone? Why is cooperation so important in cities and suburbs where there are a lot of people? What kinds of ways of behaving help people to work well together?

13. What is a community? How can working to take care of plants help to build community?

ACTIVITIES

Growing Green in the City

ACTIVITY: Complete a check-off sheet while observing plants, plant communities, the conditions that plants must survive in to grow in the city and the ways that plants make the city a nicer place to live.

GOALS: Understand the kinds of climate, growing conditions and stresses that the urban environment places on plants. Discover the variety of plant and animal life associated with living greenery. Realize the many values and benefits of urban plants.

AGE: Younger children and older children

MATERIALS: For each child, one copy of Figure 11-3, a pencil and cardboard backing or clipboard to write on, "Discussion."

PROCEDURE: Pass out one copy of *"Growing Green in the City"* (Figure 11-3) to each child, along with a pencil and hard backing to write against. Ask the children: "Do you think it is easy to be a tree or other kind of plant growing in the city? Why or why not? What would make it hard to grow in the city? How do you think plants can survive here? What kinds of plants live nearby? What kinds of animals live in or on those plants?" Review, with the children, the basic ideas found in the "Discussion" that deal with urban climate, growing conditions and plant communities.

Now inquire: "How do plants make the city a better place to live? What kinds of gifts do we receive from plants? What would it be like in the city if there were no plants here?" Discuss the many ways that trees and other plants make the city a more pleasant, hospitable environment as explained in the "Discussion."

Now take the children on a field trip to places where plants are growing near the home or school grounds. Have them search for, experience and check off as many of the discoveries described and illustrated on their *"Growing Green in the City"* check-offs as they can find. Emphasize that the idea is to look closely, not to try to find every single thing or condition described on the sheet. Instruct them to make a small check mark (√) in the corner of each illustration because they are going to color them in later on. After about 20 to 30 minutes have elapsed, bring the group together again and ask them to share their discoveries.

Note: Since the children will not have found everything on their check-off sheets, have them keep the sheets and take them home. Ask them to look for things to check off while looking out the window of the school bus, while walking home or in their own neighborhoods. They can color in the pictures once they have found everything on the list.

Triangulating Trees

ACTIVITY: Measure the height of a tree using a simple, homemade triangulation device.

GOALS: Understand what a right-angled isosceles triangle is and how it can be used to measure the heights of tall things. Practice cooperating to accomplish a group task.

AGE: Older children

MATERIALS: At least two people per group; yardsticks or measuring tapes; paper; pencils; cardboard backing or clipboards; scissors; protractor to measure the right angle while making the devices; one triangulation device per group (Figure 11-4), each made from a stiff piece of cardboard bent

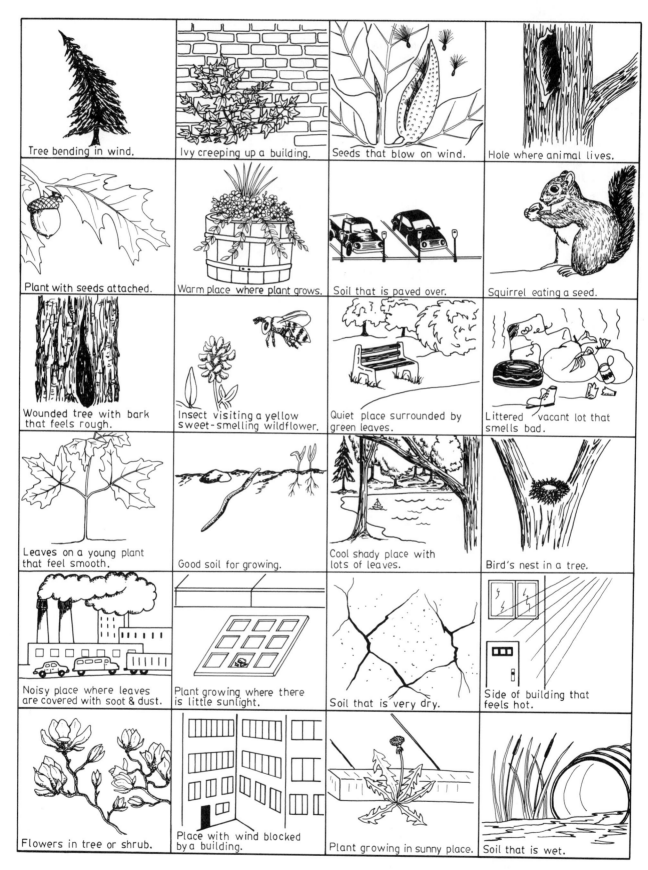

Figure 11-3. "Growing Green in the City." *Search for the things pictured in each square and check them off when you find them.*

into a right angle; one drinking straw; tape; piece of string with a light weight, such as a small stone, tied onto the end. **PROCEDURE:** Beforehand, create one triangle device for each small group of children (Figure 11-4). A hole puncher works well to make the slots in which to slip the straw. Make each cardboard leg of the device 5.5 inches (14 centimeters) long and 2 inches (5 centimeters) wide so that the drinking straw will reach across the hypotenuse and the device will be

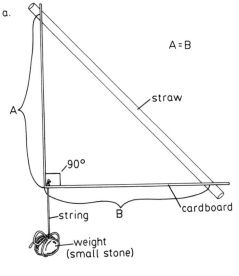

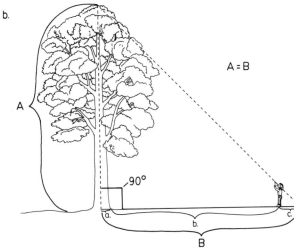

Figure 11-4. "Triangulating Trees." Have each child move the correct distance from the tree. This will be the place where she or he is looking directly at the topmost part of the tree while sighting through the straw at the same time that the string hanging from the triangulation device is parallel with the vertical edge of the cardboard triangle. The right-angled isosceles triangle in (a) above is a miniature version of the congruent triangle created in (b) below by the child and tree. In order to obtain the correct distance for B in the bottom triangle (the estimated height of the tree), one-half of the diameter of the tree must be added to the distance the child is standing from the base of the tree plus the height of the child (a+b+c=B). The child's height must be added to account for the part of the line of sight that extends behind the child and reaches to the ground.

sturdy and easy to handle. Scout out an area where large trees are growing out in the open, in which children can back up from the trees by a distance that is somewhat greater than the trees' heights. This is essential for the children to take the measurements needed to complete this activity.

Divide the children into small groups and pass out one "Tree Triangulation" device to each group. Discuss the characteristics of a right-angled isosceles triangle with the children. Share Figure 11-4 and explain the specifics of how they are going to create a giant triangle as a way of measuring the height of a large tree. Emphasize the need to cooperate to accomplish this task, just as everyone cooperated in "Blue Dawn" to retrieve the boy from the eagles.

Take the entire group outdoors to where the trees are growing. Measure out a distance of about 20 feet (6 meters) on the ground and have one child from each group pace up and down this distance, counting the number of paces she or he takes along the way. Have the children in the group calculate the average distance per pace: total distance paced divided by the number of paces. Have the pacers repeat this procedure and average the two final figures for the length of one pace.

Demonstrate to the children how they are to use the triangulation device: "Stand back from the tree by a distance that is about equal to its height. Have someone sight through the straw onto the tree's very topmost branch and move closer or farther from the tree until the plumb line (weighted string) is hanging down parallel with the vertical edge of the triangle *while* the sighter views the treetop through the straw. Have one person sight through the straw while someone else checks the plumb line. The sighter will stand at that spot while the pacer measures the distance from the sighter's feet to the base of the tree. To get a measurement for the *entire* length of the leg of the triangle that runs along the ground, the paced distance must be added to the height from the sighter's eyes to the ground and one-half of the tree's estimated diameter. This is the height of the tree." (See detail in Figure 11-4.)

Ask the children, "Why would someone want to know the height of a tree or other tall object?" Taller trees cast more shade and cooling. Someone may want to use the angle of the sun and height of the tree to calculate where the shade will be cast at different times of the year. Also, remember the cliff that Blue Dawn was taken to by the eagles. This technique could be used to sight up the cliff to calculate how high up Blue Dawn was. Review the value of plants in the city as described in the "Discussion."

Exploring Flowers of City and Suburb

ACTIVITY: (A) Search for immigrant plants from other continents. (B) Conduct a simple experiment to observe which flower colors are preferred by insects and birds. (C) Write a story about the life of a flower that has lived out its cycle.

GOALS: Discover that many plants growing nearby were actually brought from other continents. Understand why and how flowers attract insects and birds using different colors and patterns. Realize which colors insects and birds can see and are the most attracted to. Understand the process of natural selection. Understand that flowers, while different than people, also live out their lives and have a story to tell.

AGE: Younger children and older children

MATERIALS: Park, vacant lot or other area in which flowers of a variety of colors are growing. If *no* flowers can be found around the home or learning center for use in "A" and "B," flowers gathered elsewhere can be placed in vases and substituted. Likewise, dried flower stalks can be gathered elsewhere for use in "C." (A) Field guides to flowers that identify species that are introduced or "alien." (B) One thin stick at least 2 feet (61 centimeters) high for each child; brightly colored construction paper (including white), plus the major colors of the spectrum (red, orange, yellow, green, blue, indigo and violet) or shades of color as close as you can find; scissors; "Discussion" from Chapter 9; "Discussion" from this chapter; pencils; copies of Figure 11-5, "Color Them Sweet"; cardboard backing or clipboards; newsprint; marker; hand lenses. (C) Old flower stalks from last year's growth, paper, pencils, cardboard backing or clipboards, pruning shears.

PROCEDURE A: *Green Aliens in the Neighborhood. Note:* This activity is intended as a brief observation and discussion session preceding the other two activities in *"Exploring Flowers of City and Suburb."* If no flowers can be found near the home or learning center, immigrant flowers collected elsewhere and placed in vases can be substituted.

Beforehand, scout out a park, vacant lot or other habitat where a variety of different-colored flowers are growing. Using a field guide to wildflowers that identifies plants in your region and indicates the "alien" plants that were introduced from other continents, identify as many of the common flowers as you can and note which species are introduced. Some good books include the *Peterson* and *Audubon Field Guides* as well as *Newcomb's Wildflower Guide,* by Lawrence Newcomb (Boston: Little, Brown, 1977). Here is a *sampling* of some alien plants: ox-eye daisy, common mallow, bladder campion, common chickweed, wild carrot (Queen Anne's lace), mullein (lamb's ears), common and English plantains, white and red clovers, common St. Johnswort, sow-thistle, celandine, common buttercup, dandelion, butter and eggs (toadflax), purple loosestrife, hop clover, birdfoot trefoil, common tansy, dusty miller, orange hawkweed, everlasting pea, motherwort, comfrey, teasel, burdock, Canada thistle, salsify (oyster plant), grape hyacinth, nightshade and jimsonweed (these are poisonous), heal-all (self-heal), catnip, peppermint, cypress spurge, curled dock, stinging nettle and Japanese knotweed.

Take the children outdoors to the site where flowers are growing. Point out which of the plants growing there are aliens from another land. Ask the children: "Which of these plants do you know? Which ones do you like? Are there any that you do not like? Why?" Explain how some alien plants are beautiful and well-loved, but that others, such as purple loosestrife, take over and replace native plants, which often provide better food and cover for wildlife. North America is a land of immigrant plants and animals, as well as people.

PROCEDURE B: *Color Them Sweet. Note:* You will need to conduct this part of the activity on a warm, bright day when insects are most active. If no flowers can be found near the home or learning center, flowers of a variety of colors that are collected elsewhere can be placed in vases and substituted.

Beforehand, gather enough narrow sticks for each child to have one. Cut one small square (half a sheet) of brightly colored construction paper for each child. Use a variety of colors including white and others that represent the full range of the spectrum—red, orange, yellow, green, blue, indigo and violet—or colors as close to these as you can find.

Review, with the children, the reasons for flower colors and patterns and how these attract insects, birds and bats for pollination (see "Discussion" in Chapter 9). Discuss the interesting process of how bees gather pollen and nectar from flowers and how these foods are used ("Discussion" from this chapter). Explain that pollinating insects, including beetles, flies, bees, wasps, butterflies and moths, see colors differently than people do. Many insects cannot see red but can see ultraviolet color, which is not visible to human beings. Birds can see red. Then say: "Each kind of insect is attracted to certain colors. We are going to do an experiment to find out which colors the insects and birds visiting flowers in this (field, vacant lot ...) are attracted to."

Give each child a stick, a small square of brightly colored construction paper, a pencil, a copy of Figure 11-5 and backing to write on. Each color should have the same number of children observing it to create accurate results. Have them crumple up their paper into a tight ball and push it onto the top of the stick. Explain that the children are to watch their paper "flower" very closely for about 15 minutes or so. Whenever they see an insect or bird fly over to the flower (it does *not* have to land there), they are to mark a line on their data sheet next to the kind of pollinator they see. The number of lines they have at the end of their observation will record the number of visits made by each pollinator. Now set the children out in different parts of the field and have each one push the stick into the ground a bit so the stick is standing upright.

Call the children back in after about 10 minutes (younger children) or 20 minutes (older children). Give them a chance to share everything they saw that they are excited about. Now ask each child to tell you what color of paper flower she or he was observing, and the number of visits made by each pollinator. Record this information on a large sheet of newsprint. Once you have all of the children's data recorded, ask them to draw conclusions from what they found. Which colors were each kind of pollinator attracted to? Which colors are the most popular overall? Bees do not like blue-green but are very attracted to ultraviolet, which we cannot

Write down the color of your paper flower here.

_____

Make a mark next to each pollinator on this list every time that insect or bird flies up to your paper flower.

beetle _____

fly _____

bee _____

wasp _____

butterfly _____

moth _____

bird _____

Figure 11-5. "Color Them Sweet."

see. Red to purple are the favorite colors of many butterflies but they are not attracted to blue-green. Bumblebees are drawn to blue, violet and purple. Hover flies and the common cabbage white butterfly prefer yellow flowers.[6]

Now have the children repeat the entire observation process using the real flowers growing in the field. Once again, make sure equal numbers of children are observing flowers of each color to maintain the accuracy of the number of sightings at different colors relative to one another. Encourage the children to use hand lenses and look closely at the flowers before beginning their observations. Bring the children together when the observation time is up and repeat the recording of data as you did for their paper flowers. Which colors were most popular among real flowers? How do these results compare with the colors that were most often chosen on the paper flowers?

Describe the process of natural selection, through which those flowers that have the most attractive colors and patterns are most likely to become pollinated, set seed and reproduce. These flowers are "selected" by the insects and will become more and more common over time. In this way, the insects affect the evolution of flowers.

PROCEDURE C: *The Story of a Flower. Note:* This is a good winter activity. If no dried flower stalks can be found near the home or learning center, these may be collected elsewhere and substituted.

Take another trip to the field or vacant lot and look around with the children for the old, dried-up remains of last year's flowers. These stalks and their interesting sculptured seedheads where the flowers used to be have survived the winter. Each stalk has a story to tell about its life from seed to flower and back to seed again. Ask the children to find an old flower stalk and wait for you to come over and gently cut it off close to the ground. They should not pull it up because there may be roots remaining that might sprout later. As they gather these old flowers, have them look for seeds still clinging to or contained in the seedhead. Have everyone say "thank you" to the flowers by spreading around some of the old seeds from their flower or from some other old flower nearby. Ask the children to write a story about what they imagine happened during the life of their flower. What did its flower look like? How tall was it? Which kinds of pollinators visited the flower? What kinds of adventures did it have with weather, people who almost picked it, insects that ate its leaves, etc.? Ask children to be as creative and dramatic as they like. Plant lives are no less interesting than those of animals: plants simply interact with their environments differently than we do and at a slower pace. Over a period of time, plants have exciting lives, too.

Saga of a Seed Maze

ACTIVITY: Discuss the things a seed needs to germinate. Complete a maze simulating the many obstacles a seed faces in the city that may prevent it from germinating and developing into a new plant.

GOALS: Understand that seeds have basic needs for water, nutrients (soil), sunlight and certain environmental conditions to germinate and grow. Realize that a seed in the city faces difficult challenges to finding what it needs to grow, as well as facing hazards that may prevent it from germinating.

AGE: Younger children and older children

MATERIALS: "Discussion" section, crayons or pens, one copy of the *"Saga of a Seed Maze"* (Figure 11-6) for each child.

PROCEDURE: Use the "Discussion" section to review the growing conditions that plants face in the city. Ask the children: "What does a seed need to grow? What kinds of obstacles would a falling seed face in the city that might prevent it from sprouting and growing into a new plant?" Be sure they touch on the need for water, nutrients in the soil, sunlight, the proper temperature and other environmental conditions.

Pass out a copy of the *"Saga of a Seed Maze"* (Figure 11-6) to each child. Have them imagine they are seeds falling off a plant in the city. They are to begin the maze at the starting point on the outside and work their way to the inside, where a seed has successfully sprouted. Obstacles that might prevent a seed from growing appear in the maze as dead-ends. Have the children record *all* of their movements in the maze in pen or crayon. They *will* be allowed to backtrack out of the dead-ends to continue their journey toward germination. One of the rules is to not erase when they reach a dead-end, but to turn around and look for another way to find the center.

Note: You can also enlarge the maze and have the children move a real seed through it, such as an acorn or a maple seed. You could also set up a maze in the home or learning center and have the children walk through and move their seed toward germination. You might want to have the children act out their Saga of a Seed as a skit.

Once the seed mazes are complete, lead a discussion of their journeys and allow time for the children to share any questions, thoughts or stories they have. Ask how many of them "sprouted" without traveling down a single dead-end. These are the *only* seeds that would have germinated and grown into new plants.

City Plant Stewards

ACTIVITY: (A) Follow clues on a mystery trail along which are hidden ideas for plant stewardship in the city. Use letters from the clues to fill in the blanks and complete the words in a sentence. (B) Choose and implement an urban "green-up" project.

GOALS: Realize that there are many ways individuals and groups can contribute to green stewardship in the city.

Understand that, in any group project, necessary skills include empathy, listening, understanding and cooperation. Observe how human community is strengthened by helping the plant community.

AGE: Younger children and older children

MATERIALS: (A) Safe park or other natural area in which to bring the children, seven large seeds of trees or other plants native to your area, pen, paper and cardboard backing or clipboard, list of seven project ideas from this activity, rubberbands, copy of sentence for children to complete by filling in the blank letters with circled letters from the ideas along the Mystery Trail, newsprint and marker. (B) Chalkboard and chalk or newsprint and marker, other materials as needed for specific project chosen by the children, thank-you notes, appropriate books listed in this activity, supplies for a celebration, camera and film.

PROCEDURE A: *Mystery Trail.* Beforehand, visit a nearby park or other natural area and lay out an interesting trail that children will follow by using clues to get from one station to the next. Plan the route carefully so the children will be *safe* during the activity and so their foot traffic from station to station will have a minimal impact on that habitat. Younger children should be able to easily spot the next station from the one they are standing at. Older children could be clued in to a landmark or two in between each station to make the trail more challenging. For instance, a clue might say: "From this rock you can see a statue. Walk over to it. Now walk in the direction the statue is facing and you will come to a big old tree with a hole in it where the next clue is hidden." There will be seven stations along the trail corresponding with the seven project ideas listed below. Record all clues as you create the trail, and then write or type them out onto separate pieces of paper, including one of each of the following ideas along with each clue. Circle the letters as indicated:

v a c (a) n t   l o t   g a r d e n

(t) r e e   f a r m

w i l d f l o w e (r)   m e a d o w

t r e e   p l a (n) t i n g

v a c a n t   l o t   c l (e) a n u (p)

r o o f t o p   g a r d (e) n

n (e) w   n e i g h b (o) r h o o d   p a r k

Just before the excursion, use a rubberband to wrap each clue around a large seed, such as a maple, acorn or walnut (native), and hide the clues at the stations.

Divide the children into seven small groups so each group has a chance to lead to the next station at least once. Take the children out to the site and introduce them to the rules of the excursion and explain how the Mystery Trail works. Strongly

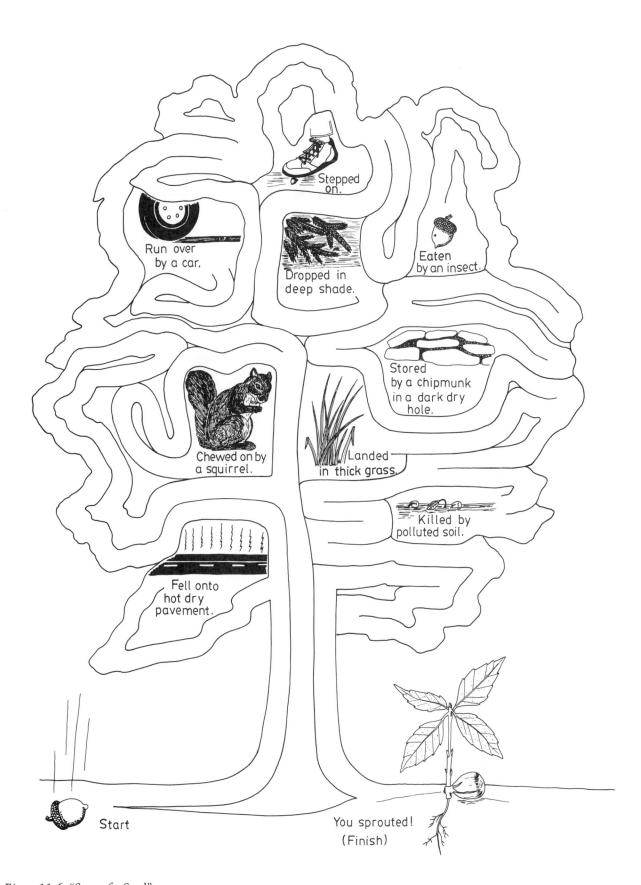

Figure 11-6. "Saga of a Seed" *maze.*

caution them to keep *safety* in mind at all times during the activity. Emphasize that this is a visit to the homes of plants and animals and that they should act respectfully while visiting: the quieter and more observant they are, the more they will see. Tell the children that, when moving from station to station, the group is to follow the leaders in single file. Ask them not to run at any time. This is a cooperative activity.

Give a verbal clue to the first station. If you are working with older children, let them conduct the entire journey with occasional tips from you if they get confused along the way. If your children have not yet learned to read, simply read the information and directions to the next site for the leaders at each stop. Ask the children to keep eyes, ears and noses alert for exciting and unexpected adventures en route. Take time to explore these interesting discoveries.

Once the children are finished finding all clues, hold up an enlarged version of this sentence, which contains four partially completed words: K _ _ p e _ s _ f _ h _ _ l _ _ t s. Ask them to use *all* of the letters that are circled on the clues to complete the words in this sentence. (The answer is "Keepers of the Plants.")

PROCEDURE B: *Green Keepers.* Have the children choose one of the projects from the "Mystery Trail" clues to carry out as a group. Ask them how they think people need to act in order to work well together. Emphasize the need for empathy, listening, understanding and cooperation in the group. Tell children: "We are going to better the plant community in our neighborhood. As we do this, and work together, we will also be doing something for the people in our community and learning how to work together as a small community of people." Now ask, "What kinds of behaviors will help us to work well together to accomplish our tasks?"

Have the children make a list of steps they will need to complete to accomplish their tasks. Whether on a vacant lot, in an existing park or near a playground, make sure the children first ask the appropriate city or town officials and neighbors for permission to carry out their project. Have the children research the information they need to work toward their objectives. These steps may include obtaining the necessary permission and permits, researching what kinds of plants to grow in your climate and where to obtain them, raising some money to purchase seeds or seedlings, gathering the necessary tools, preparing the soil at the site of planting, scheduling a work plan at the site during which at least a few adults will be able to accompany the children whenever in the field, maintaining the plantings once established, writing thank-you notes and expressing appreciation to all people from the community who helped out. The section called "Planting Trees and Shrubs" in Chapter 2 is useful here. Some helpful books are *The City Gardener's Handbook: From Balcony to Backyard,* by Linda Yang (New York: Random House, 1990); *The Terrace Gardener's Handbook,* by Linda Yang (Beaverton, Ore.: Timber Press, 1982); and *The Wildflower Meadow Book: A Gardener's Guide,* by Laura C. Martin (Chester, Conn.: Globe Pequot, 1990). Whichever project the children decide on, have them plant and grow the seeds found along the "Mystery Trail" at the site.

Once the children have begun to see the fruits of their labor, take photographs of their work and hold a celebration to congratulate them on their accomplishments. Have them schedule a "grand opening" of their new green work in the community, send out press releases and invite local officials and reporters for a children's tour of the site on a certain day. Be sure to invite everyone who helped out from the school and community.

EXTENDING THE EXPERIENCE

• Visit your local botanical garden and get involved with their educational programs and exhibits.

• Interview senior citizens and record their special memories of times spent in parks and other places where trees and other plants make visits pleasant. Ask them to share any stories they have about experiences with trees in their lives, especially trees that they planted as children.

• Hold a feast of corn dishes to celebrate the return of the rain and ripening of corn in "Blue Dawn."

• Plant a butterfly garden and attract these colorful insects to your home or learning center. An excellent guide to attracting butterflies and identifying them is *Butterflies,* by Marcus Schneck (Emmaus, Penn.: Rodale, 1990).

• Map all of the green areas near your home or learning center and try to visit each of them.

• Create your own story about a tree growing up through several generations in your community. Tell the story in the first person: "I am an old tree who has been here for many, many years …"

• Take an outing to a park or playground and play ball, fly kites and have fun.

• Use party favors—the kind that unroll when you blow into them—to mimic the action of the proboscis of a moth or butterfly. Even though, in reality, the proboscis *works* more like a partially inflated inner tube that someone squeezes, the party favors *move* much like a proboscis.

• See Chapter 14 in *Keepers of the Animals* for activities on urban and suburban wildlife.

NOTES

1. James M. Hester, "Plant Science and Human Needs," *Orion Nature Quarterly,* vol. 2, no. 4 (Autumn 1983): 24–31.

2. Friedrich G. Barth, *Insects and Flowers: The Biology of a Partnership* (Princeton, N.J.: Princeton University Press, 1991), 104.

3. Ibid., 35.

4. Ibid., 108.

5. Tom Chalkley, "High Tops and Tree Tops," *Amicus Journal,* vol. 14, no. 2 (Summer 1992): 24–27.

6. Barth, *Insects and Flowers,* 144–145.

✤ SURVIVAL ✤

The hunter became aware of a light and turned to see a woman walking toward him. The air shone all around her and as she walked he saw that her feet sank into the earth with each step.

CHAPTER 12

✤ The Woman Who Lives in the Earth ✤

(Chugach Inuit—Arctic)

The animals, the birds, the lakes and trees, even the grass—all these have something alive which dwells within them. The Chugach people call this the *shua*. And Earth itself, on which life depends, also contains a *shua*. The Chugach call this being *Nunam-shua*, the One Who Lives Within the Earth, and she is seen as a woman.

This woman who lives within the Earth also has her home in the stones and the plants. Sometimes she is known as The One Who Dwells in the Alder Trees, but she also can walk the land in the shape of a woman. A bright light shines all around her when she walks. She wears boots made of the fur of all the animals of the land. She wears a long coat, which hangs down to her knees, hangs as lichen hangs on the stones. On her coat are many tiny animals: the caribou, the arctic fox, the musk ox, the wolf, the bear, the lemming and the hare. These are the souls of the animals which she protects, all of the animals of the land. Those animals all came originally from Earth.

The people, too, came from Earth. The first children, the Inuit say, were formed out of Earth in the places where the small willow trees grow. They were covered by the willow leaves and the soil gave them food. So the human beings must always be careful what they do on Earth. They must remember Nunam-shua.

One day, during the time when the caribou migrate, a hunter went out to seek game. As he walked, he was careful where he stepped so that he did not scrape the lichen off the stones. When he moved through a thicket of small alder trees, he bent the branches gently so that they did not break. Soon he came upon the caribou herd and he stalked closer. He was careful in his movement and so was able to come very close to the caribou without frightening them. He watched them for a long time, picking out the ones which were cows with calves and the ones which were leading the herd. Those were the animals which he knew should not be killed. He chose the animal he wished to take and then spoke to its spirit as he pulled back the arrow in his bow. His shot was a good one and the animal fell dead. He could have shot more animals, but he did not need them. So he put down his weapon, took his pouch from his side and went to the fallen caribou. Before he began to cut it up, he thanked the animal's spirit for giving itself to him. Then he placed something in its mouth to show his gratitude. As he skinned and butchered the animal, he wiped his hands on his own clothing and not on the grass, remembering that the grass is sacred at the time when the caribou migrate.

This hunter did not know it, but everything he did had been watched by Nunam-shua. He became aware of a light and turned to see a woman walking toward him. The air shone all around her and as she walked he saw that her feet sank into the earth with each step. He was afraid, because he knew who this was. He knew the power of The Woman Who Dwells in the Earth. Not long ago, a man had been cutting a live alder tree and had fallen dead. The people knew that he had died because Nunam-shua lived within the alders and the man had shown no respect for the tree while cutting it.

Nunam-shua came close to the man and stopped. She looked straight into the hunter's face and he looked down at Earth to show respect.

"You have done well, child," she said to him. "You hunt the animals with care. You do not show contempt for the grass and the trees and Earth. So I give you these."

Then Nunam-shua reached up and took from her coat tiny animals in the shape of the caribou, the musk ox and the hare. The man held out his hands to take those tiny animals. As soon as he touched them, they melted like snow into his hands. When he looked up, Nunam-shua was gone. But because she had given him the gift of those animal spirits, a gift which had entered into him like rain into the soil, from that time on he was always successful whenever he hunted the animals of the land.

Waw Giwulk: The Center of the Basket

(O'odham—Southwest)

Sh hab wa chu'i na'ana. They say it happened long ago. All was well with the O'odham, the People. All was in harmony. But then a great snake came from out of Earth. It came to the place where the people lived and began to devour them. It sucked the people into its mouth. Those people who escaped the great snake called to Itoi, Elder Brother.

"Help us!" they called.

Itoi came then from his home on Waw Giwulk. He came from his house in the center of the world.

"Give me an obsidian knife and four greasewood sticks," Elder Brother said.

Then Itoi took the knife and sticks and went to meet the great snake.

The snake sucked Elder Brother into its mouth, but he stuck the first greasewood stick into the snake's mouth and wedged it open. It sucked him down into its throat, but he stuck the second greasewood stick in the great snake's throat and wedged it open. It sucked him down into its esophagus, but he stuck the third greasewood stick in and held its esophagus open. It sucked him down into its belly, but he wedged in the fourth greasewood stick and held its belly open.

In the great snake's belly, Itoi listened. He listened for the sound of its heart. With his obsidian knife he slashed the heart and then ran out of the great snake, pulling free each greasewood stick as he ran. So Itoi killed the great snake.

Elder Brother went back to the O'odham and told them the danger was over. Then he went back to his home on Waw Giwulk. *Am o wa'i at hoabdag.* That is at the center of the basket.

DISCUSSION

The stories that open this chapter come from peoples connected to two very different ecological communities: the Arctic and the desert. The Chugach Inuit say that the plants and animals protected by *Nunam-shua,* The Woman Who Lives in the Earth, came from the earth where the small willow trees grow: the Arctic and subarctic environments. Nunam-shua's being dwells within the alder trees and she can sometimes appear as a woman. All things and Earth itself possess a living essence called *shua.* Taking care of Earth

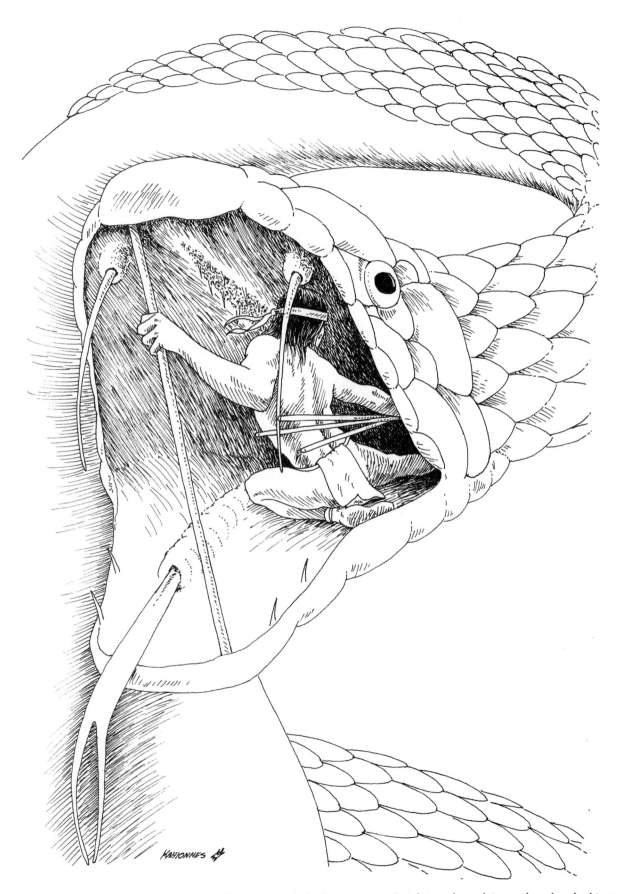

The snake sucked Elder Brother into its mouth, but he stuck the first greasewood stick into the snake's mouth and wedged it open.

demonstrates stewardship for the place from which life springs forth. One man in the story dies because he was disrespectful while cutting an alder tree. Realizing this, the hunter is careful not to damage the lichens growing on the stones, he takes care that he does not damage the alder branches and he honors the grass, which is sacred during the caribou migration. Nunam-shua gives this hunter a great gift because of his respectful ways with plants, animals and Earth.

"Waw Giwulk: The Center of the Basket" is a story from the O'odham, desert peoples of the U.S. Southwest who are also known as the Pima and the Papago. The Pima call themselves *Akimel O'odham*, "River People." The traditional name for the Papago, *Tohono O'odham*, means "Desert People." Itoi, Elder Brother, comes from Waw Giwulk, which can be seen as the dark center in the baskets of the O'odham (Figure 12-1). The four directions, south to north and east to west, are marked by two lines that cross through that circle and form the four cross-pieces on which Itoi's house rests there in the center of the maze. These lines form the maze; they reach out to each of the four directions and circle counter to the direction of the sun until the opening of Waw Giwulk at the north. There Elder Brother stands. Only he knows the way in and out of the basket maze. He will return there each time and wait in Waw Giwulk until he is needed again to help the O'odham, the People. Balance and harmony are central themes in the lives of the O'odham, and the balance of the maze design in the basket, the home of Itoi, is a perfect counterpoint to the role of maintaining that balance that Elder Brother plays when he comes out of the maze to restore order.

Figure 12-1. One basket design among the O'odham peoples shows Itoi, Elder Brother, entering the maze walking toward his home, Waw Giwulk, "the center of the basket."

This chapter discusses Arctic and desert ecological communities and how plants are able to survive in these challenging ecosystems. It also looks at plant adaptations and the nature of the interrelationships found among plants, and between plants and animals. Human impacts on the Arctic and desert are briefly examined.

Plant Adaptations and Interrelationships

The environmental adaptations of some plants can astound. Jack-in-the-pulpit sprouts in the springtime as a male (Figure 12-2). In three to five years, after accumulating the necessary energy resources, hormonal changes induce the "Jack" to become a seed-producing female. In response to drought or other severe, prolonged environmental conditions and stresses that deplete the stores of energy, the plant changes back into a male. The skunk cabbage, relative of the tropical *Philodendron* and *Dieffenbachia*, can maintain a temperature of 71.6°F (22°C) as long as the air remains above freezing. Skunk cabbage melts the spring snow above and around it. Even when it is near freezing outside, honeybees and tiny flies rest within the skunk cabbage *spathe*, the flower's hoodlike protective covering, and store heat between their foraging flights.

Plant *communities* form as a result of climate, soil, slope and other growing conditions that vary geographically, as well as the molding forces of human activities and countless intricate interactions between the living things in a given region. Plants grow together as a community with animals and other species of plants. There are many different kinds of interrelationships among living things, ranging from harmful to beneficial and from casual associations to those that are essential for the survival of one or both organisms.

Mutualism occurs when two different organisms depend on each other for survival. Some sea anemones that dwell in tide pools of the Pacific coast have single-celled algae growing in the outer tissues of their tentacles. The algae benefit from being protected in these tissues and supplied with carbon dioxide from the anemone's respiration, while the anemone obtains oxygen from the algae's photosynthesis. Algae also live symbiotically with many tropical clams and corals.

Some interactions between plants bring a necessary benefit to one of them while the other is neither harmed nor helped. Such a relationship, which exists between the epiphytic flowering plant called Spanish moss and the trees it grows in, is one of *commensalism*. Spanish moss derives an aerial perch as well as nutrients that leach off of leaves and other tree tissues, but the tree is unaffected. Many species of mosses, ferns and lichens are also epiphytic. The petals of the orchid *Trichoceros parviflorus* closely resemble the female of a certain species of fly. In attempting to copulate with this pseudo-mate, the male fly pollinates the orchid, but does not benefit itself.

Figure 12-2. The fascinating Jack-in-the-pulpit begins life as a male, matures into a female and can turn back into a male to conserve energy during times of drought or in response to other extended, energy-depleting sources of stress. (Photo by Peter Hope)

Certain interactions benefit one organism at the expense of another. Pitcher plants, sundews and other carnivorous plants (see Chapter 7) are *predators* that catch and devour prey such as small insects and spiders. *Competition* results when two plants vie for the same resource, such as food, space and water. Eventually, one competitor wins out over the other, or one either adapts to using an alternative resource or dies. No two plants can occupy the same exact niche—they cannot use identical resources in any environment. *Amensalism* occurs when an inhibitor's actions affect another organism negatively without bringing any benefit to the first organism. For instance, a mole may destroy the roots of a young seedling as the mole tunnels through the soil beneath the seedling.

A few hundred species of *parasitic* flowering plants, such as dodder and mistletoe, slowly feed on a host while it is still alive. Sometimes the host lives and sometimes it becomes so weak that it perishes, but the parasite has formed seeds to continue the next generation on a new host. The temperate and tropical species of mistletoe grow "roots" that penetrate the branches of the host and draw off water and nutrients. Although mistletoe does contain chlorophyll and carries out photosynthesis, dodder does not photosynthesize. The stems of dodder encircle the host plant, penetrate its tissues with root-like structures called *haustoria* and drain the host to death. Beech drops is a short, thin, root parasite that lives off the roots of beech trees in the understory of temperate deciduous forests. Clover, alfalfa and many other cultivated plants are weakened and killed by root parasites called broomrapes. There are thousands of species of fungal parasites, including rusts, mildews and the blight that caused the Irish potato famine. Most vines, such as lianas, grapes and ivies, are *not* parasitic.

There are many kinds of beneficial relationships between different species. One wood-boring beetle carries a fungus that consumes and softens the wood it lives in, making the wood more palatable for the beetle. In turn, the fungus is aided in its dispersal. The beetle smears its eggs with spores of this fungus and perpetuates the association into the next generation. Harvester ants inadvertently sow the plant seeds that they collect and store as food in underground nests. Leaf cutter ants purposefully cultivate fungal gardens in the leaf mulch they stockpile underground. The blossoms of carrion lily and red trillium emit a stench of rotting meat to attract pollinating flies.

The beautiful, translucent white Indian pipe is one of the few saprophytic flowering plants. Lacking chlorophyll, its roots are surrounded by leaf-decomposing fungi. *Mycorrhizal fungi* attach to the growing roots of many plants such as gymnosperms and orchids and act like root hairs (see Figure 6-5). The fungus absorbs carbohydrates from the root while the root obtains water and minerals from the fungus. Many plants cannot survive without mycorrhizal fungi. The bacteria that form root nodules on *legumes*—peas, beans and their relatives—enable the plants to obtain or *fix* nitrogen directly from the air. Other, nonleguminous plants, too, can fix nitrogen, including alder, sweet gale, silverberry, buffalo-berry and New Jersey tea.

GALLS. *Plant galls* are an intriguing natural phenomenon. Galls form swellings and bumps of all sizes and shapes on leaves, stems, trunks, roots, buds and flowers. They are caused by insects, mites, fungi, viruses, bacteria and nematodes. More than 2,000 species of North American insects create galls on such plants as goldenrods, oaks, roses and willows. More than 800 galls are formed on oaks, mostly by tiny gall-wasps of the family *Cynipidae*. Gall-forming insects also include flies, midges, aphids, mites, beetles and moths. Insects obtain shelter and food from galls. Generally, gall insects lay eggs in a certain part of a particular plant. The developing larvae secrete substances that cause plant tissues to grow into distinct, abnormal shapes. The plant is usually unaffected and does not seem to benefit, but, in some cases, can be harmed. Amazingly, the gall tissue that feeds the growing larvae contains more protein than the tissue it forms from. When the larvae have pupated into an adult, they eat their way out of the gall. In the case of the *goldenrod ball gall*, the larva tunnels a hole up to the edge of the gall, leaves a thin covering over the opening and then overwinters. When the mature fly is ready to emerge in springtime, it proceeds up the tunnel and uses an inflatable bladder between its eyes to push its way out. Without the premade tunnel the adult fly, which has no teeth, would perish, unable to escape. Gall insects are often eaten by chickadees, woodpeckers and parasites, and they also are used as fish bait. Many insects live in old, abandoned galls when the original inhabitants leave.

The *black knot gall*, which is caused by a fungus on cherry trees, is commonly seen. Each young velvety growth eventually turns hard and black, weakening the cherry by disrupting sap flow. *Witches' brooms*, a profuse growth of many stems emerging from branches, is caused by a virus. The *mossy rose gall*, a fibrous swelling that forms on a wild rose called sweetbriar or eglantine, is caused by a tiny wasp, as are the more than 50 species of round *oak bullet galls*. The beautiful *cypress flower gall* is created by the larva of a small fly.

One intriguing and common gall is the *pine cone willow gall* (Figure 12-5). A small female midge lays its eggs each spring in the opening buds on the branch tips of native willows, plants of wet places. It will not lay in weeping willow and other introduced species. Because the insect is a weak flyer, the galls are seldom more than 15 feet (4.6 meters) above the ground. Secretions from each one-eighth-inch (.3-centimeter) larva cause a swelling to form that resembles a small pine cone, complete with scales. The larva overwinters in the gall, pupates in the spring and emerges as an adult, ready to lay eggs. Each fall, the gall tissue and the stem just below it die and the scales open. Many insects take refuge here for the winter: spiders, midges, aphids, bugs, flea beetles, springtails, thrips, mites and others. The meadow grasshopper will even lay its eggs here.

OFFENSE/DEFENSE. It is easy to see that plants possess defensive adaptations that enhance their ability to survive the onslaught of animal grazing, predation and infestation. An encounter with many plants can be extremely unpleasant and even deadly because of the varieties of thorns, irritants and poisons they produce. Other plants have ingenious mechanisms for protecting themselves. The sensitive plant *Mimosa pudica* reacts quickly when contacted by a worm, insect or other creature. Whenever a spur on the stem is touched, the leaves fold up and the interloper drops to the ground or is frightened away. Numerous plant communities and adaptations are the result of evolutionary responses to the inhibiting influences of competition and predation. Certain species of seaweed that grow in the intertidal zone of the mid- to north Atlantic are found only in microscopic form during the summer, but they have a large, conspicuous

growth during the wintertime. Microscopic forms of these algae are able to endure the pressure of grazing snails, which are most active during the summer months, but the larger forms can only survive during the winter months, when snail grazing is not a major factor.

Plants also use a variety of offenses to help them survive. Many organisms produce *allelopathic* substances, which can repel, inhibit, attract or even poison other plants, animals and even people. Black walnut husks contain a substance called *juglans* that inhibits seed germination among other plants and so reduces plant growth and competition for resources near the tree. The roots of the guayule plant of Mexico produce *cinnamic acid* that poisons other plants, and the leaves of the desert brittlebush poison other seedlings. Creosote bush also emits toxins. Seaweeds that are forms of brown algae have *phenolic compounds* in their cells that inhibit the growth of microscopic algae and may even discourage grazing.

The Desert

Many desert plants are used by the traditional O'odham peoples for survival. Parts of the prickly-pear cactus, with thorns removed, are used by the Papago for food. Saguaro fruits are gathered from up high on the plants using long poles made from the ribs of the saguaro. These fruits are used for making jams, syrups and a special drink. Ropes are made from the mescal plant and baskets are fashioned out of willow and the Devil's claw plant.

Deserts cover one-fifth of Earth's total land area. North America's four major deserts—the *Great Basin, Sonoran, Mohave* and *Chihuahuan deserts*—cover approximately 500,000 square miles (1,295,000 square kilometers) in the southwestern United States and northwestern Mexico. Summer temperatures higher than 120°F (49°C) are common in places such as Death Valley, with the ground being 30° to 50°F (-1.1° to 10°C) warmer than the air. Nighttime temperatures can drop 50°F (10°C) or more. In extreme deserts the rainfall averages fewer than 5 inches (12.7 centimeters) each year. Some parts of Baja, California, receive no rain for four to five years at a time. When the rain finally returns, the land is awash with colorful flowers that bloom and set seed before the available water runs out. The Sonoran Desert experiences two rainy seasons per year: one during the summer and another during the winter. Because there is little water to leach the soils and decomposition is slow, desert soils accumulate tremendous amounts of salts and minerals. Soils in California's Imperial Valley and other areas, once irrigated, became highly fertile land. Utah's salt flats, however, are rich deposits of salt that are the remnant of an inland sea. Mosses, fungi, lichens and algae sometimes encrust and stabilize desert soils.

North America's only cold desert is the most northerly and highest in elevation. The Great Basin in Nevada and

Utah receives up to 10 inches (25.4 centimeters) of precipitation per year that comes mostly as winter snow. In higher elevations are found junipers and piñon pines that can grow up to 30 feet (9.1 meters) tall. Antelope bitterbush, four-wing saltbush, other shrubs and grasses form a desert scrub community in lower elevations. Sagebrush has a deep tap-root and a mat of shallow roots to tap into both deep ground-water stores and rainwater on the surface. When water becomes scarce this resourceful shrub sheds its leaves. Some Great Basin wildflowers include desert paintbrush, desert trumpet, lupines, desert candle, sego lily and locoweeds. Creosote bush clones in the lower Colorado Basin are the most ancient living things on Earth, having occupied the same site for about 10,000 years!

Bristlecone pine forests are found in the mountains at an elevation of around 10,000 to 11,000 feet (3,048 to 3,353 meters) to the west and north of Death Valley, the latter being the lowest point in the hemisphere at nearly 300 feet (91.4 meters) *below* sea level. Some bristlecones of the Inyo National Forest in California's White Mountains are more than 4,000 years old. Most of the roughly 8 inches (20.3 centimeters) of precipitation they receive each year falls as snow.

Each desert has its own diverse communities of plants. Some familiar plants of North America's deserts include the saguaro cactus, prickly pear, hedgehog cactus, mesquite, barrel cactus, ocotillo, evening primrose, brittlebush, Indian ricegrass, Joshua tree (a kind of yucca in the lily family), indigo bush, jojoba, pincushion cactus, wild heliotrope, desert candle, fiddleneck, tarbush, snakeweed, desert poppy, devil's claw and burrograss. *Riparian* vegetation growing along river courses, desert ditches and intermittent streams and above underground rivers includes smoke tree, burrobush, quail bush, willows, mesquite, acacias and cottonwoods.

The *saguaro* cactus can attain a height of up to 50 feet (15.2 meters) and can live for 200 years. It grows five or more arms that bear flowers with white petals and yellow centers. Ironically, although it is often used as a symbol of the sunny desert Southwest, the saguaro cactus must sprout in the shade cast by other cacti, shrubs, trees or rocks.

DESERT PLANT ADAPTATIONS. Desert plants are commonly grouped according to the kinds of adaptations they possess that enable them to survive heat and drought: (1) drought-resisting plants, (2) drought-evading plants and (3) drought-escaping plants.[1]

Drought-resistant plants grow year-round during even the harshest desert conditions. Many plants need a permanent water source beneath the surface to grow. They absorb the water they need using remarkable roots that may be massive, wide-spreading and shallow or so long and deep that they reach down to the water table. Some saguaro roots cover an area that is 90 feet (27.4 meters) across, while mesquite roots (a kind of legume) have been known to reach down as far as 175 feet (53.3 meters). The roots of creosote

bush occupy a greater amount of space than those of any other North American desert plant. Plants are often spaced far apart to avoid competition for available water. Drought-resistant plants frequently grow in low spots to take advantage of runoff that gathers there and their tissues have a low resistance to water flow. One plant, the American pygmy cedar, can grow on rock because it requires no soil water at all: it is able to absorb all the water it needs from saturated desert night air.

Other survival adaptations found among drought-resistant plants include:

- succulent habit—the ability to store water and food in roots, stems and leaves using specialized tissues and structures. The stems of many cacti can expand and contract with increasing and decreasing water content.
- spine-like and bristle-like leaves with reduced surface area or no leaves at all (photosynthesis occurs in stems).
- water-resistant cuticles. The cuticles on some cacti allow water to be lost at only .05 percent of the rate of evaporation found with open water.
- stomata that open only at night, stay closed during a drought and are located in sheltered pits and grooves.
- shapes, such as the barrel cactus, that reduce surface area relative to volume.
- tremendous water storage in stems and roots. Some barrel cacti can live for one year or more on one "load" of water, and some large cacti can store more than 11,023 pounds (5,000 kilograms) of water.
- roots that are equipped with toxic seed germination inhibitors to decrease competition for available water and space.
- thorns that prevent or decrease grazing on the plant, which results in loss of leaves, broken cuticles and increased water loss.

Like the deciduous plants of colder, northern climates, *drought-evading* desert plants survive periods of heat and drought by becoming dormant during stressful periods. Many perennials die back to the ground and then sprout anew when the rains return. The leaves of other drought evaders often curl up or are shed during a drought. Some plants have rain roots that form within a few hours following a rain and then fall off soon thereafter to prevent water loss. These plants store water and food in the surviving roots.

Drought-escaping desert plants are *ephemerals*—desert annuals that avoid long periods of heat and drought (years sometimes) as seeds that lie dormant in the desert soil. Following an above-average rainfall, the seeds sprout and the plants quickly grow, bloom and set seed to complete their life cycles during the wet period. These plants produce lots of seeds in a short time. *Summer ephemerals* grow during the showers of midsummer, and *winter ephemerals* sprout during the cooler rains of midwinter and early spring. Among certain ephemerals the timing of germination is controlled by growth inhibitors on the seed coat that become washed off by rainwater. The seeds of some other desert plants, such as the ironwood and blue paloverde, must be abraded by water rushing down gullies before they can sprout.

Pollination is accomplished among desert plants by a variety of insects, birds and bats. Verbena and larkspur are bee-pollinated, while Indian paintbrush, fiddlehead and many kinds of lilies are pollinated by butterflies. Moths and butterflies pollinate morning glory, phlox, yucca and evening primrose. Many moth-pollinated flowers are pale yellow or white and deeply fragrant. Flies, beetles and other insects pollinate California poppy, sunflower and other species.

DESERT COMMUNITIES. Complex communities have developed around desert plants. The Gila woodpecker chisels nesting cavities in the stems of the saguaro cactus, a dominant plant of the Sonoran Desert. After these holes are abandoned, the elf owl frequently makes its home there. Elf owls live *only* where saguaro cacti grow. The pygmy owl, kestrel, screech owl and certain flycatchers also make use of abandoned Gila woodpecker holes. Pack rats, mice, ground squirrels and weevil larvae eat saguaro cacti when the cactus is in the vulnerable seedling stage. Spiders, moth larvae, silverfish and other small creatures live in the protected space of the pleats running the length of the saguaro. At night the longnose bat, searching for nectar, pollinates saguaro blooms (Figure 12-3). Both the white-winged dove and the Gila woodpecker are also attracted to the fruits of the saguaro. Mourning doves may nest in the desert many miles from any source of water: they only need to take a long flight to the nearest water hole to drink every day or two. Other members of desert food webs include kangaroo rats, coyotes, jackrabbits, snakes, lizards, geckos, American kit foxes, badgers, vultures, falcons, swallows, scorpions, ants, toads, crickets and the carnivorous roadrunners.

STATE OF THE DESERT. From oil extraction to farming on irrigated land, North Americans have harvested the wealth of desert natural resources and have changed the face of millions of acres of desert habitat. Where desert soils are

Figure 12-3. Desert communities come alive at night as plants and animals take advantage of cool temperatures. This lesser longnose bat is pollinating saguaro cactus flowers as it gathers nectar with its tongue, which can extend up to a third of the bat's body length. Nectar-feeding bats are essential to the pollination of many night-blooming flowers. Size of bat: body (not including tail), 2.8 to 3.7 in. (7.0 to 9.5 cm); length of forearm, 1.8 to 2.2 in. (4.6 to 5.7 cm); weight .6 to 1 ounce (18 to 30 gm). (Illustration by Marjorie C. Leggitt)

not too salty, *irrigation* is used to supply water to vast stretches of desert, including the Rio Grande Valley and the Pecos Valley in New Mexico and Texas; the Gila and Salt River valleys in Arizona; and the San Joaquin, Sacramento and Imperial valleys of California. Water from the Grand Coulee Dam on the Columbia River in northeast-central Washington irrigates 1 million acres (405,000 hectares) of desert land. When desert soils are not irrigated properly by allowing surface water to run off, salts and other minerals build up and render previously fertile land useless for agriculture. Many native desert plants can no longer grow in such areas. Phoenix, Las Vegas, Tucson and other cities are *tapping ancient, irreplaceable ground water stores* for irrigation and other uses, drawing water levels down at alarming rates. These cities, and the surrounding suburbs, are gobbling up large areas in our diminishing deserts.

A host of other human activities threaten the deserts. *Grazing* has turned many rich desert grasslands into eroded, scrubby sagebrush habitats. Wherever the vegetation of arid lands is stripped by grazing animals, or for other uses, the ecological integrity and biological diversity of these environments decline. *Mineral extraction,* and the development associated with it, consume much desert habitat: *oil drilling* in western Texas and *mining* for uranium in Utah and New Mexico, silver in northern Mexico and copper in Nevada. In recent decades, the popularity of *off-road vehicles* and easy access into desert wilderness areas have created ecologically destructive trails, erosion and intrusions into remote wildlife habitat. Tire tracks in desert soils can leave an impact that lasts for 100 years or more, crushing animal burrows, compacting soil, preventing drainage and increasing both runoff and erosion. This access has also resulted in increased pressure on wildlife and plant populations due to a rise in collecting, *hunting and poaching.*

Deserts are not barren waste places. They are varied and rich ecosystems possessing many values, home to many intriguing plants and animals. The guayule shrub of the U.S. Southwest can be used as a viable source of rubber. Many desert plants are sources of valuable drugs, foods, fibers, dyes and ornamental plantings. To Native North Americans, desert wilderness has always been both a home and a place of retreat, for seeking solitude and closeness to Creation. From the Grand Canyon to Death Valley, from the Joshua tree forests to the Pueblo ruins at Mesa Verde and Casa Grande, desert parks, monuments and other sanctuaries are powerful magnets attracting the part of us that seeks closeness to nature in its most elemental and extreme forms.

Arctic Tundra and Alpine Communities

The Arctic reaches of North America are home to the Aleut, Inuit and related peoples who rely on the plants and animals of the tundra and the sea for their survival. Mosses are traditionally used for insulation, for diapers, as an antibacterial poultice and as a frozen lining on the bottom of sled runners. Lichens are eaten as soup and survival food by northern peoples, and they are a chief winter staple of caribou, another important human food source.

Tundra lies north of the boreal coniferous forest in Canada and Alaska and up to the permanent snow and ice toward the North Pole. This vast, open landscape is home to caribou and musk ox and is populated with lichens, mosses and sedges. Species of plants are usually more numerous than animals. Trees cannot grow in the tundra because of the effects of this extremely cold climate. *Permafrost soils* that are permanently frozen a few feet below the surface prevent tree roots from growing. Poor nutrient cycling, a result of soils that are poorly drained and soil temperatures that are inhospitable to the decomposer bacteria, fungi and insects, creates soils of low fertility. The tundra growing season lasts for about three months, during which plants must complete the growth and reproduction that will enable them to survive through the winter. At the height of the long days plants can photosynthesize for 24 hours straight.

Alpine communities are found in lofty mountain elevations, occurring higher up as one moves farther south down the spines of the Rocky Mountains, Cascades, Sierra Nevadas and Appalachians. Every 1,000-foot climb in altitude is roughly equivalent, climatically, to traveling 300 miles closer to the nearest pole (every 300-meter climb in altitude is roughly equivalent to traveling 475 kilometers toward the nearest pole). *Timberline* or *treeline,* the zone above which it is too cold for trees to grow, lies at about 13,000 to 14,000 feet (3,962 to 4,267 meters) in the tropics, at 10,000 to 12,000 feet (3,048 to 3,658 meters) in the California Sierras and northern Rockies, at about 5,000 feet (1,524 meters) in New Hampshire's White Mountains and at roughly 1,000 to 3,000 feet (305 to 914 meters) in southern Alaska.

Subalpine forest is a transitional community of a few dominant tree species that lies between the alpine above timberline and the forest below. Wind and the scouring action of windblown snow and ice sculpt trees and shrubs into bizarre shapes known as *krummholz,* German for "crooked wood." Black and white spruce, paper birch and balsam fir are common subalpine trees in the East, mountain hemlock in the Pacific Northwest and subalpine fir and Engelmann spruce in the Rocky Mountains. The dominant subalpine trees of the Sierra Nevada, Great Basin and Klamath regions are whitebark pine, foxtail pine, mountain hemlock and lodgepole pine.

ARCTIC, ALPINE AND SUBALPINE PLANT ADAPTATIONS. If you have ever walked through blowing, powdery snow on a cold winter day you experienced how snow can drift and crunch underfoot—a dry, liquid crystal desert sand. Plants must be adapted to *low temperatures and drying conditions* to survive winter in cold environments. Even though frozen soils may be saturated, the water is unavailable to plant roots and desiccating winds are common.

Some plants cope by wintering as a seed or rootstock. Deciduous plants drop their leaves while others winter as evergreens. Many cold-tolerant plants have adaptations that resemble the water-conserving measures found among desert plants: small size, rapid growth and completion of the life cycle, narrow leaves, thick waxy cuticles among evergreens, succulent leaves and stems, woolly coverings and curled-under leaf margins. These adaptations serve one or more of the following purposes: reduce water loss, protect against freezing and decrease the energy needed to complete the life cycle during the brief growing season. Since stomata are located on the undersides of leaves, curled-under leaf edges and woolly coverings limit water loss because they reduce contact between the leaf and wind and decrease wind speed over leaf surfaces, thereby lessening the rate of transpiration. In cold weather the stomata on evergreen needles remain closed to limit water loss. Some flowers can produce enough heat from stored energy to melt through spring snow cover into the sunlight. Showy flowers that attract particular insects are common among alpine and tundra plants.

On winter days when the temperatures rise above freezing, cold winds cause leaves to lose moisture at a time when the roots are in frozen ground and cannot absorb water to replace that being lost. Strong winds on warm winter days often cause patches of dead, brown foliage on evergreens. Although plants may be able to absorb some water through needles under snow cover, it is believed that plants store their limited winter water supply in the sapwood.

Deciduous and evergreen plants do not die from the cold itself; they die if the water in their cells freezes. Plants gradually become acclimated as the temperature drops and day length decreases during autumn and early winter. First, water in between the cells freezes; then, water migrates out of plant cells into the spaces in between cells. Materials in the cells become more concentrated, causing the freezing point to drop. When the temperature falls too quickly, cells will die when water trapped inside the cells freezes. This often causes brown splotches on evergreen foliage. Certain species of trees can survive extreme cold down to -112°F (-80°C), including white spruce and black spruce, red pine and jack pine, northern white cedar and balsam fir, as well as white birch, quaking aspen, balsam poplar, basswood and larch.[2]

Depending on the weather conditions and the species of plant, photosynthesis has either stopped or is very reduced among cold-tolerant plants during the long winter. In severe alpine habitats photosynthesis stops for the winter and will not even take place during brief thaws. Some photosynthesis occurs in relatively mild winter climates among evergreens, in the green bark of certain deciduous trees and even in plants under shallow snow.[3] Oak, pecan and sycamore and many other deciduous trees photosynthesize in the bark of naked twigs. Up to 15 percent of the total

Figure 12-4. This patch of alpine bunchberry, which was photographed above treeline, is snugged in a protected hollow where it is sheltered from the drying and freezing power of the wind as well as the scouring action of snow and ice. (Photo by Alan C. Graham)

photosynthesis in aspens during the growing season takes place in the bark.

Growing conditions in alpine environments are often more extreme than those found in the Arctic because of the incessant high winds and accompanying wind chills. The thinner atmosphere found here filters out less of the sun's harmful ultraviolet radiation. Due to the cold and erosion caused by strong winds and high amounts of rain and snow, there is little chance for soil to develop. Many plants survive on the leeward side of rocks, in snug rock cracks and crevices and in other protected pockets. Rock-hugging lichens persist in upper elevations below the bare rock of the highest places. Certain algae actually grow on and in glacial ice, coloring the snow with pink or red hues. These algae are coated with a protective, jelly-like film, and some species can survive several months of being frozen in ice. Most alpine flowering plants are perennial, which decreases the amount of energy needed during the growing season. Many plants have small, dense foliage to reduce the penetration of high winds into the crown of the plant (Figure 12-4).

Mechanical stress is another serious problem, particularly in alpine communities. Snow and ice, especially wet snow, under certain conditions may coat needles and branches with a layer that, in certain cases, can reach about 20 inches (50 centimeters) thick. At this thickness, a tree in the far north country that is 39.4 feet (12 meters) tall may bear a 6,614-pound (3,000-kilogram) weight of ice and snow.[4] In subalpine forests, beautiful crystalline rime ice frequently forms on needles and then sheds, taking the needles down with it. *Strong winds* often blow over large areas of trees that are rooted in the shallow soils. Windblown ice and snow crystals act like sandblasting to wear off bark and foliage, which opens the plants up to moisture loss and diminishes their ability to carry out photosynthesis. These *abrasive forces,* along with the relentless alpine and Arctic winds, often kill plants protruding above the snow line and sculpt tree crowns into shapes resembling low-growing mats, flags, broomsticks and tables. Ribbons of trees frequently grow in a row where the ground is protected under long, deep snow drifts. Temperatures inside a snow-covered mass of plants can be 68°F (20°C) higher than those of air above the snow.

Western alpine communities are larger and more diverse than those in the East. Western species of alpine flowers include beargrass, alpine buttercup, moss campion, alpine sunflower, spreading flox, glacier lily, greenleaf chiming bells, red mountain heather, alpine columbine, arctic gentian, alpine willow and Drummond's cinquefoil. With practice, in the East, one can learn to recognize most of the wildflowers found on any alpine mountaintop, such as mountain cranberry, alpine bearberry, dwarf mountain cinquefoil, alpine bluet, diapensia, bog bilberry, mountain heath, alpine goldenrod, Lapland rosebay, Mt. Washington avens, alpine azalea and moss plant.

STATE OF ARCTIC AND ALPINE COMMUNITIES.
Thin soils, permafrost and short growing seasons create fragile communities that are easily damaged or destroyed but take long to recover. Boot prints sunk in tundra soil may last for half a century or more. *Alpine trails* cause severe *erosion* and *damage to fragile plant communities* when not managed properly. Mountaintops around the world are being turned into *garbage* dumps as more and more people seek the summit on foot and leave the refuse behind, and with the advent and increasing popularity of helicopter ski-lifting of people and supplies to previously inaccessible areas.

As remote as they may seem to be, alpine and tundra ecosystems have shown us how everything on Earth really is connected to everything else. *Urban haze* has been seen hanging over tundra hollows, far from its source in cities to the south. *Radiation and other contaminants* have appeared in the tissue of caribou and other animals that feed on lichens, which readily absorb substances from the air. Alpine communities are especially sensitive and vulnerable to *damage from acid rain* and *increased incidences of ultraviolet radiation due to ozone depletion in the upper atmosphere*, which is especially severe near the poles (see Chapter 14). The gargantuan *hydroelectric projects* that have already been built, and of which more are planned for the James Bay region of Canada, are an environmental and cultural catastrophe (see Chapter 14). *Drilling for oil and natural gas* and *transport through pipelines* have fragmented Arctic ecosystems and adversely affected caribou and other animals in previously pristine environments.

* * *

Alpine meadows are ethereal wildflower gardens, miniature landscapes that pique even the most jaded sense of human curiosity. Tundra ecosystems are among the last, vast wilderness areas remaining on Earth. They are keepers of the human imagination and spirit—connections with our primal need for higher ranges and remote fringes in which to reconnect with nature and with the traditions of the Native peoples who inhabit these remarkable environments.

QUESTIONS

1.   In the story "The Woman Who Lives in the Earth," what do the Chugach Inuit mean when they refer to the *shua*? Who is Nunam-shua?

2.   Why does the hunter treat the plants and animals with such great respect? Which plants is he especially careful to treat well? How does Nunam-shua reward this hunter for his kindness?

3.   Who or what disturbs the harmony of the O'odham people in "Waw Giwulk: The Center of the Basket"? Who comes to help the people?

4.   How does Itoi, Elder Brother, defeat the great snake? Does this remind you of any stories you already know?

5.   What is an adaptation? How do adaptations help plants to survive? Can you name some plant adaptations?

6.   What is a plant community? What are some ways that plants do things that are good for other plants as well as

animals? How and why do plants harm animals and other plants?

7. What is a gall? What causes galls to form? Where have you seen galls growing near your home and what do they look like?

8. Have you ever visited a desert? What are the names of the four major North American deserts?

9. What are growing conditions like in the desert: sunlight, temperature, rainfall, soil? Are all deserts hot? Where is there a cold desert in North America?

10. What are some plants and animals that live in North American deserts? What kinds of adaptations do desert plants have that help them to survive in the dry deserts? How do they get and save water? Where does the water come from?

11. What kinds of things are people doing that are harming the deserts? Where can you go to see desert land that is protected in its natural state?

12. Why would it be hard to survive in the Arctic? What kinds of adaptations do plants have to survive where it is cold and frozen most of the year? What is the soil like in the Arctic?

13. Where else besides northern Canada and Alaska can you find habitats that are like the Arctic? Do you have any mountaintop alpine habitats near you?

14. How are people treating the Arctic and alpine habitats in North America? What kinds of things are people doing in these places?

ACTIVITIES
Survival Adaptations

ACTIVITY: (A) Match plants with descriptions or illustrations of their survival adaptations. (B) Draw pictures of plants and create your own original adaptations that will help these plants to survive among other plants and animals.

GOALS: Understand that plants are part of natural communities where they are constantly interacting with animals and other plants. Discover some different kinds of survival adaptations found on plants living nearby.

AGE: Younger children and older children

MATERIALS: (A) "Discussion"; pruning shears; clippings from local plants; illustrations or photographs of plants that are poisonous, irritating, rare or hard to find; copies of several clues for each child; scissors; large hat or paper bag. (B) One copy of an illustration of a simple plant for each child, showing roots, stems and leaves; pencils; crayons.

PROCEDURE A: *Discovering Adaptations.* Beforehand, review the section of the "Discussion" called "Plant Adaptations and Interrelationships." Wherever possible, obtain clippings from local plants that match as many of the

following clue descriptions of plant adaptations as you can find. Add clue descriptions to match specific local plants. Be careful not to cut any rare or unusual plants, such as carnivorous plants. *Use illustrations or photographs of these plants, of those that are hard to find and of those that are poisonous or irritating to the skin.*

• Thorns help to keep animals from chewing or stepping on my stems.

• I get water and nourishment from the air, so I can grow in the treetops. (an epiphyte)

• Since I take food and water from the sap of another plant, I am not rooted in the ground. (a parasite)

• Insects caught in my trap become meals for me. (a carnivorous plant)

• My petals smell sweet to attract pollinating insects.

• Flies are drawn to my flowers, which stink of rotting meat.

• Bacteria that live in my roots help to fertilize me. (pea, bean or other legume)

• Don't touch me! I protect myself by giving a terrible rash to anyone who handles me.

• I get more food and water for myself by using something that prevents the seeds of other plants from growing nearby. (black walnut husks, roots of the guayule plant, leaves of desert creosote bush, etc.)

• Thick bark protects my insides from damage caused by insects and other animals. It also helps to keep me from drying out.

• My leaves fall off every year when winter comes and water is frozen in the ground.

• Animals like to eat my fruit, and then they spread the seeds in their droppings.

Make copies of these clues, and your own, and cut them into individual strips with one clue on each strip. Every child will get clues to several plants, with the same number of clues per child. Put the clues into a large hat, paper bag or other container. Clues may be used more than once.

Place the plant clippings, illustrations and photographs on desks or tables in an open space. Hold a brief question-and-answer session with the children and discuss the kinds of survival adaptations that plants possess. Explore what it means for plants to live in a community in which they interact with animals and other plants. Have each child come up and draw several clues from the lot, without peeking. Now ask the children to mill around the plant samples and images you have set out until they have found the plants that match their clues. Ask the children to explain what they have found and how those plant adaptations work.

Note: Another variation is to conduct this activity by tagging adaptations on plants growing outdoors and creating appropriate clues to match.

PROCEDURE B: *Adaptation Art.* Beforehand, illustrate a simple plant, showing roots, stems and leaves, and make one copy of this illustration for each child. Pass these illustrations out and instruct the children to add to this imaginary plant any adaptations they think will help it to survive. Their imagination is the only limit to what they can add. The adaptations they come up with do not have to be ones that are found on plants in nature. Once the plants are completed, have the children name their plants and explain their survival adaptations to the rest of the group.

Having a Ball With Galls

ACTIVITY: (A) Perform a brief play about the life cycle of a common gall. (B) Observe galls in their natural habitats and raise a few galls indoors until the adult insects emerge in springtime.
GOALS: Understand what causes plant galls and how galls form. Realize that galls are common in nature and that they occur nearby.
AGE: Younger children (A, B) and older children (B)
MATERIALS: (A) Old sheets, cardboard boxes, scissors, tempera paints, brushes, water in containers, glue, tape, strips of newspaper and wheat paste for papier-mâché, other supplies as needed to make these props: backdrop of trees and shrubs for a shrub swamp, simple stage and curtain, fan sitting on a table to make wind, willow bud, midge egg, different kinds of seeds for flowers (ones that will drop, float away and whirlybird in the wind), colorful autumn "leaves" to drop from trees, large pine-cone-like gall (Figure 12-5) big enough for a child to fit in comfortably and with one side open so the audience can see inside, sheet for pupal case. (B) Habitat where galls are growing, field guide with information about insect galls occurring in your area, hand lenses, pruning shears, wide-mouthed jar(s), soil, water, cheesecloth and rubberband.
PROCEDURE A: *Gall Play.* Beforehand, make the props that will be used during the play, as listed in "Materials." Use Figure 12-5 as a model for creating the large pine cone willow gall prop. Set up a stage with a performance area as well as places that allow the performers to emerge, and disappear, during the play.

Ask the children whether they know what a gall is. Use information from the "Discussion" to explain what galls are, how they form and what creates them. Do not tell the children about the life cycle of the pine cone willow gall yet because that gall appears in the play.

Choose children for the roles in the following brief play. Other children will help by creating the backdrop of shrubs and trees as well as other props, and by working the props during the play. Children who are not actually in the play, or helping out during it, will be the audience. The only prop that is a bit involved to create is the pine-cone-shaped willow gall, in which a child has to be able to hide. This gall

will have an open side to it so the audience can see what the larva and fly are doing inside. The mural should include swamp trees with spring leaves, and many spring flowers. Have the children construct these props out of pieces from a cardboard box. Other props and costumes can be as simple or elaborate as the group wants to make them.

As the props are being constructed, rehearse the following play with the acting crew. A narrator will read the play, with feeling, while actors and actresses perform the scenes and actions that occur. Choose an older child who is a good reader. With younger children you may want to do the narrating or have an older child come in to help. This play does not have detailed stage directions: children simply do whatever they are supposed to as the narrator reads. Scene 1 takes place using the willow-bud prop, along with children playing the flowers that eventually mature and drop their seeds. Scene 2 makes use of the large pine cone willow gall prop in which is hiding a child who will emerge as the adult midge at the appropriate time. Once the props and costumes are complete, hold a dress rehearsal until everyone knows what they are doing, which noises they are making (if any) and when and where to enter and exit the stage. The narrator will need to read *slowly* to allow the players time to enact the parts of the play as they unfold. Every time the narrator sees the "•••" symbol he or she should pause until the players are finished.

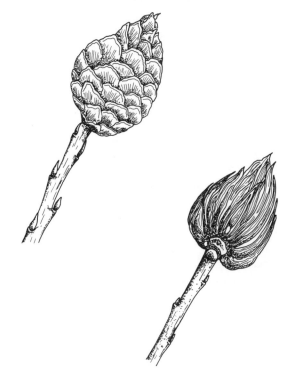

Figure 12-5. The pine cone willow gall (top) is not a pine cone at all. This intriguing gall is created by secretions from the developing larva of a midge. The tiny, 1/8-inch (.3-cm) larva can be seen in a cross-section of the gall (bottom). The midge will only lay its eggs in the branch tips of native willows.

The players are a butterfly, a honeybee and other insects that gather nectar and pollen; flowers; a midge (looks like a mosquito with feathery antennae); a midge larva; and a second midge.

GALL PLAY
Scene 1

It is a warm, sunny spring day in the swamp and the insects are buzzing around the early blooms. A butterfly sips nectar from a flower while a honeybee visits a beautiful bloom where it gathers and stores nectar and pollen to feed the hive. A strong breeze blows across the swamp and the insects have to flap their wings hard to keep from being blown away. •••

Along comes a tiny midge, searching for a place to lay her eggs. She flies over to a bud on the tip of a willow branch and hovers there for a while. Now she lands on the bud and, using the end of her abdomen, lays an egg inside. •••

Once the egg is laid, the midge flaps her wings and then flies up and away. •••

Springtime passes quickly, and then summer slips by. The flowers grow up and begin to form seeds. Meanwhile, the midge egg hidden inside the willow bud hatches into a larva. Safely inside the bud, the larva is protected from birds and other animals that might eat it. This larva gives off a liquid that makes the bud begin to grow and change shape.

(Draw the stage curtain and prepare for Scene 2 by bringing in the pine cone willow gall with the child inside dressed as a larva. Give the children who are playing the role of flowers some seeds to drop during this scene.)

Scene 2

Now it is autumn and colorful leaves are falling from the tree branches. Some flowers are dropping their seeds and others are sending their cottony seeds off on the cool breeze. •••

The larva has formed a beautiful gall out of the willow bud, which now looks like a pine cone. Inside, the larva eats the gall to stay alive. •••

Finally, when winter is nearly here, the gall larva curls up and prepares to spend the winter. •••

(Draw the stage curtain and prepare for Scene 3 by having the child dressed as a fly take the place of the one dressed as a larva in the pine cone willow gall. The fly will enter the gall wrapped up in a sheet to simulate being a pupa. Children playing flowers will stay in the scene, looking as they did in Scene 1.)

Scene 3

When spring returns to the swamp the insects are once again busily visiting flowers. •••

Inside the pine cone willow gall the larva has turned into a pupa, and big changes are happening. Slowly, the larva emerges from its pupal case as a young midge. •••

The midge leaves the gall, takes its first flight and begins to search for a mate. •••

Another midge comes flying by. •••

The life cycle of the pine cone willow gall midge is about to begin again. Soon, new eggs will be laid in the spring buds of the willows. *(Draw the curtain.)*

The End.

PROCEDURE B: *Galls Among Us.* Beforehand, scout out an area near the home or learning center where galls are growing. An old field or hedgerow is a likely habitat. Use a natural history field guide, such as *A Guide to Nature in Winter*, by Donald W. Stokes (Boston and Toronto: Little, Brown, 1976), to identify and learn about some of the galls you are seeing.

Take the children on a field trip to the habitat where you found the galls. Give the children a brief tour of the galls and tell them about the natural history of those galls. Have them observe the galls closely using their hand lenses. Do the gall shapes remind them of anything familiar?

If it is the appropriate time of year (see *Note* below), collect a few galls and bring them back to the home or learning center. Goldenrod ball galls are common and work well. Prune the plant stem off several inches above and below the gall. Place it upright in a wide-mouthed jar with cheesecloth for a lid and moist soil on the bottom. Keep the soil *damp* (not wet) so the gall plant tissue does not become too dry and hard. Store the gall in a bright place, but not in direct sunlight or near any source of heat. Only put one gall maker per jar.

Note: This is a good activity to conduct during the late winter/early spring period. Collect galls about a few weeks before spring arrives. This way they will hatch indoors and can be released after the weather warms up. Do not collect galls or any other insects during the winter, as they will hatch and become active at a time when it will be too cold outside for them to survive.

Story of Saguaro

ACTIVITY: Perform a puppet show about the saguaro (suh-wah´-roh) cactus that demonstrates some of its survival adaptations as well as interrelationships with animals in the desert community.

GOALS: Understand how the saguaro cactus is well adapted to life in the hot, dry desert. Realize how plants, such as the saguaro, and animals depend on each other for their survival needs.

AGE: Younger children and older children

MATERIALS: Four wooden studs measuring 2 inches (5.1 centimeters) by 4 inches (10.2 centimeters) by 4 feet (1.2 meters) to make the stand; nails; screws; hammer; screwdriver; saw; sandpaper; tape measure or yard (meter) stick; heavy cardboard; wide masking tape; newspaper strips; wheat paste for papier-mâché; bucket of water; large spoon; container for wheat paste; tempera paints; small containers for water and paints; paintbrushes; puppet-show script; drinking straws; small container of juice; toothpicks; modeling clay; pipe cleaners; sticks on which to mount puppets such as paint stirrers; white glue; scissors; paper; pencils; construction paper; crayons; Figure 12-6; pictures for children to use as models for the saguaro cactus and these puppets: Gila woodpecker, elf owl, cactus mouse, red-tailed hawk, longnose bat, coyote (appears in voice only).

PROCEDURE: Work with the children to make a model of a saguaro cactus and a stand to hold it up (Figure 12-6). Bend the cardboard around and join the pieces with masking tape, making the cactus around 5 feet (1.5 meters) tall and 12 inches (30.5 centimeters) in diameter. Be sure to leave two holes for Gila Woodpecker and Elf Owl, as well as two holes opposite these on the other side of the cactus so puppeteers can reach through to present these puppets from inside. Then build up the vertical ridges with papier-mâché, using toothpicks as thorns. Build on some branches with flowers on the tips that are low enough for Longnose Bat and the person in the story to reach them. (Real saguaros do not branch until they are about 15 to 25 feet [4.6 to 7.6 meters] tall or 75 years old.) The juice and straw will be built into one flower as the "nectar," and the pipe cleaners and wheat flour will be used to make the flower parts with "pollen" on them. Paint the cactus with tempera paints. The flowers have white petals with yellow centers.

Have the children prepare stick puppets for all the characters listed under "Materials."

Practice and perform this puppet play with the children. Encourage puppeteers to create and adopt voices that they think their characters would sound like. Perform for other groups.

STORY OF SAGUARO

Saguaro: Wow, is today a hot one! One hundred degrees Fahrenheit (38 degrees centigrade) and rising and it's only midmorning. I'm sure glad I have a tough waxy skin that helps to keep water from evaporating out of me. And I've got plenty of water stored in my fleshy stem. Still, if we don't get some rain soon my long roots will never get a chance to drink. They grow close to the surface so that a few hours after a rainstorm, when I grow special "rain roots," I take in up to 1 ton of water! Then my ribs unfold like an accordion. (*Gila Woodpecker glides up and starts pecking on Saguaro.*) Hey, who's sh..sh..sh..shaking m..m..m..my s..s..s..stem!

Gila Woodpecker: It's me, Gila Woodpecker. I'm boring a hole so I can lay my eggs out of the hot sun.

Saguaro: How'd you like it if someone made a hole in your skin and laid a few eggs, Gila? Why don't you just use the hole you made last spring and leave me alone?

Gila Woodpecker: Well, I could, Saguaro, it's no skin off my back. But Elf Owl is already using that hole to live in this year. Elf Owl only lives where saguaro cacti like you are found.

Elf Owl: (*comes out of hole yawning*) Whooooo called my name?

Gila Woodpecker: I did. How do you like my old house?

Elf Owl: I'd like it a lot better if there wasn't all of this construction going on. Can't you see it's bedtime? The sun is high in the sky—what are you all doing up this late?

Gila Woodpecker: No, no, no, this is daytime. You sleep now, but some of us sleep at night.

Elf Owl: You're all backwards! But could you please be quiet and respect my nap time? (*goes back in hole*)

Gila Woodpecker: Sure, Elf Owl … (*Saguaro butts in.*)

Saguaro: Okay, you two, please quiet down. I'm beginning to feel like a living high-rise apartment building. Gila's old hole gets used by Elf Owl, Pygmy Owl, Kestrel, Screech Owl and Flycatcher. (*Gila flies off.*) Ahhh (*sighs*), peace and quiet at last. (*Cactus Mouse runs up the side of Saguaro, dodging the thorns.*) Hey, who's running along my ridges?

Cactus Mouse: It's me, Cactus Mouse. You're very tall, Saguaro. How old are you?

Saguaro: I'm only 35 years old now, but I can live to be 200 and grow 50 feet (15 meters) tall! And I can weigh as much as four or five of those small cars we see whizzing by on that noisy road that passes through the neighborhood.

Cactus Mouse: Then why does such a big cactus need all those sharp spines? I passed a spider and a moth caterpillar who were taking shelter in your ridges, and we were all wondering the same thing.

Saguaro: Well, anyone who likes to eat plants and tries to take a bite out of me is going to get a mouthful of sharp thorns. So I'm protected from being eaten.

Cactus Mouse: Even I could get thorns in my mouth?

Saguaro: Even you.

Cactus Mouse: I get the point. It doesn't seem very nice but I don't blame you. After all, you can't run away when danger comes like I can. (*loudly*) Speaking of danger, I'm getting out of here! (*runs away screaming*) It's Red-Tailed Hawk! (*Red-Tailed Hawk glides over Saguaro, cries out with a loud "key-errr" and then soars away.*)

Saguaro: (*softly*) Listen, it's quiet now. I think I'll just rest here in the setting sun and wait for rain. (*Longnose Bat flies up and starts to sip nectar from one of Saguaro's flowers. He also gets dusted with pollen from the flower parts.*) Hey, stop that, it tickles!

Longnose Bat: Oh, sorry, Saguaro. I'm just collecting nectar from the center of your flower. It tastes good and sweet! Want to try some?

Saguaro: Listen, Longnose, I appreciate that you move my pollen around to fertilize my flowers as you sip the nectar, but that really tickles! (*Longnose Bat starts sipping some more nectar and Saguaro laughs.)* Stop it, I can't stand it any longer!

Longnose Bat: Oh, I forgot. Thanks for the sweets, Saguaro. *(flies off)*

(There is a pause here, and then Coyote howls in the distance.)

Saguaro: Nighttime is finally here. The calm night air is my favorite time of... *(Elf Owl interrupts.)*

Elf Owl: (sticks head out of hole and speaks brightly) Good night, Saguaro, time for me to get up!

Saguaro: What do you mean "time to get up"? It's dark out. You should be saying "good morning" when it's time to get up.

Elf Owl: But I wake up at nightfall.

Saguaro: Yes, now I remember, you were sleeping when Gila

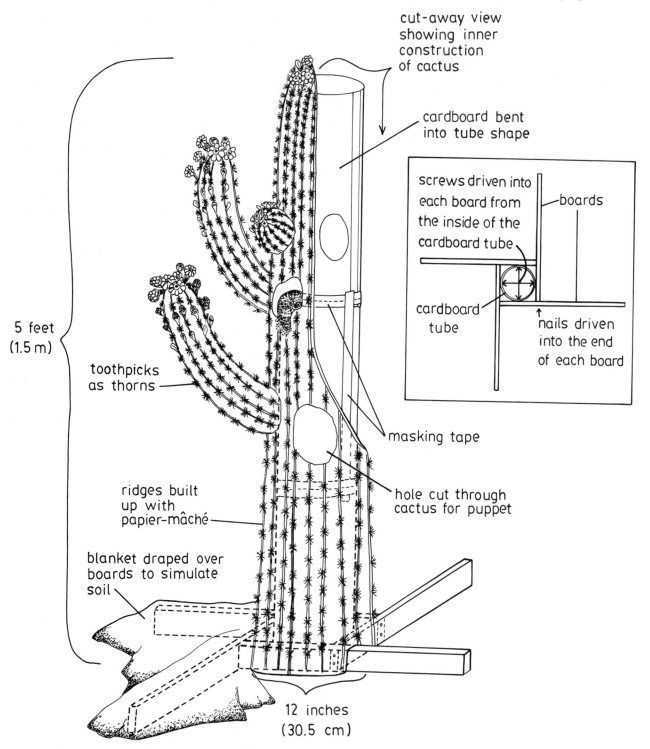

Figure 12-6. Making the saguaro cactus stage for the "Story of Saguaro" puppet show.

Woodpecker was trying to bore a hole in me earlier today.

Elf Owl: Right, and now I'm wide awake. Goodbye, Saguaro, I'm going hunting for breakfast.

Saguaro: You mean supper … Oh, I don't know what you mean! I'm going to rest. Good night!

Arctic and Desert Designs

ACTIVITY: Create plants to survive the extreme conditions in Arctic and desert environments.

GOALS: Realize that Arctic and desert plants grow in environments that are very different but face common problems such as extreme temperatures, lack of available water and drying conditions. Understand many adaptations that enable plants to survive in these conditions.

AGE: Younger children and older children

MATERIALS: Dead branches that can be used as a base for plants, balloons, clay, egg cartons, toothpicks, cotton balls and other material for insulation, pipe cleaners, straws, yarn, tape, glue, paste, construction paper, cardboard, scissors, tubes from empty rolls of toilet paper or gift wrapping, crayons, any other materials you or the children think of or need for their plant creations, photographs and illustrations of Arctic and desert plants from natural history books.

PROCEDURE: Ask the children: "What do you think growing conditions are like in Arctic environments, in desert habitats and on the tops of tall mountains where it is so cold no trees can grow?" Use the "Discussion" to discuss Arctic, alpine and desert conditions.

Arctic and alpine conditions include:
- extremely cold temperatures
- little available water during the cold months because the soil is frozen (the Arctic permafrost lies a few feet down during the summer)
- cold, saturated soils where decomposition and supplies of nutrients are poor
- cold, drying winds
- a short growing season (about 3 months)
- lots of sunlight during the growing season when many days last 24 hours (Arctic)
- strong winds that blow ice and snow so hard that the ice and snow wear bark and leaves off of plants, especially in alpine (mountaintop) habitats

Desert conditions include:
- lack of water for all or most of the year
- extremely hot temperatures (some deserts, such as the Great Basin, are relatively *cold* and dry)
- hot, drying winds
- dry soils where nutrients are not readily available

- a short growing season that lasts until the most recent rainwater runs out

Now inquire: "How do you think plants can survive in these places? What kinds of adaptations would they require to cope with each of these conditions? How can Arctic and desert plants obtain water and keep from drying out? What could a desert plant use to store water in between rainy periods? How can Arctic plants avoid freezing?"

Have the children work in small groups to create two plants: one designed to survive in the Arctic and alpine and one that possesses desert adaptations. Children will create their plants by starting with one of the dead branches as a base and adding adaptations using the clay, pipe cleaners, balloons and other materials. Have them attach as many devices (adaptations) as they think are necessary to help their plants survive. These do not necessarily have to be natural adaptations for this activity: children's imagination is the only limit.

Once the plants are finished, have each group explain how the adaptations they created for Arctic and desert conditions will help their plants to survive. Now use photographs or illustrations to share survival adaptations of real plants from Arctic and desert habitats. If you live near one of these environments, take a field trip to see the plants in their natural homes.

An Arctic Day

ACTIVITY: Take a fantasy journey as a plant growing in the cold Arctic tundra. Discuss and write your own story about what it would be like to live in such an environment.

GOALS: Understand the growing conditions found in Arctic habitats.

AGE: Younger children and older children

MATERIALS: Copy of *"An Arctic Day,"* pencils, paper.

PROCEDURE: Ask the children how it would feel to grow in the Arctic cold. "Would you like the cold winters? How would you feel about hot summer days when the sun never sets?"

Have them lie on their backs, relax and close their eyes. They are about to imagine being a plant growing in the Arctic tundra.

AN ARCTIC DAY

You are a plant rooted in the cold, wet ground of the Arctic tundra. It is summer and there are pools of water and soft, wet mounds of deep green moss all around you. A round rock off to one side is warming in the long Arctic day and you can feel the rock's heat. The smell of warm leaves, flowers and mossy soil surrounds you.

There is no nighttime in your tundra home during the summer—the sun circles and circles in the sky. It is the beginning of the day. The sun is just touching the horizon and beginning to circle.

Dark green leaves with tiny dots grow out from your stems in a thick, round cushion. Your roots reach deep into the wet soil. Gray woolly hairs cover the bottoms of your leaves and protect you from drying out. It is cooler in the middle of your branches than the warm air blowing over you. Purple flowers, each with five petals, bloom on the ends of many of your twigs. You can feel your branches shake as a few insects buzz in and out of your flowers, where they gather nectar and pollen. The sun has risen up and moved around to the other side of the sky.

A strong wind begins to blow and rustles your leaves. (*make the sound of the wind*) There, up on the rock, a furry vole, a mouse-like animal, has climbed and is munching on a berry. The reddish-brown fur on its back is parted and blown into little swirls by the wind. Suddenly it darts down off the rock and hides in your branches as a large white owl swoops and just misses its prey. The vole's heart races and its whiskers twitch as it waits a long time until feeling safe again. Slowly, cautiously, it slips away through the mosses and is gone.

Clouds move over the face of the sun and the air blows cool and hard. (*wind sound*) A few of your flower petals fly off and disappear in the breeze. Flies and other insects take shelter in the protected space inside your branches. You can feel them crawling along your twigs. The long, lonely cry of a wolf echoes and then slowly fades in the distance.

The sun has circled back and now touches the edge of the sky near where it was when the day began. Another day has passed in the Arctic tundra.

Allow a few moments of silence before asking the children to open their eyes. Then ask: "How did it feel to visit the tundra? Do you think you would like to live there? What did you like about the story? How did you think it would end?" Have the children write and share their own stories about living in the Arctic, or in a mountain alpine community. Have them write about different seasons and events happening with the plants and animals that live there.

EXTENDING THE EXPERIENCE

• Grow an epiphyte or desert plant in your home or learning center. Many kinds of tropical epiphytes and desert plants are available at nurseries and garden stores. Be sure the plants you purchase are raised domestically and are not rare species that have been collected in the wild.

• Visit a desert habitat in an arboretum or zoo. Identify adaptations among plants and animals.

• Take a field trip to a nearby bog and experience bog growing conditions. Many of the plants that grow in open bogs resemble those of the Arctic tundra. These plants usually grow far to the north and are restricted mostly to bog habitats and alpine communities south of the tundra.

• Read the Papago story "How the Butterflies Came to Be" in Chapter 8 of *Keepers of the Animals*.

NOTES

1. Natt N. Dodge, *Flowers of the Southwest Desert* (Globe, Ariz.: Southwest Parks and Monuments Association, 1976), 8.

2. Peter J. Marchand, *Life in the Cold: An Introduction to Winter Ecology* (Hanover, N.H.: University Press of New England, 1987), 55. (2nd, expanded edition released in 1992)

3. Ibid., 76–79.

4. Ibid., 81.

CHAPTER 13

✤ How Fox Brought the Forests From the Sky ✤

(Snoqualmie—Pacific Northwest)

In the old days, pine and fir and spruce and cedar trees could not be found on Earth. They were all kept in Sky Land by Moon. Moon was the chief of Sky Land.

One day, Moon decided that he would like to have some way to get down to Earth below. So Moon spoke to Spider.

"Make me a rope that will reach down to the top of those mountains."

Then Spider wove a rope which stretched from the clouds down to the mountains below. Then Moon closed the clouds at the top so that no one else could use that rope to get up into Sky Land.

But Blue Jay had sharp eyes. Blue Jay saw that rope leading down from the sky and told Fox. Blue Jay and Fox waited until it was a night when there was no moon, and then they went up that rope till they came to the bottom of the sky. Then, with his strong beak, Blue Jay pecked a hole in the clouds and the two entered the land in the sky.

While Blue Jay waited in a tree, Fox decided to look around. Before long, Fox found a lake and saw that someone had placed a trap in it to catch beavers.

"This is Moon's trap," Fox said. Then he made himself into a beaver and climbed into the trap.

When Moon came to check his trap the next morning, Moon was pleased.

"I have caught a fine beaver," Moon said. Then he carried the beaver back to his smokehouse, skinned it and threw the carcass into the corner. As soon as night came and Moon went to sleep, Fox came back to life. He pulled his skin from the wall, put it back on, went outside and looked around. There were trees everywhere: pine trees, fir trees, spruce trees, cedar trees. There were no trees like those in the world below. Fox used his spirit power. He pulled up many trees and made them so small he could carry them under his arm. Then he went back to the place where Blue Jay still waited in a tree near the hole in the sky.

"Quick," Blue Jay said, "Moon is waking up."

But Fox was still in the shape of a beaver, and he used his sharp teeth to weaken the rope which reached down to the mountains below. Then, he and Blue Jay climbed down the rope and reached Earth below. When they were far enough away, they watched to see whether Moon would follow them.

Moon was not far behind. When he woke he saw that the beaver skin was gone, and he found footprints leading away from his smokehouse.

"One of the Below People has tricked me," Moon said. He followed the footprints and came to the hole which led to the mountains below. Moon began to climb down the rope, but before he had gone far, his great weight was too much for the weakened rope to hold. The rope broke, and Moon fell down to Earth below. As soon as he struck the ground he was changed into a mountain. That mountain is Mount Si and you can still see the face of Moon on its side.

Fox and Blue Jay then went to work. They planted the trees all over the mountains. That is why, to this day, there are forests of spruce trees and fir trees and pines and cedars all over the Cascade Mountains.

Blue Jay and Fox waited until it was a night when there was no moon, and then they went up the rope till they came to the bottom of the sky.

The People of Maize
Maya

(Lacandon Maya—Middle America)
[Adapted from the *Popul Vuh* and Lacandon Maya traditions.]

The Creator and the Maker, Tepeu and Gucumatz, made people first out of earth. Out of mud they made the flesh of human beings. But it was not good. The mud was soft and it melted away. The people made of mud had no strength and they fell down. Their sight was blurred, and they could not move their heads to turn them or to look behind. These people of mud spoke, but they had no minds. The water soaked them and they could not stand.

Tepeu and Gucumatz said, "Our creatures will not be able to walk. They will not be able to multiply. Let us try again."

Then they broke up the people made of mud and returned them to Earth, to the living Earth.

Then they did a divination to see how they should make the people. And the divination said that it would be well to carve people out of wood.

So the Creator and the Maker carved people out of wood. They took the wood from the rainforest and they said, "These figures of wood will speak, they will walk about Earth."

And the people made of wood stood up and walked about. They looked like people and they spoke like people. They increased in number and spread about the land. They hunted the animals and they worked the earth. They made clearings in the rainforest to plant their milpas where their food plants could grow. But these people of wood did not have souls. They did not have minds. They had no blood and their cheeks were dry. Their feet and hands were dry. Their knees would not bend and they made no offerings. They did not offer incense to the gods. They continually hunted the animals without mercy. They continually cut the trees of the rainforest without showing thanks. They had no thought for the Creator and the Maker, for those who had created and cared for them. They did not speak with the Creator and the Maker.

So a great flood was sent down by the Heart of Heaven on the heads of the people made of wood. The face of Earth became dark. Black rain fell by day and by night. Then Xecotcovach, the great eagle, flew down to strike at the eyes of the people of wood. Camalotz, the great bat, flew down to strike at their heads. Cotzbalam, the jaguar who waits, came roaring to eat them. Tucumbalam, the tapir, came running to trample them.

Next the small animals and the large animals came to attack those people made of wood. The sticks and stones flew up to strike the people made of wood. Everything began to speak, even the water jugs and the clay plates and the grinding stones.

"You hurt us and you did not thank us," the dogs and turkeys and hens said. "You beat us and ate us, and now we will kill you."

"You tormented us every day," the grinding stones said. "You scraped our faces: *holi, holi, haqui, haqui.* Now that you are no longer human beings we will grind you up."

Some of the people made of wood tried to run away. They climbed to the top of their houses, but their houses fell down. They ran into the rainforests and climbed into the trees, but the trees threw them down. They tried to go into the caves, but the caves cast them out. At last, almost all of those people made of wood were destroyed and their villages were no more. Again the rainforest grew where their milpas had been. Only a few of those original people survived, and they became the howler monkeys who live in the rainforest.

Finally, the Creator and the Maker, Tepeu and Gucumatz, decided to try once again to make human beings. They held council to decide what would be used to make the flesh of the people. They did a divination and were told to ask help of four animals. Those four animals, the parrot, the jaguar, the coyote and the crow, told them of the yellow ears of corn and the white ears of corn. They showed the Creator and the Maker the road to Paxil. They brought the Creator and the Maker to Paxil where the corn grew.

The Creator and the Maker ground that corn and made it into dough. From that cornmeal dough they fashioned the flesh, the arms and legs and the bodies of the people. It was the blood of these new people. These new people were made out of maize.

The people made of maize were intelligent and far-seeing. They were thankful. They sang and praised the Creator and the Maker. They sang and praised the forest and the animals. But the people made of maize could see too far. They could see all of Earth and all of heaven. They saw so far that the Creator and the Maker became worried that these new people would become arrogant. So they darkened the eyes of the new people. Now the new people could no longer see into the farthest heavens. Now their sight was limited to the closest parts of Earth and Sky. Now they would not become arrogant and forget to be thankful. Now they would not forget to take care of the rainforest. The people made of maize would only remember how far they had once seen when they offered incense in the ceremonies and when they gave thanks to those who made them. As long as they remembered to give thanks and to take care of the forest, all would be well for them. So it remains to this day.

DISCUSSION

It is fitting that Fox and Blue Jay bring pine, fir, spruce and cedar trees from Sky Land in the Snoqualmie story "How Fox Brought the Forests From the Sky," for the needles among the tallest of these trees seem to brush against the clouds. Fox and Blue Jay then plant these conifers throughout the Cascade Mountains, which is the northern range of the Sierra Nevadas that stretches from northeastern California to western Oregon and Washington. The Cascades contain magnificent expanses of North America's temperate rainforest.

Prior to the coming of European cultures, traditional Native North Americans of temperate and tropical rainforests developed many ways of using local resources and living in balance with their environments. Red alder is used for smoking salmon, and the fruiting bodies of Indian paint fungus are made into a red dye. In the Pacific Northwest, the traditional Kwakiutl, Tlingit, Haida and Tsimshian make large houses and public buildings from cedar planks. The massive, elaborately carved doorways often make it appear

that people enter by walking into the jaws of an animal or a human being. Practical uses of cedar include baskets, boats, houses, gum, rope, clothes and totem poles. Parts of the cedar are used without cutting the tree down except when constructing dugout canoes and totem poles.

Far to the southwest, in the region now known as southern Mexico and northern Guatemala, a Mayan story tells how The People of Maize are formed. The first people, made of mud, are inferior and so are returned to Earth. People are then made of wood, but they lack minds and souls and do not pray to the Creator and the Maker. These people are destroyed because they do not respect the animals and trees of the rainforest. The few that remain become howler monkeys. Finally, people are made of maize. These people learn to give thanks and care for the rainforest.

Over the centuries, in the lowland tropical rainforest of what is now southern Mexico, the traditional Lacandon Maya developed a way of living sustainably with their environment. (The Lacandon Mayans are one of several Mayan groups whose traditional homeland includes parts of Mexico, Guatemala and

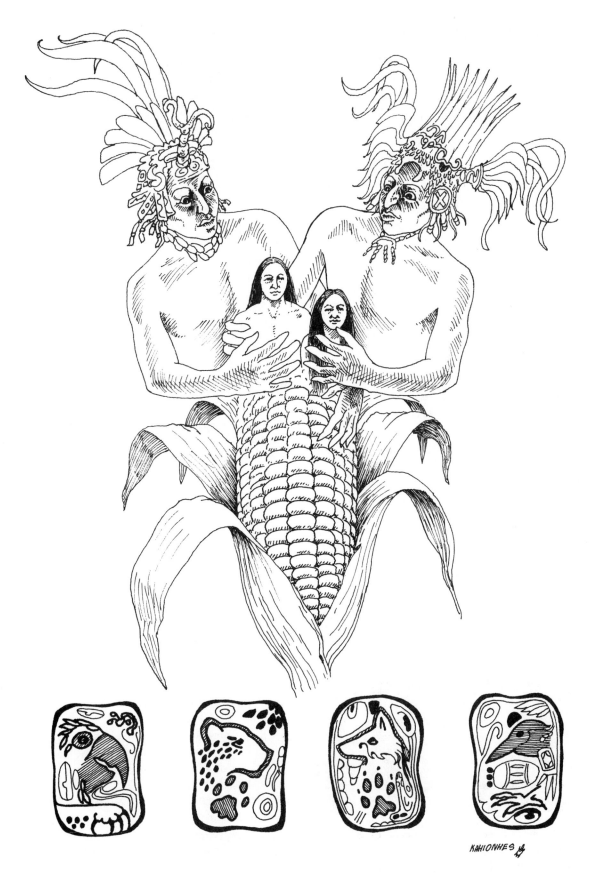

From cornmeal dough the Creator and the Maker fashioned the flesh, the arms and legs and the bodies of the people.

Belize.) Using only the available places that have well-drained rich soils, the land is cleared and planted with trees and root crops to stabilize the soil and to prevent nutrients from being lost to erosion. Maize and some 80 other crops are planted in tune with local plant cycles. This *milpa* agriculture uses diverse planting schemes, layering and companion planting. Each acre produces as much as 2.6 tons (2.4 metric tons) of shelled corn each year.[1] After three to seven years, the plot is left fallow and another garden is begun. The trees, such as rubber, cacao, citrus and balsam, which are planted in the old plot, provide abundant food and cover for many forms of wildlife, which further supplement the Lacandon diet. By hunting and collecting wild plants from the surrounding wild forest, the Lacandon Maya round out their existence. Eventually, the old milpa plot is cleared and planted once again. Relying on the cyclical use of young forest for agriculture preserves the unaltered parts of the forest.

Temperate Rainforest of the Pacific Northwest

Warm, resin-scented breezes blow upslope through the forest as a Douglas squirrel, the "chickaree," calls out its shrill alarm note to warn of approaching intruders. The wind-like voice of the river whispers in the distance. With black head and dark blue body flashing, a Stellar's jay swoops in amid the deep shadows for a closer look. Our eyes fix on wide branches of Douglas fir, western hemlock and Sitka spruce overflowing with the soft greens of mosses, lichens, liverworts and ferns—billowing communities that drape the branches several inches thick throughout the forest above the reach of winter snows (Figure 13-1). The trunk of one ancient Douglas fir, which has seen more than 1,200 springtimes, vaults branchless for 100 feet (30.5 meters) above the forest floor, and then spreads its great horizontal

Figure 13-1. Supported by abundant moisture, moss forms a soft green cover over branches in the temperate rainforests of the Pacific Northwest. In some parts of the Olympic rainforest as much as 180 in. (4.5 m) of rainfall has been recorded in one year. (Photo by Michael J. Caduto)

limbs along another 150 feet (45.7 meters) toward the sky. Life flows and drips down from the tree crowns. Flying squirrels, rufous hummingbirds and the marbled murrelet, a kind of seabird, nest in these shaggy, moist green cushions. Generations of red tree voles, a common prey of the northern spotted owl, are known to live their entire lives in the crown of a Douglas fir without ever touching Earth. Golden-crowned kinglets flit from branch to branch and pileated woodpeckers excavate impressive vertical holes in search of ants and other food. The crotch of a big-leafed maple cradles a bed of ferns and mosses. The massive, muscled trunks of the western red cedar are humbling.

Deep shadows are broken by patches of sunlight touching the lush forest floor. Here grows a foam flower, there an evergreen violet, tiger lily, blue anemone or phantom orchid. Many ferns—sword, bracken, licorice and deer—wave in forest breezes, while below a banana slug slowly consumes the cap of a mushroom. A moss- and lichen-covered fallen log has nursed a row of young conifer saplings in the thin soil along its spine. Although a standing tree may take more than 200 years to decompose in the temperate rainforest, this waterlogged old trunk may last 400 years because it is too wet for wood-rotting fungi to penetrate. An old hemlock growing nearby stands on stilt roots. When this hemlock was young it grew from the top of a nurse log. The log, straddled by the tree's roots, eventually decayed, leaving a space between the roots and the ground (Figure 13-1). Growing near a patch of red alders is a massive stump more than 10 feet (3 meters) in diameter: a remnant of an original tree hand cut from this forest with a cross-cut saw.

This is a small piece of *temperate rainforest* in the Snoqualmie National Forest of the Cascade Mountains east of Seattle, Washington. Seventy to 80 inches (177.8 to 203.2 centimeters) of rain fall here each year, mostly during the fall, winter and spring months. As little as 3 inches (7.6 centimeters) of rain may come during the summer, but the fog drip that condenses onto needles, mosses and other parts of forest plants adds up to 5 inches (12.7 centimeters) more water during the summer, better than doubling the water available for plant growth and maintenance. These conditions favor conifers over broadleaved deciduous trees. Since the temperate rainforest has only developed in the aftermath of the last glacial period, which ended about 10,000 years ago, it does not contain the incredible diversity of plant and animal life of the tropical rainforest, which has been evolving for 60 million years. However, the living mass of plants and animals in the Cascade old-growth forest is greater than anywhere on Earth except for redwood forests. Vast quantities of water and nutrients are stored in the stems and roots of old-growth trees. But the mass of living things in Cascade soils exceeds that of the trees!

Western hemlock and western red cedar are dominant trees in the Snoqualmie National Forest. Although Douglas fir can live longer and grow taller than these species, it is not a shade-tolerant tree but one that becomes established in sunlit clearings. In very old stands where ancient Douglas firs have lived out their lives and died back, hemlock and cedar prevail. Pacific silver fir replaces Douglas fir in higher elevations. (See Chapter 8 for a detailed description of the species composition and geographical range of Pacific Northwest forests.)

Every forest is unique. Fragile *interrelationships* develop among plants and animals of old-growth rainforest that are difficult to reestablish once a forest has been cut down. Each species of tree in the old-growth forest *needs* symbiotic mycorrhizal fungi (see "Discussion" in Chapter 6) to survive. Northern flying squirrels eat the fungal fruiting bodies and spread the spores throughout the forest. In springtime Clark's nutcrackers bury pine seeds where the ground first appears through melting snow: young pines later sprout in the sunlit nooks. A major source of nutrients for the old-growth forest in the Cascades is the lichen *Lobaria oregana*— a symbiotic relationship between a fungus, a green alga and a blue-green alga. Small nodules of blue-green algae scattered within the fungus fix nitrogen from the air and create a rich source of nutrients. The forest is fertilized as nitrogen leaches from the lichen to plants below and when pieces of lichen fall to the ground.[2] These lichens also provide a home for a community of organisms.

Ancient, or old-growth, forests once covered all but the higher elevations of the vast mountain ranges of Pacific northwestern Canada and the United States (see "Discussion" in Chapter 8). It takes roughly 200 years for a forest to develop *old-growth* characteristics, including a layered canopy, at least two species of trees with a range of ages and sizes, several large conifers that are at least 200 years old or greater than 32 inches (81.3 centimeters) in diameter, several large standing dead trees or "snags" and large logs lying on the forest floor and in nearby streams.[3] Nearly 130 species of birds, mammals, reptiles and amphibians make their homes in this land of moderate climate, much of which does not experience extreme summer heat or hard winter frosts, including the tailed frog, fisher, northern spotted owl and marbled murrelet. The rare Pacific giant salamander—the largest land salamander—grows to nearly 1 foot (30.5 centimeters) long and feeds on animals as large as mice and frogs. One tree may be home to more than 1,500 invertebrate animal species. In early summer, when the forest is still damp, small lightning fires release soil nutrients and help to fertilize plants. When the end of the dry season arrives in late summer, especially in forests that have not experienced a major fire in the past century or so, lightning and arson can spark tremendous infernos that consume vast acreage.

The well-being of the forest and the salmon are inextricably linked. There are five species of Pacific salmon: coho or silver, chinook or king, chum or dog, red or sockeye and pink or humpy. These salmon are *anadromous,* which means they live in salt water and return to fresh water to spawn.

Each river is a breeding ground for its own genetically distinct subspecies of salmon. Washington State alone manages 105 species and subspecies of salmon. Large woody debris in streams and rivers provides cover, traps the gravel that is essential for spawning, supports streambanks and slopes and decreases the erosive force of high waters. The pools and cascades created by logs mix and oxygenate the water and provide habitat for insects and other invertebrates eaten by salmon. *Riparian* vegetation, that growing along streams and riverbanks, is the nursery for large, woody, stream debris. Dead trees and other forest debris that washes downstream account for as much as 75 percent of the nutrients that feed some coastal ecosystems in the Pacific Northwest. More than 22 species of birds and mammals have been identified that consume the salmon that die in the rivers after spawning. In this way nutrients are returned to the forest ecosystem.

There are thousands of species in the old-growth forests of the Pacific Northwest, including some that are rare and threatened; the Pacific giant salamander, northern spotted owl, marbled murrelet and Pacific yew among them. Much attention has focused on the Pacific yew and *taxol,* a drug derived from its bark that is highly effective in treating ovarian cancer. Native Americans have traditionally used the bark of the Pacific yew—a tree that they revere—to make an anti-inflammatory. In December 1992, the U.S. Food and Drug Administration approved the use of taxol for treating advanced ovarian cancer. Taxol paralyzes cancer cells so they are not able to reproduce. It requires 100,000 pounds (45,360 kilograms) of yew bark to make enough taxol to treat ovarian cancer in one person. The yew, a diminutive tree among giants, requires 100 years to attain a height of 40 feet (12.2 meters). In 1992, 1.6 million pounds (725,760 kilograms) of Pacific yew bark were harvested. Fortunately, harvest of the threatened Pacific yew will not be necessary in the future because drug manufacturers have discovered a way to synthesize taxol from precursors found in the needles of yew trees grown on plantations in Europe and the Himalayas.[4]

Tropical Rainforest

It is a drive of several days from Mexico City, perhaps the most congested and polluted city in the world, to the highland jungles of Chiapas where the last of the Lacandon Maya live. On the third day, heading south from the great abandoned Maya city of Palenque, we passed through what had once been highland jungle. But the jungle had been clear-cut. Instead of being allowed to lie fallow and return to forest—as the old Mayan farmers always did with their small milpas—it had been sown with grass and cattle had been brought in to graze. Only single skeletal, dead trees stood here and there on hilltops, like giant telephone poles stripped of their wires. What cattle there were to be seen were thin and listless. Erosion was cutting away the thin soil from the hills, exposing stone. What had been a wonderfully diverse living ecosystem was now becoming a desert.

As we reached a hilltop and passed a sign marking the edge of the Lacandon Reserve, a protected area, we felt a change in the air. Suddenly we were into the canopy of a jungle, which arched overhead like a great verdant umbrella. Then, just as suddenly, we realized that a light rain was falling. It was the first rain we had seen for 100 miles, the moist breath of the forest. Now there were more shades of green around us than words can fully describe. Within 100 yards of travel we saw a dozen different orchids, while other flowers we could not name dropped petals onto the red dirt road. Tropical cedar, guava, *Ceiba* and even a few small mahoganies were among the many trees that cast shadows over us as we rounded another corner, passing a Lacandon man and a small boy who stood by the roadside and waved.

Mexican tropical rainforests, land of the Lacandon Maya, are home to a vast array of plants and animals (Figure 13-2). Nearly 50 species of animals have been found living on one *Cecropia* tree, including leaf-cutting ants, biting ants that live inside the hollow stems, iguanas, fruit-eating bats, monkeys, sloths and 33 species of birds feeding on flowers and fruits, including some that migrate to North America.[5] Lianas hang thick from the vaulting gray trunks of the kapok tree, which rises up to 164 feet (50 meters) before sending out a wide-reaching crown of branches that are home to many kinds of epiphytes. The compound leaves are shed during the dry season. In Mayan belief souls ascend the long trunk of a sacred kapok to heaven amid the branches. Kapok or *Ceiba* sprout in open, sunny places where they can grow up to 10 feet (3 meters) per year. White or pink, five-petaled, sour-smelling kapok flowers are pollinated by bats, which are a crucial pollinator of many flowers of the tropical rainforest. The kapok, or "silk-cotton," tree is named for the silk fibers that cover the seeds and aid in wind dispersal.

Animal life is colorful and vibrant. Trogons are stout, fruit-eating species of birds that flash intense blue, green, red and yellow as they incessantly call, "cow, cow, cow." Female plumage has a similar pattern of duller colors than the males. One kind of trogon, the 24-inch (61-centimeter) quetzal, is thought to have inspired the legend of the phoenix with its impressive size and brilliant green, golden-green and red plumage. Males possess long, attractive tail plumes. Other animals of the Mexican rainforest include spider monkeys, squirrels, pocket mice, lizards, salamanders, collared peccaries, the badger-like grison and species of opossum including the familiar American opossum that occurs farther north. The mass of insect life is greater than the mass of all other animals combined. Poisonous frogs and toads are found here and raucous treefrog calls are heard in the evening. Much-feared predators include the boa constrictor, which has been known to reach a length of more than 18 feet (5.5 meters), and several large cats such as the puma or mountain lion. El Tigre, the jaguar, is a heavy-set,

leopard-like cat that grows to a length of 6 feet (1.8 meters), weighs as much as 400 pounds (181.4 kilograms) and feeds on large prey—peccaries, birds, fish, reptiles and even deer.

The green band of *tropical rainforests* around the equator, with fingers reaching to the north and south, covers 6 percent of Earth's land area and harbors more than half of the species on Earth.[6] There are about 1.4 million *known* living species worldwide, and this figure is less than one-tenth of the total number that actually exist.[7] Rainforests on the North American continent include those of Central America and Mexico. Hawaii is home to the only lowland rainforest found within the United States. The Amazon River Basin in South America contains the largest continuous tract of tropical rainforest in the world. Warm tropical rainforests receive 80 or more inches (203.2 or more centimeters) of rain each year. Annual rainfall in the Colombian rainforest amounts to 300 inches (762 centimeters)! Plants grow all year and there are few seasonal changes except for a wet and dry cycle. Nutrients are contained in the living forests; soils are poor. When a leaf falls, it often decomposes completely within several hours—a branch within days.

Rainforests develop as many as eight different levels of vegetation, consisting of tree crowns, shrubs and herbaceous plants of different heights as well as the forest floor and soil. There may be hundreds of species of trees in the forest, but only a few individuals of any one species. Tree crowns are so dense that heavy shade suppresses growth of plants on the forest floor. It is easy to walk around in the mature rainforest. Only early stages of growth present the visitor with a thick green tangle. Animal species usually outnumber plants in tropical rainforests, and the tropical forests of arid regions have 20 to 40 percent fewer bird and plant species than rainforests. Many plants are lush, gargantuan, exotic forms of their relatives to the north, including tree-size vines and giant violets. Tree names evoke images of moist green forests with hanging vines and animals calling from hidden perches: tamarind, poisonwood, blolly, wild mahogany and gumbo limbo.

The rainforest is a world of fascinating small communities within a larger community. Treetop-dwelling epiphytes send aerial roots into cracks and nooks in tree branches where there are tiny pockets of soil containing seeds, dust, debris and often ants. Bromeliads grow in a similar way and they trap pools of up to 1 gallon (3.8 liters) of water in their leaves. Breeding frogs, aquatic insects and snails live in these treetop ponds. Leaf-shaped katydids, complete with imitation fungus spots and dewdrops, are well hidden where they call and mate in the crowns. There are beautiful orchids, parakeets, anteaters and pig-like tapirs.

State of the Rainforests

PACIFIC NORTHWEST. Temperate rainforests are endangered. Some threats originate outside of these environments, including acid precipitation (Chapter 5) and ozone pollution in the lower atmosphere (Chapter 8), global

Figure 13-2. *A rainforest community in southern Mexico, home to the Lacandon Maya. The lesser longnose bat laps bromeliad nectar. A leafcutter ant gathers clippings to culture as a fungus-growing mulch that feeds the colony. Gaudy leaf frogs have red eyes and bodies splotched white, green, blue and orange. Leaf frog eggs are attached to leaves and tadpoles drop into water when they hatch. Three-toed sloths eat leaves of the* Cecropia *and other trees and complete the nutrient cycle when they deposit droppings at the base of a tree. The resplendent quetzal eats fruit, insects and small animals. Vines called* lianas *hang from a kapok tree (upper left). Sizes (top to bottom): mahogany tree, to 164 ft. (50 m); kapok (Ceiba) tree, to 130 ft. (40 m); quetzal (including tail), 24 in. (61 cm); three-toed sloth (head and body), 24 in. (61 cm); lesser longnose bat (body, not including tail), 2.8 to 3.7 in. (7 to 9.5 cm); gaudy leaf frog (head and body), to 2.8 in. (7 cm); jaguar (head to end of tail), to 7 ft. (2.1 m); leafcutter ant, to .4 in.(9 mm);* Cecropia *tree, to 60 ft. (18.3 m). (Illustration by Marjorie C. Leggitt)*

warming and resulting climatic changes (Chapter 7) and stratospheric ozone depletion (Chapter 14). These influences work synergistically and place stress on rainforest plants and animals, diminishing their resistance. Clear-cutting and mismanagement present the most immediate threats to the continued existence of temperate rainforests. Many species require at least 1,000 acres (405 hectares) of contiguous old-growth forest.

The northern spotted owl, which is listed as a threatened species in the United States and as endangered in Canada, is a good indicator of the health of the temperate rainforest. (The Mexican spotted owl of the Southwest is also listed as threatened.) The owls feed on squirrels, red tree voles and other small mammals that are in turn supported by the forest food web. Trouble with the owls indicates that there are problems with the forest itself. And something is very wrong:

• Only 10 percent remains of the original 19 million acres of ancient forest found in Oregon and Washington. Most of this is on federal land of which only a small part is off limits to cutting. About half of the forest that remains is fragmented into such small parcels that it can no longer meet the needs of species that must have old-growth forest to survive.

• Ninety-two percent of California's ancient coastal redwoods are gone.

• Sixty percent of British Columbia's coastal old-growth forest is gone and most of it will disappear by 2020. Logging is proceeding at the rate of more than 667,000 acres (270,000 hectares) per year. One 180-square-mile (466.2-square-kilometer) clear-cut is visible from space. Only 1 of 89 large watersheds on Vancouver Island is protected from logging.

• Forty percent of Alaska's richest forest lands have been cut. Less than one-tenth of the rich forests are protected in the 16.9-million-acre (6.8-million-hectare) Tongass National Forest.

There once were 30 to 35 million acres (12.2 to 14.2 million hectares) of old-growth temperate rainforest that grew down to and overhung waterways and jammed streams and rivers with logs. Forests were so dense that waterways were cleared first and used for transportation. The infrequent natural fires created stands of trees with diverse ages. At present, 90 percent of the remaining forest consists of young trees that lack diversity in age and number of species.

The pressure to cut trees much faster than the forest can replenish itself is high because one sound old-growth tree can bring as much as $5,000 (U.S.) or more on the wholesale market, one acre of ancient forest yields $40,000 to $80,000 and 1 acre of redwood forest can be sold for $100,000. Small patches of trees are often left standing in a cut area as a ruse to claim that the land has not been clear-cut. Under these conditions the trees experience higher winds than in large tracts of forest and these shallow-rooted individuals are easily blown down. National forests are being clear-cut in patterns that resemble a patchwork quilt from the air, often reaching right up to the lower boundary of national parks. In the Olympic Mountains of Washington State, most of the forests from about 5,000 feet (1,524 meters) in elevation on down are either recently cleared or consist of young secondary growth (Figure 13-3). The remaining, higher-elevation forest in the national park is near the treeline: it is too high up and contains the wrong species to develop old-growth character. One study, which was conducted in Tongass National Forest in Alaska's coastal panhandle by U.S. Forest Service wildlife biologists, found that cutting must decrease by 25 percent or many species will disappear from much of the forest because they need old growth to survive, such as goshawks, owls, sitka black-tailed deer, brown bears, wolves and salmon. The Tongass National Forest consists of many islands; animals have no place to go when the forest is cut. But Forest Service administrators tried, unsuccessfully, to repress their own report so cutting could continue apace.[8] Another U.S. government report released in 1993 by the Forest Service Scientific Advisory Team estimates that cutting levels of the late 1970s to 1980s must be reduced at least fivefold to give the northern spotted owl an 85 percent chance of survival. However, even this reduction may not ensure the survival of other species such as the pine marten.

It is not just the *removal* of the forest that makes old-growth cutting so ecologically disastrous; it is also the demise of the *interconnections* among living things, which take around 200 years to become reestablished. When old-growth forest is clear-cut—the most widely used method of harvesting—the fragile mat of mycorrhizal fungi upon which the trees depend is broken up and destroyed by heavy equipment and dragging logs. These fungi must be reintroduced for the forest to thrive once again. What were once year-round streams dry up and flow only after heavy rains. Moss and lichen growth is nearly nonexistent and the rich remains of dead wood on the forest floor are largely gone. The dense shade beneath many even-aged, spindly trees growing close together prevents other plants from growing. A fraction of the original number of tree species now grow here and one-fifteenth the number of mosses. The red alder, which fertilizes the soil with its nitrogen-fixing root nodules, is removed chemically and artificial fertilizer is applied. Remaining forest, which consists of small, disconnected patches, does not even provide adequate travel corridors for animals to move from one stand of old growth to another.

Monoculture tree farms lack diversity and provide extremely poor habitat for plants and animals. Roads disrupt natural drainage patterns and erosion washes topsoil into waterways. The U.S. Forest Service maintains 365,000 miles (587,413 kilometers) of roads, eight times the combined length of all U.S. interstate highways. No one knows whether a forest can fully recover after several clear-cuttings during which the standing forest nutrients were removed several times over, especially when slash is burned instead of being allowed to decompose and feed the soil.

Figure 13-3. Clear-cutting has devastated many temperate and tropical rainforests. Mountainsides that have been clear-cut for timber in the Olympic National Forest, Washington, are eroding into the valleys (left). The view from Monteverde, Costa Rica, toward the Pacific Ocean shows a vast area denuded of trees for cattle grazing (right). (Photos by Michael J. Caduto {left} and Alan C. Graham {right})

Salmon suffer greatly from clear-cutting, which:
• causes erosion and washes silt into waterways, where it clogs fish gills, buries beds of spawning gravel and suffocates eggs.
• increases water temperatures to levels that stress or kill fish. Salmon require cold temperatures of about 40° to 60°F (4.4° to 15.6°C). Temperatures in the mid- to high-70s Fahrenheit (24° to 26.6° C) are lethal.
• reduces water flow.
• decreases habitat diversity, especially where dead logs are removed from the waterways.

Other decreases in salmon populations are caused by hydro-electric dams, splash dams, estuarine pollution, irrigation diversions, increases in offshore trolling and numbers of fishing vessels and the introduction of genetically inferior and less diverse strains of hatchery-bred fish.

TROPICAL RAINFORESTS. More than half of Earth's tropical rainforests have already been wiped out, and a stand of forest the size of a football field is felled every second.[9] At this rate, all of the rainforest, except that found in remote areas, will be gone in little more than two decades (Figure 13-3). Each year,

worldwide, tropical forests are destroyed at the rate of 54,826 square miles (142,000 square kilometers).[10] An additional 57,915 square miles (150,000 square kilometers) are severely degraded. This total of 112,741 square miles (292,000 square kilometers) is greater than the combined land area of Colorado and Massachusetts. From 1964 to 1986, more than one-third of Honduras' tropical forest was destroyed—16,000 acres (6,480 hectares) per year.

When tropical rainforests are cut the nutrients in the forest ecosystem are removed along with the trees and the remaining nutrients leach out of these *lateritic* soils, creating hard, infertile ground. The lack of trees, shade and water retention hastens the drying of the soils and decreases humidity and rainfall. With vegetation gone, more of the sun's heat radiates back into the atmosphere, changing global wind and rainfall patterns. With cutting, decaying and burning, the rainforest's great reservoir of carbon is continuously released into the atmosphere, where it contributes significantly to the greenhouse effect. Thirty percent of the atmospheric carbon dioxide buildup comes from the clearing of tropical forests.[11] Widespread destruction of the rainforests could return enough carbon dioxide to the atmosphere to dramatically increase Earth's temperature.

As Native peoples have gone, so have the rainforests. In the eighteenth century there were 14 million Mayans who fished, farmed and hunted in the rainforests. These were the only Native North Americans with an original written language. Their science of mathematics was far more advanced than that of Europe at the time, and their calendar is more accurate than the Gregorian calendar we use today. Two hundred years of genocide at the hands of the Spaniards, including introduced diseases, centuries of kidnapping and forced slavery, were followed by many devastating wars. The Lacandon Mayans fled north to the Chiapas lowland rainforest to escape persecution in their native Guatemala. Here, for a time, they resumed traditional milpa agriculture in peace. In the 1940s the Mexican government took the Lacandons' land in the Chiapas lowlands and encouraged more than 80,000 peasant farmers to move there who did not know how to farm sustainably in the rainforest. Poor farming practices and vast cattle ranches have destroyed much of the rainforest. In 1971 the Lacandons were forcibly relocated by the government to three small reservations of less than 20,000 total acres (8,100 hectares), far from their traditional gardens. About 400 Lacandon remain and only 1 in 5 is able to practice traditional milpa agriculture. The rest were moved en masse, against their will, into government-controlled "villages."[12]

Pesticides also threaten tropical peoples and ecosystems. Although the use of DDT was banned in the early 1970s in the United States and Canada, no such restrictions are in place in Central American countries. More than 25 percent of the pesticides exported by U.S. producers are "banned, heavily restricted or have never been registered for use here."[13] The high volumes and levels of pesticides used in the tropics are entering and poisoning food chains in tropical ecosystems. People in both Guatemala and Nicaragua have blood levels of DDT that are 31 times those found in the United States.[14] In Guatemala, cows' milk contains 90 times more DDT than is allowed by U.S. law.[15] The *circle of poison* is completed when foods that have been grown in other countries, using pesticides banned in the United States, are then shipped to the United States. Imported foods that have been found to contain pesticide residues many times those allowed under U.S. law include bananas, coffee, beans, peppers, cabbage, beef and many others. Rainforests are truly a global ecological connecting thread among peoples north and south.

Other threats to the well-being of tropical rainforests include slash-and-burn agriculture, cattle raising, firewood collecting, overpopulation, illegal trade in plants and animals, resettlement of people to escape poverty and extraction of gold and other minerals. Millions of acres of Central and South American forest are cleared each year for cattle ranching, principally for producing beef that is exported to the United States. After a few years, the poor grasses cannot support the cattle and the range is abandoned; the forest is lost, the soils destroyed. Poachers and dealers greatly deplete the populations of endangered species, including poachers who trade "rare and exotic" species on the black market. In certain highly trafficked areas, especially in Costa Rica's rainforests, unmanaged tourism is having a severe impact on local peoples and environments.

Rainforest Values and Stewardship

PACIFIC NORTHWEST. The old-growth forest of the Pacific Northwest has, for millennia, provided essential spawning habitat for salmon. The traditional Native peoples of the Pacific Northwest live in synchronicity with the cycles and seasons of the salmon. Their cultures are built around the salmon, which provide both food and skins. Today, salmon are a multibillion-dollar industry.

The many values of the old-growth northwest forest are explained throughout this chapter, from ecological guardians of the climate, soil, air and water quality of the region and source of nutrients for coastal ecosystems, to habitat for threatened and endangered species to keepers of a rich genetic diversity of plants and animals. The many utilitarian values of rainforests include their scientific and educational importance and role in providing a livelihood for people. In 1988 recreation generated $6 billion (U.S.) for the economies of Washington and Oregon. Other values are less tangible—the sound of a trout snapping up an insect meal, the smell of fir in summer heat, the reflection of sky in a drop of water pendulant from an evergreen needle.

Once gone, the forests and life therein are irreplaceable. How can wood be harvested for construction and fiber while *sustaining* the ecosystem? Can salmon stocks withstand the pressures placed on them? Since most privately owned ancient forest is already cut, the remaining land is mostly controlled by government. One model from another region that may be applied to the Northwest was developed at the Northern Arizona University School of Forestry in conjunction with the Diné (Navajo) Nation. This management system applies Native American holistic stewardship practices to forestry and considers the interdependence of plant, animal and human communities.[16] Ecological and economic concerns are seen as part of the whole and considered simultaneously.

Here are a few recommendations that have been made to better care for the well-being of old-growth forests in the Pacific Northwest:[17]
• Halt the cutting of remaining old-growth forests.
• Allow 3 acres of forest land to grow back for each acre of old growth preserved.
• Cut only what a forest can produce and sustain while retaining its ecological integrity.
• Manage forests ecologically by creating small clearings like those that would be made by fire and leaving piles of slash as homes for small animals and sources of soil nutrients.
• Maintain and cultivate diversity. Retain stands of trees that are a mix of ages and species.

• Provide corridors that connect existing old growth for plants and animals.

• Apply pressure on governments to preserve the land.

• Preserve large tracts of intact forests with sustainable cutting around the periphery.

• Practice low-impact logging. Cable logging suspends and moves trees above the forest floor to minimize stream erosion and damage to land and remaining trees.

• Support Native land claims. In 1987 the Haida won a battle for ownership of 350,000 acres (141,750 hectares) on South Moresby Island off the coast of northern British Columbia for wilderness and traditional uses. The Clayoquot people are fighting for the 22,000-acre (8,910-hectare) Meares Island off the western coast of Vancouver Island.

• Sustain jobs for people in the Northwest with wise economic management of resources. Stop exporting whole logs to Korea, Japan and China, and instead mill all lumber here. In 1988, 24 percent of all timber cut in Oregon and Washington was exported as whole logs.

• Develop sustainable harvests from living forests, such as huckleberries, mushrooms and cascara bark, which is used to make a laxative.

TROPICAL RAINFORESTS. Traditional wisdom is carried on today by Mayan peoples, but we will never know what was lost when the Spaniards destroyed centuries of Mayan writings (Figure 13-4). The mountains of Mexico, the Cordilleras, have isolated the plants and animals and encouraged the evolution of forests with distinct species and ecological character. Traditional Native peoples know best how to live in a sustainable, balanced way with the forests they inhabit and have a unique knowledge of plants and animals. Despite how they have been treated in recent centuries, indigenous peoples continue to lead others to medicinal and edible plants and share their knowledge of the curative properties of plants, insects and other parts of the rainforest.

Each genetic strain of plant has unique properties. One perennial species of wild maize, called teosinte, is found in only one place on Earth: a plot of land in Jalisco, Mexico, that is less than 5 acres (2 hectares) in size. This species provided the gene that saved U.S. corn crops from being decimated by a fungus, yet it was almost destroyed by a bulldozer before scientists discovered it. The rosy periwinkle, a plant of the imperiled Madagascar rainforest, contains two alkaloids that are extracted and used to treat childhood leukemia and Hodgkin's disease. A drug that can fight respiratory viruses was recently discovered in South American rainforests. One drug firm, Merck and Co., is cooperating with Costa Rica's nonprofit Institute of Biodiversity to collect and test plants for potential value as medicines and agricultural crops. The institute receives money up front and a royalty from the profits whenever any useful plants are found and marketed. Given the way that new inventions and discoveries are handled by Western businesses, is it not appropriate for indigenous peoples to receive credit, compensation and patent rights to the drugs and other products whose manufacture is based on the use of their traditional plants?

As the major storehouse of more than half of Earth's species, tropical rainforests are an invaluable ecological and cultural resource. Although the species and exact local conditions vary, tropical rainforests possess all of the values just discussed for temperate rainforests, as well as others mentioned throughout this discussion. Tropical forests play a major role in moderating global temperature and determining the nature and stability of global climate. Numerous schemes have been proposed and enacted for wise stewardship of these forests. We now need to:

• halt the destruction of all rainforests until a sustainable management plan is in place.

• begin a massive reforestation program to replant diverse forest communities.

• seek alternatives to the slash-and-burn cycle that destroys rainforests, such as rural development projects and sustainable agriculture. Political, economic and cultural solutions to overpopulation, poverty and poor distribution of agricultural land are needed.

• encourage and establish sustainable harvests from rainforests: extract rubber, harvest nuts, selectively harvest potential edible and medicinal varieties of plants and wisely cut *trees* for fuel and timber instead of *forests*.

• buy products that are based on sustainable use of the rainforest to encourage that kind of use. Refuse to buy products that depend on destruction of rainforests.

• create biological and cultural reserves. Two percent of the world's rainforests are nature reserves or national parks, but most have no protection and many are open to logging and other harmful activities. Biosphere reserves conserve the natural environment and indigenous cultures within large ecologically and culturally distinct regions. Two examples are the Sierra de Manantlan Biosphere Reserve in Mexico and the Comarca de Kuna Yala under the stewardship of the San Blas Kuna people of coastal Panama.

• expand educational and scientific research training programs in rainforest communities.

• promote *ecotourism* as an alternative to unmanaged tourism. The Ecotourism Society consists of conservationists, park managers and representatives of the travel industry. Trips promote conservation and tourism with a minimal impact on the local natural and ecological communities. Local guides are used along with low-impact lodging and education for travelers. Tour operators donate a percentage of proceeds to fund protection of local parks.

The help and support of many people who want to establish a sustainable coexistence with rainforests are essential if tropical forests are to survive beyond the early twenty-first century. New plans reflect the diversity of cultures and

Figure 13-4. This Mayan temple, which was built in the seventh century, stands in the ruins of the ancient city of Uxmal in the northwestern corner of the Yucatan Peninsula. One enters through the mouth of an allegorical mask. Uxmal was one of several historical Mayan cultural and ceremonial centers which housed their libraries, the collective written record of the Peoples. (Photo by Will and Jane Curtis)

natural systems they aim to protect. The proposed Tawahka Biosphere Reserve in La Mosquitia, eastern Honduras, will protect the forest and the traditional existence of indigenous Tawahka peoples, stop deforestation, protect natural resources and promote ecotourism, scientific research and sustainable development. It will create a continuous ecological link with the Rio Platano Biosphere Reserve. Such connected, holistic proposals and programs offer hope for the future as members of the international community work with local peoples and put the best interests and wishes of the forests and indigenous cultures up front.

QUESTIONS

1. What kinds of trees does Fox bring from Sky Land in the Snoqualmie story "How Fox Brought the Forests From the Sky"? How do Blue Jay and Fox outsmart Moon to bring trees to Earth?

2. What happens to Moon when he tries to climb down the rope hanging from Sky Land? Which mountain does Moon turn into? (Mount Si is located in the Cascade Range east of Seattle.)

3. Who makes the first people in the Lacandon Mayan story "The First People"? What happens when people are made out of mud? How do the people act who are made from the wood of the rainforest? What do the Creator and the Maker do to these first kinds of people?

4. What lessons do you learn by what happens to the people made of mud and wood?

5. Why do you think people are made from maize the third time around? How do the people made of maize treat the plants and animals to live well with them? Whom do the people made of maize sing to, praise and show that they are thankful?

6. Who are the native cultures that live in North America's rainforests of the Pacific Northwest? Which Native people live in tropical Mexico, Central America and South America? How do these traditional people take care of the rainforests in North America?

7. Where are the temperate rainforests in North America? What is a temperate rainforest?

8. What is the climate like in a temperate rainforest? What kinds of plants and animals live there? Can you name and describe some endangered species that live there?

9. Where do we have tropical rainforests in North America, including Mexico and Central America? What is the climate like in a tropical rainforest?

10. What kinds of plants and animals live in the tropical rainforest? Can you name and describe some of these species? Can you name some endangered species that live there?

11. What kinds of things are people doing to the rainforests that are hurting the plants, animals and Native people living there? Do people living far from the rainforest do things that hurt the rainforest? What are those things?

12. How are people changing the rainforest? How long do you think the rainforests, and the Native people who live in them, can last if no one does anything to help preserve them?

13. What gifts do you receive from the rainforest, such as food, medicine and others? How are the rainforests valuable to human beings, and to the nature and people who live in them?

14. How can the people who live in and near the rainforests work to preserve them? What does it mean to use rainforests in a way that is *sustainable*?

15. What can you do to help preserve the rainforests: the plants, animals, soil and Native people who live there? How can you help others who are working to save the rainforests?

ACTIVITIES

Rainforest Alive

ACTIVITY: Create a tropical or temperate rainforest in the home or learning center, complete with trees and other plants as well as animals.

GOALS: Realize the tremendous diversity of habitats and forms of life that exist in the many layers of the rainforest. Understand the interconnections among rainforest plants and animals that make up an ecosystem.

AGE: Younger children and older children

MATERIALS: "Discussion," reference books as listed in "Procedure" and in the Teacher's Guide from which to obtain information as well as photographs and illustrations of rainforest plants and animals, pencils, paper, strips of newspaper, wheat paste for papier-mâché, scissors, construction paper, dead branches gathered from the ground of a local forest, pipe cleaners, tempera paints and nontoxic latex paints, paintbrushes, containers of water for painting, balloons, clay, egg cartons, straws, grocery bags, yarn, tape, glue, paste, large and small cardboard boxes, tubes from empty rolls of toilet paper or gift wrapping, crayons, string, heavy rope or crepe paper to represent vines, cassette of rainforest noises, cassette player, foods from the rainforest (fruit, nuts, berries, etc.), rainforest scents, sheets, needle and thread, measuring stick or tape, toothpicks, children's stuffed animals of the rainforest, other materials as needed.

PROCEDURE: Beforehand, if possible, explore a rainforest in the wild or in an exhibit at a local zoo or botanical garden. Have the children choose the kind of rainforest they want to create: temperate or tropical. If you have a large group the children may split into two smaller groups, each of which will work on a different kind of rainforest. Help the children in each group to use the "Discussion" for identifying plants and animals from their rainforest as well as for information about those plants and animals. Round out this information with your own research from books about the rainforests. Two excellent books are *The Olympic Rainforest: An Ecological Web,* by Ruth Kirk with Jerry Franklin (Seattle: University of Washington Press, 1992), and *Wonders of the Rain Forest,* by Janet Craig (Mahwah, N.J.: Troll Associates, 1990). Other books for both children and adults are listed in the Teacher's Guide. Each group should include a representative cross-section of the plant and animal life in different parts of the rainforest. Plants need to represent the upper canopy, lower canopy, young trees, shrubs, herbaceous plants, forest floor and soil. Animals include herbivores, carnivores, omnivores and scavengers. Decomposers will be located in the soil. Construct a food web of the plants and animals in the rainforest to help plan what habitat they will be found in and which animals they will interact with in the exhibit. You may want to conduct a rainforest adaptation of the *"Ocean Food Web Wipe-Out"* activity from Chapter 5 at this point. Do not forget epiphytic plants and other exotics.

Have the children re-create a sensory immersion into a rainforest by devising ways of imitating how a rainforest would look, sound, smell, feel and even taste. How could they make these things happen? This could range from playing recordings of rainforest sounds to hanging some edible fruits, berries and nuts produced in that rainforest for people to come in and pick. These interactions will make the rainforest a lively, interesting and fun place to visit.

With information in hand, the children are ready to begin planning how they are going to turn a room, hallway, library, exhibit area or other space in the home or learning center into a three-dimensional "rainforest." Have them draw out a plan for each of the walls and the ceiling before they actually begin working. Assign specific tasks to people. The focus should be on how to situate plants and animals as realistically as possible using what the children have learned about them. This exercise is an excellent cooperative group project. It is also a perfect opportunity to get children of different ages working together, each doing something at their level that contributes to the overall creation. Children now need to make a list of the materials they will need to create the rainforest. Have them start with the list under "Materials" and add other supplies as needed.

Work with the children as they turn the space into a rainforest. This may take the form of several intense, day-long sessions, or it may be more practical to devote a segment of each day to the project. Encourage the children to bring in any stuffed animals they own that would be found in the rainforest. Once the rainforest is completed, have the children lead others on guided tours by immersing them into their fascinating sensory world and explaining the natural history of the plants and animals, the climate of the rainforest and other information they have learned.

Note: Reinforce ecological awareness by creating a rainforest from recycled materials.

People of the Rainforest Countries

ACTIVITY: Correspond with a pen-pal child from a country in a tropical rainforest region.
GOALS: Understand what it is like to live in a tropical rainforest region through the eyes of a child who lives there.
AGE: Older children
MATERIALS: Pencils, crayons, paper, envelopes, stamps, pen-pal names and addresses (see below), "Discussion," photographs and other things the children want to include.
PROCEDURE: Beforehand, acquire the names of pen pals from a region of a country containing tropical rainforest for children in your group. For free information on how to become a pen pal send a self-addressed, stamped envelope to Student Letter Exchange, 630 Third Ave., 15th Floor, New York, NY 10017, (212) 557-3312; or Worldwide Friendship International, P.O. Box 562, 3749A Brice Run Rd., Suite 1, Randallstown, MD 21133, (410) 922-2795; or World Pen Pals (ages 11 and up only), 1694 Como Ave., St. Paul, MN 55108, (612) 647-0191.

Ask the children to imagine what it would be like to live in a tropical rainforest. Lead a discussion during which children share their impressions and ask questions about life in a rainforest. What kinds of questions would they ask of children who do live in a rainforest region?

Pass out one piece of paper, a pencil and some crayons to each child, as well as one of the pen-pal names you acquired. Have the children write letters to their pen pals. Ask them to share something of their own lives with the pen pals, and to ask questions about what their pen pals' lives are like. Help very young children to write their thoughts down. Encourage the children to send photographs of themselves, as well as illustrations they have made. Have the children address and stamp their envelopes for you to mail.

Now read the sections of the "Discussion" that describe the traditions and lives of the Lacandon Mayan peoples of southern Mexico, as well as the Native peoples and traditions of the Pacific Northwest. There are paragraphs at the beginning of the "Discussion" about Native ways of relating to their environments, as well as brief descriptions of the Lacandon Mayans in the sections that discuss the nature of, and state of, tropical rainforests. A tragic story of the history of the Lacandon Mayan people is recalled in "State of the Rainforest: Tropical Rainforest." Allow time for the children to share their thoughts

Figure 13-5. A small sampling of products and materials that come from rainforests. In the center of the plate: coffee. On the plate, clockwise from the top: peanuts, cinnamon sticks, Brazil nuts, rice, millet, cashews and nutmeg. Surrounding the plate, from the top: pineapple, chocolate, bananas, avocado, latex gloves, cortisone cream, yam, mango, cocoa. On top: shirt made of rayon. Wood from rainforest trees is often used for making paper, cardboard and other paper products, such as the packages for the chocolate and cocoa. (Photo by Michael J. Caduto)

and feelings after they have listened to you read this information about Native peoples. Tell them there *is* something positive they can do to help. Encourage them to get involved in some projects that help Native peoples as described in the activity *"Heart-Wood: Completing the Circle With Rainforests,"* which appears later in this chapter.

Opening the Circle With Rainforests

ACTIVITY: Discuss the many gifts we receive from rainforests. Hold a masquerade party at which children wear a mask and dress up as a plant or animal from the rainforest and bring an example of food or some other product that is a gift of the rainforest.

GOALS: Understand the many gifts we receive from rainforests and that these gifts open a circle: a relationship with rainforests and the Native people who live in them. Realize the many values that are associated with rainforests and Native rainforest cultures.

AGE: Younger children and older children

MATERIALS: "Discussion," Figure 13-5, pictures and illustrations of rainforest plants and animals as well as copies of these images, paper, scissors, pencils, paper bag, chalk and chalkboard or newsprint and marker, rainforest reference books, rainforest products to share with others, materials as needed to create costumes of rainforest plants and animals such as old sheets, needle and thread, newspaper strips and wheat paste to make papier-mâché masks, tempera paint, paintbrushes and containers of water.

PROCEDURE: Beforehand, make a list of a representative sample of the plants and animals from temperate and tropical rainforests described in the "Discussion." Find pictures and/or illustrations of these plants and animals. (See the procedure described for preparing for the first activity, *"Rainforest Alive."*) Write the name of each plant or animal on small, separate slips of paper and put all the slips into a paper bag.

Ask the children to think of and share the names of as many foods and other products as possible that come from rainforests and other tropical environments. Write these names down where everyone can see them. Once the children have exhausted their ideas, share Figure 13-5 with them and any other ideas that they have not thought of that appear in the following list:

Pacific Northwest
- *Wood, wood products and things made from wood:* paper, cardboard, brown paper bags, houses, furniture, cabinets, floors, boats, plywood, particle board, wood I-beams, etc.
- *Fish and shellfish dependent on nutrients that wash downstream from the forests:* salmon, halibut, crabs, clams, oysters, etc.
- *Wild edible foods that are gathered for market* such as edible mushrooms
- *Medicine* such as taxol from the bark of the Pacific Yew (fights cancer)

Tropical Rainforests[18]

latex (rubber)	nutmeg	papayas
medicines	coffee	mahogany
chocolate	cinnamon	teak
rubber	cashews	millet
ebony	cocoa butter	rosewood
bananas	Brazil nuts	cortisone
bamboo	avocados	mangoes
peanuts	rice	pineapple
yams	rayon	

Share with the children some other gifts that they might not have thought of. Rainforests:

- are guardians of climate, soils, air and water quality.
- provide nutrients for other ecosystems.
- are habitat for hundreds of millions of plants and animals, including many threatened and endangered species.
- are home to many plants and animals that may become sources of food, medicines, etc.
- are places where scientific study and education are carried out.
- provide a livelihood for millions of people.
- are beautiful natural areas to visit for hiking, camping and other forms of recreation.
- are a quiet place to go to be close to nature.
- are the traditional homes of many Native cultures who have much to teach us about life, art, culture, nature and Earth stewardship.

Now have each child draw one piece of paper from the bag you prepared earlier, on each of which is written the name of a plant or animal from a tropical or temperate rainforest. These names are to be kept secret—children are not to tell anyone else which name they have chosen. Help each child to find and copy a picture of her or his plant or animal. In addition, help the children to locate some information that tells about their rainforest plant or animal.

Ask the children to work with their parents to create a costume and mask of this plant or animal. They can make any kind of costume they want, simple or elaborate. Be creative! Have the children learn about that plant or animal so they can tell the rest of the group about it. What does it eat? In what kind of a rainforest does it grow? Does it produce any fruits or nuts? What does it eat?

Also, have the children choose one thing from the list you generated of rainforest products. Each child is to bring in something made from his or her product, such as a dessert made with cashews, granola made with Brazil nuts, rubber gloves made of latex, a rubber bicycle tire or tube, sunscreen lotion made with cocoa butter, chocolate cookies, etc. Make sure a variety of products are chosen, including a number of foods, to make the celebration interesting and fun.

On the day of the masquerade, post the pictures and illustrations of the rainforest plants and animals that the children are dressed up as in a conspicuous place. Have the children try to guess which plant or animal each costumed child is supposed to be. Once everyone's identity has been revealed, have children tell the group what they learned about their rainforest plants or animals. Then have the children present the rainforest products they brought in and explain which plant or animal of the rainforest that product comes from. Now it is time to eat and enjoy the celebration!

Once the celebration is over, tell the children that there is a way they can return the gift to complete the circle with rainforests and the Native peoples, plants and animals that live there. Proceed with the next activity, *"Heart-Wood: Completing the Circle With Rainforests."*

Note: The children could work together to create and perform a play in which all of their costumed rainforest characters appear.

Heart-Wood:
Completing the Circle With Rainforests

ACTIVITY: Listen to an account of the respect that one traditional Native culture of the Pacific Northwest shows to trees that are being harvested. Choose, plan and conduct some activities to get involved in rainforest stewardship and the preservation of traditional cultures and ways of living.

GOALS: Understand that Native North American practices showing respect and reverence can serve as a link between traditional and contemporary stewardship toward the rainforest. Discover the many ways that we can complete the circle of giving and receiving by getting involved with preserving rainforests and helping Native cultures. Realize that the actions we take at and near home have an impact on environments and cultures throughout the world.

AGE: Younger children and older children

MATERIALS: Copy of "The Felling of a Tree," other materials needed for projects chosen.

PROCEDURE: Prepare the children as you would for a guided fantasy. Ask the children to sit comfortably, close their eyes, take a few slow deep breaths and relax. Tell them: "You are going to take a journey to another place in the Pacific Northwest where towering evergreens grow and salmon spawn in the rivers. Imagine that you are standing behind a tall cedar tree watching a Native person, someone from the Kwakiutl (Kwah-ke´-yut-ul) nation, cut down a tree to use for building a canoe. Use your senses as you listen to the story. What do you see, hear, smell and touch?" Now read the following script to the children.

THE FELLING OF A TREE

When the canoe maker is asked by one who hunts the porpoise to make for him a small canoe, he goes at once to the woods where the cedar for canoe building stands. Canoe builders always have a straight cedar in the woods picked out for canoe building. The man goes straight to the place, carrying his axe, straight to where that tree stands. He looks at where the tree will lie when it falls. He clears away the branches from the bottom of the tree. Then he begins to chop at the back of the cedar.

When he has chopped deeply, he stops and gathers four chips. He throws each of them in back of the foot of the tree where it will fall. As he throws the first chip, he says:

"*Wa, quasta*! Follow your power there."

Then he takes the second chip and throws it. As he does so he says:

"*Wa*, friend. Now you see your leader who says you shall turn your head and fall there."

He takes the third chip and throws it in the same way, saying:

"*Wa*, life-giver. Now you see where your power went. Now go the same way."

Finally he takes the fourth chip. He throws it, too, back of the tree's foot and says:

"*Wa*, friend. Now you will go where your heart-wood goes. You will lie on your face there."

As soon as he has said all this he speaks for the tree, answering himself like this:

"Yes, I shall fall with my top there."

Then he begins to chop again. As soon as he has chopped halfway through the trunk he stops and goes to the other side and begins chopping. He does not cut deeply into it before the tree begins to crack, and it does not take long until the cedar tree falls backward to the place that was prepared for it.

Wait a few moments after the story is completed and then ask the children to open their eyes. Emphasize that, traditionally, trees were used for many things, from baskets to clothes and lodges, and that parts were usually taken off the tree without cutting it down. Trees *were* cut down to make totem poles and dugout canoes. Say to the children: "Describe what you saw, heard, smelled and touched during the story. How did you feel about this person cutting down the tree? What do you think about how the person treated the tree as he was cutting it down? Are there any ways that you use things that come from plants and animals of the rainforest from the Pacific Northwest, and from the tropical rainforest? What are some important things that are made of wood from trees? Is it possible to affect the rainforests even though you live somewhere else in the world? How do you think we could do things differently to take care of the plants, animals and Native people who live in these rainforests? What could we do?"

Share information from the "Discussion" with the children that addresses the state of temperate and tropical rainforests and current threats to the well-being of these environments and the Native cultures who live in them. Now share the following list of ways to practice wise rainforest stewardship. Tell the children there are many ways we can complete the circle of giving and receiving with rainforests and the Native peoples who live there by getting involved with preserving rainforests and helping Native cultures. Have the children work in small groups to choose a project that they feel they can accomplish. Help them to make their decisions, conduct research to obtain the necessary information they will need, plan a course of action, gather the materials they will need and implement the plan.

Temperate Rainforest Stewardship: What You Can Do

Many steps can be taken by individuals and groups to get involved with the protection of ancient forests and to support sustainable forestry. An excellent book to consult for background information and activity ideas, which are applicable to both the U.S. and Canada, is *Saving Our Ancient Forests,* by Seth Zuckerman (Los Angeles: Living Planet Press and The Wilderness Society, 1991). Another good resource is *The Wild Wild World of Old-Growth Forests*, by Suzanne L. Rowe and Belinda Chin (Washington, DC: Wilderness Society, 1990). Both publications are available from The Wilderness Society, 900 17th St., N.W., Washington, DC 20006-2596. In Canada, write to the Sierra Club of Western Canada, 314-620 View St., Victoria, BC V8W 1J6. This group also has an office located at: Suite 701, 207 West Hastings, Vancouver, BC V6B-1H7.

• *Reduce, reuse and recycle* to decrease the demand for products made from wood fiber. Use less paper, recycle bags and use cloth bags, recycle waste paper, use both sides of paper, use recycled paper products, buy food in bulk to reduce packaging, share subscriptions to magazines with friends, get off mailing lists for junk mail, support businesses that practice rainforest conservation, use cloth diapers. (There is, however, some concern over the impacts of the use of hot water and detergents to wash cloth diapers versus the effects of using and discarding diapers made with paper and plastic.)

• *Use wood wisely.* The people of North America use more wood than those in any other part of the world: 1,000 board feet or 83.3 cubic feet (2.4 cubic meters) per year for a family of four.[19] Reuse scrap wood and purchase wood from salvage companies. If you must buy new wood, ask your local lumber company where the wood came from and do not buy wood that was cut from old-growth forests. Do not use redwood. Where possible, buy wood stamped Pacific Certified Ecological Forest Product (PCEFP), which designates wood sold in the U.S. that was obtained using sustainable forestry practices. Design your project wisely to require the least amount of wood. Houses made using truss framing and post-and-beam construction use much less wood than those made with standard stud walls. Use material other than wood wherever possible, such as brick and adobe.

• *Write to government officials* to support the preservation of remaining old-growth forests, sustainable forestry and an end to exporting whole logs. Send for The Wilderness Society's Wilderness Action Kit: Wilderness Society, 900 17th St., N.W., Washington, DC 20006.

In Canada write to:
— Minister of Forests, 1450 Government St., Victoria, BC V8W 3E7

In the United States write to:
— (Your Senator), U.S. Senate, Washington, DC 20510
— (Your Representative), House of Representatives, Washington, DC 20515
— Secretary of Commerce, Department of Commerce, 14th St. and Constitution Ave. N.W., Washington, DC 20230
— Chief, U.S. Forest Service, Department of Agriculture, P.O. Box 96090, Washington, DC 20090

— Director, Bureau of Land Management, 1849 C St., N.W., Room 5600, Washington, DC 20240
Express your views to the regional forester:
— Alaska: Regional Forester, Federal Office Building, Box 21628, Juneau, AK 99802
— British Columbia: Minister of Forests, 1450 Government St., Victoria, BC V8W 3E7
— Washington and Oregon: (1) Regional Forester, 333 S.W. 1st Ave., P.O. Box 3623, Portland, OR 97208, and (2) State Director, Bureau of Land Management, 1300 N.E. 44th Ave., P.O. Box 2965, Portland, OR 97208-2965
— California: Regional Forester, 630 Sansome St., San Francisco, CA 94111

• *Write to the heads of lumber firms* to express your views.

• *Keep well informed* by reading about forests in newspapers, magazines and other media.

• *Spread the news.* Publish your own newsletter to inform others about the situation with old-growth forests and their responsibilities to help protect the forests. Send this newsletter out to family, friends, local newspapers, scout groups, etc. Write letters to the editors of local newspapers.

• *Stage educational events* on Earth Day (April 22) and Arbor Day (April 27).

• *Support private groups that work to protect old-growth forests.* Volunteer and raise money to help local groups. Write to regional and national groups to ask how you can help.

To help save old-growth forests in British Columbia, write to:
— Western Canada Wilderness Committee, 20 Water St., Vancouver, BC V6B 1A4.
— Friends of Clayoquot Sound, Box 489, Tofino, BC V0R 2Z0.

To help save old-growth forests in the United States, write to:
— The Wilderness Society, 900 17th St., N.W., Washington, DC 20006-2596
— National Audubon Society, 700 Broadway, New York, NY 10003. (Ask about the "Audubon Activist," which provides information about how each person can help.)
— Sierra Club, 730 Polk St., San Francisco, CA 94109
— Western Ancient Forest Campaign, 1400 16th St., N.W., Washington, DC 20036

• *Plant a tree* as a symbolic statement of support for the forests and to reconnect yourself with trees and forests. (See Chapter 2 for tips, in "Planting Trees and Shrubs.") Use a local species of tree, or an old-growth species, as long as the tree is native to your part of North America. Set up a schedule to make sure the tree is cared for.

• *Have a tree planted in your name(s) to restore a forest, wetland and other natural environment.* Write to Global Releaf Heritage Forests, P.O. Box 2000, Washington, DC 22015.

• *Visit an old-growth forest* if you live nearby, or take a trip there on your next vacation.

Tropical Rainforest Stewardship: What You Can Do

• *Adapt all steps listed for temperate rainforest stewardship and apply them to tropical rainforests.*

• *Read and use: The Rainforest Book: How You Can Save the World's Rainforests,* by Scott Lewis with the Natural Resources Defense Council (New York: Berkley Books, 1993), or any of a number of available books that provide information and ideas for tropical rainforest stewardship.

• *Contact and help groups that support indigenous peoples.* Here are two suggestions:

— Cultural Survival, 215 First St., Cambridge, MA 02142

— COICA, c/o CONFENIAE, P.O. Box Casilla 4180, Quito, Ecuador.

• *Avoid buying and using materials and products that come from tropical rainforest ranches and mismanaged forests,* such as beef produced in countries where rainforests are cleared for cattle ranches. Do not buy exotic woods, such as ebony, mahogany, rosewood, teak, purpleheart and zebrawood, unless you know they were produced sustainably. Ask local stores, especially food markets, where their products come from. For more information on these products, write to:

— Rainforest Action Network, 450 Sansome, Suite 700, San Francisco, CA 94111

• *Substitute products you already use with rainforest products that are produced sustainably:* nuts, oils, fruits, cosmetics, breakfast cereals, etc. Some groups, such as Cultural Survival of Boston (see address above) and Community Products, Inc., of Montpelier, Vermont, are creating products from sustainably produced forest materials and selling them in North America and beyond. This practice also supports the livelihoods of Native people who live in rainforest regions.

• *Become a Guardian of the Rainforest* and help local peoples to protect and sustainably manage rainforest lands. Write to:

— World Wildlife Fund/Canada, 90 Eglinton Ave., E., Suite 504, Toronto, ON M4P 2Z7. World Wildlife Fund Canada offers several programs and publications that teach about tropical rainforests and get children involved with saving tropical rainforests. "Schools for the Rainforest" includes a publication and a "Protect-an-Acre" program. A video, teacher's kit and book are available under the "Rainforest Lifeline" program.

• *Join one of the many rainforest protection groups and support their efforts.*

• *Write to corporations that are exploiting rainforests and express your views.*

• *Raise money to adopt and protect an acre of rainforest.* Contact:

— Adopt-an-Acre Program, The Nature Conservancy, 1815 N. Lynn St., Arlington, VA 22209

• *Write the governor of Hawaii to express how much you value the rainforest there and want to see it protected.* Write to:

— Governor of Hawaii, Executive Chamber, State Capitol, Honolulu, HI 96813

• *View the video called The Decade of Destruction,*which is available from Bull Frog Films, P.O. Box 149, Oley, PA 19547 (800-543-FROG). Use this video in conjunction with the book of the same title, by Adrian Cowell (Henry Holt).

• *Start a wildlife refuge on the grounds of the home or learning center* and make connections with rainforest stewardship in other parts of North America.

• *Visit a rainforest.*

EXTENDING THE EXPERIENCE

• Visit a rainforest exhibit at a nearby botanical garden or zoo to experience firsthand some rainforest plants and (in a zoo) animals (Figure 13-6). Use this visit as a time to ask questions about these places as habitats: "What do you think it is like for a plant or animal to live here? Why do you think botanical gardens and zoos are important for these living things?" Get

Figure 13-6. Tropical rainforest exhibits at botanical gardens, museums and zoos are exciting environments full of opportunities for learning firsthand about the plants and animals of these fascinating ecosystems. (Photo courtesy the Missouri Botanical Garden)

involved in both the onsite educational experiences and the outreach programs offered by the place you visit.

• Create a rainforest poster to inform others about rainforest values and the need to protect them.

• Watch the movies *The Emerald Forest* and *Medicine Man* (older children) and *Fern Gully: The Last Rainforest* (younger children).

• Locate rainforests on a map of North America.

• Use the activity *"Tree of Life"* from Chapter 14 and apply it to threatened and endangered rainforest species, such as the Pacific yew, salmon and northern spotted owl in the Pacific Northwest; the jaguarundi, black howler monkey, Central American tapir or resplendent quetzel in the Mexican rainforest; or the 'Oha wai (an endangered Hawaiian bellflower).

• Read some children's books on rainforests that are listed in the Teacher's Guide bibliography.

• Visit a football field and look at it while telling the children that a tract of tropical rainforest of that same size is being cut every second. Calculate the surface area of the football field and use this figure to calculate how many football fields would fit into an area the size of your town or village. Using this information, calculate how long it would take for a rainforest the size of your town or village to be cut down at the present rate of destruction.

• Arrange for the children to have a tour of a logging operation near your community, including a question-and-answer session with the operators and loggers.

• Read the Haida story "Salmon Boy" from Chapter 9 in *Keepers of the Animals.*

• Obtain and use a copy of the rainforest curriculum called *The Vanishing Forest* for grades 2–6, available from World Wildlife Fund, P.O. Box 4866, Hampden P.O., Baltimore, MD 21211.

• Contact the following organization for tropical rainforest information, resource lists, booklets, posters, suggestions for starting grassroots programs and current legislative actions you can take:

— National Wildlife Federation International Program, 1400 16th St., N.W., Washington, DC 20036.

• Contact the following organization for information on how to get children involved with saving cloudforest land in Guatemala:

— National Audubon Society, Adopt-An-Acre Program, 2525 Wallingford, Suite 301, Austin, TX 78746.

NOTES

1. Catherine Caufield, *In the Rainforest* (Chicago: University of Chicago Press, 1991), 125.

2. Elliot A. Norse, *Ancient Forests of the Pacific Northwest* (Washington, DC: Island Press, 1990), 120.

3. Seth Zuckerman, *Saving Our Ancient Forests* (Los Angeles: Living Planet, 1991), 109.

4. Associated Press, "Yew Trees Spared by Progress With Synthetic Cancer Drug," *Boston Globe* (31 January 1993): 11.

5. John C. Kricher, *A Neotropical Companion: An Introduction to the Animals, Plants and Ecosystems of the New World Tropics* (Princeton, N.J.: Princeton University Press, 1989), 87.

6. Edward O. Wilson, *The Diversity of Life* (Cambridge, Mass.: Belknap Press, 1992), 197.

7. Ibid., 132–133.

8. States News Service, "U.S. Shelves Study Saying Logging Threatens Alaska Wildlife," *Boston Globe* (29 December 1992): 5.

9. Wilson, *Diversity of Life*, 275.

10. Norman Myers, *The Gaia Atlas of Future Worlds* (New York: Anchor/Doubleday, 1990), 28.

11. Ibid., 140.

12. Caufield, *In the Rainforest,* 126.

13. U.S. GAO, "Better Regulation of Pesticide Exports and Pesticide Residues in Imported Foods Is Essential" (Washington, DC: U.S. GAO, Rept. No CED-79-43, June 22, 1979): iii, 39. Quoted in David Weir and Mark Schapiro, *Circle of Poison* (San Francisco: Institute for Food and Development Policy, 1981), 4.

14. Final Report, Instituto Centro-Americano De Investigacion y Technologia Industrial (I.C.A.I.T.I.), "An Environmental and Economic Study of the Consequences of Pesticide Use in Central American Cotton Production" (January 1977): 128–132. Quoted in Weir and Schapiro, *Circle of Poison*, 13.

15. Weir and Shapiro, *Circle of Poison,* 13.

16. Kathryn A. Kohm, "A Native American Resource Management Planning System for Land Stewardship," *Forest Perspectives*, vol. 1, no. 2 (Summer 1991): 14. For more information, write to Native American Forestry Program, Northern Arizona University School of Forestry, P.O. Box 4098, Flagstaff, AZ 86011.

17. Zuckerman, *Saving Our Ancient Forests*, 61–68.

18. Stephen C. Crowley and Betsy Brigham, *Tropical Rainforests: The Vermont Connection* (Montpelier: Vermont Natural Resources Council, 1992), 54.

19. Zuckerman, *Saving Our Ancient Forests*, 85.

There were many seeds on the tall grass. Waynabozho used a stick to knock off many of the seeds into his bark container.

CHAPTER 14

✦ Waynabozho and the Wild Rice ✦

(Anishinabe {Ojibwa or Chippewa}—Eastern Woodland)

One day, when Waynabozho was out walking around, his grandmother called him to her lodge.

"Grandson," Nokomis said, "it is time for you to go to some distant place in the forest and fast. Then a dream may come to you to help the people yet to come."

But Waynabozho did not like the idea of walking so far.

"I will go in my canoe," he said. Then he began paddling along from lake to lake.

Waynabozho had not gone far when he saw tall grasses growing from the shallow waters at the edge of the fourth lake he entered. He liked the way that tall grass looked. There were many seeds on that tall grass, and he took a big piece of birch bark and made it into a basket. Then he used a stick to knock off many of those seeds into his bark container. When he was done, he took the seeds back to his grandmother.

"Look what I have found," he said. "The tall grass that held these seeds is very fine to look at. Let us plant these seeds along the shores of our own lake so we will have those grasses to look at from our lodge."

Nokomis did as Waynabozho asked. She helped him scatter the seeds along the edge of the lake.

"Now Grandson," she said, "you must continue on your way. You must go out and fast and hope that something good will be given to you."

So Waynabozho set out again in his canoe. He went from lake to lake and then he just leaned back in his canoe and let the boat drift. "I can wait here for a dream," he said. "Why should I trouble myself to walk?" He went without food all the rest of that day.

"This fasting is easy," Waynabozho said. "I will surely have a strong dream come to me soon." But no dream came and he fell asleep as he drifted along in his canoe.

The next day came and when Waynabozho woke up he was unable to think of anything but food. He felt hungrier than he had ever felt before. As the canoe drifted along he saw some plants growing along the shore.

"Boozhoo, Waynabozho," the plants said. "Helloo! Are you hungry? You can dig one of us up and eat the root. Then you will no longer be hungry at all."

"Ah," Waynabozho said, paddling his canoe quickly to the shore. "This must be the vision I was waiting for. I have fasted a very long time. I must do as these plants tell me to do." Then he began to dig up the plants. He did not just dig up one, he dug them all and ate their roots.

But when Waynabozho was finished eating, he began to feel very sick. Just as the plants had said, he was no longer hungry at all. He became so sick that he could not move. He lay there for three days and three nights. Finally, on the fourth day, he found enough strength to drag himself back into his canoe and paddle weakly toward home.

But when he was within sight of their lodge, he saw new plants growing from the shallow water of the lake.

"Waynabozho," these new plants said, "sometimes we can be eaten."

Carefully, Waynabozho picked some of the seedheads of those plants. He sprinkled some of the seeds back into the water before he ate. Those plants tasted good and he no longer felt weak and sick after eating them.

"What are you called?" he said.

"We are Manomin," said the wild rice plants. "You are the one who planted us here. Do you not remember?"

Then Waynabozho collected many of the seedheads of the wild rice, leaning the plants over and scraping them gently with a stick as he had done before. He made sure to let some of the seeds go into the water as he did this. That is how wild rice is gathered to this day by the Anishinabe. And as Waynabozho paddled home he knew that he would have much to tell his grandmother. He had succeeded in his quest. He had found something good for the people yet to come.

DISCUSSION

Waynabozho is generous during his quest to help future generations in the Anishinabe story "Waynabozho and the Wild Rice." When he finds the seeds of *Manomin*, wild rice, he does not eat them but helps Grandmother Nokomis plant them along the shores of their lake so they can admire the beauty of this tall grass. Later, Waynabozho gathers seeds of the wild rice, sprinkles some into the water and allows others to fall into the lake before eating any. Waynabozho shares and succeeds in his appointed task, leaving a legacy of a new food for the people.

To this day the Anishinabe and other Algonquian peoples gather wild rice in canoes by tapping the seedheads with sticks. Only about 10 to 20 percent of the seeds produced by wild rice are gathered by hand harvesting, or "ricing." Northern wild rice, *Zizania palustris,* is sown by the traditional Anishinabe in marshes and along shallow lakeshores. In fact, many ricing grounds are well known for the particular varieties of wild rice that have been cultivated there for generations. The Kakagon Slough, located along the shores of Lake Superior in the Bad River Indian Reservation, Wisconsin, offers about 400 acres (162 hectares) of wild rice to be harvested each year.[1] During the First Fruits ceremony, held during the late summer when the rice ripens, thanks and gifts are given to Gitchee Manitou and the spirits of the plants, water and Earth.

But this delicate balance has been upset. Habitat destruction and pollution have destroyed and continue to threaten many ricing grounds. Foreign cultures and alien plants who arrived during the past few centuries have outcompeted the Native peoples and their revered wild rice. One plant, purple loosestrife, takes over the habitat and overruns rice plants. The Anishinabe also struggle with legal battles for the right to gather wild rice on land located off the reservation.

In other parts of North America, where the ecosystems that Native people have been part of have been altered or destroyed and the People can no longer take care of plants such as wild rice, external forces are wreaking havoc on species after species. Texas wild rice, *Zizania texana,* which grows in the land of the Comanche and Tonkawa peoples, has been reduced by pollution, habitat destruction and boaters to one small wild patch along the San Marcos River. There may soon be nothing left but a small, captive-bred population at Southwest Texas State University.[2]

* * *

This discussion looks at endangered species and the causes of endangerment and extinction. Any discussion of endangered species and extinction evokes feelings of sadness and, at times, even despair. However, there is indeed *hope* for endangered species and for us human beings who hold their fate in our hands. This chapter ends with a discussion of success stories describing species that have been saved from extinction—some of which are out of immediate danger. There is also a section describing how people can work to make Earth a safe home for plants as well as specific actions to take to help save endangered species.

The Values of Species

Why is every species so important? Human beings tend to place far more emphasis on endangered animals than we do on endangered plants, but plants are an integral and essential part of the ecosystems that support all life in the wild. *All* species contribute to the whole, interdependent system. Consider the many irreplaceable *values* that every species possesses:

• *ecological,* as sources of genetic and biological diversity and stability, as warnings or signs of environmental health, as threads in the web of life and, with plants, as sources of life-giving oxygen and energy at the base of the food chain

• *utilitarian and economic (commercial),* since plants are used for food and drink, clothing, shelter, medicine, fuel and many products (building materials, rubber, paper, rope, lubricants ...)

• *educational and scientific,* as teachers to help us understand our environments and ourselves

- *historical,* connecting us with our own cultural past and that of Earth
- *recreational,* for our enjoyment while we are engaged in outdoor activities
- *aesthetic and symbolic,* as sources of beauty, inspiration and wildness
- *spiritual,* as sources of our connections with all our relations on Earth, both human and wild, and satisfying our subconscious need for *biophilia,* which means connections with the rest of life on Earth, including wilderness untouched by human hands[3]
- *inherent or intrinsic,* the value a species possesses simply by virtue of its existence and being, regardless of whatever values people do or do not attribute to it
- *ethical,* that species have the right to exist, and that human beings play a stewardship role to preserve, not destroy, other species

Figure 14-1. All species possess a full range of values worth protecting. The Tiburon mariposa lily, which grows only on one site in Marin County, California, is the first state-listed plant to have its status upgraded from endangered to threatened. The lily's existence had been jeopardized by residential development and off-road vehicular traffic until the Nature Conservancy purchased and protected its habitat. Size: about 20 in. (50 cm) tall. (Photo by Richard York, courtesy the California Native Plant Society)

Biological diversity, or *biodiversity,* is an overriding ecological principle that recognizes that every species and each habitat possesses the full range of values just described. Every plant has unique, genetically endowed qualities of pest resistance, drought tolerance, adaptability to various soils, tolerance to heat and cold, nutritional and medicinal uses and flavors (Figure 14-1). When a species or habitat is lost, its particular values are gone forever, decreasing the biological diversity of an ecosystem. Biodiversity measures the adaptability of any ecosystem, even the global ecosphere, and is a major determinant of whether or not that ecosystem can survive. The greater the number and variety of species and habitats, the greater chance an ecosystem has to adapt to and survive change. The increasing population of humanity and the stresses we place on the ecosphere are decreasing biodiversity to a level not seen since the dinosaurs disappeared 65 million years ago at the end of the Mesozoic Era.[4] It took 5 million to 10 million years for Earth's diversity to recover after that great extinction. At the current rate of extinction, more than half of Earth's species will be wiped out by the mid-twenty-first century.

Threats to Species Survival

The effects of people on wild plant populations have been devastating. *Threats* to the continued well-being, and even existence, of many species are serious and widespread, including:

- *burgeoning human populations* and competition with plants for available resources
- *habitat destruction and decimation,* including urbanization, deforestation, landfills for the disposal of human refuse, mining and desertification and the resulting erosion
- *the introduction of exotic species* that compete with indigenous plants for food, water and cover
- *the introduction of alien diseases* that often accompany exotic species
- *the overcollecting of plants* for ornamentals, medicines and other commercial plant "products"
- *poaching and other uncontrolled, illegal activities* that decimate plant populations
- *global warming* (the *greenhouse effect*) and the expected *sea-level rise* that will result
- *acid rain* and other forms of *air pollution*
- *ozone depletion* and the resulting increased exposure to harmful solar ultraviolet radiation
- *pesticides, herbicides and other toxic compounds* that poison the food chain
- *surface- and ground-water pollution*
- *toxic waste* buildup and environmental contamination
- *disturbance and stress* caused by contact with humans involved in recreational activities such as hiking, photography, boating and skiing
- *the gradually deteriorating quality of the ecosphere* that all of these problems produce

Overpopulation is the greatest threat to the existence of many plant species due to the effects of our direct contact with plants, habitat destruction, pollution and other human impacts. Today's population of more than 5 billion people is expected to double to 10 billion in 50 years. Ninety percent of this growth will occur in developing countries where rainforests grow.

We compete with plants for available water, habitat and other resources. We gather plants in the wild and grow the varieties we prefer in the habitats from which we have displaced native species. We use plants for everything from sustenance to construction and ornamentation. With the survival of millions of species on the line, how far are we willing to go in living closer to our *needs* versus fulfilling our *desires,* to reduce the consumption that is driven by materialism?

Wild plants are companions in leisure; we fill our homes with their verdure and seek the green surroundings of nature while camping, hiking, photographing wildflowers and during other *recreational activities.* We prize the sight of rare and endangered plants. Certain forms of recreation, however, such as the use of off-road vehicles in sand dunes and deserts, are destroying the last known habitats for many plant species. Even well-meaning contact with plants in the wild often beats down and destroys their habitats. In some areas, such as rainforests, tourism is having disastrous effects on the habitats of native species. Many activities help people to be more aware of the plight of these plants, but how do these activities affect the plants' chances for survival?

Without an environment to meet a plant's needs it cannot survive. If *habitat destruction* continues at the present rate, we will lose 20 percent of the species alive today within the next 30 years. Vast amounts of natural habitat are used for logging, grazing, agriculture and urban development. The astounding rates at which tropical and temperate rainforests are being cleared (see Chapter 13) are causing extinctions among many known species and others that are not yet identified. Destruction of plant habitat spells disaster for animal species. The drop in the populations of migratory North American songbirds in recent years has been linked to decreases in their wintering habitats in the tropical forests of Mexico, Central America, the Caribbean and the West Indies. This alarming decline—averaging 3 percent each year since the late 1970s—is also due to the large-scale loss and fragmentation of summer breeding habitat in North America because of agriculture, urbanization and other developments, as well as to disturbance by feral cats, dogs, raccoons and other animals.

The activities associated with energy production have altered, polluted and destroyed significant amounts of plant habitat. Acid runoff from coal mines poisons passing streams and bodies of water downstream, killing algae and other aquatics. Oil spills in marine habitats disrupt the base of the food chain and degrade the quality of affected habitat for years to come.

Hydroelectric dams have flooded vast amounts of North American habitat. Half of the 15 sites originally identified where giant helleborine, a threatened plant in Canada, has been found growing were flooded by hydroelectric projects. The enormous hydroelectric dams and reservoirs in the James Bay region of Canada are a catastrophe for plant habitat, indigenous wildlife and the Cree and Inuit peoples of that region. James Bay I flooded 4,440 square miles (11,500 square kilometers) of habitat, including fish spawning areas, caribou calving grounds and migratory bird habitat. Areas where bush and forest once grew were flooded. High ground is mostly just exposed rock. (See "The Coniferous Forests" in the "Discussion," Chapter 8, for a description of the boreal forest of this region.) Other impacts of this project include:[5]

• the loss of vast areas of forest land, increasing the greenhouse effect as the carbon dioxide absorption capacity of those trees is lost. The decaying vegetation also releases carbon dioxide, methane and other "greenhouse gases," further accelerating the greenhouse effect.
• the disruption of the seasonal flow of fresh water into the seas, especially during the growing season, severely decreasing the productivity of plants at the base of estuarine food chains.
• the leaching of naturally occurring methyl mercury out of flooded soils, causing this heavy metal to enter the food chain, poisoning people, fish and other wildlife.

Changes of this kind are eroding the Native cultural, environmental and spiritual contexts that are so tightly intertwined with the local environment. The Cree, Inuit and Innu peoples of northern Quebec have suffered greatly from many changes, including:

• the flooding of villages, as well as hunting, trapping and fishing grounds.
• the depletion and destruction of native fisheries due to mercury poisoning and the destruction of spawning grounds.
• mercury poisoning among people who have eaten tainted fish and wildlife, particularly children, who are the most susceptible and for whom, traditionally, the first solid food is mashed whitefish. The limited alternatives in this remote land are to either eat contaminated fish or go without.
• a shift from the traditional subsistence life to a monetary economy. Jobs are few and mostly involved with building the dam. Some Native people left the local community and tried to assimilate elsewhere, where racism, poverty and alienation led to a high rate of drug abuse, alcoholism and suicide.

The proposed James Bay II project would flood an additional 1,614 square miles (4,180 square kilometers) of land, in addition to creating a 774-square-mile (2,005-square-kilometer) storage reservoir by flooding Lake Bienville. If James Bay II is completed by Hydro-Quebec, the total area that is actually flooded (the *impacted* area will be far greater) by both James Bay projects will exceed the combined land area of the states of Connecticut and Rhode Island.

East of James Bay II, two large hydroelectric dams have been proposed by Newfoundland and Labrador Hydro for the lower Churchill River in *Nitassinan,* the homeland of the Innu people, the Quebec/Labrador Peninsula. The *Innu* (Montagnais Naskapi) are related culturally and linguistically to the James Bay Cree. The Churchill Valley is rich in plant diversity, but these two dams would flood 66 square miles (172 square kilometers), almost the entire river valley, to generate power for sale to Hydro-Quebec. These dams are linked to the completion of the Trans-Labrador Highway, which would fragment the habitat and provide easy access to the area for clear-cutting, mines (aluminum smelting), development, outfitters and non-Innu hunters.

Introducing *exotic species* to an area can contribute to major declines in native plant populations and significant ecological disturbances. Roughly 1,800 exotic or *alien* plant species have been introduced into, and become established in, North America's habitats. About 170 species of alien ferns and other plants have invaded the state of Florida and now account for 16 percent of Florida's plant species. Many of these plants outcompete native species, reduce their former range and decrease diversity in native ecosystems. In many cases, the foreign diseases that often accompany introduced species have all but wiped out entire native populations. Examples of the impacts that alien species and diseases are having on native plants are seemingly without end:

• Water hyacinth, an aquatic weed from South America, is choking waterways in the south.
• Canada thistle (originally from Eurasia) is outcompeting the native Colorado butterfly plant.
• American chestnut blight, caused by a fungus from Asia, has reduced this once-dominant tree of the eastern forests (now a threatened species in Canada) to mere root sprouts throughout its range.
• Tall fescue from Europe displaces native eastern grama-grass and other plants on the Texas prairie.
• Ecosystems in western states and provinces have been overrun with exotic species, including Pampas grass and brooms on cut slopes and other environments, European beach grass in Pacific coast dune habitats and Eurasian grasses and forbs in California's Central Valley.
• Populations of Eurasian milfoil are ballooning and choking waterways in the East.
• Dutch elm disease, a fungus spread by a bark beetle, continues to kill the remaining trees of the once-common American elm.
• Australian fireweed is spreading throughout the U.S. Southwest and the pine-like Australian *Casuarina* tree grows so thickly on sandy beaches in Florida that sea turtles and alligators cannot rest or nest.
• Kudzu vine from Asia has overrun enormous tracts of southeastern countryside like an alien invader out of a grade B movie.

• Purple loosestrife from Europe crowds out native marsh species, which are more valuable for wildlife food and cover, in marshes from Newfoundland to Minnesota down to North Carolina.
• Lantana in Hawaii is driving some native species to extinction.

The negative effects of human activity upon plants are not always inadvertent. Many threatened and endangered plants are *collected* and *poached* for international *commercial trade,* including the lucrative *ornamental plant market* (Figure 14-2). Cacti and orchids are prized by plant collectors and poachers. Texas has been hard hit, especially regarding small, spherical cacti that work well as potted plants for the window sill. About a half-million such cactus plants were collected each year in Texas during the mid-1970s.[6] One species of cactus, *Epithelantha bokei,* which grows inside Big Bend National Park, has been so heavily poached that it is now a threatened species.

It is predicted that *global warming*—the *greenhouse effect*—will have a profound effect upon plants, especially those species living in the cold temperate and polar regions. (See Chapter 7 for information and activities on the greenhouse effect.) As the climate warms, those plants living in the Arctic and subarctic, as well as plants in other habitats where the climate is altered, would perish, especially species that could not adapt or "migrate" quickly enough to suitable climates. In addition, as the polar ice caps melt and sea levels rise several feet, coastal habitats would be flooded and weather patterns around the globe altered, resulting in widespread droughts and floods.

Acid rain (acid precipitation) is a pervasive form of air pollution at the leading edge of a general decline in the quality of the global environment. (See Chapter 5 for information and activities on acid rain.) Acidity has killed life in hundreds of waterways worldwide, especially in industrialized nations. Acid rain is also causing a decline in the growth of conifers at high elevations and has been implicated in the decline of numerous deciduous trees in eastern forests.

Another atmospheric pollution problem, *depletion of the ozone layer* in the upper atmosphere, is also affecting plants. Ozone-destroying chemicals such as chlorofluorocarbons (CFCs), which are found in refrigerants and air conditioners, and bromine, which is contained in household fire extinguishers and fumigants, are causing significant seasonal losses of ozone in polar and midlatitude areas.[7] Since ozone filters out the sun's harmful ultraviolet (U.V.) "B" radiation, increasingly more U.V. is reaching Earth's surface as the ozone layer is depleted. The effects of ozone loss and exposure to this U.V. radiation over time include increases in skin cancers and cataracts among humans and other animals, suppression of the immune systems in plants and animals, decreases in crop productivity and harvests as well as suspected damage to the ocean's vital plant life, particularly the microscopic phytoplankton that comprise the base of the marine food chain.[8]

The combined impacts of several environmental hazards often produce a *synergistic* effect, in which the damage done is greater than the sum total of the harm expected to be caused by the two agents. A plant or animal whose resistance has been lowered, for example, is more susceptible to the ill effects of diseases and environmental toxins.

DDT and other contaminants pose a serious threat to many species and have brought some perilously close to extinction. Pesticides, herbicides and other toxins become incorporated into the tissues of plants at the bottom of the food chain. Through *biomagnification,* certain toxins become concentrated in the tissues of those animals near the top of the food chain. Each time a sparrow, for instance, eats contaminated seeds, it absorbs and stores more toxin. Peregrine falcons and other predators concentrate toxins in their tissues with each sparrow they consume. Declines in populations of contaminated animals, such as the peregrine falcon, bald eagle and brown pelican, have served as important indicators of environmental health. (See Chapter 17 in *Keepers of the Animals.*)

Endangerment and Extinction

Rare or *vulnerable species* do not face an immediate threat but are likely to become threatened in time because their numbers are declining and/or they occur in a restricted range. Some species may be listed as rare in one region while they may even be abundant somewhere else. If the surviving population of a species is so low that the species could face extinction if the population declined further, it is a *threatened species.* Members of an *endangered species* are so threatened they are in immediate danger of becoming *extinct,* of being wiped out completely from the face of Earth. A species has been *extirpated* from part of its range when it no longer exists in an area it once inhabited. Some species that are *extinct in the wild* now exist only in captivity, such as in botanical gardens, seed banks and zoos.

During Earth's 4.5 billion years there have been five periods of mass extinction. Human beings are causing the sixth. Of Earth's estimated 30 million species of plants, animals and microbes, one-quarter or more will become extinct by 2010 if we do not act now. Some species will be gone before they are discovered. At the present, accelerating rate of extinction, around 400 plant species become extinct worldwide each year. From 15 to 25 percent, about 40,000, of all known species of higher plants will be lost by the year 2000.[9] There are about 11 animal species in the world for each species of plant: 50 to 100 animal species become extinct each day.

Figure 14-2. Orchids, such as the beautiful pink and white showy lady's slipper, have been overpicked to the point that they are rare in many places. As with numerous plants, habitat destruction reduced the number of lady's slippers over much of their range, causing them to become so vulnerable that it is illegal to collect them from the wild in many states. Size: 1 to 3 ft. (30.5 to 91.4 cm). (Photo by Alan C. Graham)

Records kept by the Center for Plant Conservation (figures include Hawaii) indicate the status of native plants in the United States: 228 plants have become extinct in the United States during the past 200 years and nearly 700 U.S. plants (mostly in southern regions) are threatened with extinction by the year 2000. Better than 97 percent of Hawaii's native species are threatened, more than 800 are endangered and more than 273 have already become extinct. California's floristic province, which stretches from southern Oregon to Baja, California, contains one-quarter of all species of plants found in both the United States and Canada. About one-half, 2,140 species, grow nowhere else in the world. This environment, especially the central and southern coasts of California, is being destroyed by urban expansion and conversion of land to agriculture.

THREATENED AND ENDANGERED NORTH AMERICAN PLANTS.
In the United States, threatened and endangered species are protected by the Endangered Species Act of 1973, which is administered by the Endangered Species Program of the U.S. Department of the Interior, Fish and Wildlife Service.[10] About 1,100 species are expected to be on the list of *Endangered and Threatened Wildlife and Plants* by 1996. Of the more than 760 species now listed, about 200 are holding steady or increasing and the rest are in decline. Just 5 species have recovered enough to be removed from the list. Seven *registered* endangered species have become extinct over the past 20 years but more than 80 plants and animals have become extinct since 1973 while *waiting* to be reviewed and placed on the endangered species list.[11] The waiting list of vulnerable species now stands at about 400. Three thousand more are being evaluated whose status is considered to be less tenuous. Only 1 plant and 4 animals have recovered and been removed from the list. On the average, only 120 individuals remain in populations of listed plants.

In Canada, the government group that determines and monitors the status of wildlife species is the Committee on the Status of Endangered Wildlife in Canada (COSEWIC).[12] This is a coalition of governmental conservation agencies and private environmental groups. Endangered species are also protected from international trade in endangered wildlife and wildlife products by the Convention on International Trade in Endangered Species of Wild Flora and Fauna (CITES). Under CITES, signature countries restrict and control the import and export of species on the list. Enforcement of CITES is spotty. TRAFFIC (Trade Record Analysis of Flora and Fauna in Commerce) is an organization that monitors international trade in species.

Some species are threatened and/or endangered in both Canada and the United States. *Furbish's lousewort* is a small perennial with variable red and yellow flowers that grows in small patches along shady, eroded banks of the St. John River between Maine and New Brunswick. This species is listed as endangered in both countries and has stopped several dams proposed by the U.S. Army Corps of Engineers that would have flooded nearly all of its remaining habitat.

Some such dam proposals are still pending. Few projects, however, are actually blocked by the U.S. Endangered Species Act. Just 19 of 71,808 proposed development projects reviewed by the government between 1987–1991 were stopped because of consideration for endangered species.[13]

Among the rarest blooms in North America are the diminutive, greenish-yellow flowers of the *small whorled pogonia,* an orchid that is listed as endangered in both the United States and Canada. Only about 1,500 plants remain scattered in 30 or so colonies. In Canada, the small whorled pogonia is restricted to a single site in southwestern Ontario, while in the United States it occurs in numerous eastern and southeastern states and as far west as Missouri.

American ginseng is thought to be an aphrodisiac and a cure for an array of ailments from coughs and headaches to rheumatism. Ginseng bears a delicate head of white or yellowish flowers with a tinge of greenish pastel. It grows in the deep shade of rich, moist woodlands throughout eastern North America but is not common in many areas. Because ginseng is heavily collected throughout and is scarce in the northern U.S. and southern Canada, it is listed as threatened in southern Ontario, southwestern Quebec and in many states. Ginseng is an endangered species in certain states. Export is prohibited in Ontario and Quebec and export permits are needed under the CITES treaty.

The *eastern mountain avens* is endangered in Canada: it occurs only on Brier Island in western Nova Scotia. Small with bright yellow flowers, this rare plant is also found in the high alpine communities of New Hampshire's White Mountains. It prefers sphagnum bogs, wet coastal habitats and exposed mineral soil.

Many Canadian plant species are listed as threatened (T) or endangered (E) (Figure 14-3). Several species, including the *southern maidenhair fern* (E) and *giant helleborine* (T), grow around hot springs at the northern edge of their range. Other listed Canadian species include:

nodding pogonia (T)	Tyrrell's willow (T)
pink milkwort (E)	small white lady's slipper (E)
slender bush clover (E)	cucumber tree (E)
pitcher's thistle (T)	eastern prickly pear cactus (E)
pink coreopsis (E)	heart-leaved plantain (E)
water pennywort (E)	hoary mountain mint (E)
mosquito fern (T)	American chestnut (T)
Athabasca thrift (T)	bluehearts (T)

The list of endangered and threatened species found throughout the United States is long and growing (Figure 14-3). Here are a few examples:

Arizona agave (E)	Minnesota trout lily (E)
four-petaled pawpaw (E)	Ash Meadows blazing-star (T)
Loch Lomond coyote-thistle (E)	Texas wild rice (E)
Bradshaw's desert-parsley (E)	Robbins' cinquefoil (E)
Eureka dunegrass (E)	sandplain gerardia (E)
Key tree-cactus (E)	salt-marsh bird's-beak (E)

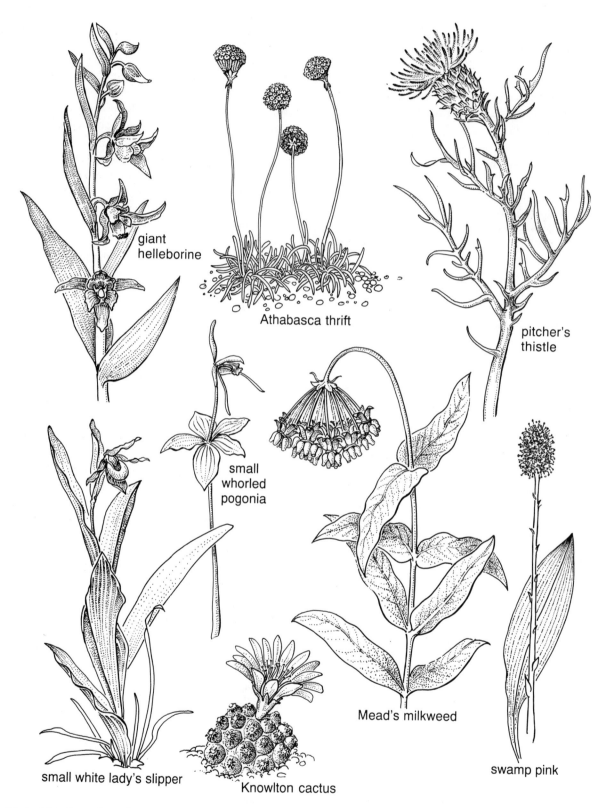

Figure 14-3. Some plants that are threatened or endangered in Canada (Can) and/or the United States (US). Sizes are given after the name of each plant. (Clockwise from the upper left): giant helleborine (Can), 1 to 3 ft. (30.5 to 91.4 cm); Athabasca thrift (Can), 6 to 10 in. (15.2 to 25.4 cm); pitcher's thistle (Can), to 3.3 ft. (1 m); swamp pink (US), 1 to 3 ft. (30.5 to 91.4 cm); Mead's milkweed (US), to 2 ft. (61 cm); Knowlton cactus (US), to 1.5 in. (3.8 cm); small whorled pogonia (Can, US), 4 to 10 in. (10.2 to 25.4 cm); small white lady's slipper (Can), 6 to 15 in. (15.2 to 38.1 cm). (Illustration by Marjorie C. Leggitt)

Mead's milkweed (T) Alabama streak-sorus fern (T)
Na'ena'e (E) Tennessee yellow-eyed grass (E)
Peebles Navajo cactus (E) swamp pink (T)

Back From the Brink: Species Recovery

While some plants now exist only in domestic cultivation, such as the small southern tree *Franklinia alatahama*, which was last seen in the wild in the late 1700s, many efforts to save plants now focus on preserving habitat. Threatened and endangered species require a minimum of *critical habitat*—the land, water and air space needed to meet the needs of a species and assure its survival. The Nature Conservancy has preserved habitats all around the world, including many large areas that encompass entire ecosystems. Other groups, such as the Society for Ecological Restoration in Madison, Wisconsin, restore, create and manage critical species habitat. You, too, can help. One gardener in southern Florida created a 1-acre pine rockland habitat with 200 to 300 species of plants, many of which have largely disappeared outside Everglades National Park.

Still, endangered plant species do not receive the attention given to endangered animals. As far as recovery plans for particular species go, which would include captive breeding and efforts at reintroduction to former habitats, Canadian biologists assert that, with the exception of Furbish's lousewort in Canada, "Too little is being done about the plant species to warrant a detailed summary." One plant that was extinct in the wild and has been reestablished in its native habitat is a kind of Hawaiian mallow, *Hibiscadelphus giffardianus*.

THE ROAD TO RECOVERY. Saving the threatened and endangered species of the world is going to require *conservation; habitat protection,* particularly for critical habitat; *sharing* of Earth's resources, not hoarding them to the exclusion of others; *sacrifices* to help plants by getting back to our needs and doing without some of our wants; and a sustained *commitment.*

Edward O. Wilson, the noted specialist in biodiversity, estimates that if we take strong action to preserve plants and their habitats now we may be able to keep the loss of species to around 10 percent of those that presently exist over the next 30 years.[14] Worldwide, there is a need to survey the existing flora and fauna, to preserve the remaining species and habitats, to instill in people an awareness of the value of biological wealth in order to create a desire to preserve species, to restore wild populations and to promote sustainable development. The specific steps required during the long, difficult journey to recovery for an endangered species include:

- *legal protection* and listing on the register of threatened and endangered species
- the design and implementation of a *recovery plan*
- *habitat protection*
- *habitat cleanup,* such as the ban on DDT
- *habitat management* to maintain and restore conditions required by that species
- *captive breeding and propagation*

- *reintroduction into former habitat* in the wild
- a substantial *investment* of human energy and financial resources
- *coordinated efforts* of both governmental and private conservation agencies and groups
- *education* for public awareness

Botanical gardens and *seed banks* are a survival safety net for plants that are rare or even extinct in the wild, and they preserve a genetic pool of plants and seeds of threatened and endangered species. Here, plants are grown under controlled conditions and seeds are stored for the long term. Governments worldwide have stored more than 2 million plant seeds and tissues in this way. More than 30 full-time botanists at the Missouri Botanic Gardens in St. Louis focus on finding and cataloging plants that have yet to be identified and recorded. Other plant preservation banks include those at the University of California, Irvine, and the Pacific Tropical Botanical Garden on the island of Kauai, Hawaii.

Although plants and seeds are relatively easy to acquire, research and monitor in botanical gardens and seed banks, the high cost of keeping plants this way often limits the varieties saved to "useful" species. In captivity, the natural selection and evolution that would occur in the wild cease and populations become genetically stagnant. Other places to preserve plants in their natural habitats are *natural plant reserves,* which are, in their present state, often an unintended benefit derived from protecting wild and scenic lands. It can, however, be difficult and time-consuming to breed, monitor and research plant species, and can leave plants vulnerable to poaching or to succumbing to the needs of subsistence peoples or development pressures.[15]

There is a need for Native farmers and others to keep growing indigenous plant varieties locally. Seed banks must be expanded and land preserved as habitat for wild and domesticated varieties to be preserved. The *Seed Saver's Exchange* on Heritage Farm in Decorah, Iowa, grows and saves heirloom seeds and preserves the folklore associated with Native plants. This group, in association with *Native Seeds • SEARCH,* helps to sustain Native varieties and seeds for future planting by Native communities. They have distributed traditional varieties back to dozens of Native communities in the southwestern United States and in Mexico. Both Seed Saver's Exchange and Native Seeds • SEARCH, which operates a seed bank that includes more than 1,200 collections of endangered crop varieties, distribute seeds to gardeners, family farmers, researchers and Native peoples. Native Seeds • SEARCH is working to reintroduce crops and diets that help to control diabetes among indigenous peoples of the U.S. Southwest.

Plant conservation cannot occur in a vacuum. Cultural and economic concerns must be considered. Several large biosphere reserves have been established to provide for the needs of Native peoples *and* their environments. *Biosphere reserves* are protected areas designed to preserve, intact, entire ecological communities and the Native subsistence cultures living within them. Plants are preserved in their natural habitats where Native peoples are engaged in traditional uses of plants and animals, free from outside interference. Cultural survival, agricultural stability and diversity and wildlands preservation are combined in an integrated approach to conservation. Two examples are the Sierra de Manantlan Biosphere Reserve in Mexico and the Comarca de Kuna Yala, under the stewardship of the San Blas Kuna people of coastal Panama, which has been proposed as an expanded biosphere reserve called Nusagandi Park.

Since people have brought plant species to their present predicament, both economics and the human condition are important aspects of species preservation. Money is needed for plant research and preservation, for assistance to developing countries and for family planning programs to control human population. Corporations need to minimize the ecological cost of their activities and demonstrate ecological responsibility. The impacts on ecological stability and sustainability over the long term need to be considered. What is the cost of a refrigerator, automobile or other product in terms of declining species and the environmental harm caused to create that product? Since the use of ozone-damaging CFCs is banned in most countries beginning in 1996, many manufacturers are developing CFC-free refrigerators and air conditioners. The most environmentally conscious corporations use a voluntary program of environmental goals called the "International Chamber of Commerce's Business Charter for Sustainable Development," which consists of 16 internationally accepted principles that exceed presently mandated environmental regulations. Economic growth and material consumption cannot increase indefinitely in a world of finite resources that is governed by ecological processes and limits.

QUESTIONS

1. Why does Waynabozho's grandmother send him off to a distant forest in the Anishinabe story "Waynabozho and the Wild Rice"? Does he succeed in his task?

2. What does Waynabozho do with the seeds of wild rice when he first finds them? What would you have done?

3. When Waynabozho finds rice growing where he and his grandmother planted it, why does he first sprinkle some seeds back into the water before he eats? What do the Anishinabe call wild rice?

4. Why are species of plants important?

5. What is biological diversity, or biodiversity? Why is it better for an ecosystem to have a lot of species of plants and animals, rather than just a few?

6. What will happen if a species disappears in an ecosystem where there are only a few species? What will happen if a species disappears in an ecosystem where there are a lot of species living?

7. What is an endangered species? What is a threatened species? What does it mean to say that a plant is rare? What has happened to a plant that has become extinct?

8. How are people causing species to disappear on Earth? What kinds of things are people doing that harm plant species?

9. Can you name some North American plants that are threatened or endangered? Where are they found? Why are they in trouble?

10. What are people doing to bring back threatened and endangered plants? Why is it important to save not only plants but also the Native people who live with and take care of those plants?

11. What are some things you can do to help? What is a commitment? Are you willing to make a commitment to help threatened and endangered species? What are you prepared to do?

ACTIVITIES
Species Generosi-Tree

ACTIVITY: Adorn the branches of a tree with illustrations and photographs of threatened and endangered plants with a list of their gifts and a "thank you" to each species on the back. Make small paper "axes" to represent the threats faced by endangered and threatened species. Hold a tree-planting ceremony and plant a tree.

GOALS: Realize the values of and the many gifts we receive from plant species and discover ways to show appreciation and return those gifts. Understand that the well-being and continued existence of endangered and threatened species are threatened by the actions of people as well as by natural events. Develop a connection to a living tree by planting it.

AGE: Younger children and older children

MATERIALS: Small live tree, large waterproof bucket for holding the ball of plant roots, water, extra bucket of rich soil, shovel, old sheet, pencils, posterboard, scissors, tape, string, glue, paste, stapler and staples, chalkboard and chalk or newsprint and marker, field guides and other reference books from which to obtain pictures and illustrations of endangered plants listed in "Discussion," construction paper, crayons, "Discussion."

PROCEDURE: This activity is best when conducted in early spring or late fall, which are good times for transplanting trees.

Beforehand, obtain a small, live tree that is native to your area. Trees are available from local nurseries, or you many want to transplant one (with permission) from private property. Place the balled-up roots into a large, waterproof bucket and bring the plant into the home or learning center. Cover the roots with several layers of cloth and keep the ball of roots moist. Dig a hole outside where you will plant this tree. Now make a stencil in the shape of the outline of a small axe. Use this stencil to trace and cut about 30 small "axes" out of posterboard.

Using newsprint or the chalkboard, draw the outline of a giant gift box with a bow on top. Ask the children to think of and share the many gifts people, animals and other parts of nature receive from plants, such as food, oxygen, shelter, clothing, soil, medicine, rubber, beauty, wood, paper, cardboard and cellophane. List all of these gifts inside the gift box where the children can see them. Review the list of some recognized values of plants from the "Discussion" and list these in the gift box next to the list of children's ideas about the gifts of plants. Explain biodiversity and why it is important. Keep these lists in a prominent place.

Find as many pictures or illustrations as you can of the threatened and endangered North American plants listed in the "Discussion" section or others you may know of. Each child will choose one threatened or endangered plant that he or she would like to thank. Have her or him draw that plant on a piece of construction paper or cut out a picture of the plant and paste it onto construction paper. Using field guides and reference books, help the children to find out about their plant: where and in what kinds of habitat it lives, what the status of its population is, what kinds of particular values it possesses and specific threats to its continued existence. On the back of each illustration or picture of a plant, have each child create a "thank you" for the gifts that plant gives to her or him, other people and the rest of nature, as well as creating a list of the gifts from that plant. Children can refer back to the lists of gifts and values in the gift box. This "thank you" could take the form of a poem, a list, a story, an illustration—anything the child wants to use to express gratitude to that plant. Children will attach a string to the top of their species' photograph or illustration in order to hang it. When the children have created the images of their plants and recorded their "thank you" for the gifts from that species, have them take turns going up and hanging the images on the "Species Generosi-Tree." Each time a child hangs the "thank you" up she or he will share what has been learned about that threatened or endangered plant and the gifts we receive from it.

Ask the children what kinds of harmful things and events plants face in the natural world and from the actions of people. Record these ideas up front for all to see. Allow enough time for children to respond until their ideas are exhausted. Fill their ideas in with other human-caused threats they may have missed from the list provided in the "Discussion" at the beginning of the section called "Threats to Species Survival." Do not forget to include natural threats, such as insect damage, disease, fire, hurricanes and other kinds of extreme weather. Pass out the posterboard "axes" you made earlier and have the children write or draw one threat on each of these axes to represent the full range of threats that plant species must deal with. Have the children hang these threats from the ceiling above the "Species Generosi-Tree."

Hold a ceremony outdoors and plant the tree used in this activity on the grounds of the home or learning center as one final group thanks to plant species. (See Chapter 2 for tips in "Planting Trees and Shrubs.")

Tree of Life

ACTIVITY: Take action to conserve threatened and endangered species. "Grow" a *"Tree of Life"* mural by adding new branches and leaves over time as a record of the acts taken on behalf of threatened and endangered species. Visit a botanical garden, zoo, nature preserve, national forest or other habitat to see and learn about endangered plants and habitats.

GOALS: Discover ways of returning the gifts from species. Help to conserve endangered and threatened plants.

AGE: Younger children and older children

MATERIALS: Chalkboard and chalk or newsprint and marker; construction paper (including lots of green); tape; paste; stapler and staples; scissors; newsprint; tempera paints; paintbrushes; containers of water; crayons; list of "Stewardship Ideas for Saving Species" with the groups' ideas added; materials as needed for specific stewardship projects chosen by the children; transportation to a botanical garden, zoo, museum or a natural habitat to see threatened and endangered species.

PROCEDURE: *Note:* An excellent way to broaden this activity is to take the children on a field trip to see and learn about threatened and endangered plants found in local habitat exhibits such as at a local botanical garden, zoo, museum, national park, bog or nature center. Have the children choose or "adopt" a plant species, say "thank you" to that species, make a commitment to help preserve it in the wild and practice stewardship toward that particular species. Model this experience after the activity called *"Zoos and Endangered Species"* in Chapter 14 of *Keepers of the Animals.*

Ask the children: "What are some ways you can help to make sure endangered and threatened species are able to survive? What can *you* do?" List their ideas in a prominent place as the children come up with them. Give value to even the smallest bit of help, such as recycling one container. Once you and the children have exhausted your ideas, add others that the children missed that are found at the end of this activity in the "Stewardship Ideas for Saving Species." Discuss actions that biologists take to save species as described in the "Discussion."

Have the children agree on a level of commitment they will make to help species survival. Suggest that they each do one thing per week from the list of ideas. It is important that they understand that they will be expected to fulfill this commitment once it is made.

Use newsprint and construction paper to create a giant mural silhouette of a tree that has a trunk and branches but no leaves. The children will complete this tree by doing things to preserve threatened and endangered plant species. Each time someone does something to help a plant species, she or he will cut a leaf out of green paper and write or draw with crayon on the leaf to describe the accomplishment. This paper will be attached to a branch of the mural as a bit of "foliage," working from the bottom branches up to the top. Gradually, as the children do more and more to help species, the tree will leaf out and symbolically turn green, recording their care and concern for threatened and endangered plants. One final act of stewardship is to recycle all of the materials used here, including the waste products used to make the "tree" earlier in this activity.

Stewardship Ideas for Saving Species

Additional ideas can be adapted from the activity "Heart-Wood: Completing the Circle With Rainforests" in Chapter 13.

• Refuse to eat, use or buy the products made from all plants that are threatened or endangered.

• Refrain from using goods that, when produced, destroy the habitats of endangered species. Boycott foods that harm endangered species while the food is being captured, grown or processed.

• Encourage and support environmentally concerned producers who make their products using sustainable agricultural and forestry practices. A good resource is the book *Rain Forest in Your Kitchen: The Hidden Connection Between Extinction and Your Supermarket,* by Martin Teitel (Washington, D.C., and Covelo, Calif.: Island Press, 1992).

• Do not buy cacti, carnivorous plants or other wild plant species unless proof is provided that those plants have been grown from seed in a nursery, not collected in the wild (Figure 14-4).

• Keep informed and up-to-date on threatened and endangered plants and related issues by reading newspapers, magazines and books.

• Write to and join local, national and international conservation groups that help save threatened and endangered plants. Donate some of your time and money to help these groups. Find out how to help these groups in their efforts.

• Fight to stop development projects that threaten rare plants and their habitats.

• Get permission to visit natural areas nearby that are going to be developed. Collect and save rare species from these habitats.

• Use museums and libraries to set up displays on plant endangerment and extinction. Encourage public and school libraries to purchase relevant books and subscribe to conservation periodicals.

• Visit botanical gardens and zoos near you and get involved with their educational and stewardship programs on threatened and endangered species. If these organizations near you are not involved with threatened and endangered species, encourage them to begin programs such as protecting and propagating species by establishing seed banks or by creating live, endangered-plant habitat exhibits and research programs. Support these programs if they already exist.

• Use the media to educate others about the plight of threatened and endangered plants and habitats: write letters to the editor, get on public access radio and television, write a newsletter.

• Get endangered species lists from local and federal governments, universities, garden clubs, etc.

• Use less electricity to reduce the need to build new power plants that destroy habitat and consume resources to generate electricity (turn off lights when not being used, keep the refrigerator door closed, turn the television off when not in use, etc.).

• When buying new appliances, choose models that conserve energy and are less harmful to the environment while being made and used. For instance, refrigerators will soon be available that do not use ozone-harming CFCs.

• Reduce use of resources by *using only what you need:* paper, glass, cans, bottles, wood, etc.

• Reuse and recycle those things that you can: paper, glass, cans, bottles, plastics, wood, etc.

• Use less gasoline, heating oil and other petroleum products: drive less frequently in cars; use buses, trains and other mass transit; ride a bicycle; use a skateboard or scooter or walk; keep houses cooler in winter; use clothes of cotton and other natural fibers and less of synthetic fibers made from oil; use less plastic that is made from oil (use cellophane made from trees instead) and reuse plastic articles (wash plastic bags, cups and bottles and reuse).

• Help keep plant species' habitats clean and free of pollution by not using toxic chemicals such as pesticides, herbicides and other household toxic compounds. Do not litter, and pick up litter that you find, being careful to not get hurt on broken glass and ragged, rusty metal cans.

• Reduce the production and use of synthetic fertilizers, and thus the release of nitrous oxide into the atmosphere—a gas that contributes to global warming.

Figure 14-4. Be careful when buying a potted plant that it is not a threatened or endangered species and that it has been cultivated in a nursery, not collected in the wild. This is a mammilaria cactus in bloom. Size: to 12+ in. (30.5+ cm). (Photo by Michael J. Caduto)

• Promote local, national, state, provincial and territorial laws to protect plant species. Write to government officials to tell them you care and want particular plants to stay (or become) listed as threatened or endangered.

• Create local communities of *native* plants that maintain species and reintroduce them to depleted populations. Some people in the Midwest are planting small patches of prairie in city lots and on private land. Cacti are being planted in Arizona. These habitats also provide homes for insects, birds and associated plants.

• Plant a garden to save traditional Native American plant varieties and other heirloom plants that are becoming rare. (See seed sources under "Extending the Experience.")

• Alert homeowners of any threatened and endangered species found on their land and encourage them to preserve those species.

• Eat a variety of foods to encourage the continued growth of diverse plant culture.

• Grow your own seeds to help preserve plant varieties.

• Share Earth's resources with plants that live here.

• Make a commitment to keep doing everything you can to help a plant until it recovers and has a healthy population, or until it disappears and you have done all you can to save it.

Fate of Furbish's Lousewort

ACTIVITY: Conduct a role-playing exercise during which the players air their views, take and defend a particular stand regarding the fate of the Furbish's lousewort and its habitat and related issues and engage in a simulation of cross-cultural dialogue.

GOALS: Understand the various stands that people take for and against habitat preservation for endangered species. Explore the issues and controversies surrounding habitat protection and endangered species preservation, such as the difference between developing a hydroelectric dam out of want versus need, traditional Native North American stewardship of habitat and plants, materialism and economics and their effects on the well-being of plants and their habitats. Practice sharing ideas and opinions and listening to the ideas and opinions of those with whom you do not agree as you search for a common solution to a difficult problem. Consider the needs, wants and beliefs of traditional Native North American cultures during a decision-making process affecting habitat and species on their traditional lands.

AGE: Older children

MATERIALS: Pencils, large index cards, cardboard and felt-tipped marking pens to create name plates for government officials, props and clothing for children to use to dress up in the roles they are playing, large tables or desks and 10 chairs for Department of Environmental Management (DEM) representatives and federal, provincial and state authorities to sit at as they preside over the meeting. Copies of "History of Furbish's Lousewort," the "Furbish's Lousewort Management Plan" and the "Descriptions of the Interest Groups" from this activity, Figure 14-5.

PROCEDURE: *Note: Although this activity is, in part, based on factual information about the history and fate of the Furbish's lousewort and Native peoples of the St. John River Valley, it is a fictional exercise. Any similarity between individuals and organizations portrayed in this exercise and those in real life is strictly coincidental and unintentional.*

Begin this activity at least one week before you want the children to conduct the actual role-playing exercise. This will give them time for research, interviews and other background preparations. We find that when children are heavily invested in their roles they take the entire exercise more seriously and, for a time, "become" their role-playing identities.

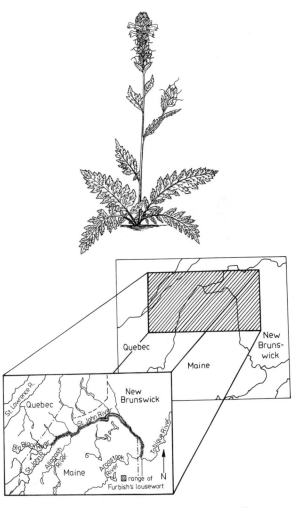

Figure 14-5. Furbish's lousewort and its range. This perennial with its fernlike leaves is endangered in both the United States and Canada. The lousewort's clusters of yellow flowers resemble those of its close relative, the snapdragon. Size: 1 to 3 ft. (30.5 to 91.4 cm).

Beforehand, prepare the cards describing each interest group's identity and position regarding the Furbish's Lousewort Management Plan.

Have each child take turns reading as you review the parts of the "Discussion" section that deal with habitat destruction, habitat preservation and the fate of endangered and threatened plants. Now tell the children they are each going to prepare for a role-playing activity during which they will take on the identity of a person with a particular stand about the fate of the Furbish's lousewort and its habitat. Share the illustration of the Furbish's lousewort and map of its range in Figure 14-5 with the children. Emphasize that the children are going to take their roles *seriously* and defend their positions as though they *really are* the persons they are role-playing. Even if the children are asked to take a position they do not personally agree with, for the purpose of the activity they will advocate and defend that position. Read the following:

History of Furbish's Lousewort

Furbish's lousewort is a small perennial with variable red and yellow flowers that grows in patches along parts of the steep, shady, eroded banks of the St. John River, which flows along an international border between what is now called Maine (United States) and New Brunswick (Canada). The lousewort habitat requires the kind of erosion and ice gouging that occurs during late winter "ice-out" and early spring floods along free-flowing rivers in the north country. Some 34 other species of rare plants are also found in the subarctic climate and habitat of the Upper St. John Valley.

The lousewort's habitat is in the traditional land known by Native North American peoples as *Wabanaki*, "The Dawn Land." This endangered plant grows in the traditional land of the Passamaquoddy and Maliseet nations, two of the many Wabanaki peoples. For thousands of years the Wabanaki have lived as stewards of this land. Traditionally, wild plants are harvested only if the patch is large enough to support a thinning of the plants growing there. Permission is first asked of the Creator and the plant, and then a gift is left where the plant is harvested—often some seeds to grow new plants. Out of respect, the tallest, "Grandmother" plant is never picked for it is the one that gave birth to the others. Only what is needed of the plant is picked and nothing is wasted. Words of thanks are spoken to the plant and the Creator for the gift of life presented by the plants.

The St. John River, which is free-flowing for the 200-mile (322-kilometer) stretch from the headwaters to the first dam at Grand Falls, New Brunswick, is the longest remaining free-flowing river in the northeastern United States. The lousewort's population consists of a number of patches found along both banks of a 28-mile (45-kilometer) stretch of the St. John River. It is now listed and protected as an endangered species in both countries and became well known when dams were proposed by the U.S. Army Corps of Engineers that would have flooded nearly all of its remaining habitat.

The governments of both the United States and New Brunswick continue to propose dams that would destroy the habitat of Furbish's lousewort if built.

Furbish's Lousewort Management Plan

As a result of pressure from the Wabanaki, numerous conservation groups, provincial and state authorities and the general public, the federal governments of both the U.S. and Canada have proposed protecting all habitat of the Furbish's lousewort and a ban on picking or disturbing this plant in any way. This will assure that the population of Furbish's lousewort will remain healthy as a recovery program is put into effect to improve numbers along the St. John River and to introduce the lousewort to other suitable habitat found along the region's rivers. A public hearing has been scheduled to consider the issues surrounding this proposal, known as the Furbish's Lousewort Management Plan.[9]

Have the children choose their roles and pass out the cards that identify the interest groups and their positions to players so all sides are represented. Now allow the children a week or longer to prepare for their roles through research and (if possible) interviews with people involved with similar issues in real-life situations. It is important to set aside specific time for this background preparation and to offer as much support and guidance as possible. During this period of preparation, the children need to decide who will be the spokesperson for their group and what comments of support the other members of the group will make at the hearing. Help the children representing the federal, provincial and state authorities to decide which of the four positions they want to advocate at the hearing. They are to prepare a position statement while remaining open to changing it as a response to testimony given at the public hearing.

When time for the role-playing arrives, children will play their roles as people present at the public hearing, which will be conducted by the six representatives from the joint Canadian/U.S. task force for the Departments of Environmental Management (DEM). During the hearing, each side will have a maximum of 10 minutes to present its views until all sides have been heard.

Descriptions of the Interest Groups

These descriptions of the interest groups and their stands on the issues are to be written on index cards and passed out to the children. Make up as many cards as indicated so each player has his or her own card.

• *Department of Environmental Management officials: Joint Canadian/U.S. Task Force* (total of six—three each from New Brunswick and Maine)

You are a representative of either New Brunswick's or Maine's Department of Environmental Management (DEM). You are to work with the other five DEM representatives. First, read DEM's Furbish's Lousewort Management Plan to the entire group that has assembled. Then, tell the assembly that each interest group will be allowed *10 minutes only* to submit testimony during the hearing, until all who want to have shared. Appoint an official timekeeper from among yourselves to stop testimony after 10 minutes for each group.

• *Passamaquoddy and Maliseet representatives* (one spokesperson plus any number of representatives)

We have used the native plants from this region for thousands of years. Some of the Creation stories say that human beings came from the trees. Plants are an important part of our culture and traditional way of life. We have always treated plants with great respect, asking permission, taking no more than we need and returning the gift with gratitude. We do not pick plants unless they are abundant. There was never any problem with the population of the Furbish's lousewort or other native plants until people came from other lands and began harvesting plants at will and destroying their habitats. How can the Furbish's lousewort, or any wild plant, survive if it has no place to live and people are picking the few that are left and destroying their homes? We support this ban in every way and will do whatever we can to help carry it out. (Other Maliseet and Passamaquoddy people add their own comments.)

• *Hydro-North Power Company* (one spokesperson plus any number of representatives)

Why should you single out this stretch of the St. John River for protection? What are you going to do for power when the demand outgrows the supply in this region? We have a strong environmental record. It is only a few insensitive power companies that have destroyed habitat without regard for the environment and we are not one of them. We strongly urge the federal governments to amend the Furbish's Lousewort Management Plan to allow a limited amount of the habitat to be flooded by a moderate-size hydroelectric dam while the remaining population of Furbish's lousewort, and its habitat, are protected and a reintroduction program is started in habitat along other suitable rivers in the region. (Other power company officials add their comments.)

• *Conservationists for the Preservation of the Furbish's Lousewort* (a spokesperson plus any number of representatives)

For many generations the free-flowing rivers of the north country have been dammed, first for mechanical power and later for hydroelectric power. The St. John is one of the last long free-flowing rivers in northeastern North America. The Upper St. John Valley harbors an extensive community of more than 30 rare and endangered plants. This unique ecosystem will be forever and irrevocably altered if the development of more hydroelectric dams is permitted. Our figures show that if the Furbish's Lousewort Management Plan is not enacted and enforced, and the population of Furbish's lousewort declines any further, the plant will not be able to sustain itself and will be driven to the brink of extinction within a decade. We strongly recommend approval of this plan as it is now written. (Other conservationists add their comments.)

• *Citizen-Watch for the St. John River Valley and other members of the general public* (non-Native members of local wildflower clubs, employees of power companies, construction contractors, trout fishers, environmental rights activists and others)

Some of you will be for, and some against, the Furbish's Lousewort Management Plan. Decide who will take which stand and take your 10 minutes to say how you feel about the issues and why. Be sure some representatives are present from each side of the issue.

• *Federal, provincial and state authorities* (one spokesperson, six present—two each from both Maine and New Brunswick and one each from the federal governments of both the U.S. and Canada)

Once all testimony has been heard, the six representatives of the federal, provincial and state authorities will (1) retire for a few minutes to consider the testimony; (2) take a vote on the resolution and decide either to support or reject the Furbish's Lousewort Management Plan, or to offer an alternative course of action; and (3) report their decision to the group as a whole. If the first vote ends in a tie, the authorities must remain in their closed meeting to discuss the issues until a vote is taken during which a majority (at least four members) vote for a particular plan.

Four possible courses of action by the federal, provincial and state authorities are offered here: (1) a decision in support of the Furbish's Lousewort Management Plan (FLMP); (2) a decision to reject support of the proposed FLMP, but to propose instead to monitor the existing situation more closely; (3) a decision during which the provincial authorities offer their support for an amended version (of their own design) of the FLMP; and (4) an open option in which the provincial authorities design a completely original response to the FLMP and the situation at hand.

Once the authorities' plan, and their reasons for so deciding, have been shared with the entire group, ask the various members of each interest group to share how they feel about the process and what their thoughts and feelings are about the decision.

Finally, facilitate a discussion that includes the concepts of need versus want, traditional plant-gathering techniques versus modern-day views of relating to wild plants, materialism and economic demand (including the need for electric power generation) and the effects of these forces on plant populations in the wild. Ask the children: "Did anyone personally disagree with the position he or she represented? How did that feel? Did you change your mind at all or did your beliefs become stronger? Did it help you to understand people who have opinions different from yours?"

EXTENDING THE EXPERIENCE

• Prepare an endangered species impact statement on products that you buy and use. Take into consideration the list of threats to species found in the "Discussion."

• Obtain native wild rice: prepare some recipes, plant some seeds, compare wild with white rice.

• *Seed Savers.* Purchase and plant heirloom seeds and the seeds of plants that are native to North America as a means of helping to preserve traditional varieties of plants that are quickly disappearing. *Seeds of Change* produces a wide selection of organically grown, traditional, heirloom, unusual and nutritious plant varieties as a way of reintroducing diversity into the food chain. It also conducts research and an educational program. For information and a catalog, contact Seeds of Change, 621 Old Santa Fe Trail #10, Santa Fe, NM 87501, (505) 983-8956.

The *Seed Saver's Exchange* lists more than 5,000 varieties of heirloom seed stocks that are being planted and preserved by its members and that you can obtain: Seed Saver's Exchange, 3076 North Winn Rd., Decorah, IA 52101, (319) 382-5990.

Sources of Native North American seed varieties can be obtained from *Native Seeds • SEARCH,* 2509 North Campbell Ave. #325, Tucson, AZ 85719, (602) 327-9123. This organization also has available VHS tapes, slides and curriculum materials that teach about the work of finding and preserving Native seeds in the Southwest, as well as their work using Native crops of the Southwest to control diabetes.

• Read *Night Flying Woman: An Ojibway Narrative,* by Ignatia Broker (St. Paul/Minneapolis: Historical Society Press, 1983)

• Hold a celebration to honor and thank those species that are threatened, endangered and extinct.

• Report any sightings of plant poaching to the toll-free hotline maintained by the National Parks and Conservation Association at (800) 448-NPCA.

• Find out how you can help to support Native peoples of Canada who are threatened by hydroelectric dams and development. Write to the Arctic to Amazonia Alliance, P.O. Box 73, Strafford, VT 05072.

• Conduct the activities *"Biodiversity Breakdown"* and *"The Population Shuffle"* from Chapter 17 in *Keepers of the Animals.*

• For the current list of U.S. endangered and threatened plants and wildlife, and other pertinent information about threatened and endangered plants, contact the U.S. Department of the Interior, Fish and Wildlife Service, Endangered Species Program, Washington, DC 20240.

• For information on the current status of Canadian threatened and endangered species, contact Coordinator, Threatened Species, Environment Canada, Canadian Wildlife Service, Ottawa, ON K1A 0H3.

• For posters, activity ideas and fact sheets describing endangered species and wilderness, contact World Wildlife Fund/Canada, 90 Eglinton Ave., E., Suite 504, Toronto, ON M4P 2Z7.

• For information about habitat protection in Canada, contact Wildlife Habitat Canada, 1704 Carling Ave., Suite 301, Ottawa, ON K2A 1C7, (613) 722-2090.

• For a copy of the 1989–1990 supplement *Endangered Species,* contact Teachers Clearinghouse for Science and Society Education, Inc., 1 West 88th St., New York, NY 10024.

• Contact the Superintendent of Documents, P.O. Box 371954, Pittsburgh, PA 15250-7954 to order copies of the posters called *Endangered Means There Is Still Time* (stock no. 024-010-00693-5) and *Endangered Means There Is Still Time: Desert Species* (stock no. 024-010-00698-6).

• Contact the Department of Agriculture about federally regulated plant species and importing or exporting pets and birds.

• Check the reference books and directories at your local library to learn more about endangered species and ways you can help to save them.

NOTES

1. Gary Paul Nabhan, *Enduring Seeds: Native American Agriculture and Wild Plant Cultivation* (San Francisco: North Point, 1989), 113.

2. Ibid., 111–112.

3. Edward O. Wilson, *The Diversity of Life* (Cambridge, Mass.: Belknap Press, 1992), 350.

4. Edward O. Wilson, "Threats to Biodiversity," *Scientific American,* vol. 261, no. 3 (September 1989): 108–116.

5. According to figures from the Arctic to Amazonia Alliance, Strafford, Vermont.

6. Harold Koopowitz and Hilary Kaye, *Plant Extinction: A Global Crisis* (Washington, D.C.: Stonewall Press, 1983), 181.

7. Dianne Dumanoski, "Scientists Report North Pole Ozone Loss," *Boston Globe* (1 May 1992): 13.

8. Ibid.

9. Koopowitz and Kaye, *Plant Extinction,* 6.

10. For information about and a list of threatened and endangered species, write to U.S. Department of the Interior, Fish and Wildlife Service, Endangered Species Program, Washington, DC 20240.

11. Dianne Dumanoski, "Group Says Species Die Out While U.S. Delays," *Boston Globe* (9 August 1986): 17.

12. For more information, write to Coordinator, Threatened Species, Environment Canada, Canadian Wildlife Service, Ottawa, ON K1A 0H3.

13. Donella Meadows, "Saving Endangered Species," *Valley News,* Lebanon, N.H. (17 April 1993): 26.

14. Maura Dolan, "Fatal Impact: Our Population Boom May Threaten Plant's Other Species," *Valley News,* Lebanon, N.H. (24 August 1992): 13.

15. Nabhan, *Enduring Seeds,* 89–90.

✠ HEALING OUR RELATIONS ✠

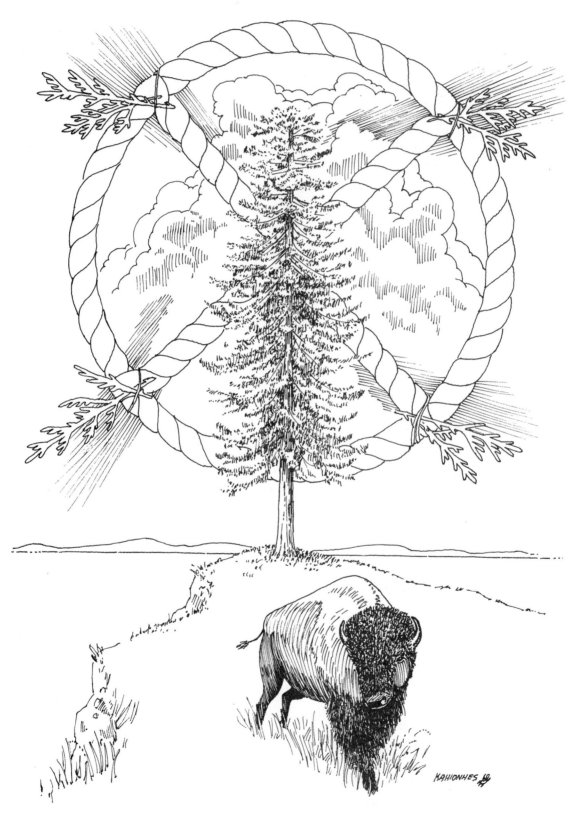

"When the Little Ones make these their symbols," Cedar said, *"they will live to see their own hair white with age as they travel the Path of Life."*

CHAPTER 15

✦ The Buffalo Bull and the Cedar Tree ✦

(Osage—Plains)

When the Osage people came down from the sky, they wandered the world seeking guidance and help. They wanted to learn the right ways to live and they trusted the beings they met to guide them.

The first being they met was the great Bull Buffalo. It lowered its head and bellowed with anger. It pawed earth, throwing up red dust. Then a man of the Peace Clan fired an arrow. That arrow was fletched with Eagle's down feathers, feathers stained red with pokeberry juice to make them a symbol of peace and the dawn. The arrow entered the open mouth of the Buffalo Bull and that great one grew quiet from the magic of peace.

"I will be a great symbol for you, Little Ones," the Bull Buffalo said. Then it rolled on the ground four times. Each time it rolled, thunder rolled overhead. Then, where it had rolled, healing plants grew. The green gourd and the yellow striped gourd, the poppy mallow and the blazing star grew up from earth where the buffalo rolled.

"I give these plants for you to use," the Buffalo Bull said to the people. "Use them and you will see old age as you travel the path of life."

"Of what will our children make their bodies?" the people asked.

Then the Buffalo Bull made the red corn grow. Then the Buffalo Bull made the red squash grow. The Buffalo Bull made blue corn and black squash. The Buffalo Bull made speckled corn and speckled squash. The Buffalo Bull made yellow corn and yellow squash.

"When your children use these plants as food, they will see old age. They will reach the days when life is filled with calm and peace."

So the Buffalo Bull said to the people. Then he told the Osage, "You may have my body. You may use it for food, shelter, clothing and tools."

As the people continued to travel on, they saw the leaves falling from the trees. They had come to the earth in the time of autumn. They continued to travel and the days grew colder and now all of the trees were bare of leaves. But then they came to the edge of a cliff and there before them they saw a tree whose boughs were still green. Its scent was fragrant. It was Cedar. They looked at that tree and, as she stood in the midst of the four winds, sending forth her fragrance whichever way the wind blew, she spoke to them.

"I stand here on this cliff," Cedar said, "so that the Little Ones may make of me their medicine. Look at my roots, a sign of my old age. When the Little Ones make me their symbol they, too, will live to see their toes gnarled with age. Look at my branches, how they bend. With these as symbols, the People will live to see their own shoulders bent with age. Look at the feathery tips of my branches. When the Little Ones make these their symbols, they will live to see their own hair white with age as they travel the Path of Life."

So it was that the Osage people accepted the cedar tree as their symbol of the Tree of Life.

DISCUSSION

At the beginning of the story "The Buffalo Bull and the Cedar Tree," a man from the Peace Clan uses an arrow flecked with feathers stained red from pokeberry juice to bring peace to the Buffalo Bull. Healing plants grow where Buffalo rolls on the ground. Buffalo then gives the people different kinds of corn and squash to eat and, finally, Buffalo offers himself as food, shelter, clothing and tools. Cedar becomes medicine, a symbol of longevity to the People—the Tree of Life. The Osage people ultimately discover ways to live well because Buffalo Bull and Cedar give openly of themselves.

Today, we human beings often put ourselves on a level far above that of the plants and animals. Science and psychology tell us how highly developed our brains are compared to those of other animals, even while the theory of evolution traces our lineage back to the same ancestors in antiquity as those of other modern animals. Indeed, the human capacity for conceptual thinking, for the use of second-order thought—reflection, intelligence and imagination—has led us to create forms of art and invention that are marvelous and ingenious.

In many Native North American oral traditions, plants and animals come before human beings. Plants and animals know how to live well on Earth; they are more at ease and at home here. The trees drop their leaves and become dormant during the cold winter months, the bear sleeps away the winter in its den, the woodchuck has a snug home in its burrow, the chickadee always finds food even on the coldest winter days. As in the story of the Buffalo Bull and the Cedar Tree, plants teach people and animals how to survive. Humans need their great intellect to compensate for a plant's ability to sustain itself, and for the adaptations that animals are born with. We develop weapons in place of fangs and claws; clothes in place of fur, feathers and bark; homes in place of caves, nests and burrows. Plants and animals are a source of great power and wisdom for those who are willing to learn from them.

Individuals and families in many Native North American cultures are closely associated with plants and plant families. Many creation stories say that people first formed from plants. In the Lacandon Mayan tradition people are fashioned by the Creator and the Maker from maize. The first Abenaki people step live from an ash tree with hearts growing and green wherever Gluskabe, the Transformer, shoots arrows of life into the tree. Among the Abenaki of the Northeast certain families have adopted the butternut tree as their family name.

Healing

In this Osage story, healing plants grow where the Buffalo Bull rolls on the ground: green- and yellow-striped gourds, blazing star and poppy mallow. From aspirin to cortisone and Novocaine®, native medicinal plants, and the knowledge handed down by Native cultures of the Americas, seem inexhaustible. Consider the following native plants and their medicinal properties:

Figure 15-1. *Female trees of the Pacific yew produce poisonous, scarlet, berry-like seed "cones." Bark of the Pacific yew is the source of a potent cancer-fighting drug called Taxol. Size: to 50 ft. (15 m). (Illustration by Marjorie C. Leggitt)*

- Balsam root, from *Balsamorhiza sagittata,* is used to create a salve for healing wounds. The resinous bud coating on balsam poplar or tacamahac forms the base for a healing ointment.
- Dogwood reduces fever.
- Milkweed sap promotes healing and wards off infection. Milkweed root is used to treat coughs.
- Witch hazel sap is boiled down for an astringent.
- Pacific yew is traditionally used as an anti-inflammatory by Native peoples of the Pacific Northwest (Figure 15-1). Taxol, a powerful cancer-fighting drug, is extracted from yew bark.
- Salicin from willow, a chemical precursor to modern-day aspirin, is used to relieve headaches and rheumatism and the bark is dried and smoked to alleviate the symptoms of asthma.
- White pine tea—made from boiling the needles—has more vitamin C than orange juice. It is used to treat symptoms of scurvy and colds. White pine sap cures boils and abscesses.
- Ash bark is used to make a poultice for treating sores and hemorrhoids and for a tea that is an effective diuretic for women.
- Bark from the Cascara buckthorn is used by Pacific Northwest peoples as a cathartic laxative.
- Root-bark tea from oak is an astringent, helps wounds to heal and treats coughs.
- Quinine from bark of the Peruvian quina-quina is used to treat malaria.
- The roots of three species of yams (*Dioscorea*) in eastern Mexico contain a steroid, *diosgenin*. This compound is used to create synthetic cortisone, a treatment for skin disorders,

rheumatoid arthritis and ulcerative colitis. From diosgenin scientists also learned to create birth-control pills.

• Procaine (Novocaine®) and xylocaine are synthetic drugs patterned after the chemical composition of cocaine to produce similar anesthetic effects.

In numerous Native North American cultures, many people of the bear clan are healers. They spend years studying families of plants and their healing properties. Plants within particular families tend to possess healing qualities toward specific classes of disease. It is no surprise that many communities in North America bear healing names, such as Medicine Bow Forest, Wyoming, and Medicine Hat, Alberta.
THE HEALING VISION. Native North American traditional *medicine* is much more than a pill to cure a particular ailment. It is a sacred thing—the source of one's strength, wisdom and power in the cosmos. Medicine encompasses all aspects of life that act on body, mind and spirit, as well as one's attitude toward them. This includes all forms of knowledge such as the advice of elders, natural and cultural laws and proverbs.[1] Medicine is sought through ceremony, fasting, the vision quest and seeking life's satisfaction. Many people carry a *medicine bag*, which contains natural objects that represent and bear testimony to the power received through one's life experiences, particularly during the fast and vision quest.

Giving thanks is often linked to healing and medicine: giving thanks to the Creator and all of creation's manifestations as plants, animals and their surroundings. "All my relations" is a greeting spoken upon entering certain places for thanksgiving. Thanks are offered in the form of smoke from a pipe. Many different barks, plants and tobacco smoke are used that carry thanks on the wind to the Creator. Cedar and other aromatics are commonly used like an incense.

Thanks are offered to the four directions, as well as to Father Sky and Mother Earth.[2] Four is an important number that appears in many stories and traditions. In the Osage story "The Buffalo Bull and the Cedar Tree," the Buffalo Bull rolls on the ground four times and Cedar stands in the midst of the four winds to send forth her fragrance. The roots of the *Haudenosaunee's* (Iroquois') great white pine, the tree of peace, grow out to the four sacred directions to symbolize peace and charity and to lead other peoples to its truth. These four directions, along with Earth, Sky and the center that lies within each of our hearts, are the *seven directions* that symbolize connection, completion and balance in the sacred hoop or circle.

Today, we need a way to change, to make a positive transformation. We, humankind, through our great numbers, technological and industrial powers and political and economic conflicts have created a crisis in our relationship with Earth in the form of inestimable ecological damage. Through habitat destruction, overhunting, overfishing and pollution we have driven tens of thousands of our relations to the threshold of oblivion.

The way back, the healing, should not be sought by using more force. It needs to occur through a metamorphosis in our relationships with plants, animals, other people and all of creation. To make this change, we need to reorient our moral, ethical, spiritual, intellectual and scientific energies away from manipulation and control toward peace, preservation and the perpetuation of the ecosphere. We can take our inspiration from the Peace Clan of the Osage who use feathers stained with pokeberry juice to symbolize peace and the dawn. We have a responsibility to recognize a higher order and to extend the equivalent of human rights to all species.

The Giving Circles

The thin, living membrane covering Earth is only one one-thousandth of Earth's diameter, like a skin 1 inch thick covering a sphere more than 83 feet in diameter (or a skin 1 millimeter thick covering a ball 1 meter in diameter). Yet the *center* of existence for each of us walking upon Earth is within; as the Oglala Lakota (Sioux) scholar Black Elk says, the center is everywhere. We move on this living circle and can only maintain its entirety by completing our circles, by giving back every time we receive Earth's bounty, by living in balance and by keeping each gift moving.

To Native North Americans, and many other traditional cultures, a *gift* gains importance and power every time it is given to another. A gift is not meant to be kept forever; it is given to be held in trust for a time before it is passed on to another. Each gift circles among the people. The same gift may someday come back to one who had already received it and passed it on, but, more likely, other gifts will come to that person instead. Thus, the circles overlap and interconnect. In fact, the less one knows about the giving, and the less *control* one has over where that gift will travel to once it has been given away, the stronger the power in that act of giving.

When Europeans first encountered the generous Native North American *circle of giving and receiving* and found themselves expected to eventually pass a gift on after they had received it, they erroneously labeled Native North Americans as "Indian givers." In fact, the European tradition of acquiring without giving back and taking without limit has proven that a gift moving one way soon depletes its source. Linear, extractive thinking and ways of living with Earth and other people have failed both socially and ecologically.

This circular, interconnected ecological community of sentient beings, composed of body, mind and spirit, is our habitation, our *Oikos*, our ecosphere. Plants provide us with food, drink and healing medicines and, in Cedar, become the Tree of Life as a symbol for longevity.

Living in Balance

Our relationships with plants can be used to explore the Native concept of *balance*. The ultimate symbol that plants provide, through their intimate ecological relationship with the sun, soil, water and air, and as Keepers of Life in the biosphere, is their example of how it is possible to live in ways that sustain and support life on Earth. *Living in balance* is a strong, central aspect of traditional Native North American cultures. This tradition can be a model for *Earth stewardship*. Based on the *cycles of nature* and the *circles of life* (Figure 4-1), a positive, nurturing existence connected to the plant world and all of nature is the foundation for a sustainable future on Earth. The Abenaki traditions concerned with the gathering of plants to be used for any purpose show a deep respect for the circle of giving and receiving (see "Plants in the Wild: To Collect or Not to Collect" in Chapter 2). These traditions are an example of a reciprocal, sharing relationship with plants, which can be used as a model for contemporary ways of living in balance in today's world.

The traditional stewardship perspective of Native North American cultures is one of considering the long-term effects of our actions upon Earth and humanity. It is often expressed in terms of doing things wisely and carefully while keeping in mind the repercussions every action will have upon the next *seven generations* of children to come. Decisions are made considering the wisdom of the ancestors of seven generations ago. Each of us *is* a seventh generation.

In our way of life, in our government, with every decision we make, we always keep in mind the seventh generation to come. It's our job to see that the people coming ahead, the generations still unborn, have a world no worse than ours—and hopefully better. When we walk upon Mother Earth we always plant our feet carefully because we know the faces of our future generations are looking up at us from beneath the ground. We never forget them.[3]

—Chief Oren Lyons
Onondaga

QUESTIONS

1. How does the great Buffalo Bull help the Osage people who come down from the sky in the story "The Buffalo Bull and the Cedar Tree"? What gifts does he give the People?
2. What makes the Buffalo Bull peaceful? What grows from the ground where he rolls? Why is the buffalo an important animal to Native North Americans?

3. Where does Cedar grow? From how many directions are the winds blowing that spread Cedar's fragrance? How many times does the Buffalo Bull roll on the ground? Why do so many things happen in fours in Native North American stories? Why is the number 4 important?
4. What are Cedar's gifts to the People? What does Cedar become a symbol of? Name some other giving plants and describe how they help human beings.
5. Where do Native North American stories say people first came from? Are people really related to plants and animals? Why do you think so, or why not?
6. In what ways are plants and animals better adapted to live in the natural world than are people?
7. What advantages do plants and animals have over people? What advantages do we have over plants and animals?
8. How are plants used for healing and medicine by Native North Americans? Can you think of any healing plants? What medicines do you use that first came from plants?
9. What does "medicine" mean to Native North Americans? How is this different from what it means to people who are not Native North American? What does it mean to you?
10. Why is giving thanks important in Native North American traditions? Do you think giving thanks is important? Why or why not?
11. What does "all my relations" mean to Native North Americans? Who are our Earth relations?
12. How can we heal our relationships with plants and animals? What changes must we make?
13. What do we need to do to take care of "all our relations"? What can you do?
14. Why is it important to do things in the way of a circle to keep our relations well and our families strong on Earth? What is the circle of giving and receiving?
15. What do you think of when someone says "Indian giver"? What is the real story behind this term? How do Native peoples keep the circle of giving and receiving strong?
16. What does it mean to live in balance? Why is this important to becoming wise Earth stewards?
17. What does it mean to live each day and care for each other and Earth with the next seven generations in our hearts?

ACTIVITIES
Growing Your Green Heart

ACTIVITY: Take a fantasy journey to find the seed in your heart. Grow into a green plant that spreads its branches and roots to reach out and connect with all life in a caring way. Make a "green heart" to represent the strength and qualities of the plant you choose to become.

GOALS: Visualize the green branches and roots of a plant that connect you to all parts of Earth. Understand how to bring to life a seed growing inside of you, by watching, listening and being quiet and receptive. Imagine how a seed, and your green heart, can grow into a nurturing plant that helps you to touch, heal and have a positive relationship with the life in your surroundings.

AGE: Younger children and older children

MATERIALS: Copy of the fantasy *"Growing Your Green Heart,"* pencils, crayons, felt-tipped pens, writing paper and construction paper, scissors, strips of newspaper, wheat paste, water, paintbrushes, tempera paints, other supplies needed for chosen projects, calming music and equipment on which to play it (optional).

PROCEDURE: Prepare the children for the fantasy as described under "Leading the Guided Fantasies" in Chapter 2. They are going to feel and experience the events that happen during the fantasy and can grow into any plant they desire as they discover the seed of their green heart. It could be a plant they know or an entirely new kind of plant. Now read *"Growing Your Green Heart"* to the children.

Note: You may want to play calming music as you read this journey.

GROWING YOUR GREEN HEART

You are a small seed sitting on top of a beautiful hill in some rich, deep, brown soil that is warm and moist. The bright sun is warming you inside and out. From this place you can look out over Earth in all directions. Every place you look the land is covered with rolling hills, green forests and fields. Some puffy gray clouds blow over the face of the sun and a gentle rain begins to fall. The sweet scent of fresh rain surrounds you. Soon, the clouds pass and the warm rays of sunlight return. Take some time to look around you in all directions. (*Pause*)

Slowly, you feel something inside of you pushing down into the soil. A root breaks through the coat on your seed and starts to branch down into the soil. You can feel the root absorbing water and minerals to help you grow.

Now a shoot emerges from the top of the seed and grows up toward the sky. You are growing in both directions: down into the rich earth and up into the fresh air that swirls around you. Each sinking root and rising branch keeps forking and following more new pathways. Your roots grow slowly, but they are amazingly strong as they push their way through the soil. Green leaves use the bright sunlight to create food that flows through your sap to feed all parts of you. Leaves and flowers begin to form on your branches. Listen to the wind rustling your leaves. Smell the petals of your flowers.

Imagine what you look like. What color of green are your leaves? Which color do your flower petals form? How big are you? As your flowers grow, what do they turn into: fruits, nuts, vegetables or something new that you have never seen before?

These branches, these roots, are your new way of reaching out and touching the world around you. The air passing into the pores on your leaves is a breath shared with all other living things. The water being taken up by your roots has been part of other living things before you, and will again become part of other plants and even animals once it evaporates from your green leaves and forms new rain clouds. Listen to the sap flowing through you. The soil feeding your new growth will one day be fed by your remains when you die and decompose.

An animal walks by and picks some food off your branches. How does it feel to give food to that animal?

You are part of all Earth, and it is part of you. You now have a growing, green heart that cares and wants to be cared for. It is up to you to connect in a good way with Earth, both those things that are alive and those, like the soil, that are not alive. Because you and Earth are one, what you do to Earth, you do to yourself. Use the patient wisdom of your green heart to heal and live in a good way.

Have each child draw a picture of the plant she or he became and take on a name for that plant. Invite the children to share the illustration with the group. Emphasize that it is their choice to share or not share. Have those who share describe their plant, say its name and tell the others what it smells like, what the wind sounds like blowing through its branches, how deep its roots go and how high its branches reach, how the sap tastes. Ask each child to describe how his or her plant reaches out to other parts of Earth, and what good qualities the plant has because of its caring green heart, such as kindness, generosity and gentleness. Tell the children that, in Abenaki tradition, the first people stepped alive from an ash tree with hearts that were growing and green wherever Gluskabe, the Transformer, shot arrows of life into the tree.

Have the children create a story of how their plant, their green heart, is going to help them to care for and heal Earth around them. Help them to brainstorm and think of ways to help all plants, and especially those they have chosen to be. Ask each child to commit to follow through on some specific projects that will put these ideas into action.

Help each child to create a small papier-mâché heart. Have her or him paint the heart green, and then draw a picture of her or his plant upon it. Their green hearts will give them the strength and qualities of their plant. Encourage the children to use their plant names whenever they want.

Make up your own activities to continue the children's relationships with their plants and the healing qualities those plants represent. Keep referring back to these caring plants as you continue using the stories and activities throughout this book. Encourage the children to use their green hearts to help them care for, heal and take care of Earth and other people.

Seventh-Generation Stewardship

ACTIVITY: Plant and nurture a flower, tree or other plant over the course of seven visits. List the survival needs of plants and the gifts plants give to people. Discuss threats to the well-being of plants. Create an ongoing story of the experience and a "seventh-generation" necklace.

GOALS: Understand the circle of sharing, of giving and receiving, and the meaning of living in balance. Develop the awareness and the communication skills necessary for nurturing plants physically and through supportive words and empathic caring feelings. Understand what plants need to survive and how to help them obtain these needs. Realize the many threats that plants face in their existence. Incorporate seventh-generation stewardship into daily life.

AGE: Younger children and older children

MATERIALS: Appropriate area in which to plant; one plant (preferably a tree, shrub or perennial flowering plant) and a few seeds for each child; pails of water; hose or other water supply; rich loam for fill; shovels, sticks, twine and rubber tubing for staking out trees and shrubs; shears; hammer; wheelbarrow or cart to transport trees or shrubs in or on; chalk and chalkboard or markers and newsprint; bar of soap; towels, paper, pencils, crayons, construction paper, paste, scissors, clay and other materials for stories; one piece of string for each child (with one end of each string glued and dried into a point to prevent fraying); seven *wooden* beads for each child; materials as needed for the children's gifts to the plants during their visits; "Discussion" from Chapters 8 and 9.

PROCEDURE: Beforehand, decide where you would like the children to plant their trees, shrubs or perennial flowers and obtain appropriate permissions to visit that land for the course of this activity. Comb the site thoroughly to be sure it is free of all dangerous litter such as broken glass and rusted cans. Acquire the seeds or plant supplies needed for the initial visit to the site and leave them at the site just prior to bringing the children out for the planting. Review "Planting Trees and Shrubs" in Chapter 2.

We highly recommend that each child be given a tree seedling or sapling to plant—something she or he can take pride in over the year as it grows. If space is limited you might have children plant a hedgerow, perhaps as a visual screen at the edge of the home or learning center grounds. Or, where space is very tight, flower beds or planter boxes with perennials work well.

Cut one 30-inch (76-centimeter) piece of string for each child. Dab some white, nontoxic glue on the end of each string, mold into a point and let dry. This is the end to use for stringing.

Note: We suggest a 3-to-1 ratio of children to adults for this activity.

Ask the children to describe what *sharing* means. Explain that one of the great circles of life is that of giving and receiving in a sharing, circular relationship with the natural world. Brainstorm ways that we can give to plants, and gifts that we receive from them. An important part of *living in balance* is to keep the circle of giving and receiving strong. Describe how we can empathize and communicate with

plants—plants respond well to kind words and soothing music but poorly to harsh feelings and sounds. Plants can sense and react to human emotions.

Review the "Discussion" sections from Chapters 8 and 9. Focus on the descriptions of the state of the forests and forest stewardship. Describe to the children the threats that trees, forests and other plants face. Say, "You are about to begin a journey to care for trees and other plants."

Now explain: "Each one of us is going to begin a circle of giving and receiving with a plant of our own by planting it outdoors. We are then going to practice good *stewardship* by taking care of that plant and protecting it from harm."

Take the children outdoors and demonstrate the proper way to plant those particular plants. Help the children to complete their planting and encourage them to speak kindly and to sing to and nurture their plants as they work with them. Clean up the children, the tools and the site.

Now gather the group together and ask the children to call out the gifts they have just given to the plants. Record their answers on newsprint: water, a home, soil (food, a footing) and love, for example. Ask them to think of other things that plants need for survival: space to grow, carbon dioxide and oxygen, sunlight, appropriate climate, animals to pollinate flowers and spread seeds, etc. Have them think of the gifts they have received from the plants: oxygen from the leaves, exercise, satisfaction, beauty, hope for the future of the plant and themselves, something to care for, positive feelings in return for those they gave the plants. Brainstorm other gifts we receive from plants such as food, shelter and materials for building, creating art and making medicines. (See the list of values [gifts] of plants in the "Discussion" for Chapter 14, as well as the description of plants' survival needs where Chapter 5 discusses photosynthesis.)

Have each child create a first "story" of his or her circle with this plant. This could take the form of a poem, an illustration, a tale of the day's experience or inspired by the experience or even a clay or other kind of model representing the story. Encourage the children to use their imaginations.

When all have finished their stories, discuss that Native North American cultures keep the circle of life strong by planning for the next seven generations and by considering how today's actions will affect the children to come. The children have now completed their first visit, gifting and story about their experience. Pass out one string and one bead to each child and explain that they will add one bead after each visit and story until the necklaces have seven beads. Instruct them to find the hard, glued end of the string to use for stringing and to not put the string in their mouths. Tell them that each bead also stands for one of the seven letters in the word *balance* (Figure 15-2). Some children like to write the appropriate letter on each bead as they string it.

Over the coming weeks and months, have the children visit their plants to water, weed and maintain their green friends. Ask them to speak kindly to the plants, and to give

Figure 15-2. This child is making a necklace as a reminder to consider the effects of our actions on the next seven generations to come. The seven wooden beads also represent the letters in the word "balance," and are symbolic of living a life of wise stewardship. (Photo by Nancy J. Fellows)

their plants a *simple* gift during each visit. Besides watering and maintenance, gifts could take the form of:
•   playing soothing music to the plant, such as classical music
•   singing to the plant
•   hanging a personal object of beauty on the plant (once its branches are strong enough)
•   reading the plant a story or poem, especially one with a positive message for plants and in which plants are well cared for
•   placing some rich soil at the base of the plant for fertilizer

A strong connection and symbol result when the children's gifts represent something they would give to coming generations of children. The next generation will be their own children!

Encourage the children to continue building an empathic relationship with the plants. After each visit, gift and the completion of that story another bead will be added.

Once their seventh-generation necklaces are completed, lead a discussion to refresh their memories about the mean-ing of the seven beads. Remind the children that each bead also stands for one of the letters in the word B•A•L•A•N•C•E. Ask the children to share other ways they can be and things they can do as good stewards of plants. Have them wear their necklaces and keep the next seven generations in mind as they share other stories and activities in this book.

Note: Although this activity would ideally be conducted as described above, variations could include (1) having small groups of children work with each plant if you have a large learning group and/or limited resources or (2) leaving a total of seven *gifts* for the plants over fewer visits when time is short.

EXTENDING THE EXPERIENCE

•   Celebrate the Circle of Life. Share the *"Round Dance of Unity and Thanksgiving"* in Chapter 4.
•   Make a medicine bag of natural objects that are important to you. These could be gifts, things you found in your special places outdoors or other natural objects that mean something special to you.
•   Make a pile of Earth-keeping stones. Add a stone each time you do something good for Earth.
•   Read *The Man Who Planted Trees*, by Jean Giono (Post Mills, Vt.: Chelsea Green, 1985), and listen to the accompanying cassette.
•   Write letters to future children in your home or learning center. In these letters, describe who you are, what is important to you and how you feel about caring for other people and Earth.
•   See Chapter 14 for information and activities about endangered plant species and making a commitment to help save a species.
•   Study and gather information about your favorite plants. Emphasize the importance of these plants, why they are needed in the world and, thus, the need to maintain and preserve their essential habitats. Share this information with the rest of the group to make everyone aware of even more plants, their habitat needs and their wonderful gifts to us.
•   Encourage the children to visit, enjoy and give to their *"Seventh-Generation Stewardship"* plants over the years. It is deeply rewarding to watch a tree or shrub you planted grow as you get older.

NOTES

1. Frances G. Lombardi and Gerald Scott Lombardi, *Circle Without End: A Sourcebook of American Indian Ethics* (Happy Camp, Calif.: Naturegraph Publishers, 1982), 29.

2. John G. Neihardt, *Black Elk Speaks* (Lincoln, Nebr.: University of Nebraska Press, 1932, 1972), 2–3, 181, 197–200.

3. Harvey Arden and Steve Wall, *Wisdomkeepers: Meetings With Native American Spiritual Elders* (Hillsboro, Ore.: Beyond Words, 1990), 68.

Glossary and Pronunciation Key to Native North American Words and Names

The following rules are used for the phonetic description of how each word is pronounced:

1. A line appears over long vowels. Short vowels are unmarked. For instance, "date" would appear as d̄at, while "bat" would appear as bat.
2. An accent mark (´) shows which syllable in each word or name is the one emphasized.
3. Syllables are broken with a hyphen (-).
4. Syllables are spelled out as they are pronounced. For instance, "Cherokee" appears as chair-oh-key.

Where appropriate, the culture from which each word or name comes is given in brackets [ ], followed by the meaning of that word or name or an explanation of its significance as it appears in the text.

Aataensic (Ah´-tah-en-sik) [Huron]. "Ancient Woman."

Abenaki (Ab´-er-na-kee or Ab´-eh-na-kēē). People living at the sunrise, "People of the Dawn." A northeastern Algonquian group.

Aleut (Al´-ēē-ūt). *See* Aleutian Islands.

Aleutian Islands (Ah-lū´-shun). A string of islands stretching from the southwestern tip of Alaska almost to the coast of Siberia. "Aleut" is the name the Russians gave to the people of these islands. They call themselves *Unangan*, literally "Those of the Seaside." They are related to the Inuit-Inupiaq people (Eskimo).

Algonquian (Al-gon´-kēē-en). Large, diverse grouping of Indian peoples related by a common linguistic root. Algonquian Indians live in the Atlantic coastal regions from what we now call the Maritime Provinces to the southeastern United States, west to the Prairie Provinces and down through the central states into Wyoming and Montana.

all my relations. Words spoken when entering or leaving a sweat lodge. A translation of the Lakota Sioux words *Mitakuye oyasin* (Mē-tah´-koo-yeh oh-yah´-sēēn).

Am o wa'i at hoabdag (Am oh wah´ee at ho-ahb-dahg) [O'odham]. "That is at the center of the basket."

Anishinabe (Ah-nish-ih-nah´-bey) or Anishinabeg. The Native people found in the central and northern Great Lakes areas of North America. They are the same people known as the Ojibway and the Chippewa, names applied to them in the past few centuries and used widely today by Anishinabe people themselves. *Ojibway* (O-jib-i-weg) was a name given them by their neighbors and probably means "Those Who Make Pictographs." *Anishinabe* means "First Men" or "Original Men." *Chippewa* is a variant of Ojibway. (Ojibway is also translated as "puckered up," referring to their moccasin style, which is puckered in front.) Currently the Anishinabe are one of the largest Native groups, with a U.S. and Canadian population of more than 160,000.

Aniyunwiya (Ah-nee-yoon-wi´-yah). The Cherokee people, whose original homelands included the areas now known as Tennessee, Kentucky and North Carolina. *Aniyunwiya* means "Real People." *See* Cherokee.

Appanaug (Ahp´-puh-nawg) [Wampanoag]. "Clambake" or "seafood cooking."

Black Elk (1863–1950). A Lakota (Sioux) visionary and medicine man of the late nineteenth and early twentieth centuries. The story of his life, as recorded by John Neihardt, *Black Elk Speaks: Being the Life Story of a Holy Man of the Oglala Sioux*, is regarded as a minor classic of American literature. The words of this *wichasha wakan* (holy man) are also recorded in *The Sacred Pipe*, by Joseph Epes Brown, and in *The Sixth Grandfather*, edited by Raymond J. DeMaille.

cacique (kah´-sēēk). Spanish word used to refer to Native chiefs in areas now or formerly dominated by the Spanish, as among the Pueblos of the American Southwest. Origin is Native West Indian, from the Arawak word *kassequa*.

Camalotz (Kahm-ah´-lots) [Maya]. "Great Bat."

Cherokee (Chair-oh-key´). Corruption of a Lenni Lenape [Delaware] Indian name (*Talligewi* or *Tsa la gí*) for this very large southeastern tribe who called themselves *Ani Yunwiya* (Ah-nee Yuhn-wi-yah)—"Real People." One of the so-called (by whites) Five Civilized Tribes. *See* Aniyunwiya.

Cheyenne (Shy-ann´). Name commonly used for the northern plains Native people who call themselves *tsitsitsas*, "The Striped Arrow People." From the Dakota word *shalyena*, meaning "Those Who Speak Strangely."

chief. This is one of the most widely used and misunderstood words applied to Native people today. All too often, every Indian man is called "Chief" by non-Indians. In some cases, this can be seen as an insult, especially if that man is *not* a chief. Other Native men, who, indeed, are "chiefs," do not mind having that word applied to them. Early Europeans thought a "chief" among the Native peoples of the Americas was like a king, and they even called many traditional leaders "king" (e.g., King Philip, who was known as Metacomet by his own *Wampanoag* [Wom-pah-nō´-ag] people). In general, a chief was a person chosen by his people to lead them. He was not all-powerful and the roles of such chiefs varied widely from one part of North America to another. In many tribal nations, if a chief did not behave properly, he was taken out of office by the people. Sitting Bull once explained that a chief, by definition, has to be a poor man because he must share everything he has. "Chief," therefore, is not a term to be used lightly.

Chief Seattle (1786?–1866). Seattle, sometimes called Sealth, was a leader of the Duwamish League of Puget Sound and a strong U.S. ally during the wars between the United States and a number of northwestern Native nations between 1855 and 1860. The present-day city of Seattle, Washington, bears his name. He is best remembered for a speech ascribed to him that sets out eloquently the relation between human beings and the natural world.

Chippewa (Chip´-ah-wah). *See* Anishinabe.

Chugach Inuit (Chew´-gatch). Inuit people in the area of Alaska near present-day Anchorage.

circle. The circle is seen as a special symbol for many Native people. It is continuous and all-embracing. When people gather and form a circle, the circle can always be made larger to include more. Those who sit in the circle are all at the same height, and all are the same distance from the center—thus it promotes and stands for equality. The "Sacred Hoop" referred to by many of the Native people of the plains is another vision of the circle and stands for life itself, continuing, never-ending, as well as standing for "the nation."

clan. Among most Native peoples the concept of "clan" exists. A term also applied to Scots and other European peoples, *clan* refers to groups of people within a nation who are "born into" a particular group, though they are not necessarily related by blood. Among the Mohawk there are three clans—Turtle, Wolf and Bear. A person *always* belongs to the clan of his or her mother. If a person from another nation (including a white person) entered a tribal nation, that person had to be adopted by a clan mother and was then of her clan. Among many Native nations, people were not supposed to marry someone of their own clan. Further, if a member of the Bear Clan among the Mohawk, for example, met a person of the Bear Clan from another Native nation, she or he might regard that person as a sister or a brother. Clans, therefore, created links among people and nations, as well as a sense of belonging to a special group.

clan mother. Elder woman regarded as the head of a particular clan. Among matrilineal people such as the Haudenosaunee (Iroquois), a clan mother has great power and is a major political force. Among the Haudenosaunee, the women have a strong, central role. Each clan is headed by an elder woman, a clan mother, chosen by the others of her clan to lead. The clan mothers and the other women of the clan have many duties—such as choosing the men who will be "chiefs" among the Haudenosaunee. If a Haudenosaunee chief does not do his job well, the clan mother warns him three times and then, if he still fails to behave appropriately, she takes away his chieftaincy. The roles of clan mothers varied, and in some Native nations of North America there were no clan mothers per se.

Clayoquot Nootka. *See* Nootka.

Comanche (Ko-man´-chē). Corruption of the Ute word *komon´teia*, "One Who Wants to Always Fight Me." A people of the southern Great Plains whose own name for themselves is *Nermurnuh* (New-mer´-noo), or "True Human Beings."

Cooper, Vernon. A contemporary elder of the Lumbi Nation.

Cotzbalam (Kohts´-bah-lam) [Maya]. Jaguar Chief.

Crazy Horse (1842–1877). An Oglala Lakota (Sioux) noted for his reckless courage. Crazy Horse was one of the leaders of the Native resistance against the U.S. encroachment on Lakota lands in the period following the U.S. Civil War. As a war leader, he is credited with many victories, the most famous being the Battle of Little Big Horn in 1876. After surrendering to the army in 1877, he was bayoneted by a soldier while being taken forcibly into a prison cell and died shortly thereafter.

Cree (Krē). A primarily subarctic people whose various tribal nations stretch from Quebec in eastern Canada to Alberta in the West, a stretch of close to 2,000 miles. In the area around Hudson Bay and James Bay, the traditional hunting and fishing subsistence lives of the Cree are threatened today by several James Bay power projects. The dams from these projects will block the major rivers of this region, creating a number of enormous lakes that will inundate much of that part of the North American continent, with disastrous ecological and cultural impacts.

da neho (dah ney-hō´) [Seneca]. Literally, "It is finished." A conventional way to end a story among the Iroquois.

Dakota (Dah-kō´-tah) [Sioux]. One of the seven main "council fires" of the Sioux people. *Dakota* in the Santee Sioux dialect means "Allies" and refers to the Sioux of the eastern plains of Minnesota. Sioux called themselves *Ocheti Shakowin* (Oh-che-ti Shah-kō-win), "The Seven Council Fires."

Delaware. *See* Lenni Lenape.

Diné (Dih-nēy´) [Navajo]. It means "The People."

Eastman, Charles Alexander. *See* Ohiyesa.

Eskimo (Es´-kih-mō). Cree word meaning "Fish Eaters," applied to the people who call themselves *Inuit*—"The People." *See* Inuit.

Fast Turtle. Wampanoag name for Russell Peters, a contemporary Wampanoag elder.

Gitchee Manitou (Gih-chee´ Man´-ē-too) [Anishinabe]. The Great Spirit.

Gluskabe (Gloos-kah´-bey) [Abenaki]. "Storyteller," the trickster and changer hero who lived on Earth before the human beings.

Grandmother. The term *grandmother* is used among many Native people to refer in a respectful way to a female elder, whether human or animal.

Grandmother Spider. Grandmother Spider is a central character in many stories of the U.S. Southwest. She is seen in some stories as the Creator of many things. She introduced weaving to the

people, and the rays of the sun are sometimes seen as part of her great web. She is a benevolent force in the Native world of such people as the Diné (Navajo) and Pueblo nations.

Great League [Iroquois]. The alliance of peace forged among the formerly warring five nations of the Iroquois about 500 years or more ago by The Peacemaker and Hiawatha; also known as the League of Peace. The Great League is still active among Iroquois peoples.

Great Mystery or Great Spirit. A translation of various Native names for the Creator, such as the Anishinabe term *Gitchee Manitou* or the Abenaki term *Ktsi Nwaskw* (T-see´ Nah-wahsk´).

Gucumatz (Goo´-koo-matz) [Maya]. The Maker.

Gumbs, Harriet Starleaf. A contemporary woman elder of the Wampanoag nation.

hageota (hah-gey-ōh´-tah). Iroquois word for a person, usually a man in middle age, who travels from lodge to lodge telling stories and being rewarded for his efforts by being given small gifts, food and a place to stay.

Haida (Hĭ´-dah). Pacific Northwest Indian group of Queen Charlotte Islands, British Columbia, and the southern end of Prince of Wales Island, Alaska. Called *Kaigani* in Alaska, they are known for their beautiful carvings, paintings and totem poles.

Hako (Hah´-kō) [Pawnee]. A ceremony involving a number of rituals taking place in spring, summer and fall that affirm the Pawnee belief in a harmonious and orderly universe.

Handsome Lake. Seneca chief whose visionary experience, called "The Good Message," at the start of the nineteenth century resulted in a cultural revival among the Iroquois. Handsome Lake is a literal translation of the name, inherited from one chief to the next, Ganio-dai-yo, meaning "It is a beautiful lake."

Haudenosaunee (Ho-dē-nō-shōw´-nē) [Iroquois]. Iroquois name for themselves, which means "People of the Longhouse."

Hiawatha (Hi-ah-wah´-tha) [Mohawk]. One of the historical founders of the League of the Haudenosaunee.

holi, holi, haqui, haqui (ho-lee´ ho-lee´ hah-key´ hah-key´) [Maya]. Words imitating the sound of a grinding stone.

huib (weeb) [Isleta Pueblo]. Game played by running and kicking a stick.

Huron (Hyu´-ron). A Native people of the St. Lawrence Valley and Ontario region of present-day Canada. Name drawn from the French *hure*, "disheveled head of hair."

Itoi (Ē´-ē-tōy) [O'odham]. Elder Brother, Our Creator.

Illinois (Ill-ih´-noy). A Native confederation that was located in what is now present-day Illinois, Iowa and Wisconsin. Name means "Human Beings."

Inca (in´-kah). A highly organized confederation of Native peoples of the Andean region of South America.

Innu (ihn´-yu). Native people of present-day Labrador. Name means "The People."

Inuit (In´-you-it) [Eskimo]. "The People," name used for themselves by the Native peoples of the farthest Arctic regions, Iceland and Arctic Asia. Not regarded by themselves or Indians as North American Indian.

Iowa (Eye-oh´-wah). A Native people of Kansas and Oklahoma, once part of the Winnebago nation in the Great Lakes region. "Sleepy Ones."

Iroquois (Ear´-oh-kwah). Corruption of an Algonquian word *ireohkwa*, meaning "real snakes." Applied commonly to the Six Nations, the "Haudenosaunee." *See* Haudenosaunee.

Isleta Pueblo (Is-leht´-ah Pweb-lo). One of the oldest of the Pueblo communities, located just south of present-day Albuquerque, New Mexico.

Kahionhes (Gah-hē-yōn´-heys) [Mohawk (Iroquois)]. Name meaning "Long River."

Kanienkahageh (Gah-nee-en-gah-hah´-gey) [Mohawk]. The Mohawk, "People of the Land of the Flint."

Kanietakeron (Gah-nee-dah-gay´-loo). This traditional name for David Kanietakeron Fadden, who was born in the month of March, means "Patches of Snow." A member of the Wolf Clan from the Mohawk community of Akwesasne, he is a museum educator at the Iroquois Indian Museum in Howes Cave, New York. In addition to stories illustrated for *Keepers of Life*, his work has appeared in *Keepers of the Night*, *Keepers of the Animals* and various Native publications including *Akwesasne Notes*, *Indian Time* and materials for the Six Nations Indian Museum, where he works to preserve Haudenosaunee traditions.

Kehtean (Kay´-tyahn) [Wampanoag]. "Great Spirit."

Ketci Niweskwe (kuh-tsee´nah-wah´-skwah) [Micmac]. "Great Mystery."

Kishelemukong [Lenape]. "Great Spirit."

Klamath (Klah´-muth). A Native people of present-day southern Oregon. Their name for themselves is Auksni (awks´-nee), "People of the Lake." The name *Klamath* may come from a Lutuami Indian word meaning "community."

Knight, Charlie. A contemporary Ute elder and medicine man.

Koluskap (Kōh-loos´-kahp) [Micmac]. *See* Gluskabe.

Kurahus (koor´-ah-hus) [Pawnee]. A priest of the hako ceremony.

Kwakiutl (kwah-gyuhlt´). A people of the Pacific Northwest and the British Columbia coast. Sometimes referred to as *Kwaguilth* or *Kwa-Gulth*.

Lacandon Maya. Native people of the highland jungles of Chiapas province in Mexico.

Lahks (lahx) [Passamaquoddy]. "Wolverine," who is a dangerous trickster figure.

Lakota (Lah-kō´-tah) [Sioux]. *See* Dakota. "Sioux" Native people of the northern plains, Nebraska and the Dakotas.

Lenni Lenape (leh-nee´ lay-nah´-pee). "We, the people," the name that the people sometimes called Delaware, whose traditional lands include present-day New Jersey and Pennsylvania, call themselves. Many Lenape now live in Oklahoma, having been forcibly resettled there almost two centuries ago.

longhouse. Large traditional dwelling of Iroquois people. Framework of saplings covered with elm bark with central fires and, to each side, compartments for families.

Lumbee or Lumbi (Lum´-bee). A large nation (more than 40,000) of Native people in present-day North Carolina. Formerly called the "Croatoans," they are said to have absorbed the white survivors of Sir Walter Raleigh's lost colony in the 1580s.

Lyons, Chief Oren. Contemporary Faithkeeper for the Turtle Clan of the Onondaga Nation and frequent spokesman for the Six Nations Iroquois Confederacy.

Maliseet (Mah´-luh-seet). Wabanaki nation located primarily in present-day New Brunswick, Canada. Name means "Broken Talkers" in Micmac. They call themselves Walastawkwiyak (Wah-lah-stawk´-wee-yahk), "People of the Beautiful River."

Malsom (mahl´-sum) [Micmac]. "Wolf."

Manabozho (Man-ah-bō´-zo). Algonquian trickster hero, "Old Man."

Mandan (Man´-dan). An agricultural people of the Great Plains whose traditional homelands are in North Dakota.

manomin (mah-no´-min) [Anishinabe]. Wild rice.

Maushop (Maw´-shop). Culture hero of the Wampanoag people.

Maya (My-uh). A Native people of Mexico and Central America.

medicine. As this word is used in contemporary Native cultures it refers both to medicinal preparations used for curing illnesses and to things that may bring good fortune or a certain kind of power.

Micmac (mik´-mak). Wabanaki nation located in present-day Newfoundland and Maritime Provinces of Canada. Name means "Allies."

milpa (mihl-pah) [Mayan]. A cultivated field in the rainforest.

Miwok (Mee´-wohk). Native people of the part of California surrounding the San Francisco Bay area and east of the bay.

Mohawk (Mo´-hawk). From an Abenaki word indicating "enemies." The Mohawk are the easternmost of the Six Nations of the

Iroquois, the "Keepers of the Eastern Door." Their name for themselves is "People of the Land of the Flint."

Montagnais (Mon-tun-yeys´). From the French for "mountain people," an Algonquin-speaking nation of northeastern Canada. *See* Innu.

Mooin (moo´-in) [Micmac]. Bear.

Narragansett (Nayr-ah-gahn´set). The "People of the Small Bay" were one of the largest tribal nations of the area now known as southern New England. Present-day Rhode Island approximates their traditional lands. Their current tribal offices are in Charlestown, Rhode Island.

Navajo (Nah´-vah-hō). *See* Diné.

nda (un-dah´) [Abenaki]. No.

Nokomis (Nok-kōh´-miss). Anishinabe term for grandmother; grandmother of Manabozho in stories.

Nootka (Newt-kah). A Wakashan-speaking group of the Pacific side of Vancouver Island in the Pacific Northwest. Many distinct Nootkan tribes are associated with the multitude of islands, sounds and inlets found along the coastline, including the Clayoquot Nootka of Meares Island. Nootka country is dominated by coastal coniferous forest with up to 262 inches (655 centimeters) of rain each year in the Vancouver Island Maritimes.

Nunam-shua [Chugach Inuit]. "The Dweller in Earth."

Oglala Lakota (Ō-glo´-lah Lah-ko´-tah). One of the branches of the western Lakota (Sioux) people.

Ohiyesa (oh-he-yeh-sah) [Dakota]. "The Winner." The Dakota name of Charles Alexander Eastman (1858–1939), whose autobiographical novel *Indian Boyhood* told of his traditional upbringing. A graduate of Dartmouth and Boston University, Ohiyesa became a practicing physician and one of the founders of the Boy Scouts of America.

Ojibway (Ōh-jib´-wah). *See* Anishinabe.

Oktehrakenrahkowa (Ohk-dey-lah-gen-lah-gō´-wah) [Mohawk]. "Great White Root," one of the four roots which must be followed to bring people together in harmony under the Great Tree of Peace.

Oktomkuk (ohk-tahm´-kook) [Passamaquoddy]. Island off the coast of Maine.

Onondaga (On-un-dah´-gah) [Iroquois]. The centralmost of the six nations, the "Fire-keepers." Name for themselves is *Onundagaono*, "People on the Hills."

O'odham (Ōh-ōh´-dum). Southwest Indian group of southern Arizona. Nomadic horticulturalists and prolific basket weavers. Two-thirds of the roughly 13,500 Papagos today live on reservations located mostly in Pima County, Arizona, with some living in Sonora state, Mexico. Sometimes referred to as *Tohono O'odham*, "People of the Desert." *See also* Pima.

Osage (Ō´-sāj). The people who call themselves *Ni-U-kon´-Skah*, "The People of the Middle Waters." Their lands formerly included the area where Missouri, Kansas, Arkansas and Oklahoma meet, but today their communities are mostly in Osage County, Oklahoma.

Ottawa (Ah´-tō-wah). From *adawe*, "to trade." Native nation whose traditional lands are in present-day Canada and the United States along Lake Superior, Lake Michigan and Lake Huron.

Palenque (pah-len´-kay). Ancient Mayan city famous for its pyramids, in the current state of Chiapas in Mexico.

Papago (Pah´-pah-gō). *See* O'odham.

Passamaquoddy (Pass-uh-mah-kwah´-dee). Wabanaki nation of the eastern coast of Maine. Their name comes from *Peskedemakddi*, "plenty of pollock."

Penobscot (Pen-ahb´-skaht). Wabanaki nation of southern Maine. Their name comes from *Penaubsket*, meaning "it flows on rocks."

Peters, Russell (Fast Turtle). [Wampanoag]. Author and former president of the Wampanoag Indian Tribal Council.

Pima (Pee´-mah). Native people of the Sonoran Desert region of present-day Arizona and Mexico who call themselves *Akimel O'odham*, "River People." The name "Pima" appears to originate from a phrase the O'odham used to answer the many questions asked them by the Spanish, "*Pi nyi maach*," which means "I don't know." *See also* O'odham.

Popponesset (Pah-po-nah´-sit). A bay off the coast of Martha's Vineyard in Massachussetts.

Pueblo (Pweb´-lō). Spanish for "town," refers to a number of "town-dwelling" Native peoples along the Rio Grande in New Mexico who live in large adobe buildings like apartment complexes.

Sachem (sah´-chum) [Algonquin]. A chief.

Salish (say´-lish) [Okanagan]. Sometimes called "Flatheads," the Salish are one of the divisions of the Okanagan peoples of the Pacific Northwest. Okanagan (oh-kah-nah´-gun) is usually translated as "People Who See to the Top."

San Blas Kuna (Cuna) (kyew´-nah). A Native people of the coast of present-day Panama.

Santee Dakota (San-tēē Dah-kō´-tah). A division of the eastern Dakota (Sioux) peoples living in Minnesota.

Sekatau, Dr. Ella W. T. (Seh´-kah-taw). A Narragansett ethnohistorian and cultural education consultant who is also well known for her fine weavings and embroidery.

Seneca (Sen´-eh-ka). Corruption of Algonquian word *O-sin-in-ka*, meaning "People of the Stone." Refers to the westernmost of the Six Nations, "Keepers of the Western Door." The Iroquois who called themselves *Nundawaono*, "People of the Great Hill."

Sequoia or Sequoyah (Suh-kwoy´-yah). A Cherokee scholar of the early nineteenth century who, in 1821, introduced a syllabic form of writing his native language that was adopted by virtually all of the Cherokee people within a decade.

Sh hab wa chu'i na'ana (shuh-hab wah chu´ēē nah´-ahnah). This means, "They say it happened long ago" in O'odham.

Shenandoah, Audrey. A clan mother of the Onondaga Nation and recording secretary of the Haudenosaunee Council of Chiefs.

Shinnecock (Shin´-eh-cok). A Native people of present-day Long Island whose reservation is located near Southampton.

shua (shoo´-ah) [Inuit]. The living spirit that dwells within all life.

sickissuog (sik´-ih-soo-ahg) [Wampanoag]. "Clams that spit."

Sioux (Su). *See* Dakota. Corruption of an Anishinabe word meaning "Snakes," which refers to those who call themselves *Dakota* or *Lakota* or *Nakota* or *Ocheti Shakowin* (Oh-che-ti Shah-ko-win), "The Seven Council Fires."

Snoqualmie (Snōw-kwal´-mē). One of the Native peoples of present-day Washington.

Sonkwaiatison (Son-kway-ah-dee´-sō) [Seneca]. The Holder-Up of the Heavens, the Creator.

Standing Bear, Chief Luther (1868–1939). An Oglala Lakota author whose widely read books include *My People the Sioux* (1928) and *Land of the Spotted Eagle* (1933).

Swamp, Chief Jake. Contemporary Mohawk elder known for planting "trees of peace" throughout the world.

Ta-kee-whee kay-ee (tah-key´-whee kay´-ee). Formulaic way of ending an Isleta Pueblo story, roughly meaning "that is all."

Tawahka (Ta´wah-kah). A Native people of Honduras.

Ten Bears. Civil chief of the Yampahreekuh Comanche, Ten Bears (Par-roowah Sermehno) delivered his famous speech in 1867 at the Medicine Lodge Creek Council.

Tepeu (Tey´-pyu) [Mayan]. "The Creator."

tipsin root. A member of the pea family with a large root the size of a hen's egg used widely as a food by the Native peoples of the Great Plains.

Tlingit (Klin´-kit). A Native people of the Pacific Northwest.

Tonkawa (tahn´-kah-wah). A Native people of what is now Texas.

tribe. From Latin *tribus*. A term used by both Indians and non-Indians to refer to groups of Native North Americans sharing a common linguistic and cultural heritage. Some Native North American people prefer to speak not of "tribe" but of *nation*.

Tsalagi. *See* Cherokee.

Tsimshian (Shim´-shē-un). A Native people of the Pacific Northwest coast, from present-day southeast Alaska into British Columbia. The name, *Tsimshian* means "People Inside of the Skeena River."

Tsioneratisekowa (See-own-eh-la-dih-say-go´-wah) [Mohawk]. The Tree of Peace.

Tucumbalam (Too-coom-bah-lahm´) [Mayan]. "Tapir."

Ute (Yōōt). Native people for whom the state of Utah is named. Their homeland included Colorado, Utah and part of New Mexico. An important division of the Shoshonean nations, most live today in Colorado. They call themselves *Nu Ci* (New´ Chi), which means "Person." The word *Ute* is a corruption of the Spanish term *Yuta*, which is of unknown origin.

vision quest. The practice of sending a young person out to an isolated place, as directed by one or more elders, to sit alone without food or sleep for a period of time to obtain spiritual guidance.

Wabanaki Confederacy (Wa´-bah-na-kēē). A loose union of a number of Abenaki nations circa 1750–1850, possibly echoing an earlier confederacy and influenced by the Iroquois League. Allied Micmac, Maliseet, Passamaquoddy, Penobscot and Abenaki nations. Wampum belts were introduced and triannual meetings held at Caughnawaga, Quebec.

Wampanoag (Wom-pah-nō´-ag). Means "Dawn People"; sometimes called *Pokanoket*. Algonquian linguistic group of eastern woodlands who once occupied what are now Bristol County, Rhode Island, and Bristol County, Massachusetts. Many were killed, along with the Narragansetts, by the colonists in King Philip's War in 1675 (King Philip was the colonists' name for Chief Metacomet, son of Massasoit). At least 500 Wampanoag live today on Martha's Vineyard, Nantucket and other places in the region.

Waw Giwulk (waw gee´-woolk) [O'odham]. "The center of the basket."

Waynabozho (Way-nah-bō´-zō). *See* Manabozho.

Winnebago (Win-eh-bey´-gō). "People of the Dirty Water." A Native people of the area of present-day southeastern Wisconsin. Name comes from the Anishinabe word *winnipig*, meaning "filthy water."

Xecotcovach (Hey-kot-kō-vatch) [Mayan]. "Great Eagle."

Yamparika Comanche (Yahm-pah´-ree-kuh). The northernmost of the 13 different bands of the Comanches, whose territory included present-day Kansas. "Eaters of the Yap Root."

Zimo (zēē´-moh) [Abenaki]. "The Planter."

✤ Other Versions of Native North American Stories ✤

Joseph Bruchac

In choosing the stories to be included in this book and in its two predecessors, I followed several rules. First, I chose stories with levels of meaning a general audience can understand. (Each story has additional levels of meaning to be perceived by those who are close to the individual tribal nation each story comes from.) Second, I did not tell "restricted" stories, stories only to be shared with those who are, in some way, "initiated." Third, I only included stories with earlier versions already in print or in public circulation through recordings or film. I do not wish to be the first to take a story out of the oral tradition. Fourth, the versions included in this book (and in *Keepers of the Earth* and *Keepers of the Animals*) are my own retellings and may differ from other versions already recorded. I have tried to make my versions closer to the oral traditions from which they came or to include important information left out in other recorded tellings.

My retellings of each of the stories have been based on assistance from other Native storytellers and writers and on my knowledge of other written versions of these tales. The following is an acknowledgment of those tellers and a suggestion of places to look for other written tellings of the stories.

The Corn Spirit (Seneca/Tuscarora). My thanks to Marion Miller, Seneca storyteller. There are many other versions of the corn spirit story. In some cases the corn spirit is a woman, in others a man. See Arthur Parker's *Seneca Myths and Folk Tales* (University of Nebraska Press, 1989); *Seneca Fiction, Legends and Myths* by J. N. B. Hewitt (Washington, D.C.: Bureau of American Ethnology Bulletin 32, 1911).

The Sky Tree (Huron). Thanks to my Huron (Wyandot) friends Eleonore Jiconsaseh Sioui and George B. Sioui. See *The Huron* by Nancy Bonvillian (Chelsea House, 1989).

How Kishelemukong Made the People and the Seasons (Lenape). Special thanks to Jack Forbes (Lenape/Renape) for his work in preserving and explaining Lenape traditions. See *The Lenapes* by Robert S. Grumet (Chelsea House, 1989).

The Thanks to the Trees (Seneca). This section from the traditional Seneca Thanksgiving Address, which is given at the start of most important gatherings, is adapted and translated from a Long Opening Thanksgiving Address given in 1972 by Enos Williams/Quivering Leaves at Seneca Longhouse, Six Nations, Ontario. The full text of a Mohawk version entitled *Thanksgiving Address: Greetings to the Natural World*, illustrated by Kahionhes and edited by John Stokes, is available from The Tracking Project, PO Box 266, Corrales, NM 87048. It is not for sale, but contributions are accepted to keep the book in print. (I suggest offering at least $5.)

The Circle of Life and the Clambake (Wampanoag). Russell Peters is my primary source for this story. *Wampanoag Tales: Legends of Maushop* (Story Stone), an audiocassette by Wampanoag storyteller Medicine Story and in *Spirit of the New England Tribes: Indian History & Folklore, 1620-1984* by William S. Simmons (University Press of New England, 1986).

Fallen Star's Ears (Cheyenne). Thanks to Lance Henson for keeping Cheyenne traditions and helping me understand them. See *Star Legends Among the American Indians* by Clark Wissler, American Museum of Natural History Science Guide #91; *The Rolling Head* by Henry Tall Bull and Tom Weist (Montana Indian Publications).

Koluskap and Malsom. Several versions of this story, which is much like the Iroquois tradition of the twin sons of Sky Woman's daughter, are told among the different Wabanaki nations, including my own Mississquoi Abenaki people. See *The Wabanakis of Maine and the Maritimes* prepared and published for the Maine Indian Program by the American Friends Service Committee.

Why Some Trees Lose Their Leaves (Cherokee). Gayl Ross and Murv Jacob are foremost among the Cherokee storytellers and artists who have helped me. See *The Path to Snowbird Mountain* by Traveller Bird (Farrar, Straus & Giroux, 1972); *Myths of the Cherokee* by James Mooney (Washington, D.C.: Bureau of American Ethnology Report 19, 1902).

The Bitterroot (Salish). Thanks to Vi Hilbert and Johnny Moses. See *Indian Legends from the Northern Rockies* by Ella E. Clark (University of Oklahoma Press, 1988).

Indian Summer (Penobscot). Penobscot storyteller Joe Mitchell of Old Town, Maine, is only one of a number of contemporary Abenaki storytellers. See *Penobscot Tales and Religious Beliefs* by Frank G. Speck, *Journal of American Folklore* No. 187.

The First Basket (Mandan). See *Prairie Smoke* by Melvin R. Gilmore (Minnesota Historical Society Press, 1987).

The Woman Who Lives in the Earth (Chugach Inuit). Mary Peters, an Inuit storyteller, was kind enough to spend several hours sharing stories with me when I visited her in 1992 on Baffin Island. Much of my understanding of her people and their stories comes from her and the other elders who were so generous to me. See *Powers Which We Do Not Know: The Gods and Spirits of the Inuit* by Daniel Merkur (University of Idaho, 1991).

Waw Giwulk: The Center of the Basket (O'odham). Thanks

to Larry Evers. See "Pima and Papago Legends," by Mary L. Neff, *Journal of American Folklore* 25, 1912.

How Fox Brought the Forests from the Sky (Snoqualmie). See *Indian Legends of the Pacific Northwest* by Ella E. Clark (University of California Press, 1953).

The People of Maize (Maya). Thanks to Victor Montejo of the Jkaltek and Chan Kin, the 120-year-old patriarch of the Lacandon Mayan village of Naha, shared many stories with me when I visited his people in 1992 in the Mexican rain forest. The best-known written version of this tale can be found in the *Popol Vuh: The Sacred Book of the Ancient Quiche Maya* by Adrian Recinos as translated by Goetz and Morley (University of Oklahoma Press, 1983).

Waynabozho and the Wild Rice (Anishinabe). See *Wild Rice and the Ojibway People* by Thomas Vennum, Jr. (Minnesota Historical Society Press, 1988).

The Buffalo Bull and the Cedar Tree (Osage). *Osage Life and Legends* by Robert Liebert (Happy Camp, Calif.: Naturegraph, 1987); *The Osage Tribe* by Francis LaFlesche (Washington, D.C.: Bureau of American Ethnology Report 35, 1918).

✤ Index of Activities by Subject ✤

USING THIS INDEX

1) Look in this index and find the subject you want to teach. For quick reference, the broad subject headings are listed prior to the detailed subject headings.

2) Find the number(s) given under the subject headings to the right of the subject you want to teach. These numbers identify the appropriate activities in the chronological list found on this page. The page number for each activity is given to the right of that activity in this list. The suggested learning level for each activity is given to the left of the page number: (Y) indicates younger children (roughly ages 5 to 8 years), and (O) indicates older children (roughly 9 to 12 years).

LIST OF ACTIVITIES AND THEIR LOCATIONS IN THE TEXT

The numbers given to the left of the name of each activity correspond with the numbers listed in this index. Page numbers are listed to the right of each activity.

BROAD SUBJECT HEADINGS FOR ACTIVITIES

Note: Page numbers here refer to the listing of these subjects in this index.

DETAILED SUBJECT HEADINGS FOR ACTIVITIES

Note: Numbers given here are activity numbers, *not* page numbers. See "Using This Index" section. "Plant," as used in this index, refers to all plants and plant-like organisms.

Human Impacts on Plants

✤ General Index ✤

✣ Notes ✣

✢ Notes ✢

The Keepers Series

A complete line of books and tapes that teach children responsible stewardship toward the Earth and all living things

By Michael J. Caduto and Joseph Bruchac

KEEPERS OF THE ANIMALS
Native American Stories and Wildlife Activities for Children
Michael J. Caduto and Joseph Bruchac
Illustrations by John Kahionhes Fadden
ISBN 1-55591-088-2, LC91-71364, 8 $^1/_2$ x 11, b/w photographs, 35 original illustrations, 286 pages, cloth $22.95

KEEPERS OF THE ANIMALS TEACHER'S GUIDE
ISBN 1-55591-107-2, 8 $^1/_2$ x 11, bibliography, reading lists, 66 pages, paperback $9.95

NATIVE AMERICAN ANIMAL STORIES
Told by Joseph Bruchac
Illustrations by John Kahionhes Fadden
ISBN 1-55591-127-7, LC92-53040, 7 x 10, line drawings, two-color, 140 pages, paperback $11.95

KEEPERS OF THE ANIMALS AUDIOCASSETTE
Native American Animal Stories
Told by Joseph Bruchac
ISBN 1-55591-128-5, two audiocassettes, 110 minutes $16.95

New Music in the Keepers series!

ALL ONE EARTH
Songs for the Generations
Performed by Michael J. Caduto
   Twelve exciting songs for families add a new dimension to the lessons of the Keepers books. Ten original compositions. Lyrics included, 47 minutes of music.
Cassette $9.95, ISBN 1-55591-209-5
CD $14.95, ISBN 1-55591-210-9

KEEPERS OF THE EARTH
Native American Stories and Environmental Activities for Children
Michael J. Caduto and Joseph Bruchac
Illustrations by John Kahionhes Fadden
ISBN 1-55591-027-0, LC88-3620, 8 $^1/_2$ x 11, b/w photographs, 32 original illustrations, 234 pages, cloth $22.95

KEEPERS OF THE EARTH TEACHER'S GUIDE
ISBN 1-55591-040-8, 8 $^1/_2$ x 11, bibliography, reading lists, 52 pages, paperback $9.95

NATIVE AMERICAN STORIES
Told by Joseph Bruchac
Illustrations by John Kahionhes Fadden
ISBN 1-55591-094-7, LC90-85267, 7 x 10, line drawings, 160 pages, paperback $11.95

KEEPERS OF THE EARTH AUDIOCASSETTE
Native American Stories
Told by Joseph Bruchac
ISBN 1-55591-099-8, two audiocassettes, 133 minutes $16.95

KEEPERS OF THE NIGHT
Native American Stories and Nocturnal Activities for Children
Michael J. Caduto and Joseph Bruchac
Story Illustrations by David Kanietakeron Fadden
Chapter Illustrations by Jo Levasseur and Carol Wood
ISBN 1-55591-177-3, 7 x 10, b/w photographs, original illustrations, 160 pages, paperback $14.95

All of these Fulcrum titles are available at your favorite bookstore or call us directly at **(800) 992-2908** to place an order

Fulcrum Publishing
350 Indiana Street, Suite 350
Golden, Colorado 80401